SHANG-CHI

EARTH'S MIGHTIEST MARTIAL ARTIST

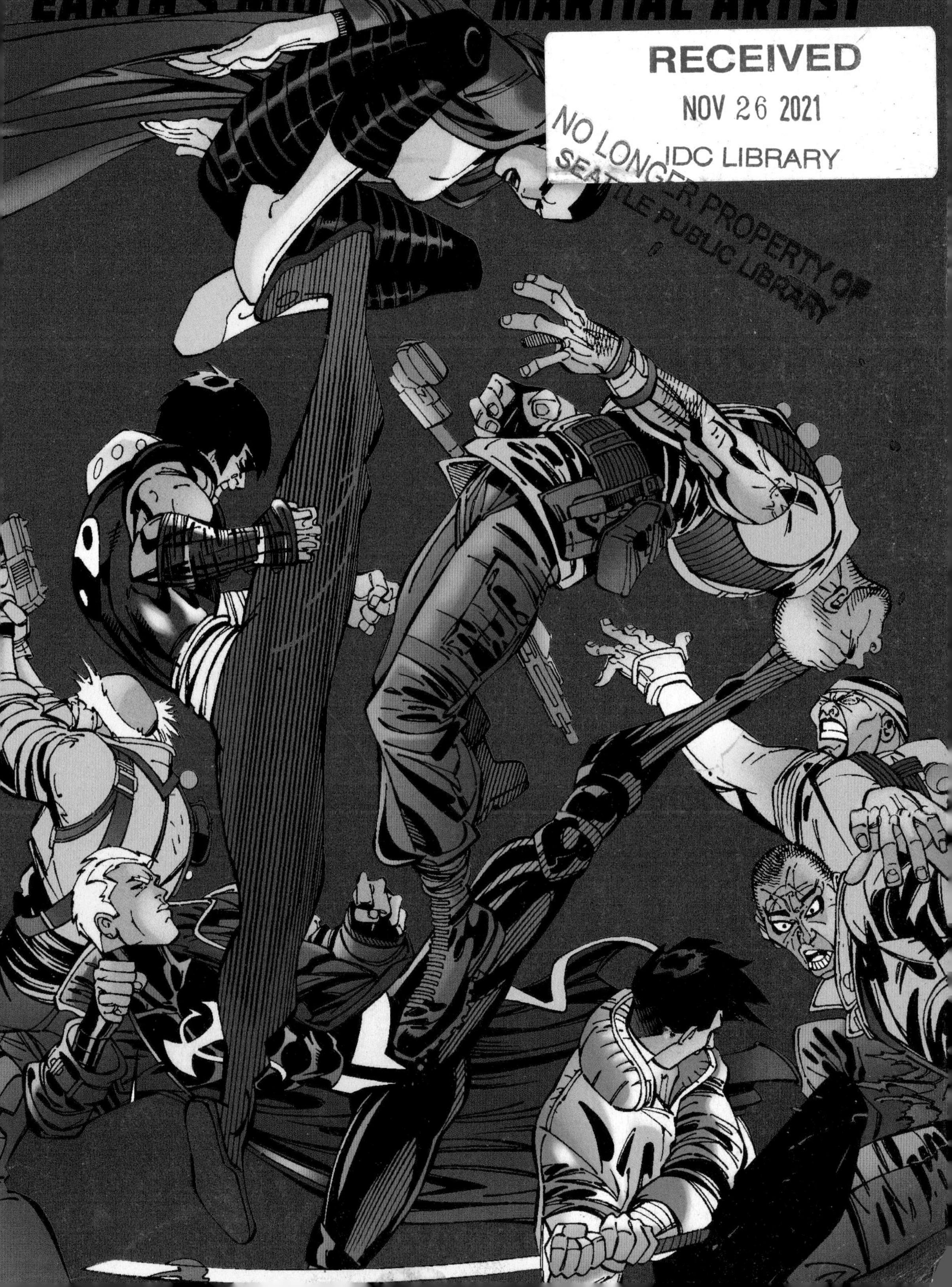

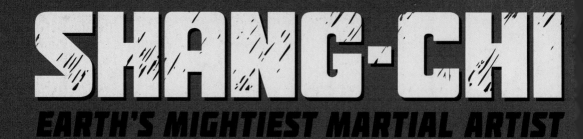

SHANG-CHI

EARTH'S MIGHTIEST MARTIAL ARTIST

WRITERS: Scott Lobdell, Ben Raab, John Ostrander, Dan Slott, Warren Ellis & Jonathan Hickman

PENCILERS: Carlos Pacheco, Pasqual Ferry, Paulo Siqueira, David Aja & Mike Deodato Jr.

INKERS: Art Thibert, Jaime Mendoza, David Aja & Mike Deodato Jr. with Pasqual Ferry, Amilton Santos, Roland Paris & Paulo Siqueira

COLORISTS: Christian Lichtner, Aron Lusen, Liquid!, Joe Rosas, Fabio D'Auria, David Aja & Frank Martin

LETTERERS: Jon Babcock, Dave Lanphear, VC's Joe Sabino & Cory Petit, and Richard Starkings & Comicraft's Albert Deschesne & Emerson Miranda

ASSISTANT EDITORS: Jason Liebig, Lysa Kraiger, Tom Brennan & Jake Thomas

ASSOCIATE EDITORS: Mark Powers & Lauren Sankovitch

EDITORS: Bob Harras, Mark Bernardo, Stephen Wacker & Tom Brevoort with Lauren Sankovitch

FRONT COVER ARTISTS: Gil Kane & Dan Adkins

BACK COVER ARTIST: David Aja

COLLECTION EDITOR: Jennifer Grünwald
ASSISTANT EDITOR: Daniel Kirchhoffer
ASSISTANT MANAGING EDITOR: Maia Loy
ASSISTANT MANAGING EDITOR: Lisa Montalbano
ASSOCIATE MANAGER, DIGITAL ASSETS: Joe Hochstein
VP PRODUCTION & SPECIAL PROJECTS: Jeff Youngquist
RESEARCH: Jess Harrold
PRODUCTION: Joe Frontirre
BOOK DESIGNER: Adam Del Re
SVP PRINT, SALES & MARKETING: David Gabriel
EDITOR IN CHIEF: C.B. Cebulski

SHANG-CHI: EARTH'S MIGHTIEST MARTIAL ARTIST. Contains material originally published in magazine form as X-MEN (1991) #62-64, HEROES FOR HIRE (1997) #18-19, SHADOWLAND: SPIDER-MAN (2010) #1, SECRET AVENGERS (2010) #18 and AVENGERS (2012) #11. Second printing 2021. ISBN 978-1-302-92527-7. Published by MARVEL WORLDWIDE, INC., a subsidiary of MARVEL ENTERTAINMENT, LLC. OFFICE OF PUBLICATION: 1290 Avenue of the Americas, New York, NY 10104. © 2021 MARVEL No similarity between any of the names, characters, persons, and/or institutions in this magazine with those of any living or dead person or institution is intended, and any such similarity which may exist is purely coincidental. **Printed in the U.S.A.** KEVIN FEIGE, Chief Creative Officer; DAN BUCKLEY, President, Marvel Entertainment; JOE QUESADA, EVP & Creative Director; DAVID BOGART, Associate Publisher & SVP of Talent Affairs; TOM BREVOORT, VP, Executive Editor; NICK LOWE, Executive Editor, VP of Content, Digital Publishing; DAVID GABRIEL, VP of Print & Digital Publishing; JEFF YOUNGQUIST, VP of Production & Special Projects; ALEX MORALES, Director of Publishing Operations; DAN EDINGTON, Managing Editor; RICKEY PURDIN, Director of Talent Relations; JENNIFER GRÜNWALD, Senior Editor, Special Projects; SUSAN CRESPI, Production Manager; STAN LEE, Chairman Emeritus. For information regarding advertising in Marvel Comics or on Marvel.com, please contact Vit DeBellis, Custom Solutions & Integrated Advertising Manager, at vdebellis@marvel.com. For Marvel subscription inquiries, please call 888-511-5480. **Manufactured between 6/18/2021 and 7/20/2021 by FRY COMMUNICATIONS, MECHANICSBURG, PA, USA.**

10 9 8 7 6 5 4 3 2

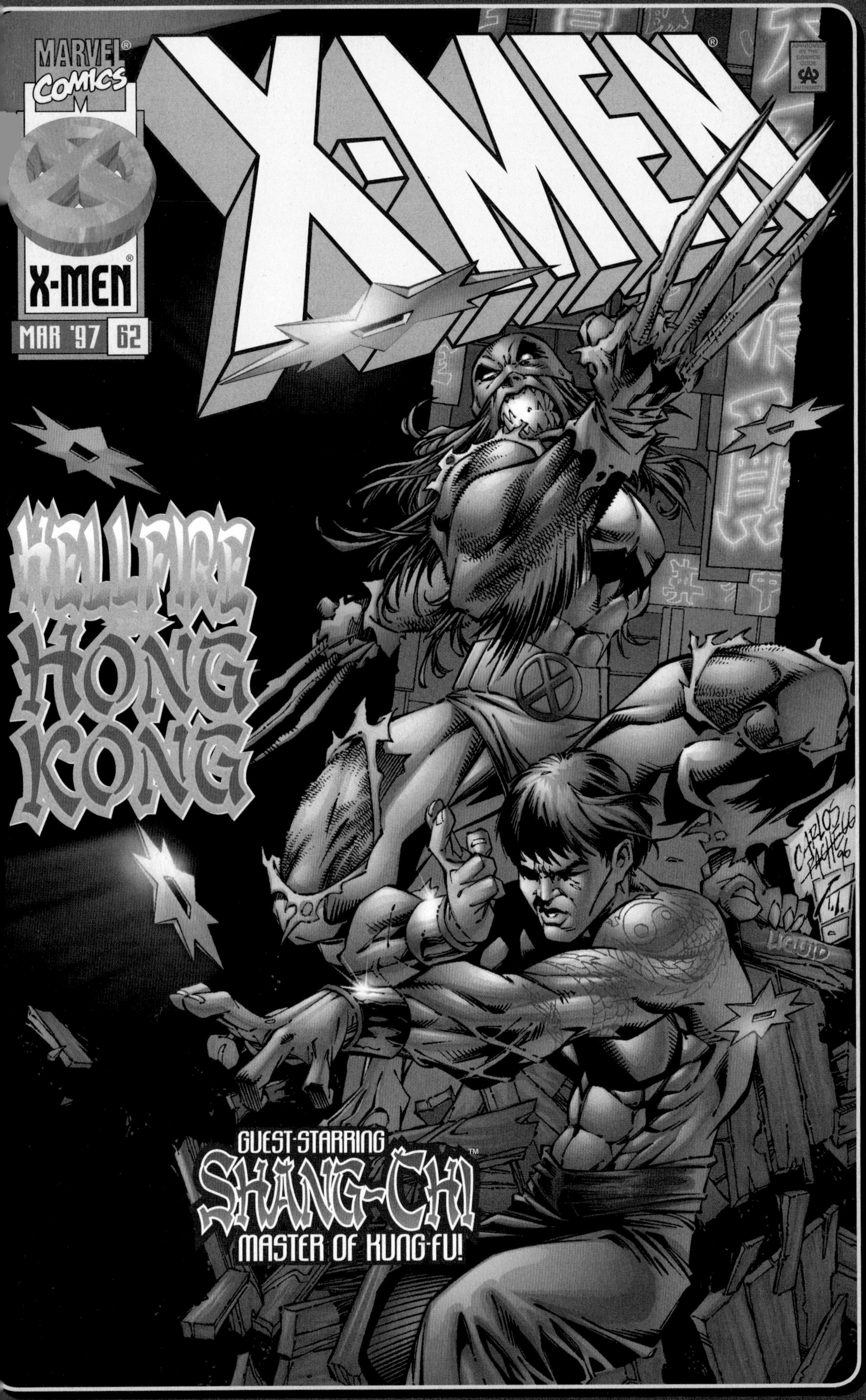
MARVEL COMICS
X-MEN
X-MEN
MAR '97 62
APPROVED BY THE COMICS CODE AUTHORITY
HELLFIRE HONG KONG
GUEST-STARRING
SHANG-CHI
MASTER OF KUNG-FU!
CARLOS PACHECO '96
LIQUID

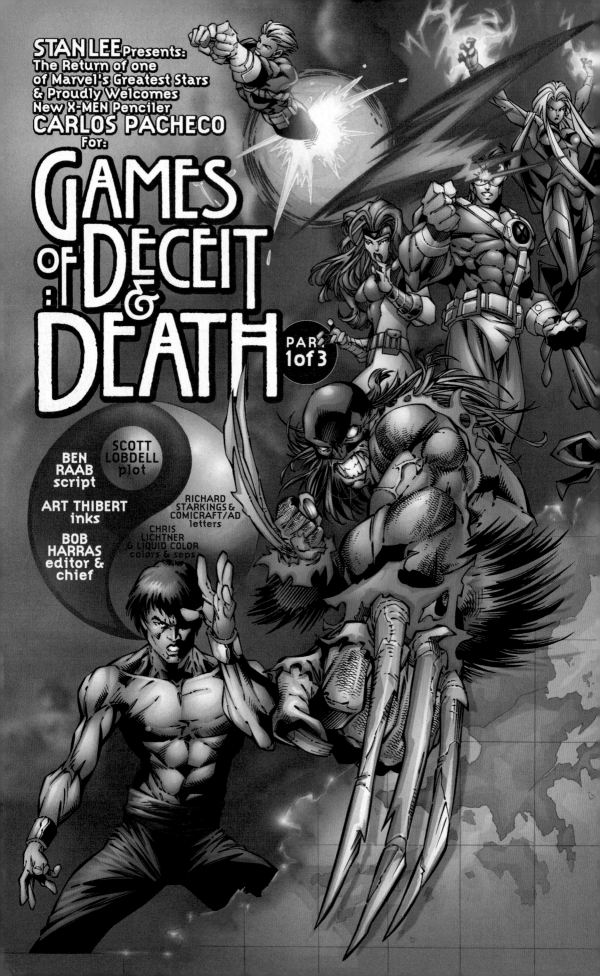

STAN LEE presents:
The Return of one
of Marvel's Greatest Stars
& Proudly Welcomes
New X-MEN Penciler
CARLOS PACHECO
For:

GAMES OF DECEIT & DEATH
PART 1 of 3

SCOTT LOBDELL plot

BEN RAAB script

ART THIBERT inks

BOB HARRAS editor & chief

RICHARD STARKINGS & COMICRAFT/AD letters

CHRIS LICHTNER & LIQUID COLOR colors & seps

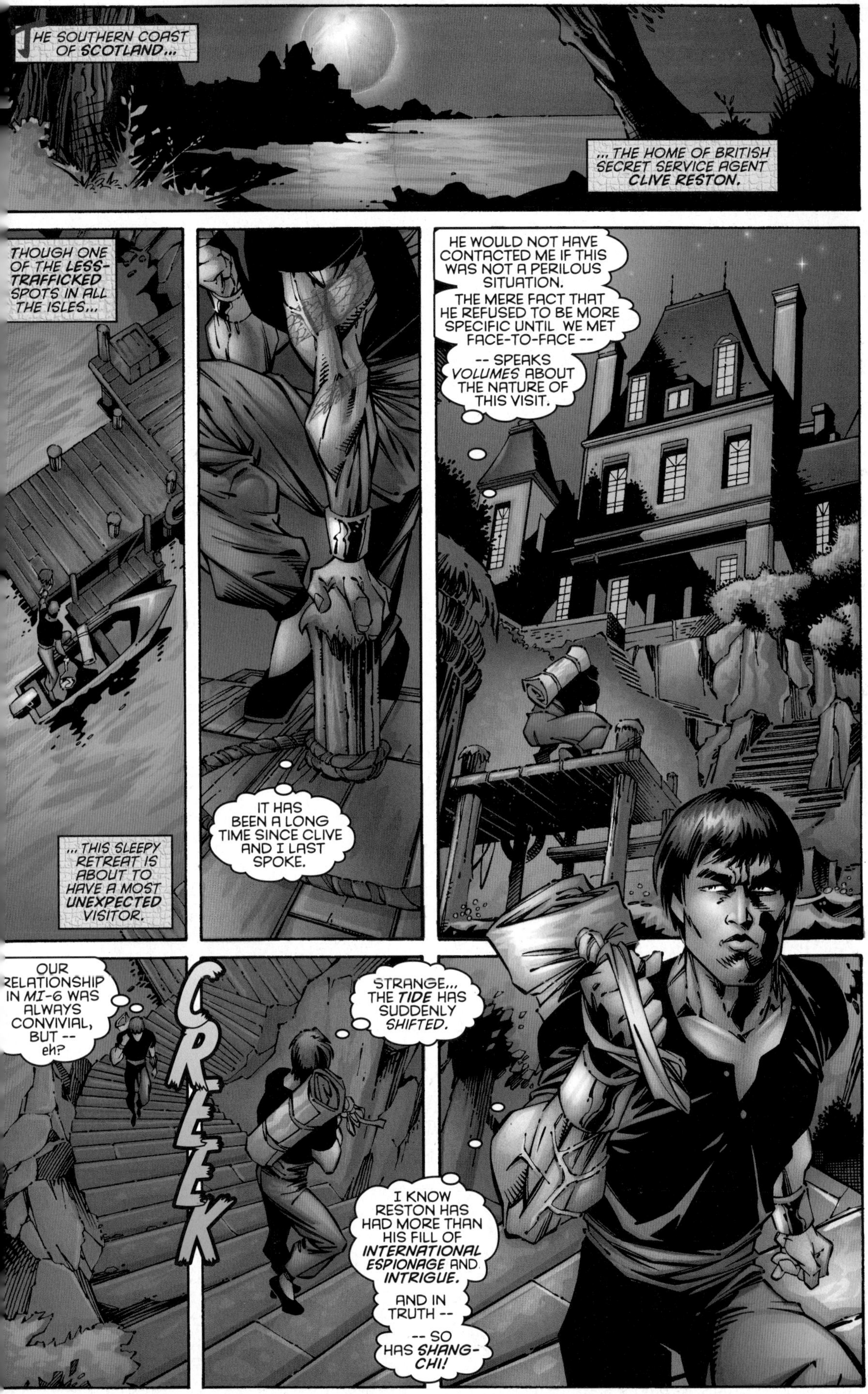
THE SOUTHERN COAST OF SCOTLAND...
...THE HOME OF BRITISH SECRET SERVICE AGENT CLIVE RESTON.
THOUGH ONE OF THE LESS-TRAFFICKED SPOTS IN ALL THE ISLES...
...THIS SLEEPY RETREAT IS ABOUT TO HAVE A MOST UNEXPECTED VISITOR.
IT HAS BEEN A LONG TIME SINCE CLIVE AND I LAST SPOKE.
HE WOULD NOT HAVE CONTACTED ME IF THIS WAS NOT A PERILOUS SITUATION.
THE MERE FACT THAT HE REFUSED TO BE MORE SPECIFIC UNTIL WE MET FACE-TO-FACE --
-- SPEAKS VOLUMES ABOUT THE NATURE OF THIS VISIT.
OUR RELATIONSHIP IN MI-6 WAS ALWAYS CONVIVIAL, BUT -- eh?
CREEK
STRANGE... THE TIDE HAS SUDDENLY SHIFTED.
I KNOW RESTON HAS HAD MORE THAN HIS FILL OF INTERNATIONAL ESPIONAGE AND INTRIGUE.
AND IN TRUTH --
-- SO HAS SHANG-CHI!

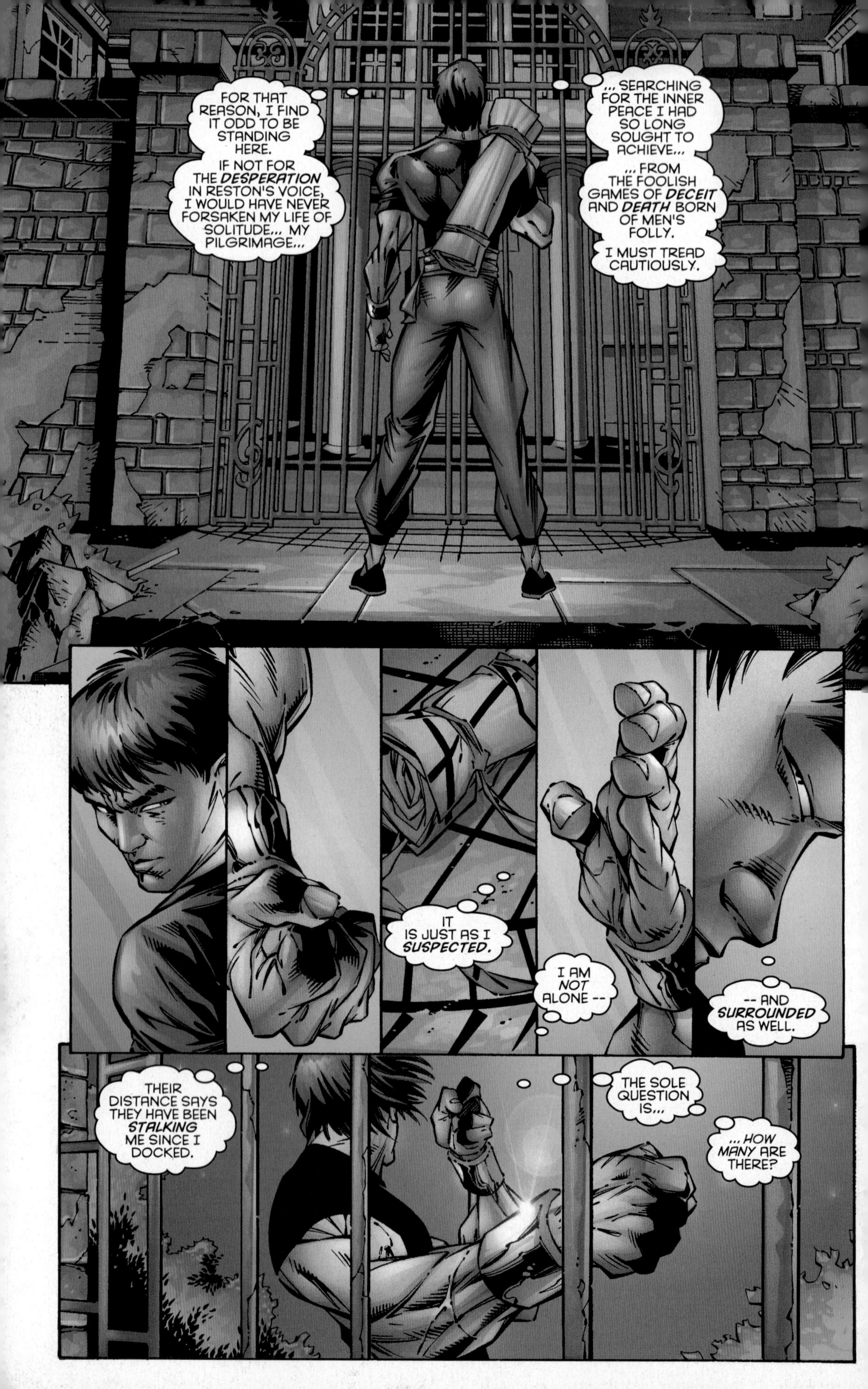
FOR THAT REASON, I FIND IT ODD TO BE STANDING HERE.
IF NOT FOR THE DESPERATION IN RESTON'S VOICE, I WOULD HAVE NEVER FORSAKEN MY LIFE OF SOLITUDE... MY PILGRIMAGE...
... SEARCHING FOR THE INNER PEACE I HAD SO LONG SOUGHT TO ACHIEVE...
... FROM THE FOOLISH GAMES OF DECEIT AND DEATH BORN OF MEN'S FOLLY.
I MUST TREAD CAUTIOUSLY.
IT IS JUST AS I SUSPECTED.
I AM NOT ALONE --
-- AND SURROUNDED AS WELL.
THEIR DISTANCE SAYS THEY HAVE BEEN STALKING ME SINCE I DOCKED.
THE SOLE QUESTION IS...
... HOW MANY ARE THERE?

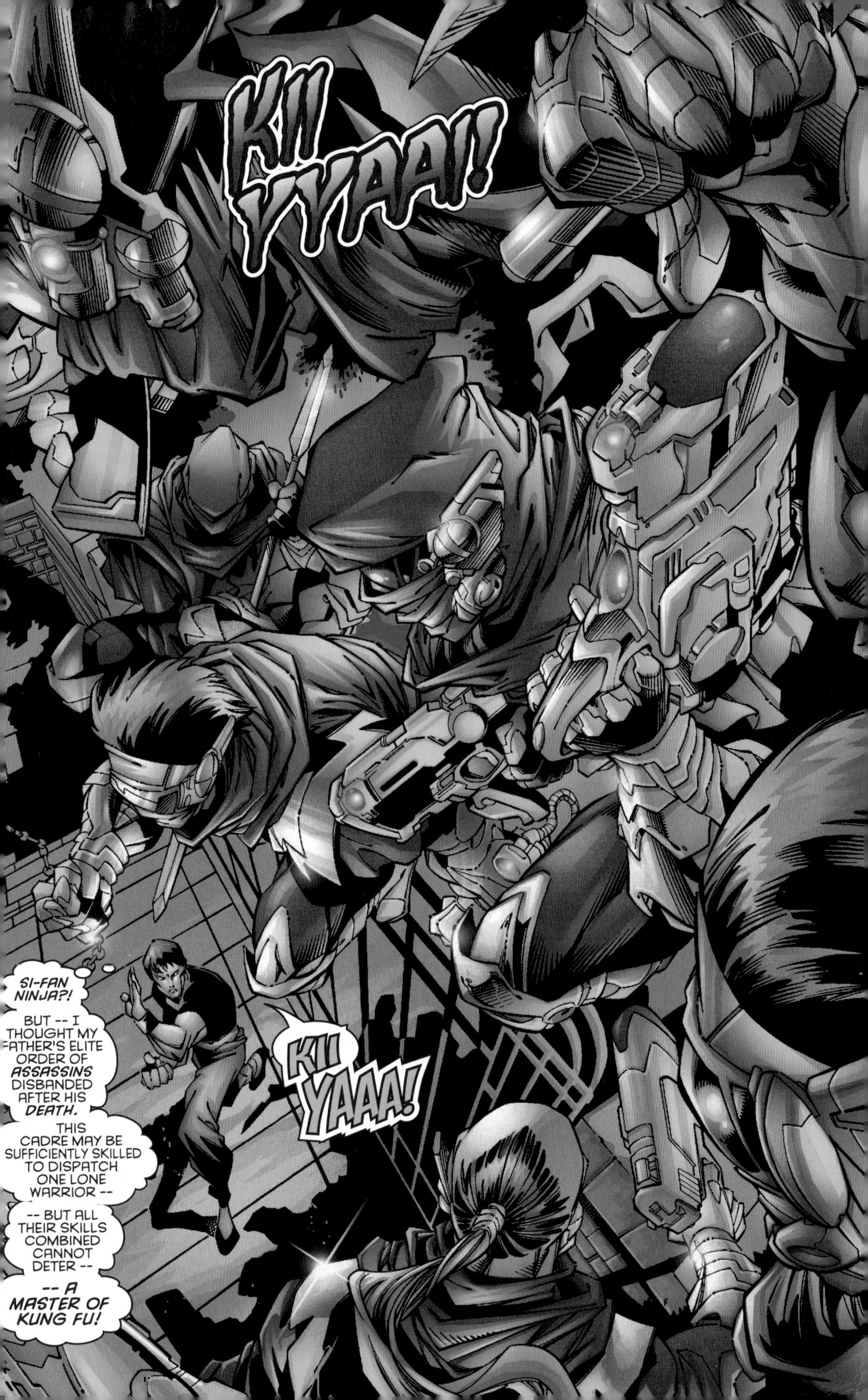
KII YYAAI!
SI-FAN NINJA?!
BUT -- I THOUGHT MY FATHER'S ELITE ORDER OF ASSASSINS DISBANDED AFTER HIS DEATH.
THIS CADRE MAY BE SUFFICIENTLY SKILLED TO DISPATCH ONE LONE WARRIOR --
-- BUT ALL THEIR SKILLS COMBINED CANNOT DETER --
-- A MASTER OF KUNG FU!
KII YAAA!

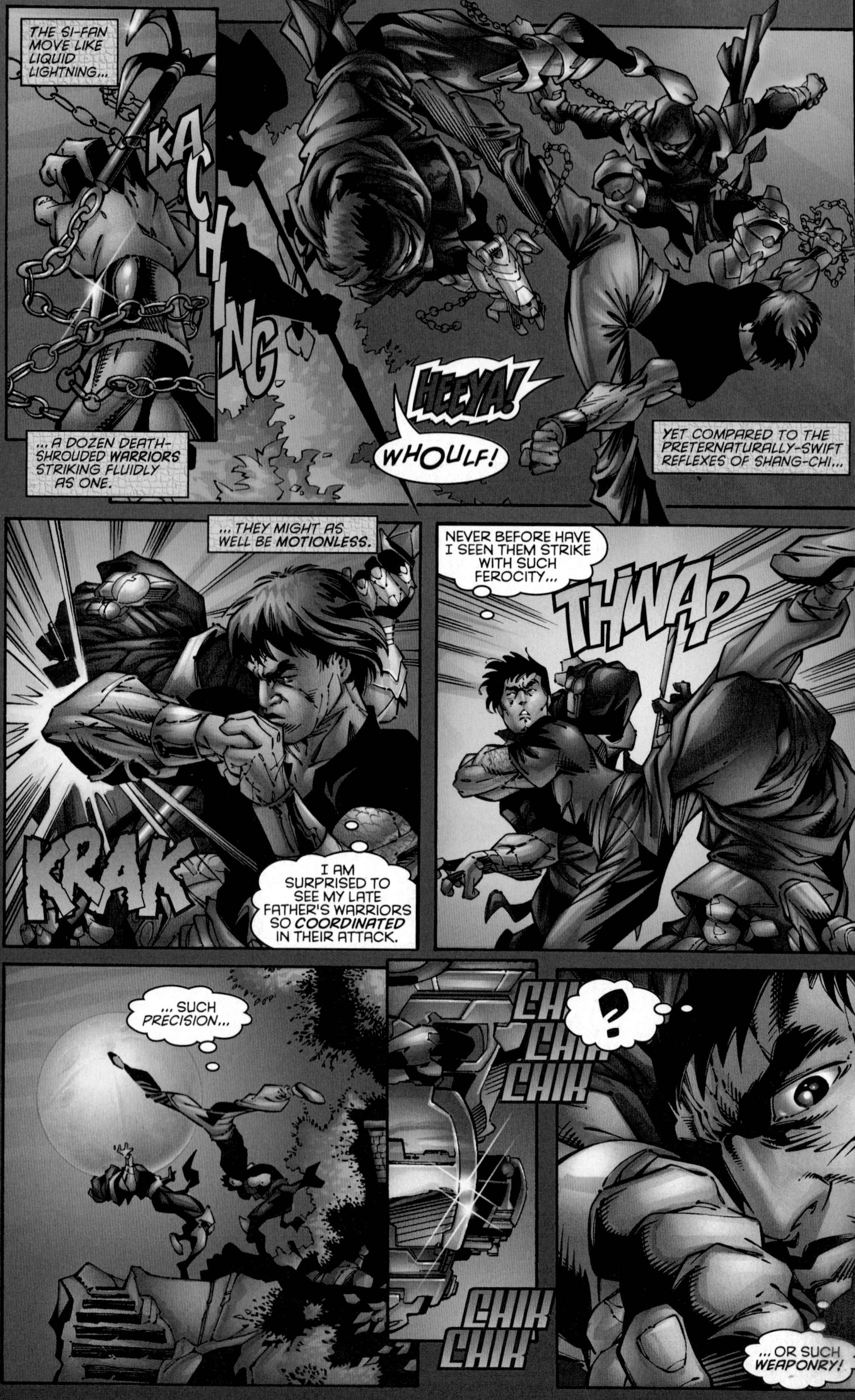
THE SI-FAN MOVE LIKE LIQUID LIGHTNING...
KACHING
...A DOZEN DEATH-SHROUDED WARRIORS STRIKING FLUIDLY AS ONE.
HEEYA!
WHOULF!
YET COMPARED TO THE PRETERNATURALLY-SWIFT REFLEXES OF SHANG-CHI...
...THEY MIGHT AS WELL BE MOTIONLESS.
KRAK
I AM SURPRISED TO SEE MY LATE FATHER'S WARRIORS SO COORDINATED IN THEIR ATTACK.
NEVER BEFORE HAVE I SEEN THEM STRIKE WITH SUCH FEROCITY...
THWAP
...SUCH PRECISION...
CHIK CHIK CHIK
?
CHIK CHIK
...OR SUCH WEAPONRY!

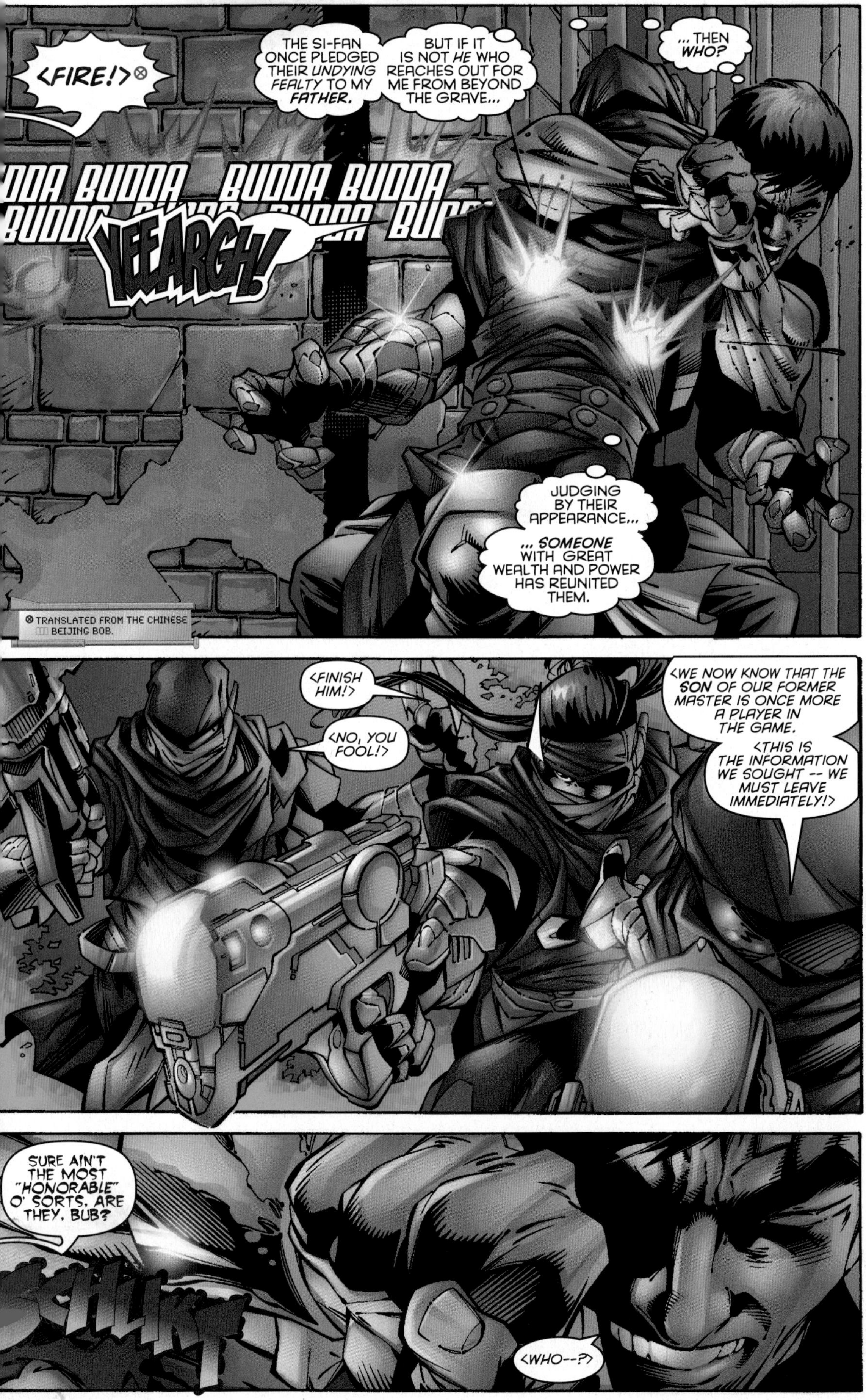
<FIRE!>⊗
THE SI-FAN ONCE PLEDGED THEIR *UNDYING FEALTY* TO MY **FATHER.**
BUT IF IT IS NOT *HE* WHO REACHES OUT FOR ME FROM BEYOND THE GRAVE...
...THEN *WHO?*
BUDDA BUDDA BUDDA BUDDA
YEEARGH!
JUDGING BY THEIR APPEARANCE...
...SOMEONE WITH GREAT WEALTH AND POWER HAS REUNITED THEM.
⊗ TRANSLATED FROM THE CHINESE BEIJING BOB.
<FINISH HIM!>
<NO, YOU FOOL!>
<WE NOW KNOW THAT THE **SON** OF OUR FORMER MASTER IS ONCE MORE A PLAYER IN THE GAME.
<THIS IS THE INFORMATION WE SOUGHT -- WE MUST LEAVE IMMEDIATELY!>
SURE AIN'T THE MOST "HONORABLE" O' SORTS, ARE THEY, BUB?
SCHLIKT
<WHO--?>

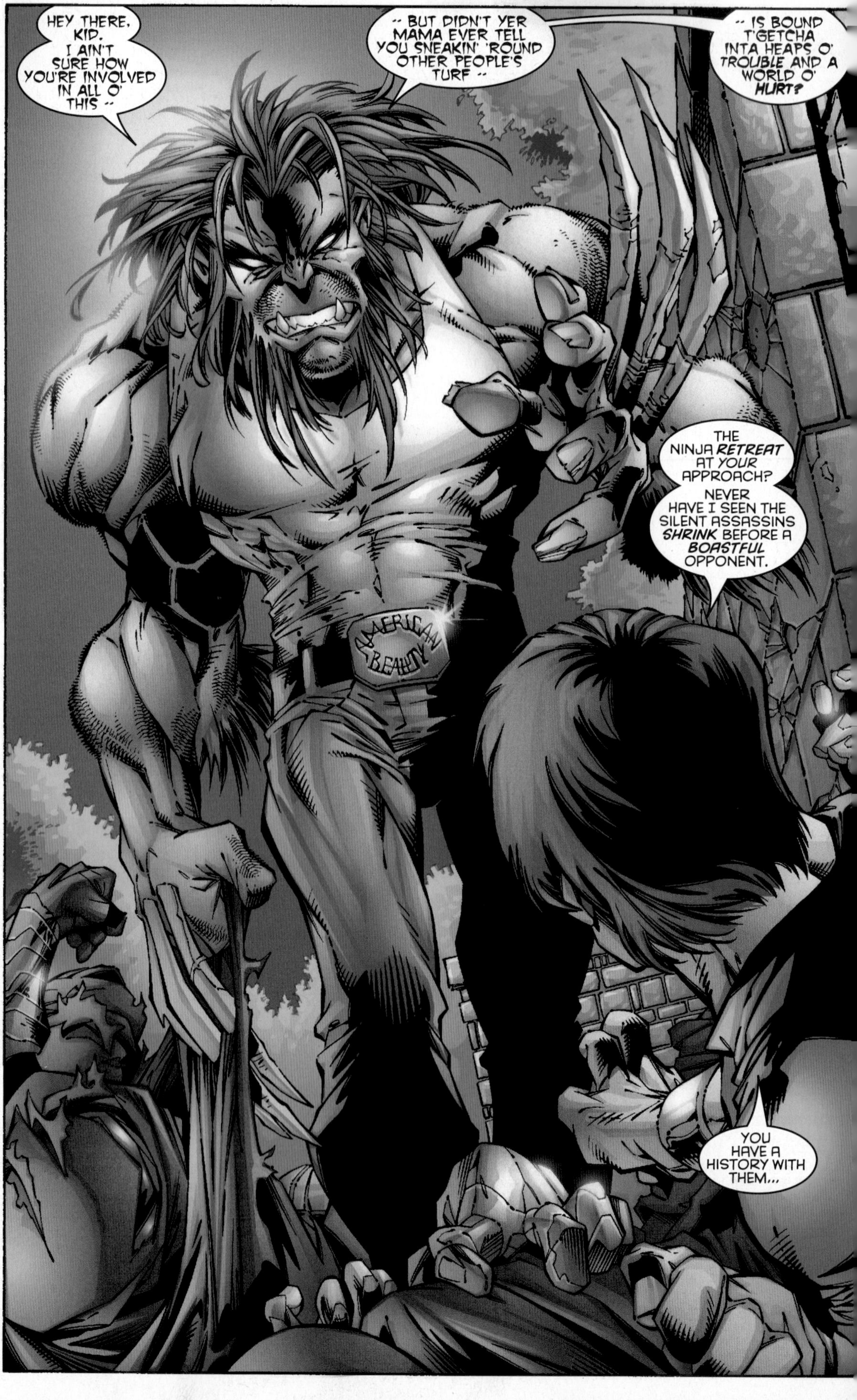
HEY THERE, KID. I AIN'T SURE HOW YOU'RE INVOLVED IN ALL O' THIS --
-- BUT DIDN'T YER MAMA EVER TELL YOU SNEAKIN' 'ROUND OTHER PEOPLE'S TURF --
-- IS BOUND T'GETCHA INTA HEAPS O' TROUBLE AND A WORLD O' HURT?
AMERICAN BEAUTY
THE NINJA RETREAT AT YOUR APPROACH?
NEVER HAVE I SEEN THE SILENT ASSASSINS SHRINK BEFORE A BOASTFUL OPPONENT.
YOU HAVE A HISTORY WITH THEM...

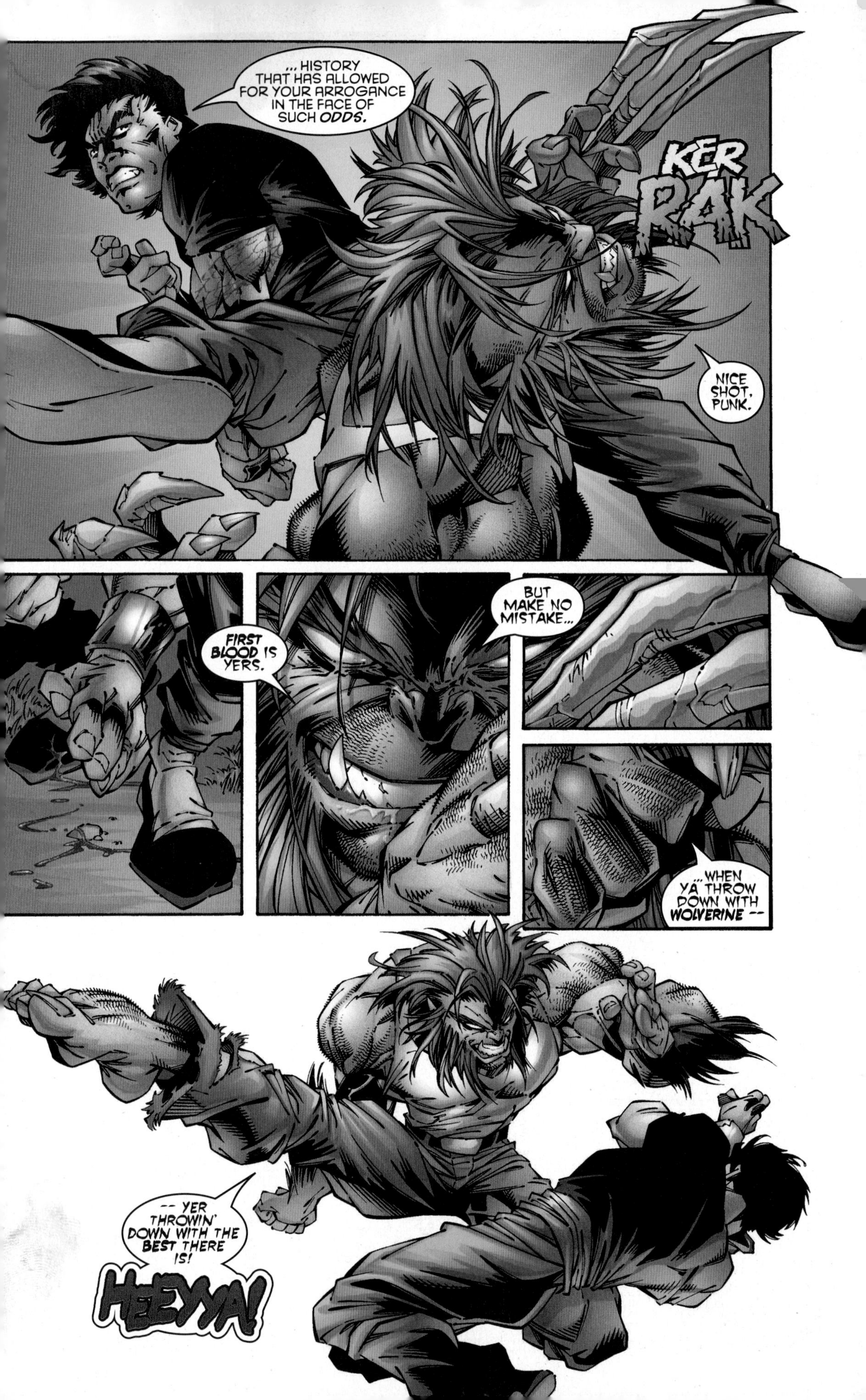
...HISTORY THAT HAS ALLOWED FOR YOUR ARROGANCE IN THE FACE OF SUCH ODDS.
KER RAK
NICE SHOT, PUNK.
FIRST BLOOD IS YERS.
BUT MAKE NO MISTAKE...
...WHEN YA THROW DOWN WITH WOLVERINE --
-- YER THROWIN' DOWN WITH THE BEST THERE IS!
HEEYYA!

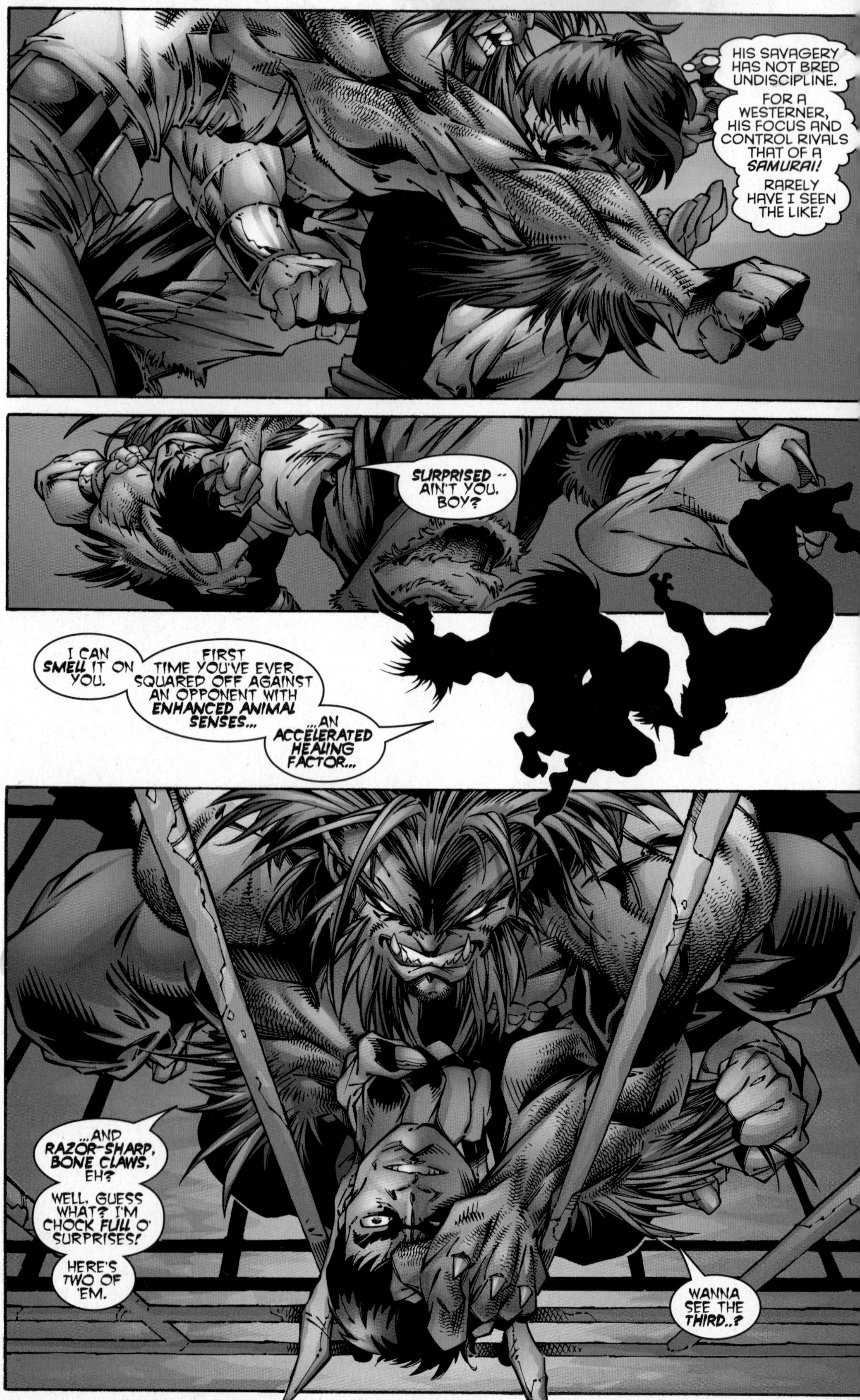
HIS SAVAGERY HAS NOT BRED UNDISCIPLINE.
FOR A WESTERNER, HIS FOCUS AND CONTROL RIVALS THAT OF A SAMURAI!
RARELY HAVE I SEEN THE LIKE!
SURPRISED -- AIN'T YOU, BOY?
I CAN SMELL IT ON YOU.
FIRST TIME YOU'VE EVER SQUARED OFF AGAINST AN OPPONENT WITH ENHANCED ANIMAL SENSES...
...AN ACCELERATED HEALING FACTOR...
...AND RAZOR-SHARP, BONE CLAWS, EH?
WELL, GUESS WHAT? I'M CHOCK FULL O' SURPRISES!
HERE'S TWO OF 'EM.
WANNA SEE THE THIRD..?

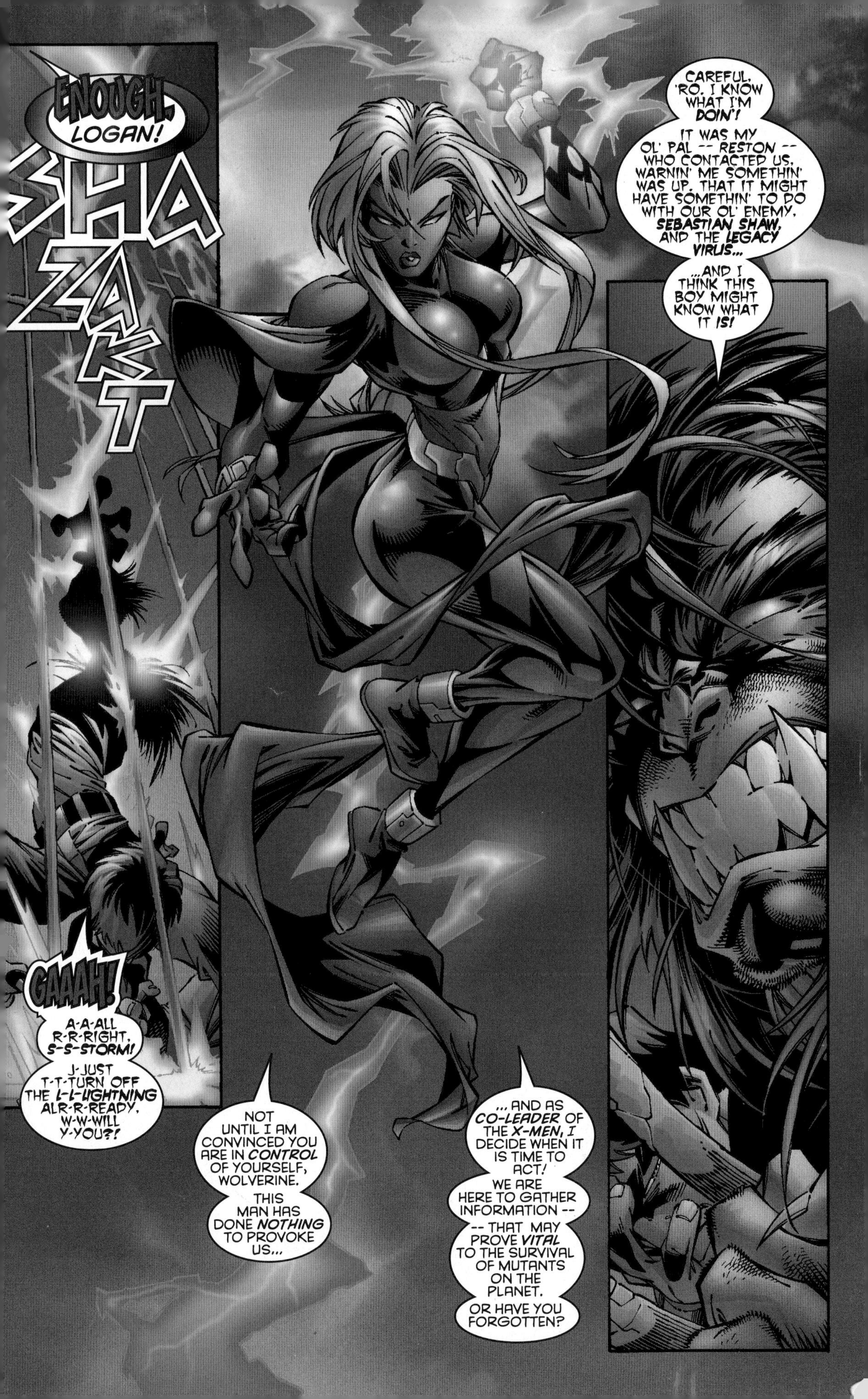

ENOUGH, LOGAN!
SHA ZAKT
GAAAH!
A-A-ALL R-R-RIGHT, S-S-STORM!
J-JUST T-T-TURN OFF THE L-L-LIGHTNING ALR-R-READY, W-W-WILL Y-YOU?!
NOT UNTIL I AM CONVINCED YOU ARE IN CONTROL OF YOURSELF, WOLVERINE.
THIS MAN HAS DONE NOTHING TO PROVOKE US...
... AND AS CO-LEADER OF THE X-MEN, I DECIDE WHEN IT IS TIME TO ACT!
WE ARE HERE TO GATHER INFORMATION --
-- THAT MAY PROVE VITAL TO THE SURVIVAL OF MUTANTS ON THE PLANET.
OR HAVE YOU FORGOTTEN?
CAREFUL, 'RO. I KNOW WHAT I'M DOIN'!
IT WAS MY OL' PAL -- RESTON -- WHO CONTACTED US, WARNIN' ME SOMETHIN' WAS UP. THAT IT MIGHT HAVE SOMETHIN' TO DO WITH OUR OL' ENEMY, SEBASTIAN SHAW, AND THE LEGACY VIRUS...
...AND I THINK THIS BOY MIGHT KNOW WHAT IT IS!

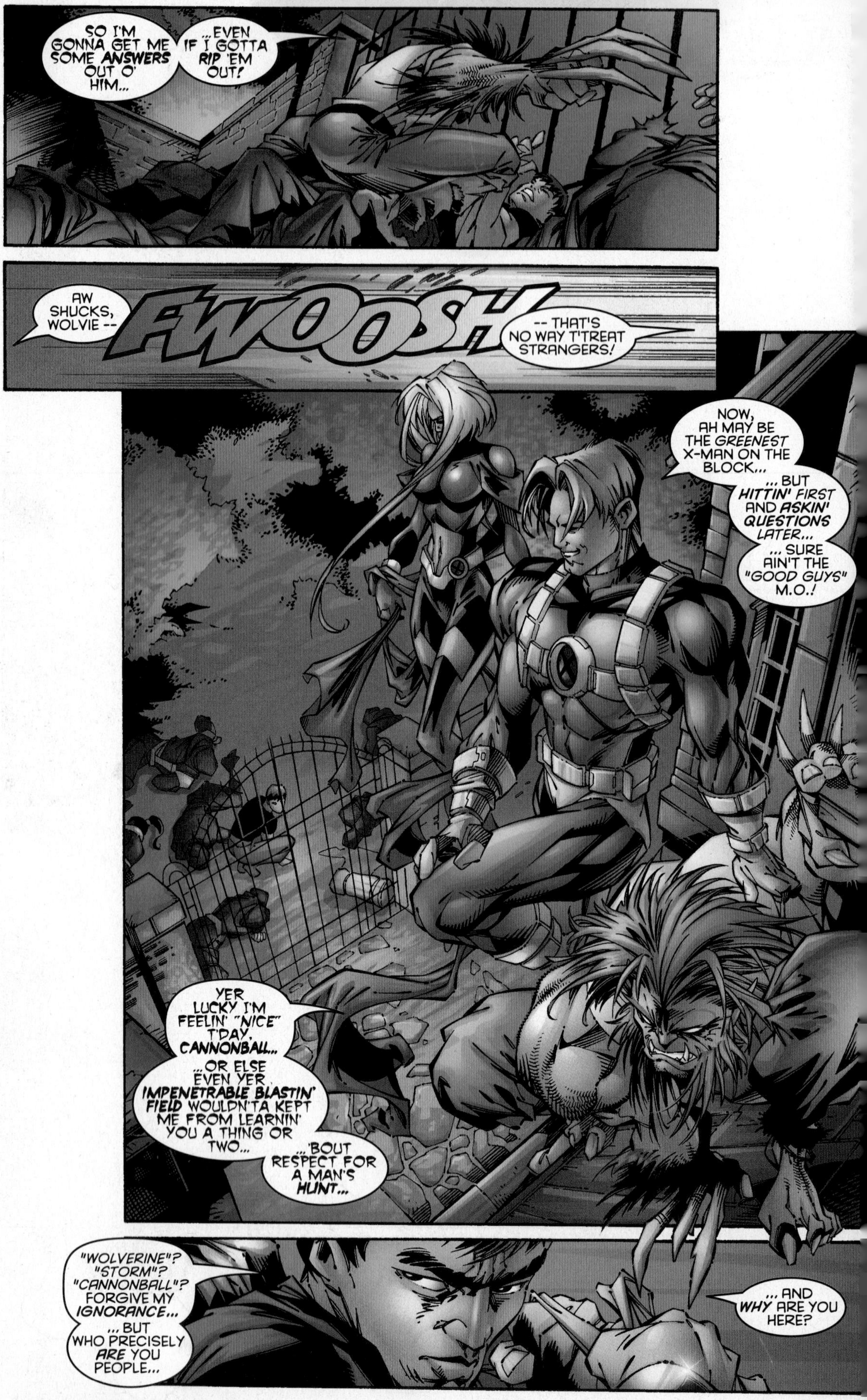
SO I'M GONNA GET ME SOME ANSWERS OUT O' HIM...
...EVEN IF I GOTTA RIP 'EM OUT!
AW SHUCKS, WOLVIE --
FWOOSH
-- THAT'S NO WAY T'TREAT STRANGERS!
NOW, AH MAY BE THE GREENEST X-MAN ON THE BLOCK...
...BUT HITTIN' FIRST AND ASKIN' QUESTIONS LATER...
...SURE AIN'T THE "GOOD GUYS" M.O.!
YER LUCKY I'M FEELIN' "NICE" T'DAY, CANNONBALL...
...OR ELSE EVEN YER IMPENETRABLE BLASTIN' FIELD WOULDN'TA KEPT ME FROM LEARNIN' YOU A THING OR TWO...
...'BOUT RESPECT FOR A MAN'S HUNT...
"WOLVERINE"? "STORM"? "CANNONBALL"? FORGIVE MY IGNORANCE...
...BUT WHO PRECISELY ARE YOU PEOPLE...
...AND WHY ARE YOU HERE?

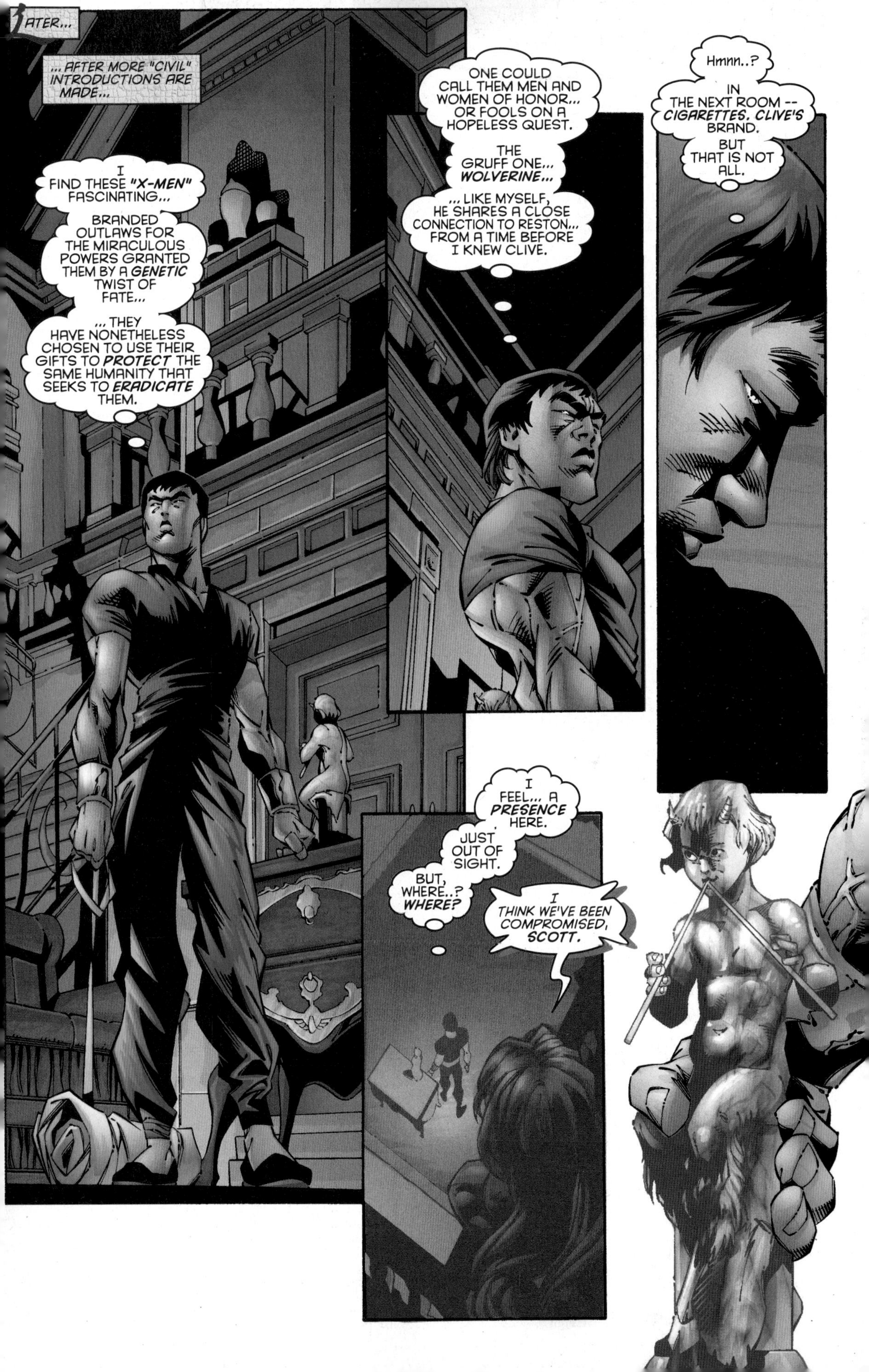
LATER...
...AFTER MORE "CIVIL" INTRODUCTIONS ARE MADE...
I FIND THESE "X-MEN" FASCINATING...
BRANDED OUTLAWS FOR THE MIRACULOUS POWERS GRANTED THEM BY A GENETIC TWIST OF FATE...
...THEY HAVE NONETHELESS CHOSEN TO USE THEIR GIFTS TO PROTECT THE SAME HUMANITY THAT SEEKS TO ERADICATE THEM.
ONE COULD CALL THEM MEN AND WOMEN OF HONOR... OR FOOLS ON A HOPELESS QUEST.
THE GRUFF ONE... WOLVERINE...
...LIKE MYSELF, HE SHARES A CLOSE CONNECTION TO RESTON... FROM A TIME BEFORE I KNEW CLIVE.
Hmmn..?
IN THE NEXT ROOM -- CIGARETTES. CLIVE'S BRAND.
BUT THAT IS NOT ALL.
I FEEL... A PRESENCE HERE.
JUST OUT OF SIGHT.
BUT, WHERE..? WHERE?
I THINK WE'VE BEEN COMPROMISED, SCOTT.

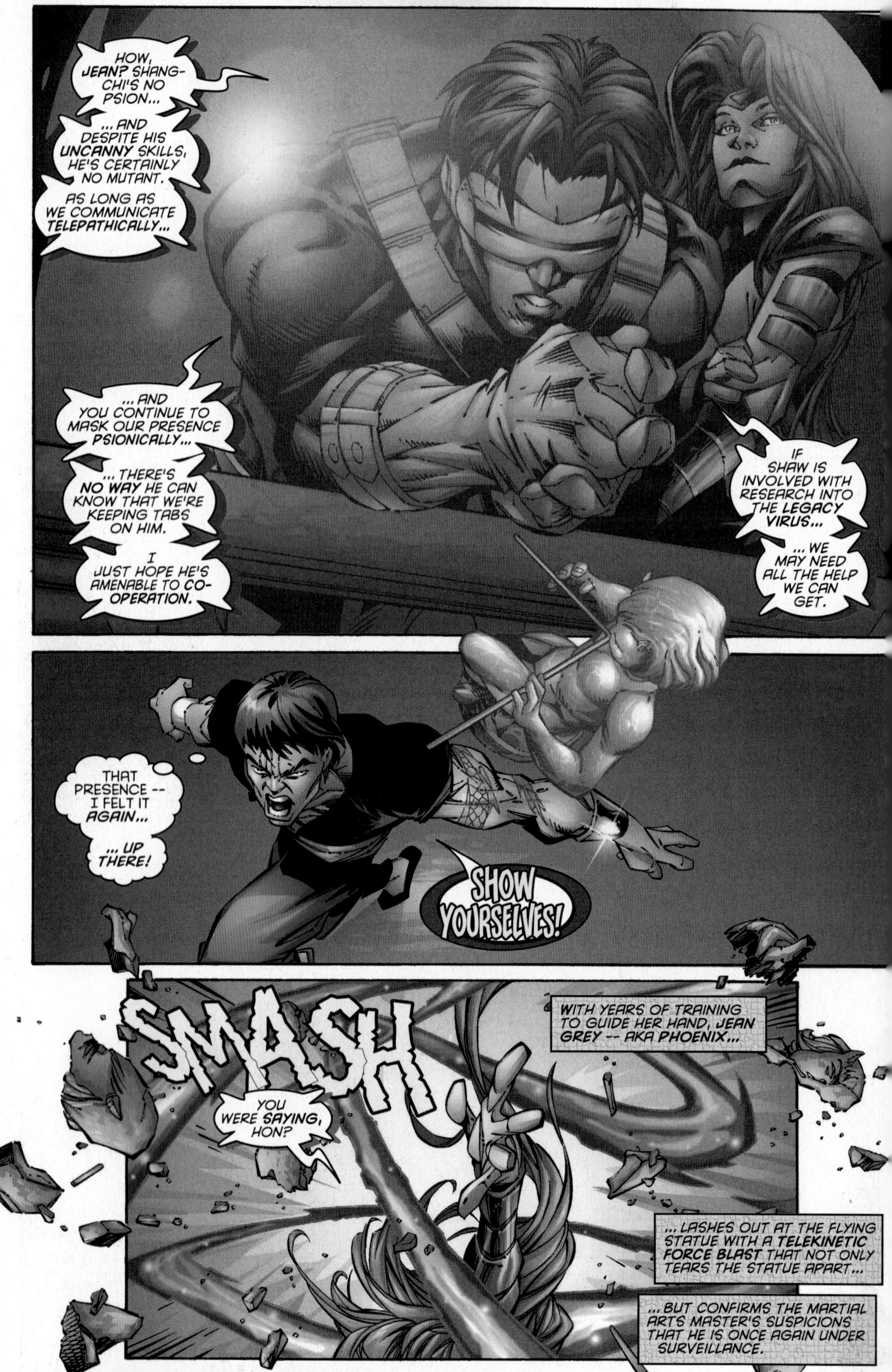
HOW, JEAN? SHANG-CHI'S NO PSION...
...AND DESPITE HIS UNCANNY SKILLS, HE'S CERTAINLY NO MUTANT.
AS LONG AS WE COMMUNICATE TELEPATHICALLY...
...AND YOU CONTINUE TO MASK OUR PRESENCE PSIONICALLY...
...THERE'S NO WAY HE CAN KNOW THAT WE'RE KEEPING TABS ON HIM.
I JUST HOPE HE'S AMENABLE TO CO-OPERATION.
IF SHAW IS INVOLVED WITH RESEARCH INTO THE LEGACY VIRUS...
...WE MAY NEED ALL THE HELP WE CAN GET.
THAT PRESENCE -- I FELT IT AGAIN...
...UP THERE!
SHOW YOURSELVES!
SMASH
WITH YEARS OF TRAINING TO GUIDE HER HAND, JEAN GREY -- AKA PHOENIX...
YOU WERE SAYING, HON?
...LASHES OUT AT THE FLYING STATUE WITH A TELEKINETIC FORCE BLAST THAT NOT ONLY TEARS THE STATUE APART...
...BUT CONFIRMS THE MARTIAL ARTS MASTER'S SUSPICIONS THAT HE IS ONCE AGAIN UNDER SURVEILLANCE.

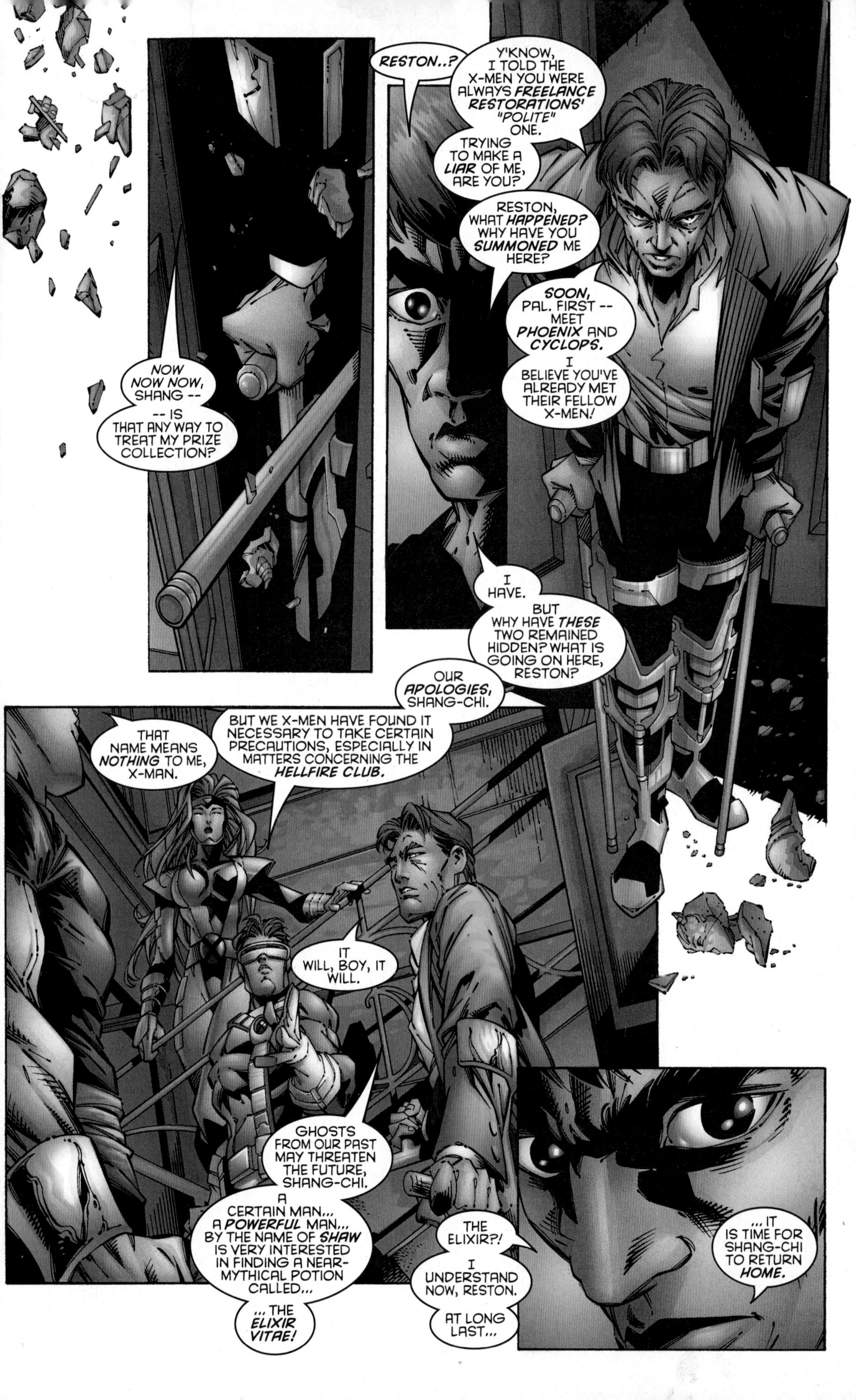

NOW NOW NOW, SHANG --
-- IS THAT ANY WAY TO TREAT MY PRIZE COLLECTION?
RESTON..?
Y'KNOW, I TOLD THE X-MEN YOU WERE ALWAYS FREELANCE RESTORATIONS' "POLITE" ONE.
TRYING TO MAKE A LIAR OF ME, ARE YOU?
RESTON, WHAT HAPPENED? WHY HAVE YOU SUMMONED ME HERE?
SOON, PAL. FIRST -- MEET PHOENIX AND CYCLOPS.
I BELIEVE YOU'VE ALREADY MET THEIR FELLOW X-MEN!
I HAVE.
BUT WHY HAVE THESE TWO REMAINED HIDDEN? WHAT IS GOING ON HERE, RESTON?
OUR APOLOGIES, SHANG-CHI.
BUT WE X-MEN HAVE FOUND IT NECESSARY TO TAKE CERTAIN PRECAUTIONS, ESPECIALLY IN MATTERS CONCERNING THE HELLFIRE CLUB.
THAT NAME MEANS NOTHING TO ME, X-MAN.
IT WILL, BOY, IT WILL.
GHOSTS FROM OUR PAST MAY THREATEN THE FUTURE, SHANG-CHI.
A CERTAIN MAN... A POWERFUL MAN... BY THE NAME OF SHAW IS VERY INTERESTED IN FINDING A NEAR-MYTHICAL POTION CALLED...
... THE ELIXIR VITAE!
THE ELIXIR?!
I UNDERSTAND NOW, RESTON.
AT LONG LAST...
... IT IS TIME FOR SHANG-CHI TO RETURN HOME.

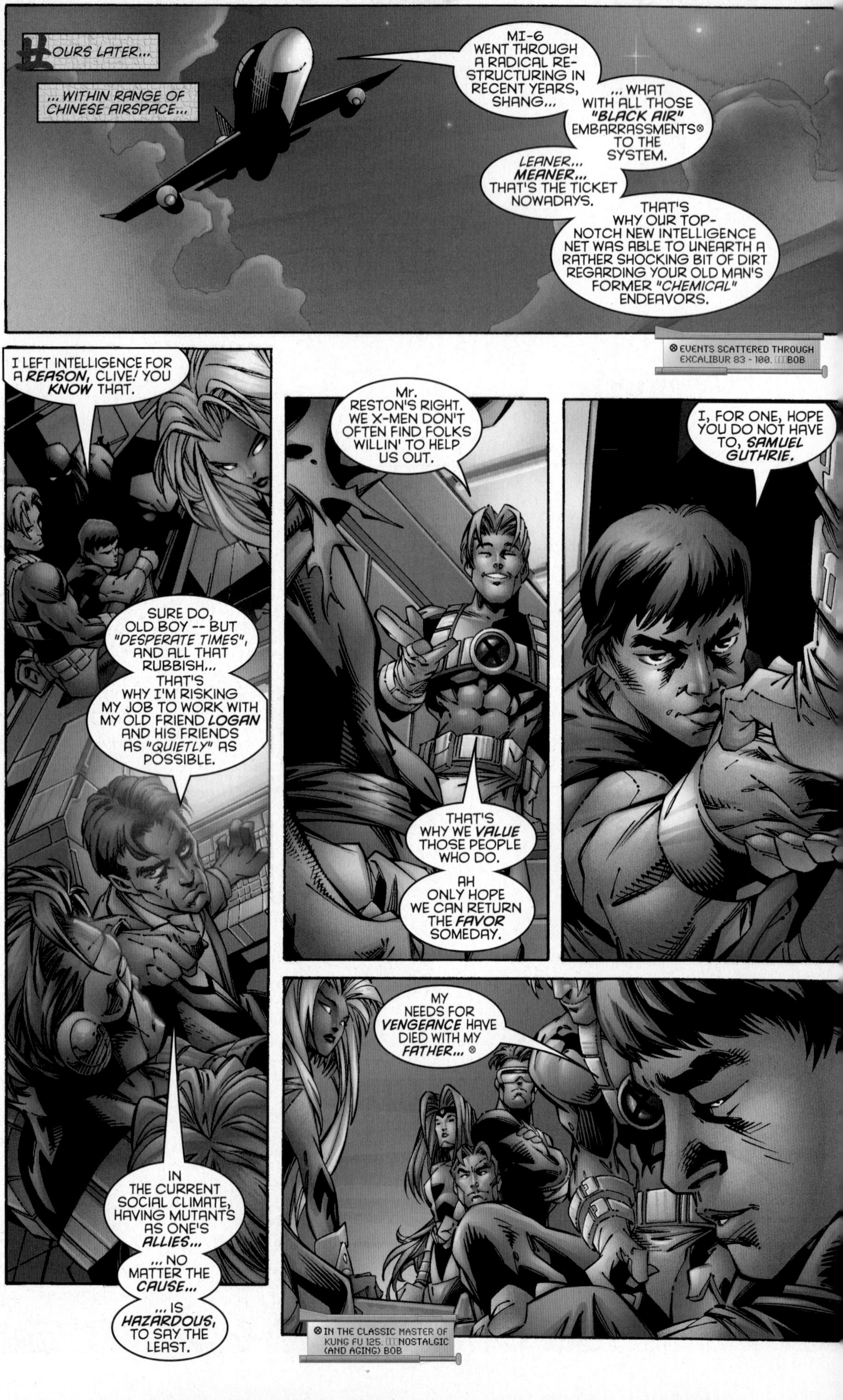

HOURS LATER...
...WITHIN RANGE OF CHINESE AIRSPACE...
MI-6 WENT THROUGH A RADICAL RE-STRUCTURING IN RECENT YEARS, SHANG...
...WHAT WITH ALL THOSE "BLACK AIR" EMBARRASSMENTS⊗ TO THE SYSTEM.
LEANER... MEANER... THAT'S THE TICKET NOWADAYS.
THAT'S WHY OUR TOP-NOTCH NEW INTELLIGENCE NET WAS ABLE TO UNEARTH A RATHER SHOCKING BIT OF DIRT REGARDING YOUR OLD MAN'S FORMER "CHEMICAL" ENDEAVORS.
⊗ EVENTS SCATTERED THROUGH EXCALIBUR 83 - 100. ——BOB
I LEFT INTELLIGENCE FOR A REASON, CLIVE! YOU KNOW THAT.
SURE DO, OLD BOY -- BUT "DESPERATE TIMES", AND ALL THAT RUBBISH...
THAT'S WHY I'M RISKING MY JOB TO WORK WITH MY OLD FRIEND LOGAN AND HIS FRIENDS AS "QUIETLY" AS POSSIBLE.
IN THE CURRENT SOCIAL CLIMATE, HAVING MUTANTS AS ONE'S ALLIES...
...NO MATTER THE CAUSE...
...IS HAZARDOUS, TO SAY THE LEAST.
Mr. RESTON'S RIGHT. WE X-MEN DON'T OFTEN FIND FOLKS WILLIN' TO HELP US OUT.
THAT'S WHY WE VALUE THOSE PEOPLE WHO DO.
AH ONLY HOPE WE CAN RETURN THE FAVOR SOMEDAY.
I, FOR ONE, HOPE YOU DO NOT HAVE TO, SAMUEL GUTHRIE.
MY NEEDS FOR VENGEANCE HAVE DIED WITH MY FATHER... ⊗
⊗ IN THE CLASSIC MASTER OF KUNG FU 125. ——NOSTALGIC (AND AGING) BOB

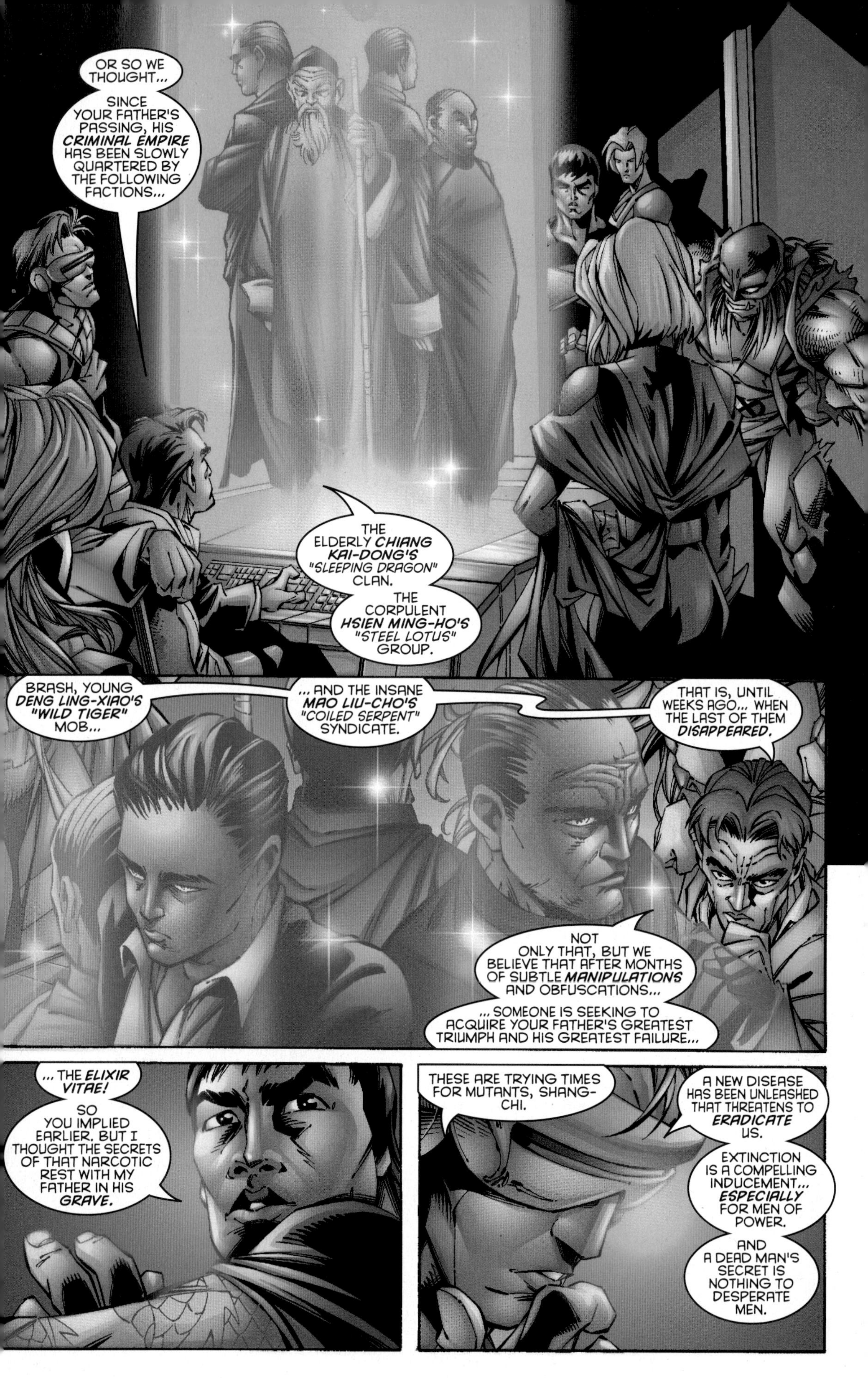
OR SO WE THOUGHT...
SINCE YOUR FATHER'S PASSING, HIS *CRIMINAL EMPIRE* HAS BEEN SLOWLY QUARTERED BY THE FOLLOWING FACTIONS...
THE ELDERLY *CHIANG KAI-DONG'S* "SLEEPING DRAGON" CLAN.
THE CORPULENT *HSIEN MING-HO'S* "STEEL LOTUS" GROUP.
BRASH, YOUNG *DENG LING-XIAO'S* *"WILD TIGER"* MOB...
...AND THE INSANE *MAO LIU-CHO'S* "COILED SERPENT" SYNDICATE.
THAT IS, UNTIL WEEKS AGO... WHEN THE LAST OF THEM *DISAPPEARED.*
NOT ONLY THAT, BUT WE BELIEVE THAT AFTER MONTHS OF SUBTLE *MANIPULATIONS* AND OBFUSCATIONS...
...SOMEONE IS SEEKING TO ACQUIRE YOUR FATHER'S GREATEST TRIUMPH AND HIS GREATEST FAILURE...
...THE *ELIXIR VITAE!*
SO YOU IMPLIED EARLIER. BUT I THOUGHT THE SECRETS OF THAT NARCOTIC REST WITH MY FATHER IN HIS *GRAVE.*
THESE ARE TRYING TIMES FOR MUTANTS, SHANG-CHI.
A NEW DISEASE HAS BEEN UNLEASHED THAT THREATENS TO *ERADICATE* US.
EXTINCTION IS A COMPELLING INDUCEMENT... *ESPECIALLY* FOR MEN OF POWER.
AND A DEAD MAN'S SECRET IS NOTHING TO DESPERATE MEN.

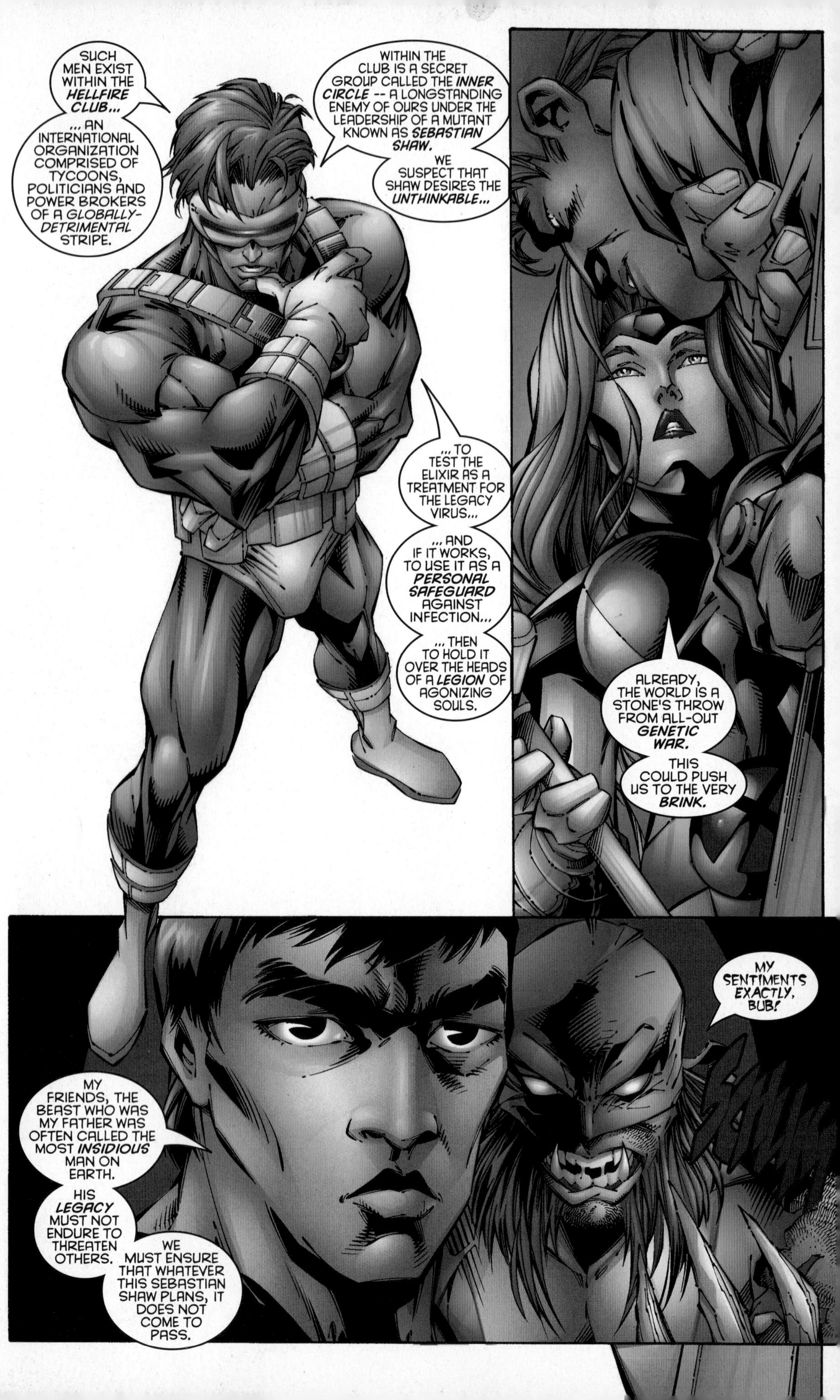
SUCH MEN EXIST WITHIN THE HELLFIRE CLUB...
...AN INTERNATIONAL ORGANIZATION COMPRISED OF TYCOONS, POLITICIANS AND POWER BROKERS OF A GLOBALLY-DETRIMENTAL STRIPE.
WITHIN THE CLUB IS A SECRET GROUP CALLED THE INNER CIRCLE -- A LONGSTANDING ENEMY OF OURS UNDER THE LEADERSHIP OF A MUTANT KNOWN AS SEBASTIAN SHAW.
WE SUSPECT THAT SHAW DESIRES THE UNTHINKABLE...
...TO TEST THE ELIXIR AS A TREATMENT FOR THE LEGACY VIRUS...
...AND IF IT WORKS, TO USE IT AS A PERSONAL SAFEGUARD AGAINST INFECTION...
...THEN TO HOLD IT OVER THE HEADS OF A LEGION OF AGONIZING SOULS.
ALREADY, THE WORLD IS A STONE'S THROW FROM ALL-OUT GENETIC WAR.
THIS COULD PUSH US TO THE VERY BRINK.
MY FRIENDS, THE BEAST WHO WAS MY FATHER WAS OFTEN CALLED THE MOST INSIDIOUS MAN ON EARTH.
HIS LEGACY MUST NOT ENDURE TO THREATEN OTHERS.
WE MUST ENSURE THAT WHATEVER THIS SEBASTIAN SHAW PLANS, IT DOES NOT COME TO PASS.
MY SENTIMENTS EXACTLY, BUB!

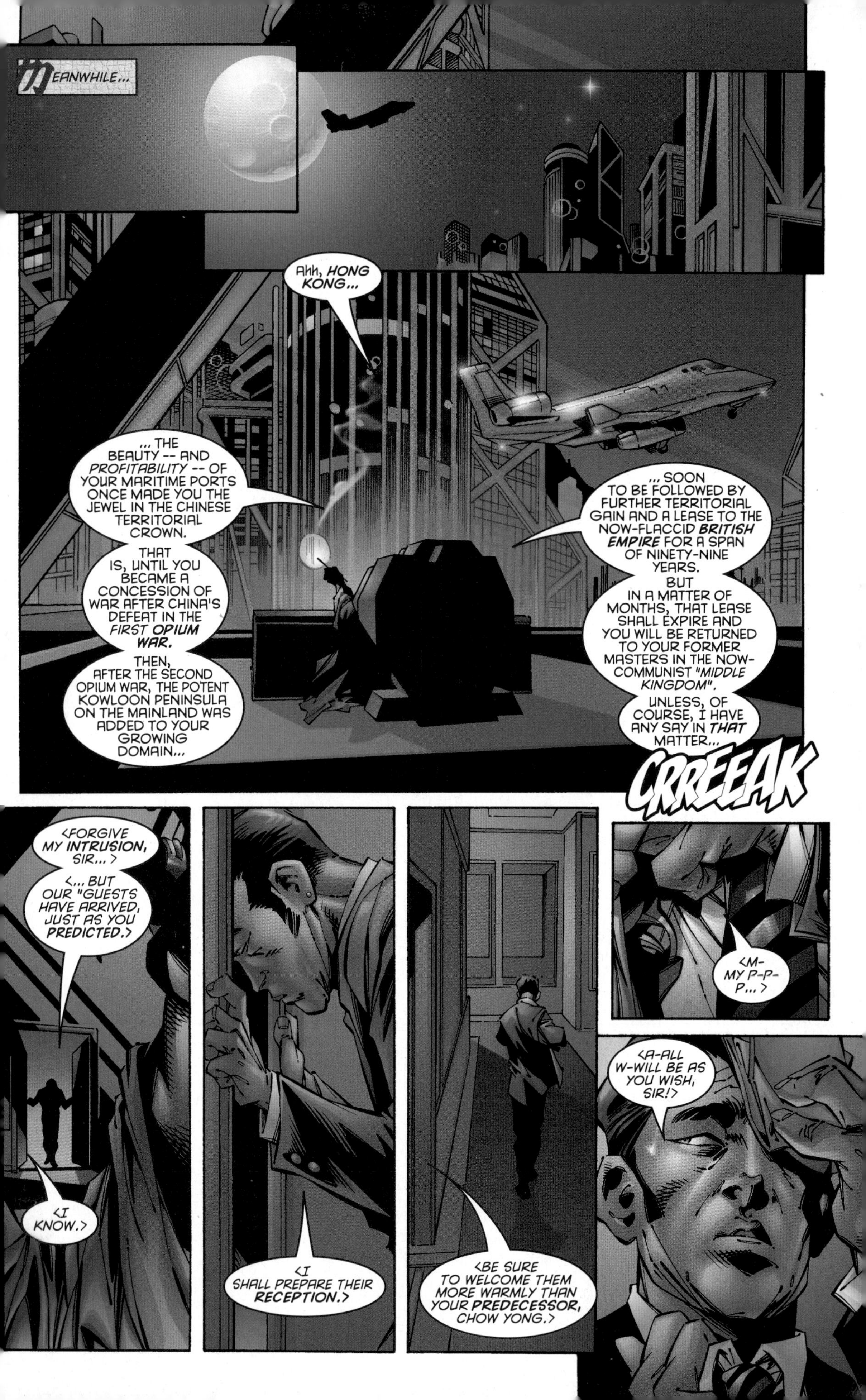
MEANWHILE...
AHH, HONG KONG...
... THE BEAUTY -- AND PROFITABILITY -- OF YOUR MARITIME PORTS ONCE MADE YOU THE JEWEL IN THE CHINESE TERRITORIAL CROWN.
THAT IS, UNTIL YOU BECAME A CONCESSION OF WAR AFTER CHINA'S DEFEAT IN THE FIRST OPIUM WAR.
THEN, AFTER THE SECOND OPIUM WAR, THE POTENT KOWLOON PENINSULA ON THE MAINLAND WAS ADDED TO YOUR GROWING DOMAIN...
... SOON TO BE FOLLOWED BY FURTHER TERRITORIAL GAIN AND A LEASE TO THE NOW-FLACCID BRITISH EMPIRE FOR A SPAN OF NINETY-NINE YEARS.
BUT IN A MATTER OF MONTHS, THAT LEASE SHALL EXPIRE AND YOU WILL BE RETURNED TO YOUR FORMER MASTERS IN THE NOW-COMMUNIST "MIDDLE KINGDOM".
UNLESS, OF COURSE, I HAVE ANY SAY IN THAT MATTER...
CRREEAK
<FORGIVE MY INTRUSION, SIR... >
<... BUT OUR "GUESTS HAVE ARRIVED, JUST AS YOU PREDICTED.>
<I KNOW.>
<I SHALL PREPARE THEIR RECEPTION.>
<BE SURE TO WELCOME THEM MORE WARMLY THAN YOUR PREDECESSOR, CHOW YONG.>
<M-MY P-P-P... >
<A-ALL W-WILL BE AS YOU WISH, SIR!>

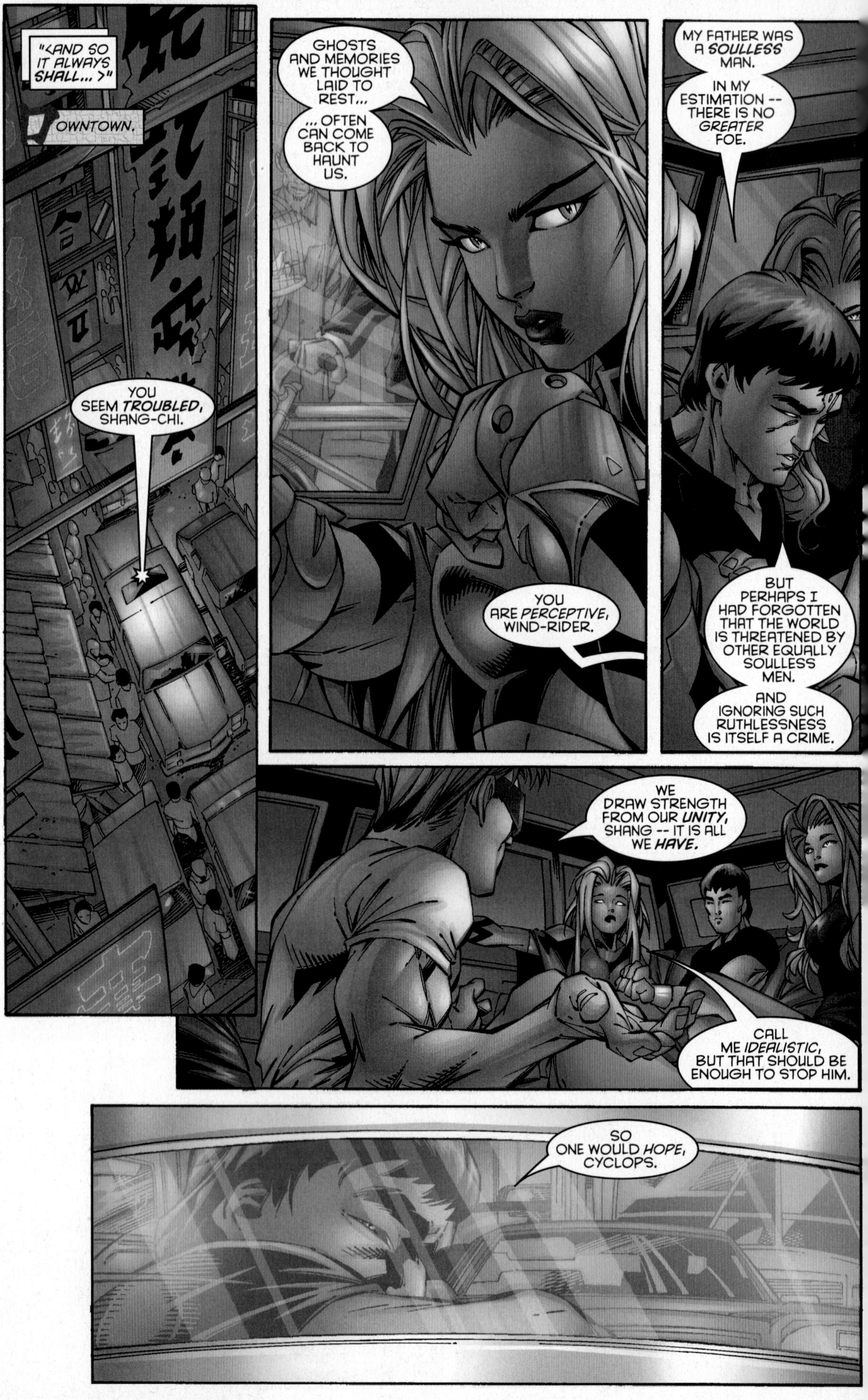
"<AND SO IT ALWAYS SHALL... >"
DOWNTOWN.
YOU SEEM TROUBLED, SHANG-CHI.
GHOSTS AND MEMORIES WE THOUGHT LAID TO REST...
... OFTEN CAN COME BACK TO HAUNT US.
YOU ARE PERCEPTIVE, WIND-RIDER.
MY FATHER WAS A SOULLESS MAN.
IN MY ESTIMATION -- THERE IS NO GREATER FOE.
BUT PERHAPS I HAD FORGOTTEN THAT THE WORLD IS THREATENED BY OTHER EQUALLY SOULLESS MEN.
AND IGNORING SUCH RUTHLESSNESS IS ITSELF A CRIME.
WE DRAW STRENGTH FROM OUR UNITY, SHANG -- IT IS ALL WE HAVE.
CALL ME IDEALISTIC, BUT THAT SHOULD BE ENOUGH TO STOP HIM.
SO ONE WOULD HOPE, CYCLOPS.

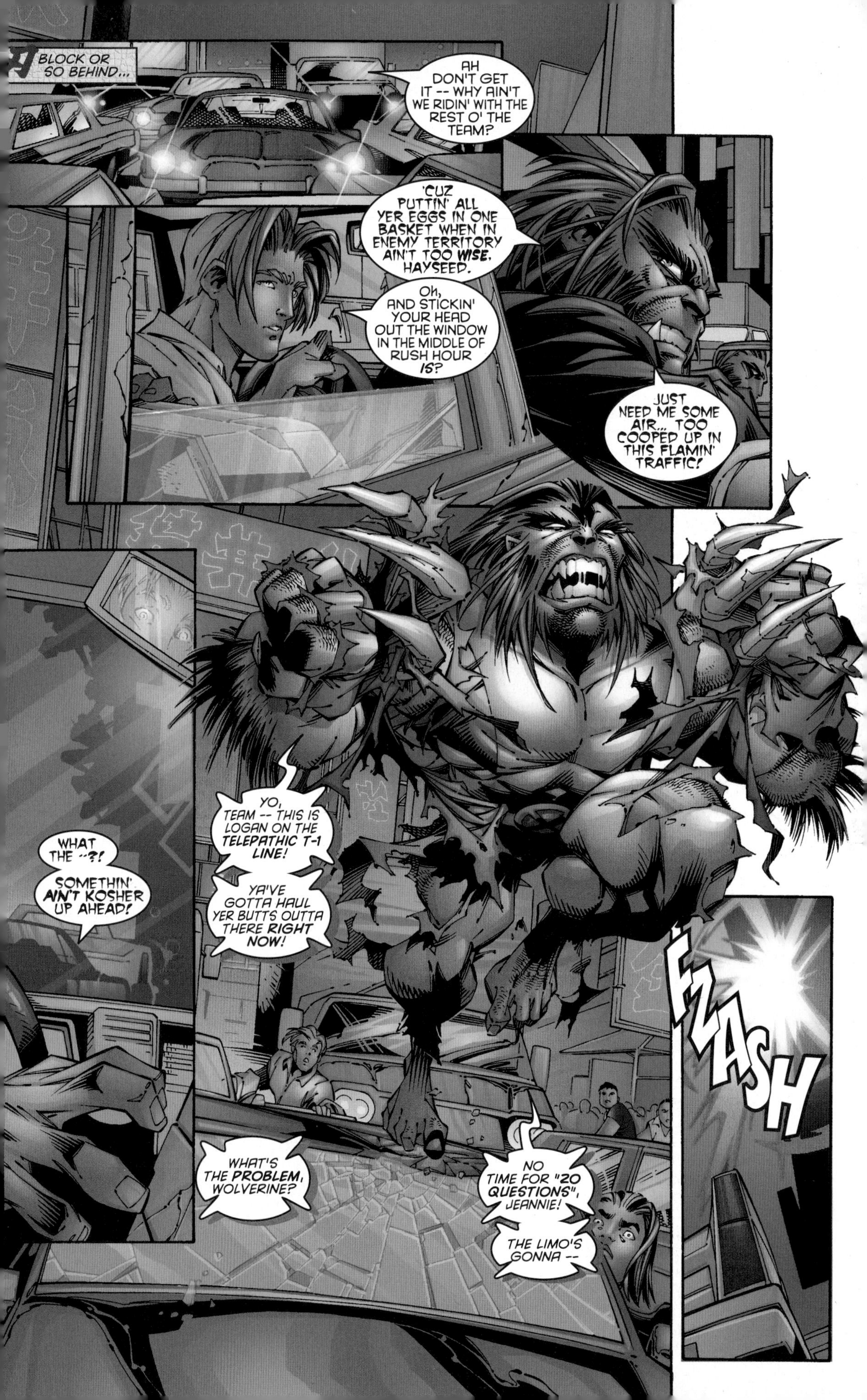
A BLOCK OR SO BEHIND...
AH DON'T GET IT -- WHY AIN'T WE RIDIN' WITH THE REST O' THE TEAM?
'CUZ PUTTIN' ALL YER EGGS IN ONE BASKET WHEN IN ENEMY TERRITORY AIN'T TOO WISE, HAYSEED.
OH, AND STICKIN' YOUR HEAD OUT THE WINDOW IN THE MIDDLE OF RUSH HOUR IS?
JUST NEED ME SOME AIR... TOO COOPED UP IN THIS FLAMIN' TRAFFIC!
WHAT THE --?!
SOMETHIN' AIN'T KOSHER UP AHEAD!
YO, TEAM -- THIS IS LOGAN ON THE TELEPATHIC T-1 LINE!
YA'VE GOTTA HAUL YER BUTTS OUTTA THERE RIGHT NOW!
WHAT'S THE PROBLEM, WOLVERINE?
NO TIME FOR "20 QUESTIONS", JEANNIE!
THE LIMO'S GONNA --
FZASH

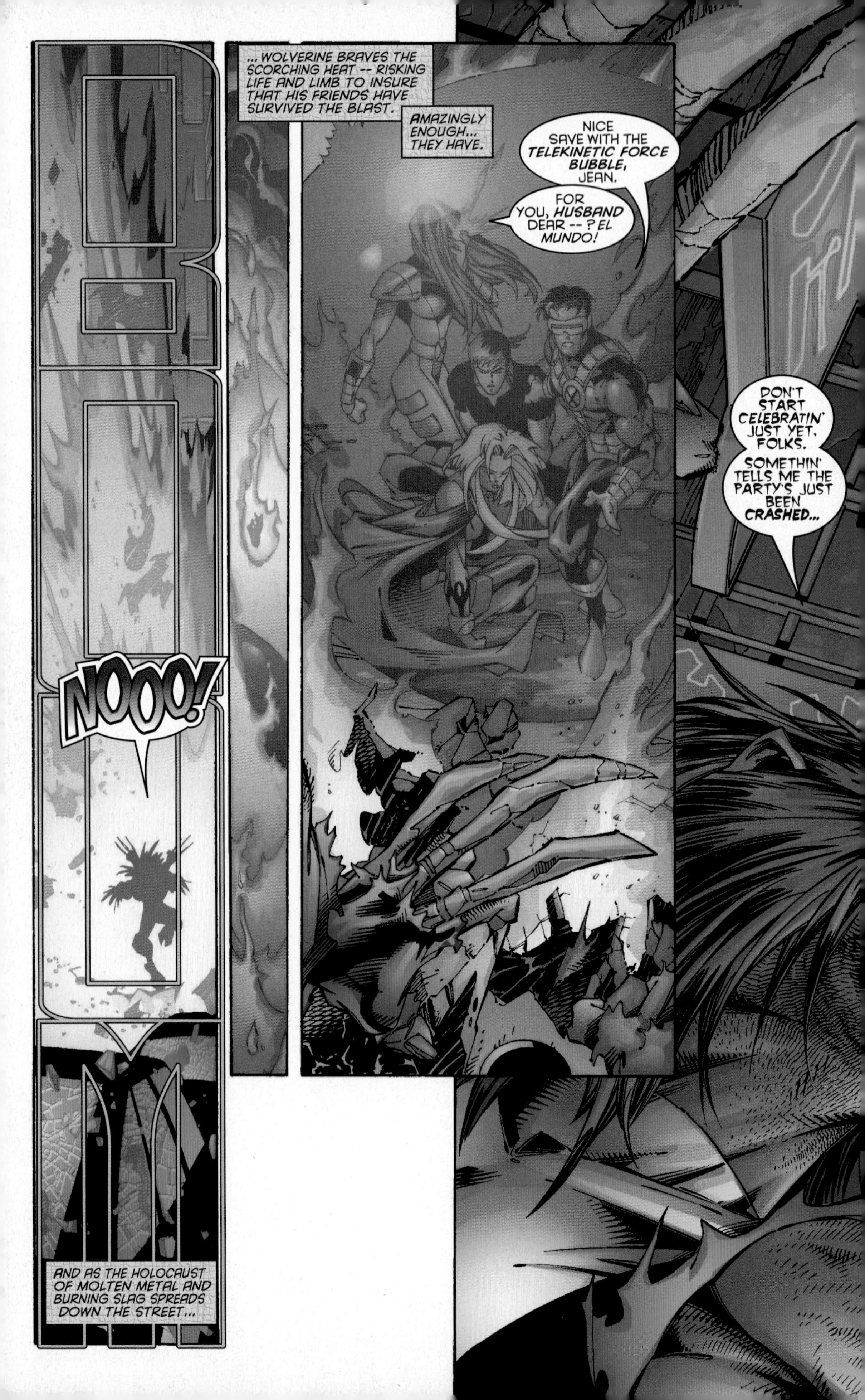

NOOO!
AND AS THE HOLOCAUST OF MOLTEN METAL AND BURNING SLAG SPREADS DOWN THE STREET...
... WOLVERINE BRAVES THE SCORCHING HEAT -- RISKING LIFE AND LIMB TO INSURE THAT HIS FRIENDS HAVE SURVIVED THE BLAST.
AMAZINGLY ENOUGH... THEY HAVE.
NICE SAVE WITH THE TELEKINETIC FORCE BUBBLE, JEAN.
FOR YOU, HUSBAND DEAR -- ?EL MUNDO!
DON'T START CELEBRATIN' JUST YET, FOLKS.
SOMETHIN' TELLS ME THE PARTY'S JUST BEEN CRASHED...

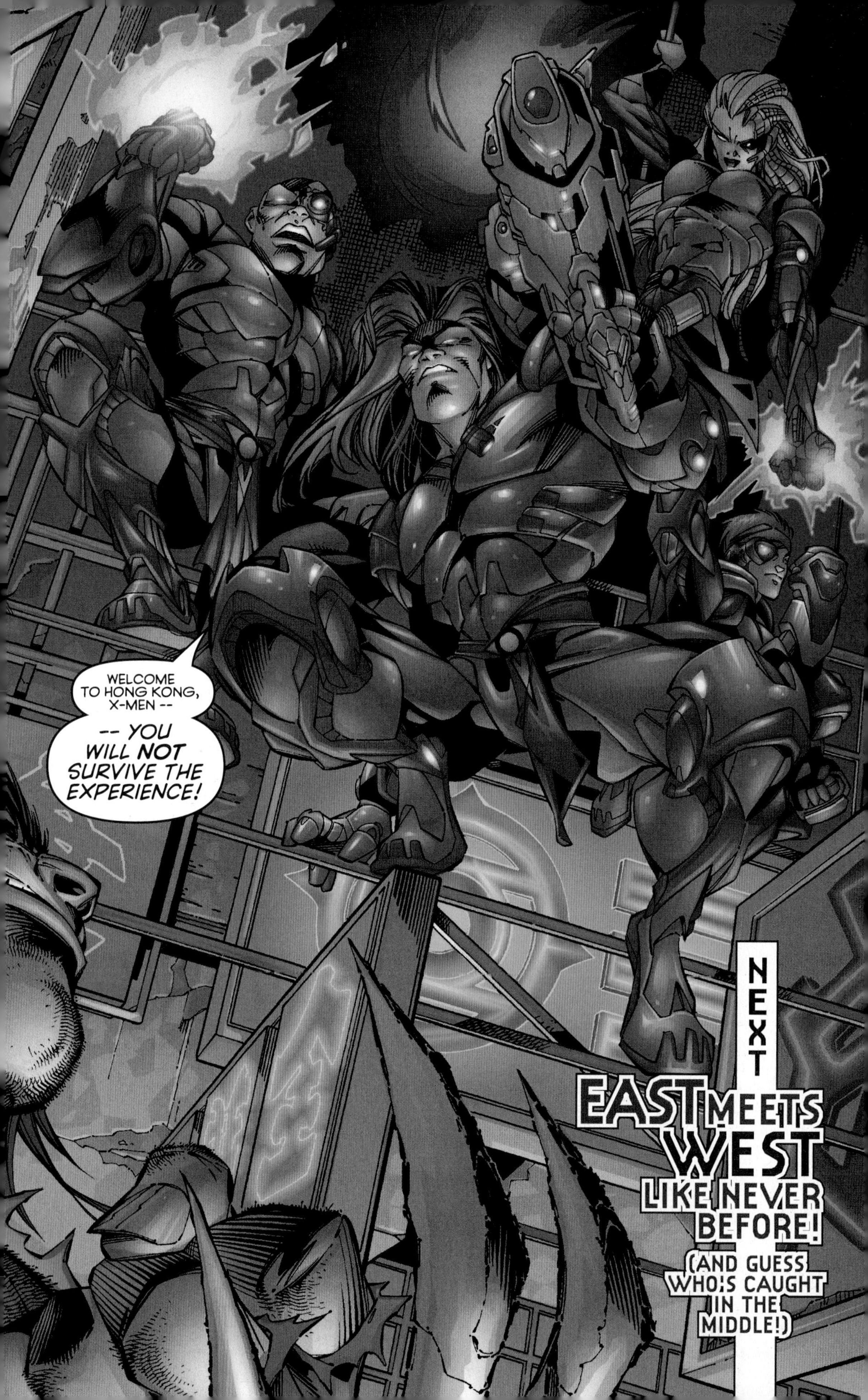
WELCOME TO HONG KONG, X-MEN --
-- YOU WILL NOT SURVIVE THE EXPERIENCE!
NEXT
EAST MEETS WEST LIKE NEVER BEFORE!
(AND GUESS WHO'S CAUGHT IN THE MIDDLE!)

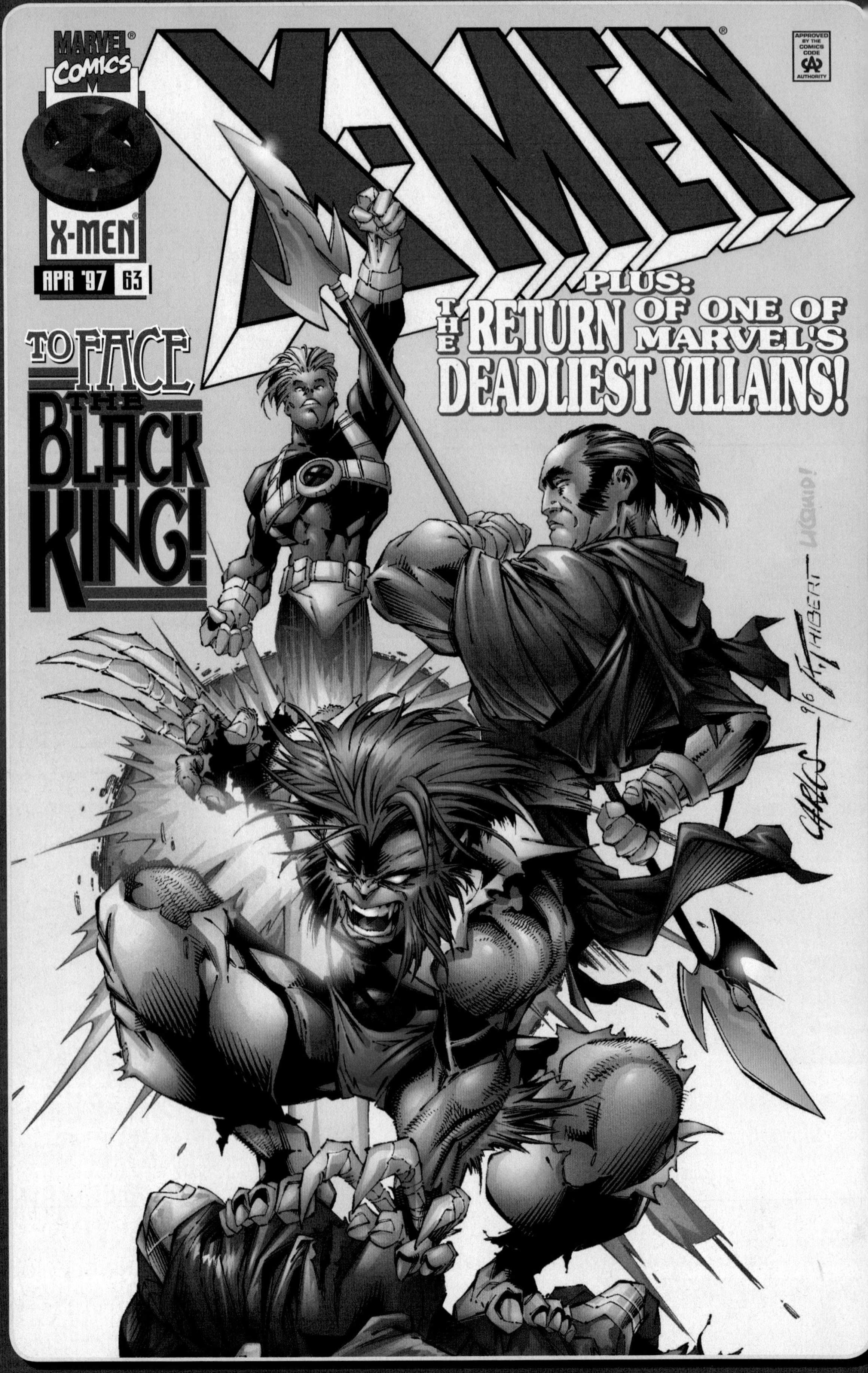
MARVEL COMICS
X-MEN
APR '97 63
APPROVED BY THE COMICS CODE AUTHORITY
X-MEN
PLUS:
THE RETURN OF ONE OF MARVEL'S DEADLIEST VILLAINS!
TO FACE THE BLACK KING!

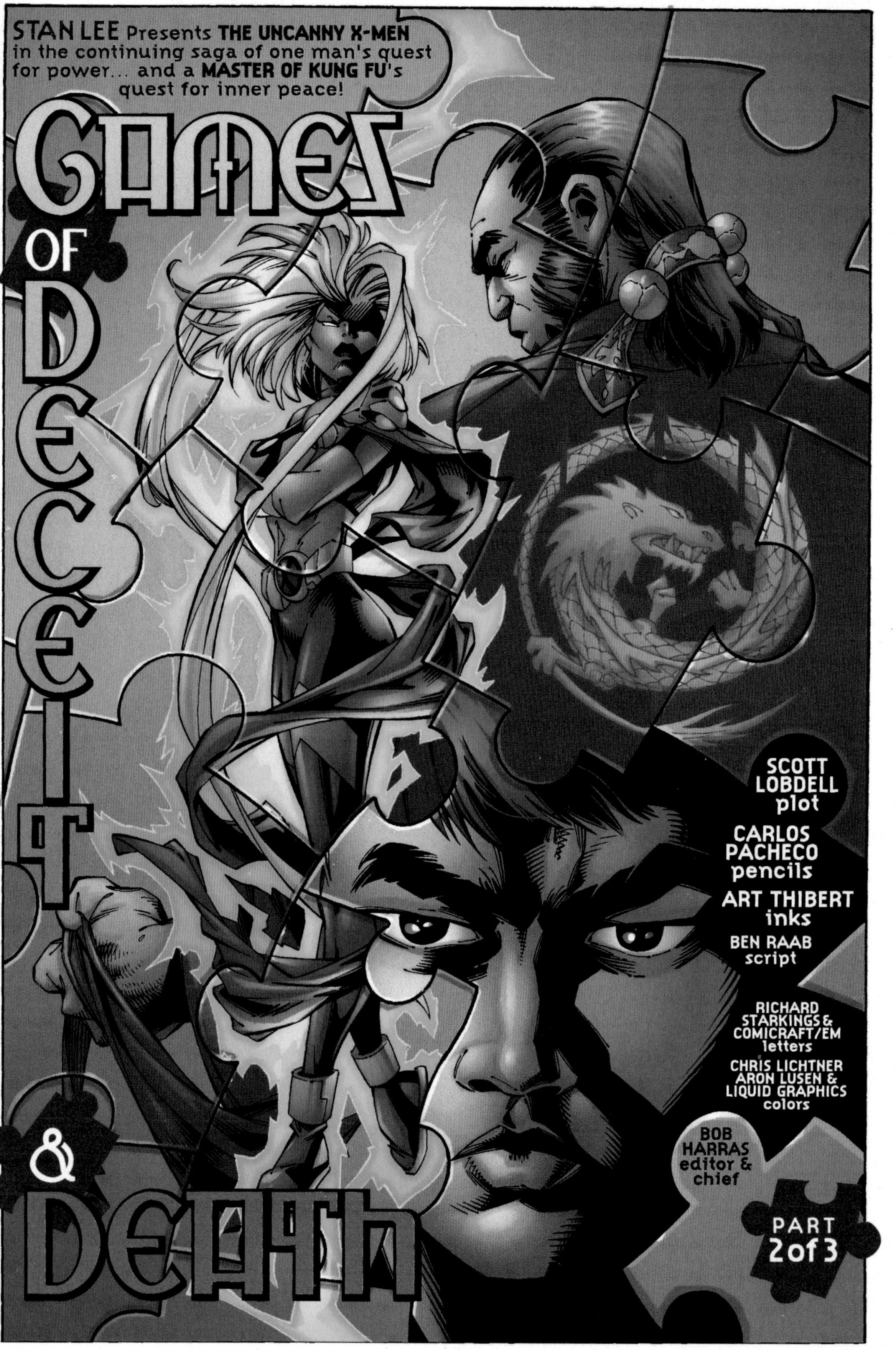
STAN LEE Presents THE UNCANNY X-MEN in the continuing saga of one man's quest for power... and a MASTER OF KUNG FU's quest for inner peace!
GAMES OF DECEIT & DEATH
SCOTT LOBDELL plot
CARLOS PACHECO pencils
ART THIBERT inks
BEN RAAB script
RICHARD STARKINGS & COMICRAFT/EM letters
CHRIS LICHTNER ARON LUSEN & LIQUID GRAPHICS colors
BOB HARRAS editor & chief
PART 2 of 3

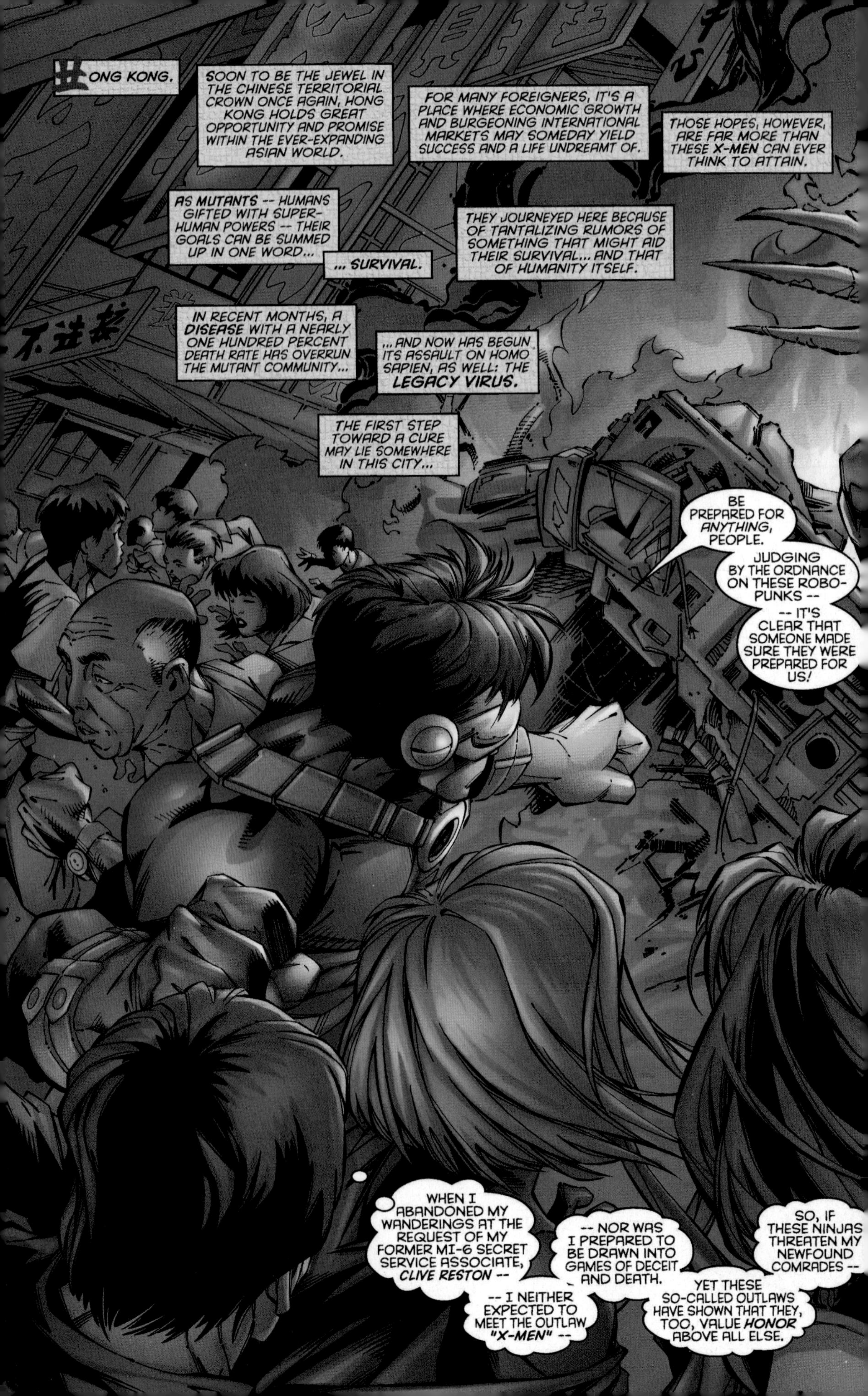
HONG KONG.
SOON TO BE THE JEWEL IN THE CHINESE TERRITORIAL CROWN ONCE AGAIN, HONG KONG HOLDS GREAT OPPORTUNITY AND PROMISE WITHIN THE EVER-EXPANDING ASIAN WORLD.
FOR MANY FOREIGNERS, IT'S A PLACE WHERE ECONOMIC GROWTH AND BURGEONING INTERNATIONAL MARKETS MAY SOMEDAY YIELD SUCCESS AND A LIFE UNDREAMT OF.
THOSE HOPES, HOWEVER, ARE FAR MORE THAN THESE X-MEN CAN EVER THINK TO ATTAIN.
AS MUTANTS -- HUMANS GIFTED WITH SUPER-HUMAN POWERS -- THEIR GOALS CAN BE SUMMED UP IN ONE WORD...
... SURVIVAL.
THEY JOURNEYED HERE BECAUSE OF TANTALIZING RUMORS OF SOMETHING THAT MIGHT AID THEIR SURVIVAL... AND THAT OF HUMANITY ITSELF.
IN RECENT MONTHS, A DISEASE WITH A NEARLY ONE HUNDRED PERCENT DEATH RATE HAS OVERRUN THE MUTANT COMMUNITY...
...AND NOW HAS BEGUN ITS ASSAULT ON HOMO SAPIEN, AS WELL: THE LEGACY VIRUS.
THE FIRST STEP TOWARD A CURE MAY LIE SOMEWHERE IN THIS CITY...
BE PREPARED FOR ANYTHING, PEOPLE.
JUDGING BY THE ORDNANCE ON THESE ROBO-PUNKS --
-- IT'S CLEAR THAT SOMEONE MADE SURE THEY WERE PREPARED FOR US!
WHEN I ABANDONED MY WANDERINGS AT THE REQUEST OF MY FORMER MI-6 SECRET SERVICE ASSOCIATE, CLIVE RESTON --
-- I NEITHER EXPECTED TO MEET THE OUTLAW "X-MEN" --
-- NOR WAS I PREPARED TO BE DRAWN INTO GAMES OF DECEIT AND DEATH.
YET THESE SO-CALLED OUTLAWS HAVE SHOWN THAT THEY, TOO, VALUE HONOR ABOVE ALL ELSE.
SO, IF THESE NINJAS THREATEN MY NEWFOUND COMRADES --

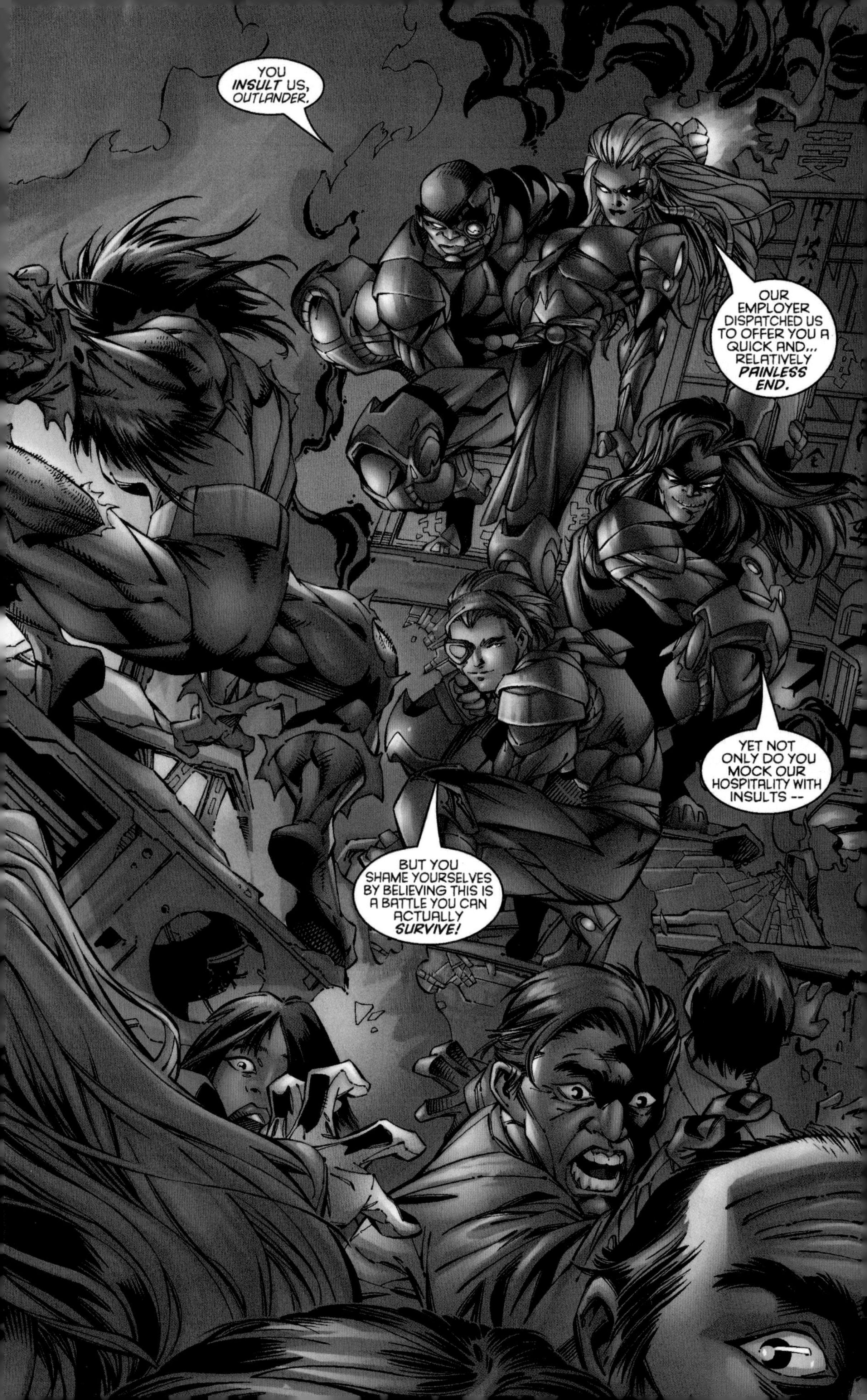
YOU INSULT US, OUTLANDER.
OUR EMPLOYER DISPATCHED US TO OFFER YOU A QUICK AND... RELATIVELY PAINLESS END.
YET NOT ONLY DO YOU MOCK OUR HOSPITALITY WITH INSULTS --
BUT YOU SHAME YOURSELVES BY BELIEVING THIS IS A BATTLE YOU CAN ACTUALLY SURVIVE!

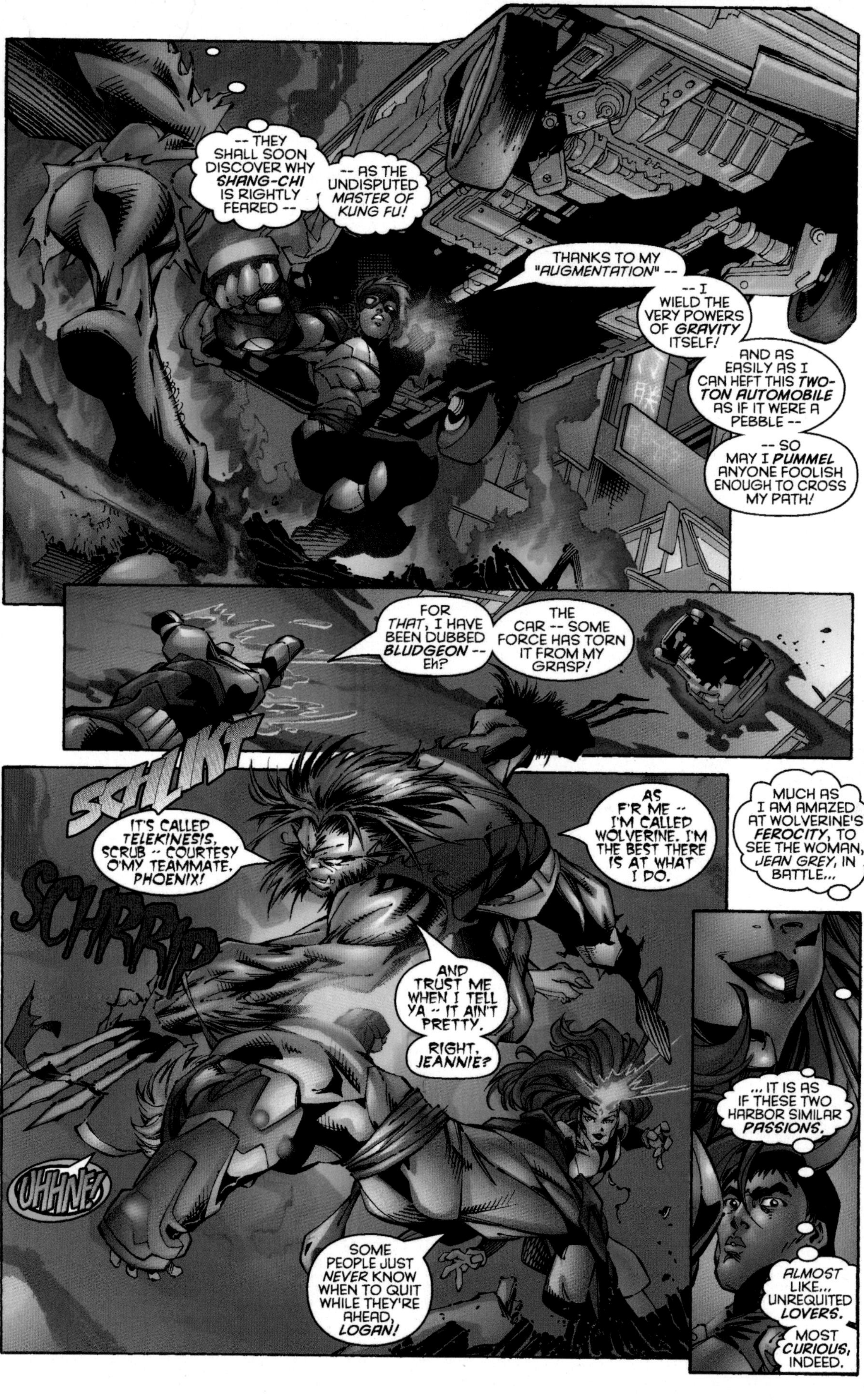
-- THEY SHALL SOON DISCOVER WHY SHANG-CHI IS RIGHTLY FEARED --
-- AS THE UNDISPUTED MASTER OF KUNG FU!
THANKS TO MY "AUGMENTATION" --
-- I WIELD THE VERY POWERS OF GRAVITY ITSELF!
AND AS EASILY AS I CAN HEFT THIS TWO-TON AUTOMOBILE AS IF IT WERE A PEBBLE --
-- SO MAY I PUMMEL ANYONE FOOLISH ENOUGH TO CROSS MY PATH!
FOR THAT, I HAVE BEEN DUBBED BLUDGEON -- Eh?
THE CAR -- SOME FORCE HAS TORN IT FROM MY GRASP!
SCHLIKT
IT'S CALLED TELEKINESIS, SCRUB -- COURTESY O'MY TEAMMATE, PHOENIX!
AS F'R ME -- I'M CALLED WOLVERINE. I'M THE BEST THERE IS AT WHAT I DO.
SCHRRIP
AND TRUST ME WHEN I TELL YA -- IT AIN'T PRETTY.
RIGHT, JEANNIE?
UHHNF!
SOME PEOPLE JUST NEVER KNOW WHEN TO QUIT WHILE THEY'RE AHEAD, LOGAN!
MUCH AS I AM AMAZED AT WOLVERINE'S FEROCITY, TO SEE THE WOMAN, JEAN GREY, IN BATTLE...
... IT IS AS IF THESE TWO HARBOR SIMILAR PASSIONS.
ALMOST LIKE... UNREQUITED LOVERS.
MOST CURIOUS, INDEED.

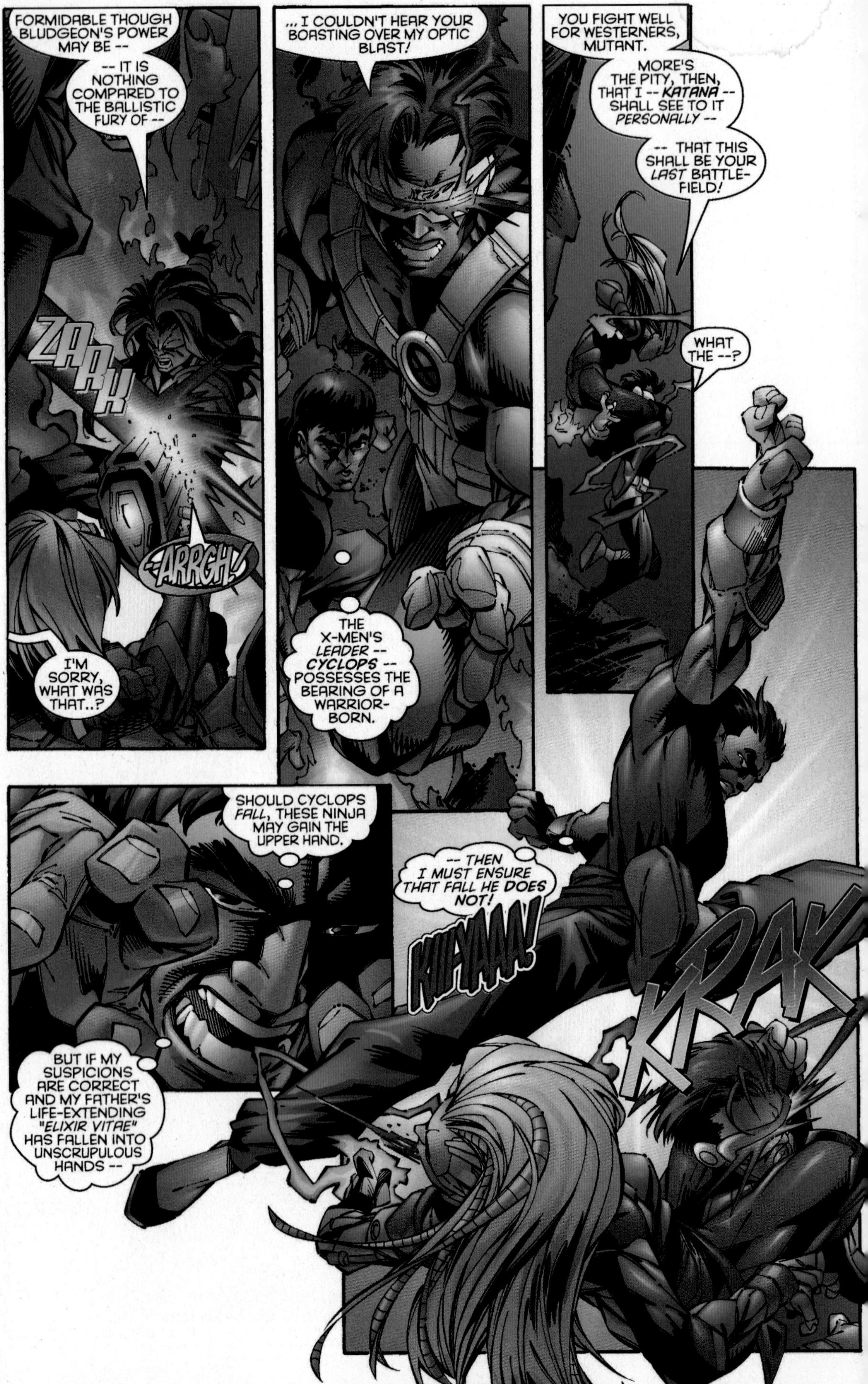

FORMIDABLE THOUGH BLUDGEON'S POWER MAY BE --
-- IT IS NOTHING COMPARED TO THE BALLISTIC FURY OF --
ZAARK
ARRGH!
I'M SORRY, WHAT WAS THAT..?
... I COULDN'T HEAR YOUR BOASTING OVER MY OPTIC BLAST!
THE X-MEN'S LEADER -- CYCLOPS -- POSSESSES THE BEARING OF A WARRIOR-BORN.
YOU FIGHT WELL FOR WESTERNERS, MUTANT.
MORE'S THE PITY, THEN, THAT I -- KATANA -- SHALL SEE TO IT PERSONALLY --
-- THAT THIS SHALL BE YOUR LAST BATTLE-FIELD!
WHAT THE --?
SHOULD CYCLOPS FALL, THESE NINJA MAY GAIN THE UPPER HAND.
BUT IF MY SUSPICIONS ARE CORRECT AND MY FATHER'S LIFE-EXTENDING "ELIXIR VITAE" HAS FALLEN INTO UNSCRUPULOUS HANDS --
-- THEN I MUST ENSURE THAT FALL HE DOES NOT!
KIIIYAAA!
KRAK

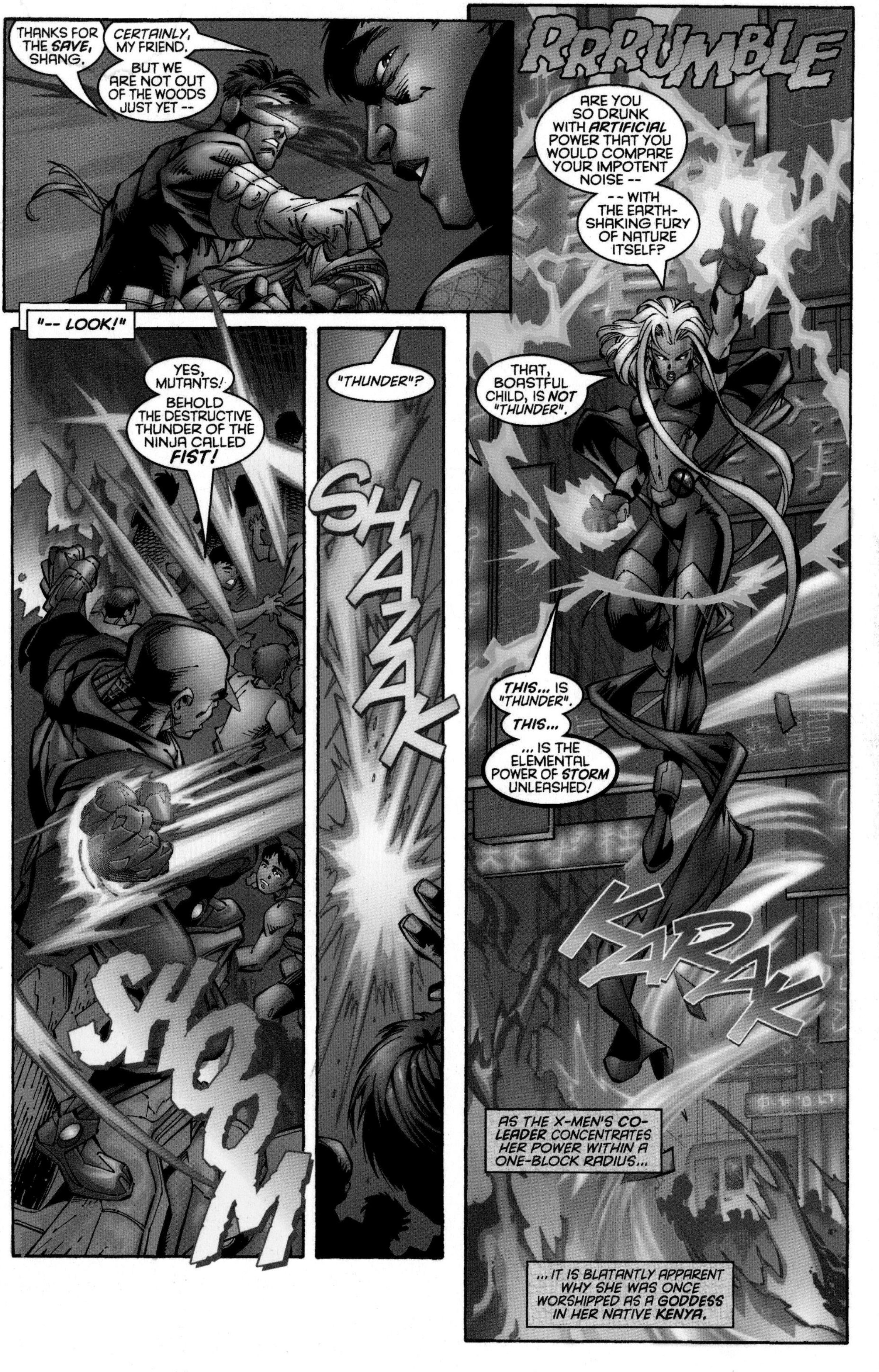
THANKS FOR THE SAVE, SHANG.
CERTAINLY, MY FRIEND.
BUT WE ARE NOT OUT OF THE WOODS JUST YET --
"-- LOOK!"
YES, MUTANTS! BEHOLD THE DESTRUCTIVE THUNDER OF THE NINJA CALLED FIST!
SHOOM
"THUNDER"?
SHANAK
RRRUMBLE
ARE YOU SO DRUNK WITH ARTIFICIAL POWER THAT YOU WOULD COMPARE YOUR IMPOTENT NOISE --
-- WITH THE EARTH-SHAKING FURY OF NATURE ITSELF?
THAT, BOASTFUL CHILD, IS NOT "THUNDER".
THIS... IS "THUNDER".
THIS...
... IS THE ELEMENTAL POWER OF STORM UNLEASHED!
KARAK
AS THE X-MEN'S CO-LEADER CONCENTRATES HER POWER WITHIN A ONE-BLOCK RADIUS...
... IT IS BLATANTLY APPARENT WHY SHE WAS ONCE WORSHIPPED AS A GODDESS IN HER NATIVE KENYA.

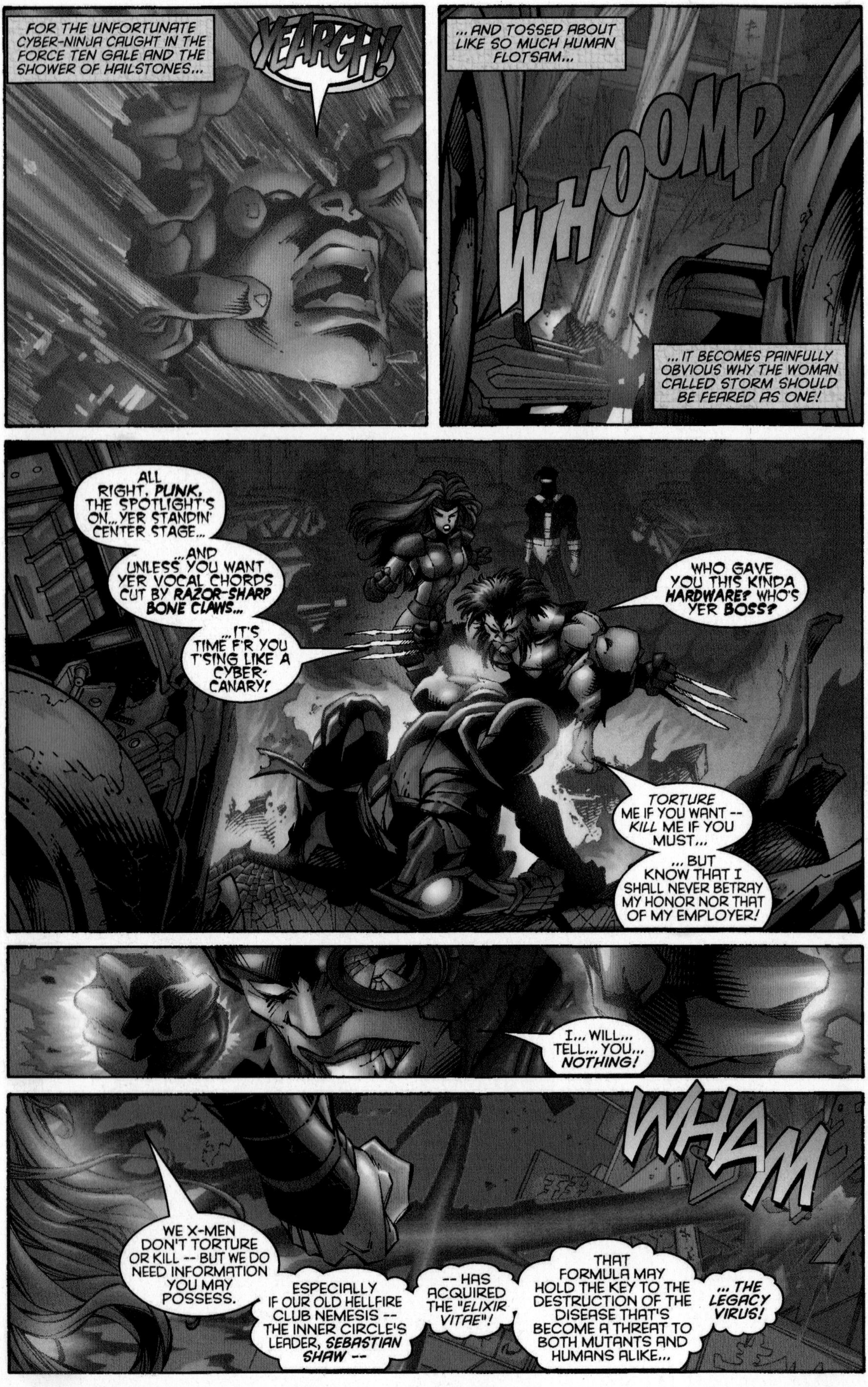

FOR THE UNFORTUNATE CYBER-NINJA CAUGHT IN THE FORCE TEN GALE AND THE SHOWER OF HAILSTONES...
YEARGH!
...AND TOSSED ABOUT LIKE SO MUCH HUMAN FLOTSAM...
WHOOMP
...IT BECOMES PAINFULLY OBVIOUS WHY THE WOMAN CALLED STORM SHOULD BE FEARED AS ONE!
ALL RIGHT, PUNK, THE SPOTLIGHT'S ON...YER STANDIN' CENTER STAGE...
...AND UNLESS YOU WANT YER VOCAL CHORDS CUT BY RAZOR-SHARP BONE CLAWS...
...IT'S TIME F'R YOU T'SING LIKE A CYBER-CANARY!
WHO GAVE YOU THIS KINDA HARDWARE? WHO'S YER BOSS?
TORTURE ME IF YOU WANT -- KILL ME IF YOU MUST...
... BUT KNOW THAT I SHALL NEVER BETRAY MY HONOR NOR THAT OF MY EMPLOYER!
I... WILL... TELL... YOU... NOTHING!
WHAM
WE X-MEN DON'T TORTURE OR KILL -- BUT WE DO NEED INFORMATION YOU MAY POSSESS.
ESPECIALLY IF OUR OLD HELLFIRE CLUB NEMESIS -- THE INNER CIRCLE'S LEADER, SEBASTIAN SHAW --
-- HAS ACQUIRED THE "ELIXIR VITAE"!
THAT FORMULA MAY HOLD THE KEY TO THE DESTRUCTION OF THE DISEASE THAT'S BECOME A THREAT TO BOTH MUTANTS AND HUMANS ALIKE...
...THE LEGACY VIRUS!

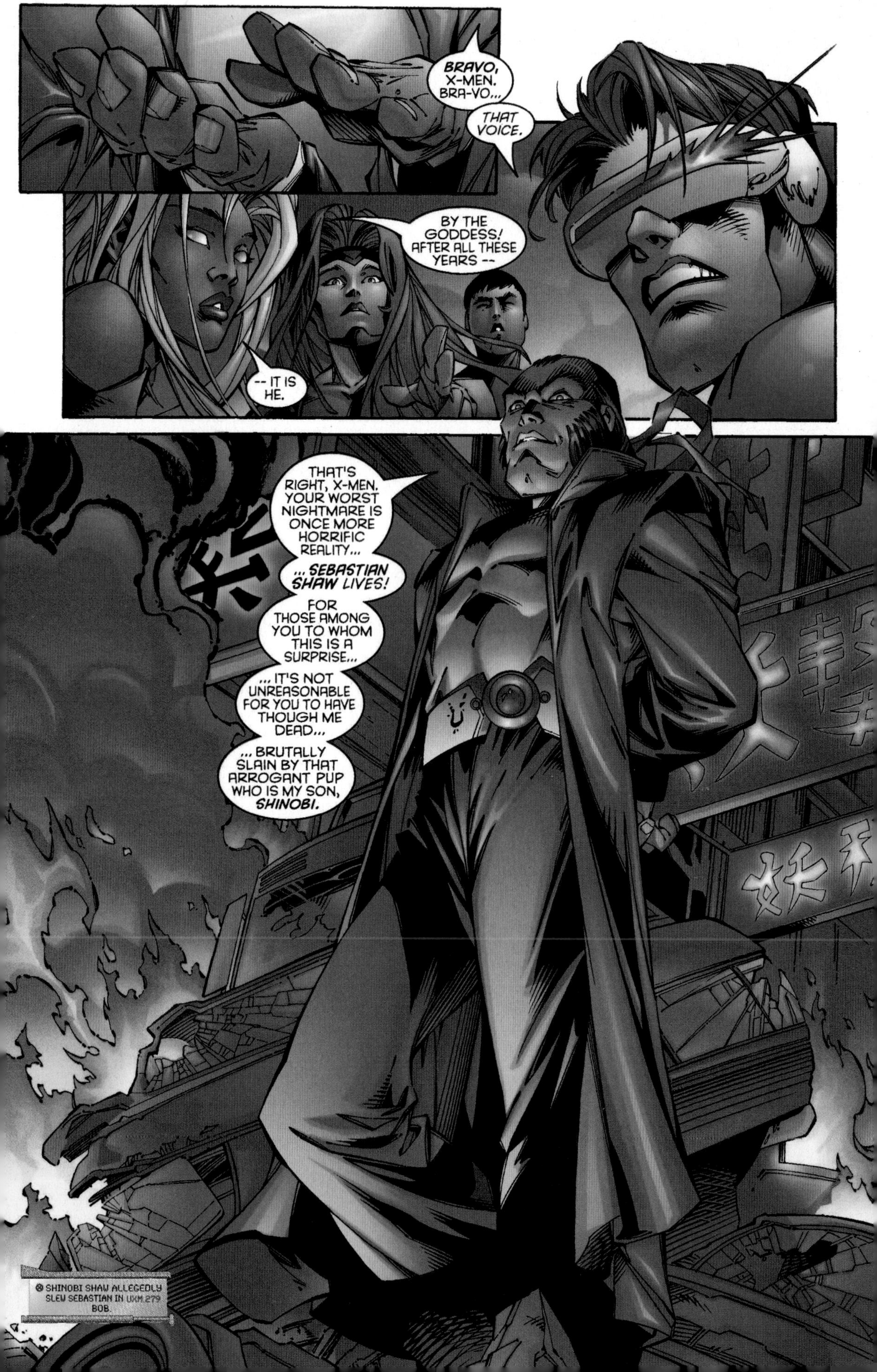
BRAVO, X-MEN. BRA-VO...
THAT VOICE.
BY THE GODDESS! AFTER ALL THESE YEARS --
-- IT IS HE.
THAT'S RIGHT, X-MEN. YOUR WORST NIGHTMARE IS ONCE MORE HORRIFIC REALITY...
...SEBASTIAN SHAW LIVES!
FOR THOSE AMONG YOU TO WHOM THIS IS A SURPRISE...
...IT'S NOT UNREASONABLE FOR YOU TO HAVE THOUGH ME DEAD...
...BRUTALLY SLAIN BY THAT ARROGANT PUP WHO IS MY SON, SHINOBI.
SHINOBI SHAW ALLEGEDLY SLEW SEBASTIAN IN UXM 279
BOB.

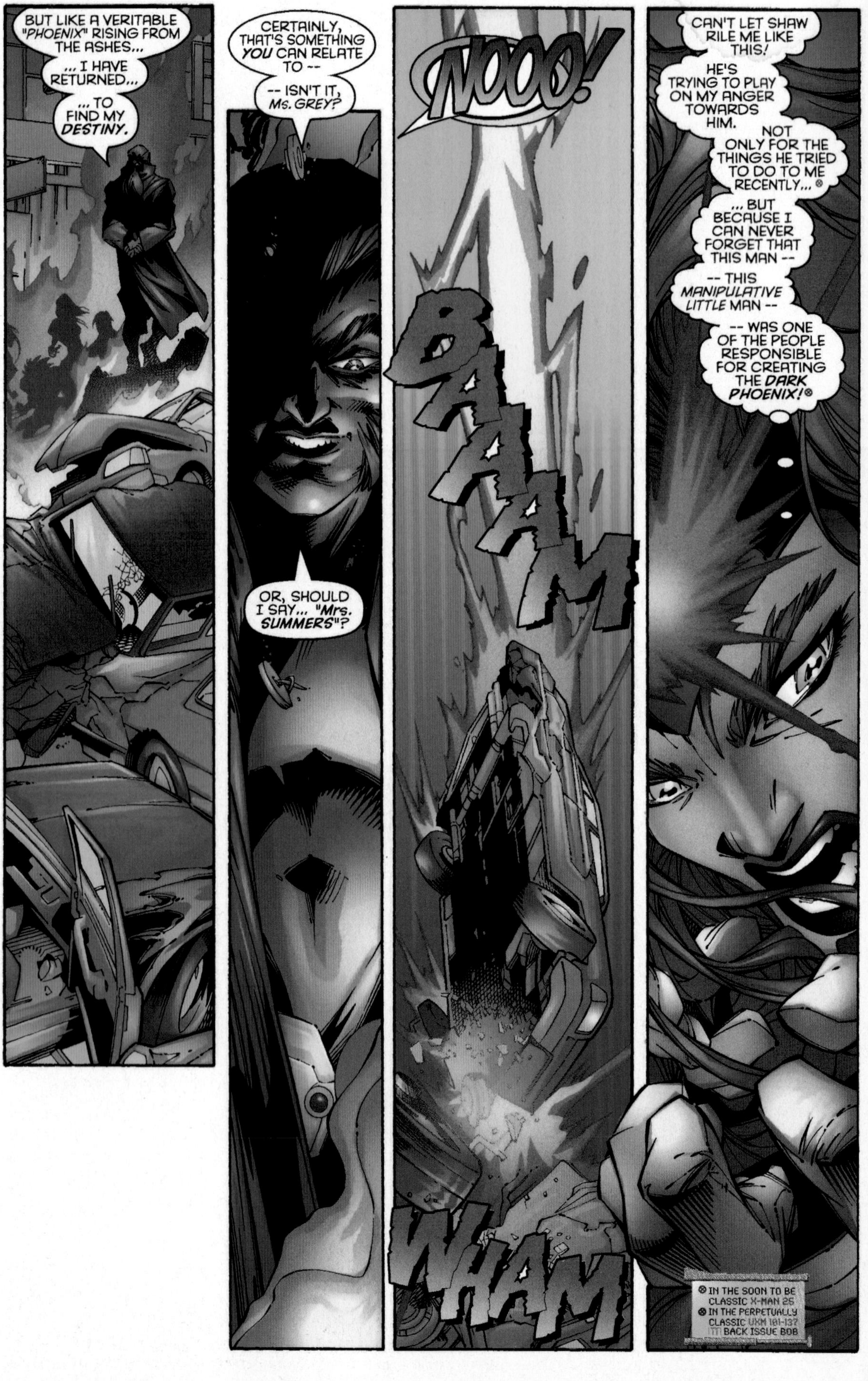
BUT LIKE A VERITABLE "PHOENIX" RISING FROM THE ASHES...
... I HAVE RETURNED...
... TO FIND MY DESTINY.
CERTAINLY, THAT'S SOMETHING YOU CAN RELATE TO --
-- ISN'T IT, Ms. GREY?
OR, SHOULD I SAY... "Mrs. SUMMERS"?
NOOO!
BAAAM
WHAM
CAN'T LET SHAW RILE ME LIKE THIS!
HE'S TRYING TO PLAY ON MY ANGER TOWARDS HIM.
NOT ONLY FOR THE THINGS HE TRIED TO DO TO ME RECENTLY...
... BUT BECAUSE I CAN NEVER FORGET THAT THIS MAN --
-- THIS MANIPULATIVE LITTLE MAN --
-- WAS ONE OF THE PEOPLE RESPONSIBLE FOR CREATING THE DARK PHOENIX!
IN THE SOON TO BE CLASSIC X-MAN 25
IN THE PERPETUALLY CLASSIC UXM 101-137
BACK ISSUE BOB

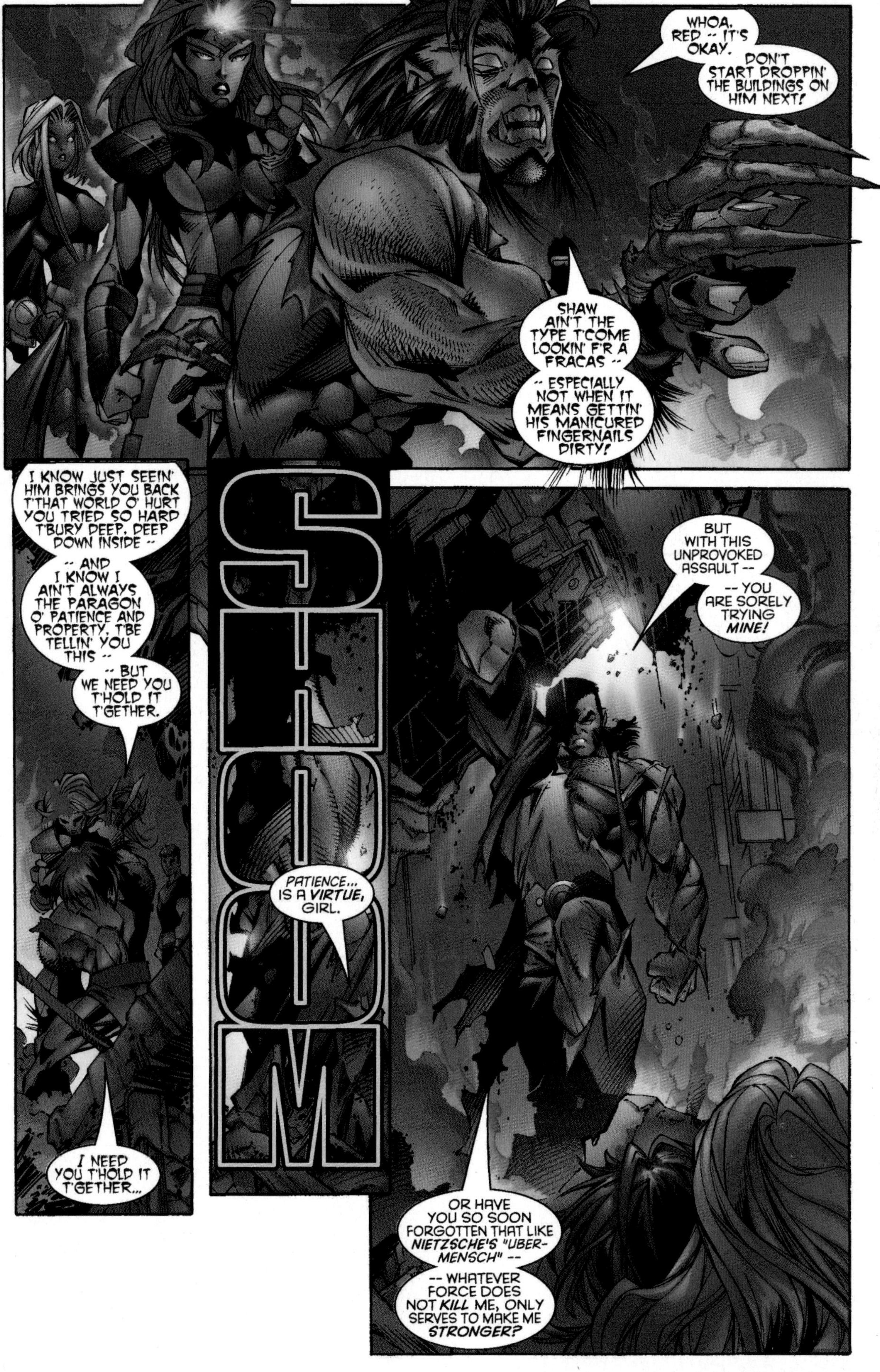

WHOA, RED -- IT'S OKAY. DON'T START DROPPIN' THE BUILDINGS ON HIM NEXT!
SHAW AIN'T THE TYPE T'COME LOOKIN' F'R A FRACAS --
-- ESPECIALLY NOT WHEN IT MEANS GETTIN' HIS MANICURED FINGERNAILS DIRTY!
I KNOW JUST SEEIN' HIM BRINGS YOU BACK T'THAT WORLD O' HURT YOU TRIED SO HARD T'BURY DEEP, DEEP DOWN INSIDE --
-- AND I KNOW I AIN'T ALWAYS THE PARAGON O' PATIENCE AND PROPERTY, T'BE TELLIN' YOU THIS --
-- BUT WE NEED YOU T'HOLD IT T'GETHER.
I NEED YOU T'HOLD IT T'GETHER...
SHOOM
PATIENCE... IS A VIRTUE, GIRL.
BUT WITH THIS UNPROVOKED ASSAULT --
-- YOU ARE SORELY TRYING MINE!
OR HAVE YOU SO SOON FORGOTTEN THAT LIKE NIETZSCHE'S "UBER-MENSCH" --
-- WHATEVER FORCE DOES NOT KILL ME, ONLY SERVES TO MAKE ME STRONGER?

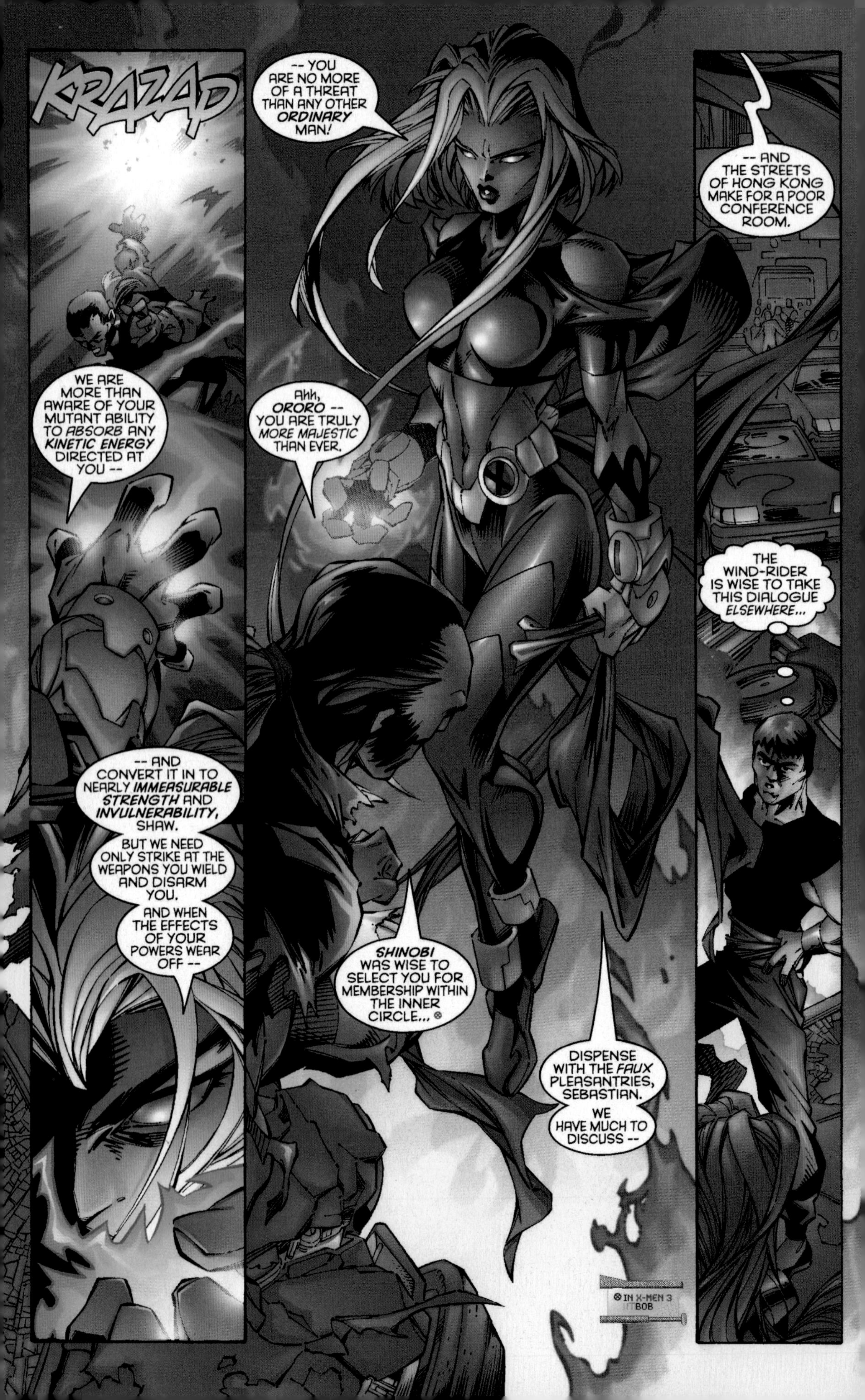
KRAZAP
-- YOU ARE NO MORE OF A THREAT THAN ANY OTHER ORDINARY MAN!
-- AND THE STREETS OF HONG KONG MAKE FOR A POOR CONFERENCE ROOM.
WE ARE MORE THAN AWARE OF YOUR MUTANT ABILITY TO ABSORB ANY KINETIC ENERGY DIRECTED AT YOU --
AHH, ORORO -- YOU ARE TRULY MORE MAJESTIC THAN EVER.
THE WIND-RIDER IS WISE TO TAKE THIS DIALOGUE ELSEWHERE...
-- AND CONVERT IT IN TO NEARLY IMMEASURABLE STRENGTH AND INVULNERABILITY, SHAW.
BUT WE NEED ONLY STRIKE AT THE WEAPONS YOU WIELD AND DISARM YOU.
AND WHEN THE EFFECTS OF YOUR POWERS WEAR OFF --
SHINOBI WAS WISE TO SELECT YOU FOR MEMBERSHIP WITHIN THE INNER CIRCLE...
DISPENSE WITH THE FAUX PLEASANTRIES, SEBASTIAN.
WE HAVE MUCH TO DISCUSS --
IN X-MEN 3
BOB

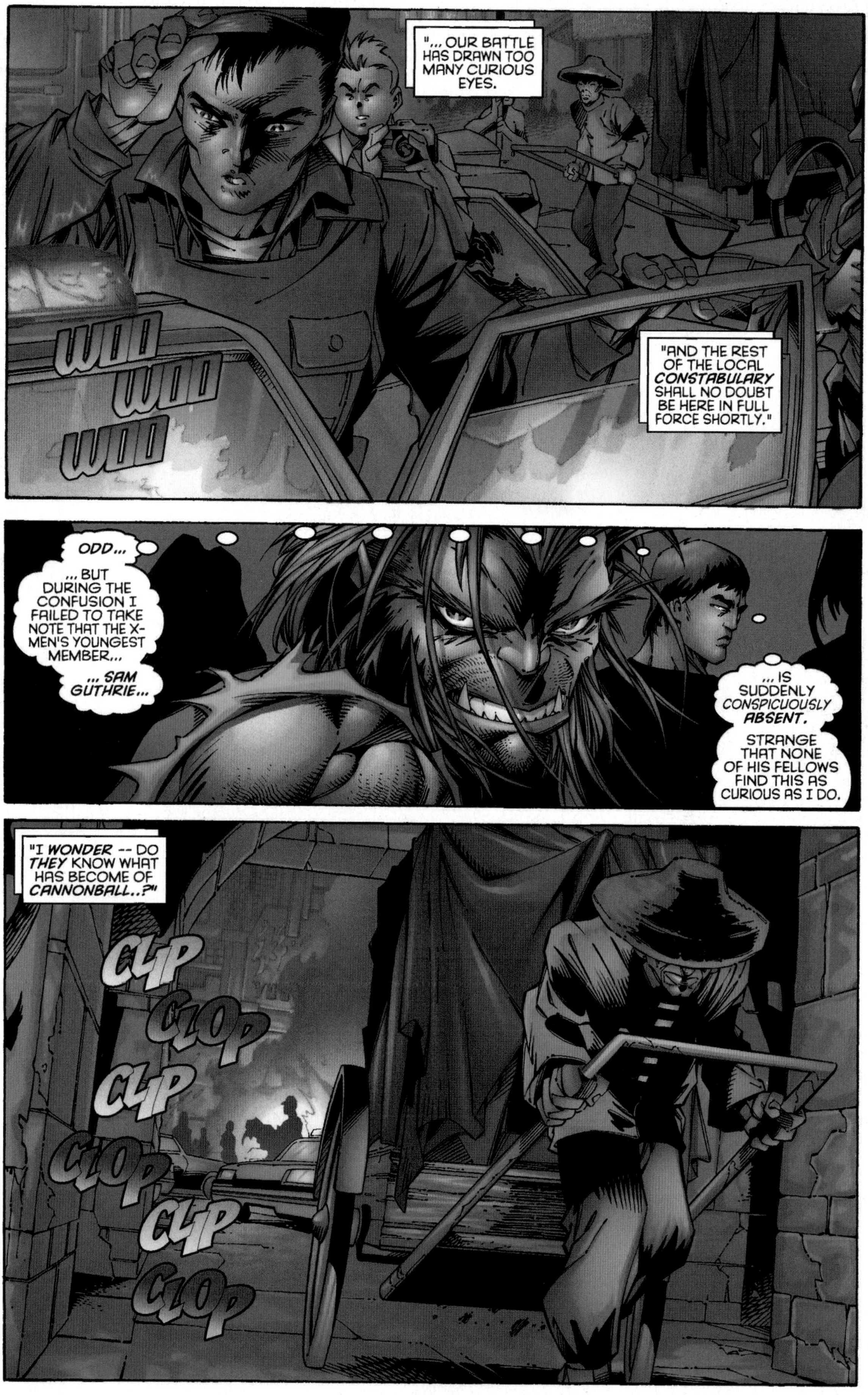
"... OUR BATTLE HAS DRAWN TOO MANY CURIOUS EYES.
WOO
WOO
WOO
"AND THE REST OF THE LOCAL CONSTABULARY SHALL NO DOUBT BE HERE IN FULL FORCE SHORTLY."
ODD...
... BUT DURING THE CONFUSION I FAILED TO TAKE NOTE THAT THE X-MEN'S YOUNGEST MEMBER...
... SAM GUTHRIE...
... IS SUDDENLY CONSPICUOUSLY ABSENT.
STRANGE THAT NONE OF HIS FELLOWS FIND THIS AS CURIOUS AS I DO.
"I WONDER -- DO THEY KNOW WHAT HAS BECOME OF CANNONBALL..?"
CLIP
CLOP
CLIP
CLOP
CLIP
CLOP

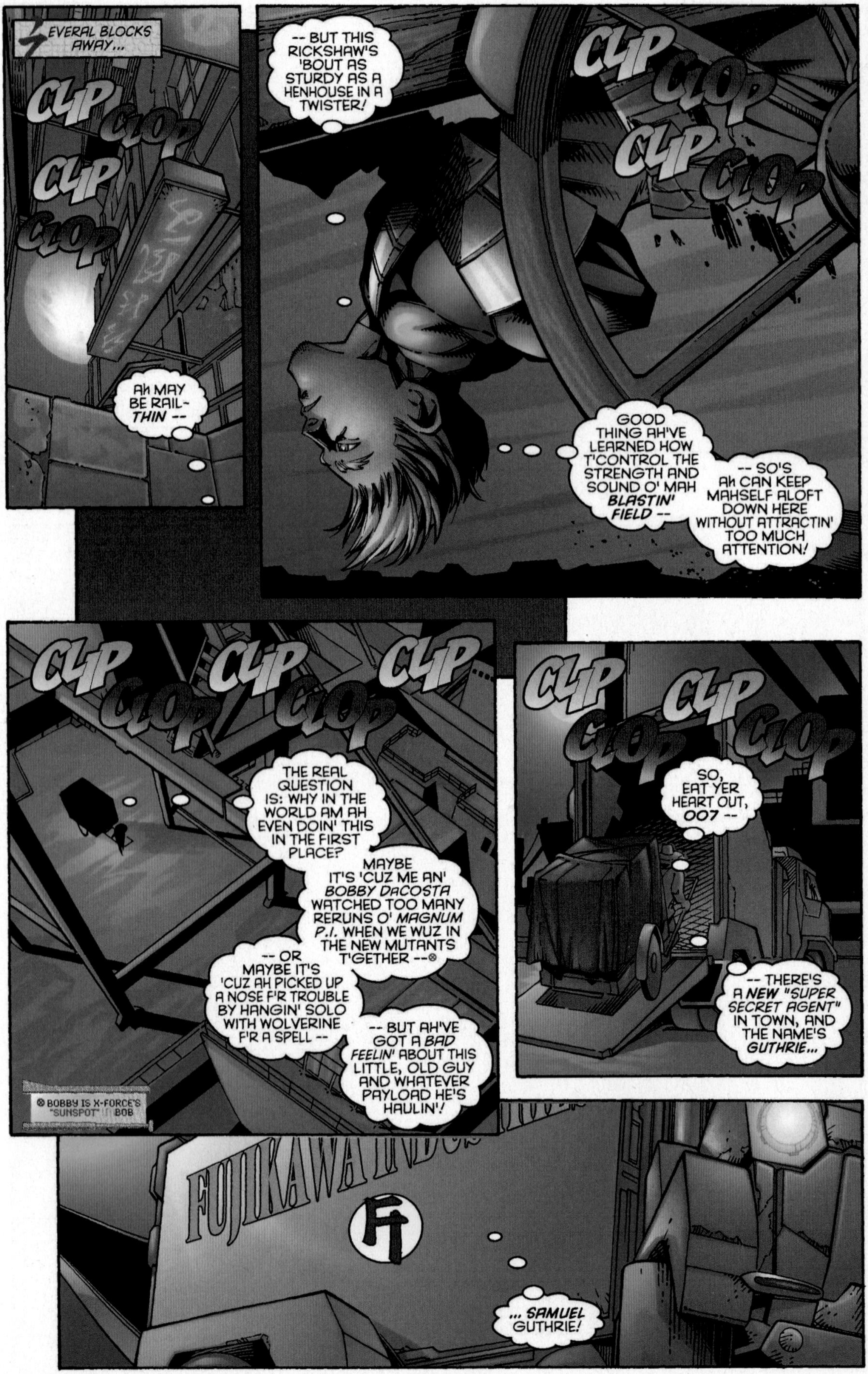
SEVERAL BLOCKS AWAY...
CLIP CLOP CLIP CLOP
AH MAY BE RAIL-THIN --
-- BUT THIS RICKSHAW'S 'BOUT AS STURDY AS A HENHOUSE IN A TWISTER!
CLIP CLOP CLIP CLOP
GOOD THING AH'VE LEARNED HOW T'CONTROL THE STRENGTH AND SOUND O' MAH BLASTIN' FIELD --
-- SO'S AH CAN KEEP MAHSELF ALOFT DOWN HERE WITHOUT ATTRACTIN' TOO MUCH ATTENTION!
CLIP CLOP CLIP CLOP CLIP
THE REAL QUESTION IS: WHY IN THE WORLD AM AH EVEN DOIN' THIS IN THE FIRST PLACE?
MAYBE IT'S 'CUZ ME AN' BOBBY DACOSTA WATCHED TOO MANY RERUNS O' MAGNUM P.I. WHEN WE WUZ IN THE NEW MUTANTS T'GETHER --⊗
-- OR MAYBE IT'S 'CUZ AH PICKED UP A NOSE F'R TROUBLE BY HANGIN' SOLO WITH WOLVERINE F'R A SPELL --
-- BUT AH'VE GOT A BAD FEELIN' ABOUT THIS LITTLE, OLD GUY AND WHATEVER PAYLOAD HE'S HAULIN'!
⊗ BOBBY IS X-FORCE'S "SUNSPOT" BOB
CLIP CLOP CLIP CLOP
SO, EAT YER HEART OUT, 007 --
-- THERE'S A NEW "SUPER SECRET AGENT" IN TOWN, AND THE NAME'S GUTHRIE...
FUJIKAWA IND
...SAMUEL GUTHRIE!

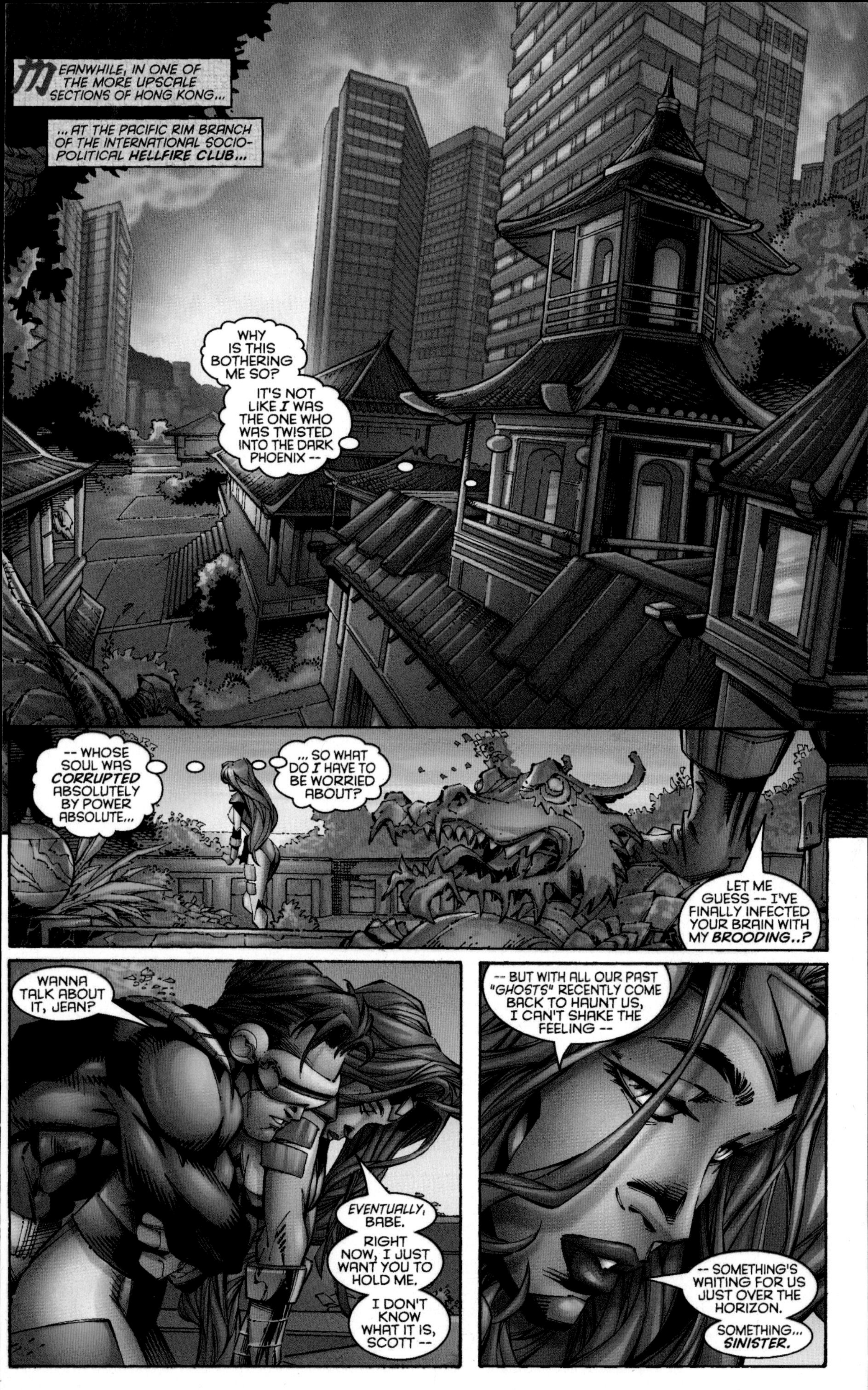
MEANWHILE, IN ONE OF THE MORE UPSCALE SECTIONS OF HONG KONG...
...AT THE PACIFIC RIM BRANCH OF THE INTERNATIONAL SOCIO-POLITICAL HELLFIRE CLUB...
WHY IS THIS BOTHERING ME SO?
IT'S NOT LIKE I WAS THE ONE WHO WAS TWISTED INTO THE DARK PHOENIX --
-- WHOSE SOUL WAS CORRUPTED ABSOLUTELY BY POWER ABSOLUTE...
... SO WHAT DO I HAVE TO BE WORRIED ABOUT?
LET ME GUESS -- I'VE FINALLY INFECTED YOUR BRAIN WITH MY BROODING..?
WANNA TALK ABOUT IT, JEAN?
EVENTUALLY, BABE.
RIGHT NOW, I JUST WANT YOU TO HOLD ME.
I DON'T KNOW WHAT IT IS, SCOTT --
-- BUT WITH ALL OUR PAST "GHOSTS" RECENTLY COME BACK TO HAUNT US, I CAN'T SHAKE THE FEELING --
-- SOMETHING'S WAITING FOR US JUST OVER THE HORIZON.
SOMETHING... SINISTER.

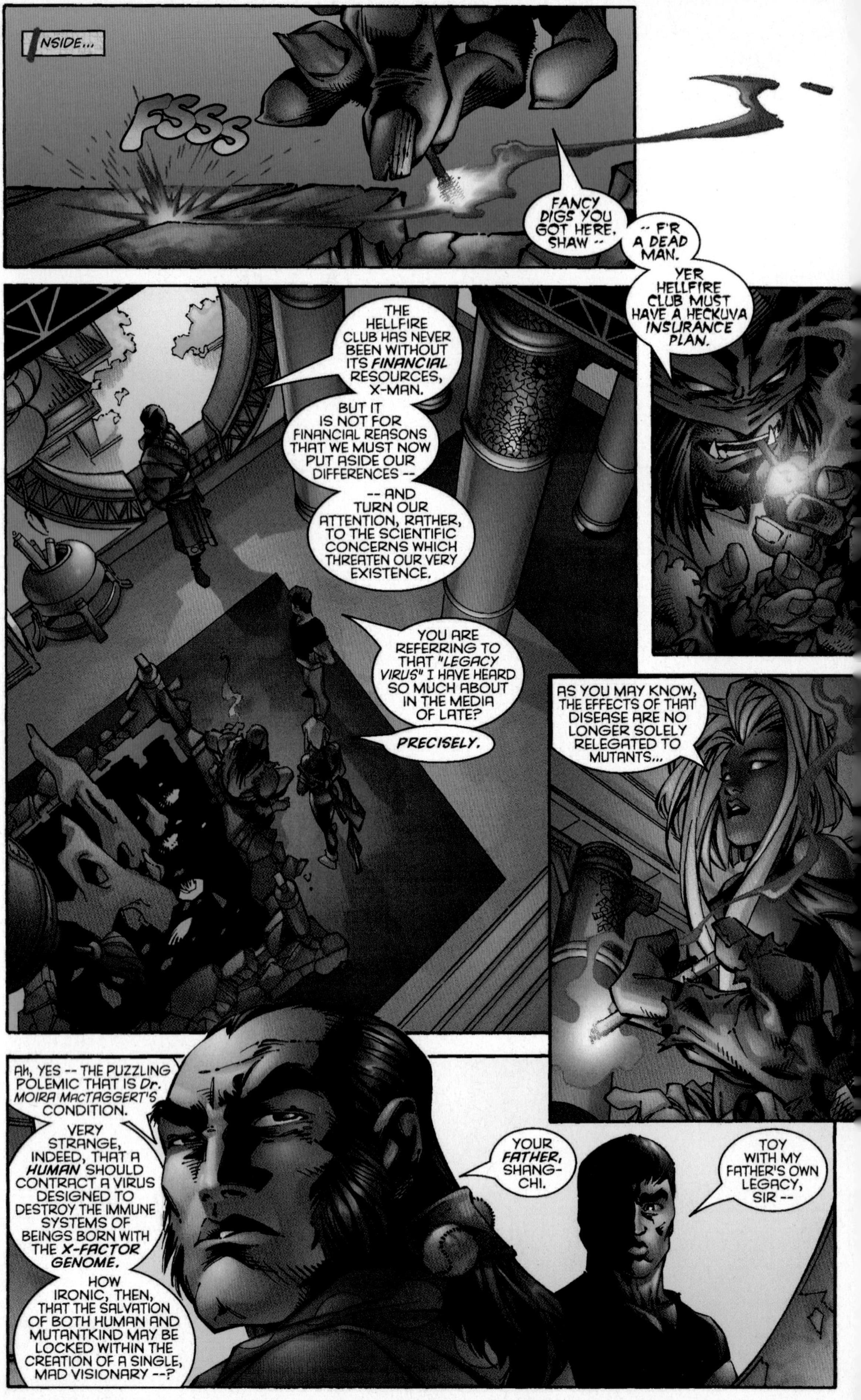
INSIDE...
FSSS
FANCY DIGS YOU GOT HERE, SHAW --
-- F'R A DEAD MAN.
YER HELLFIRE CLUB MUST HAVE A HECKUVA INSURANCE PLAN.
THE HELLFIRE CLUB HAS NEVER BEEN WITHOUT ITS FINANCIAL RESOURCES, X-MAN.
BUT IT IS NOT FOR FINANCIAL REASONS THAT WE MUST NOW PUT ASIDE OUR DIFFERENCES --
-- AND TURN OUR ATTENTION, RATHER, TO THE SCIENTIFIC CONCERNS WHICH THREATEN OUR VERY EXISTENCE.
YOU ARE REFERRING TO THAT "LEGACY VIRUS" I HAVE HEARD SO MUCH ABOUT IN THE MEDIA OF LATE?
PRECISELY.
AS YOU MAY KNOW, THE EFFECTS OF THAT DISEASE ARE NO LONGER SOLELY RELEGATED TO MUTANTS...
Ah, YES -- THE PUZZLING POLEMIC THAT IS Dr. MOIRA MacTAGGERT'S CONDITION.
VERY STRANGE, INDEED, THAT A HUMAN SHOULD CONTRACT A VIRUS DESIGNED TO DESTROY THE IMMUNE SYSTEMS OF BEINGS BORN WITH THE X-FACTOR GENOME.
HOW IRONIC, THEN, THAT THE SALVATION OF BOTH HUMAN AND MUTANTKIND MAY BE LOCKED WITHIN THE CREATION OF A SINGLE, MAD VISIONARY --?
YOUR FATHER, SHANG-CHI.
TOY WITH MY FATHER'S OWN LEGACY, SIR --

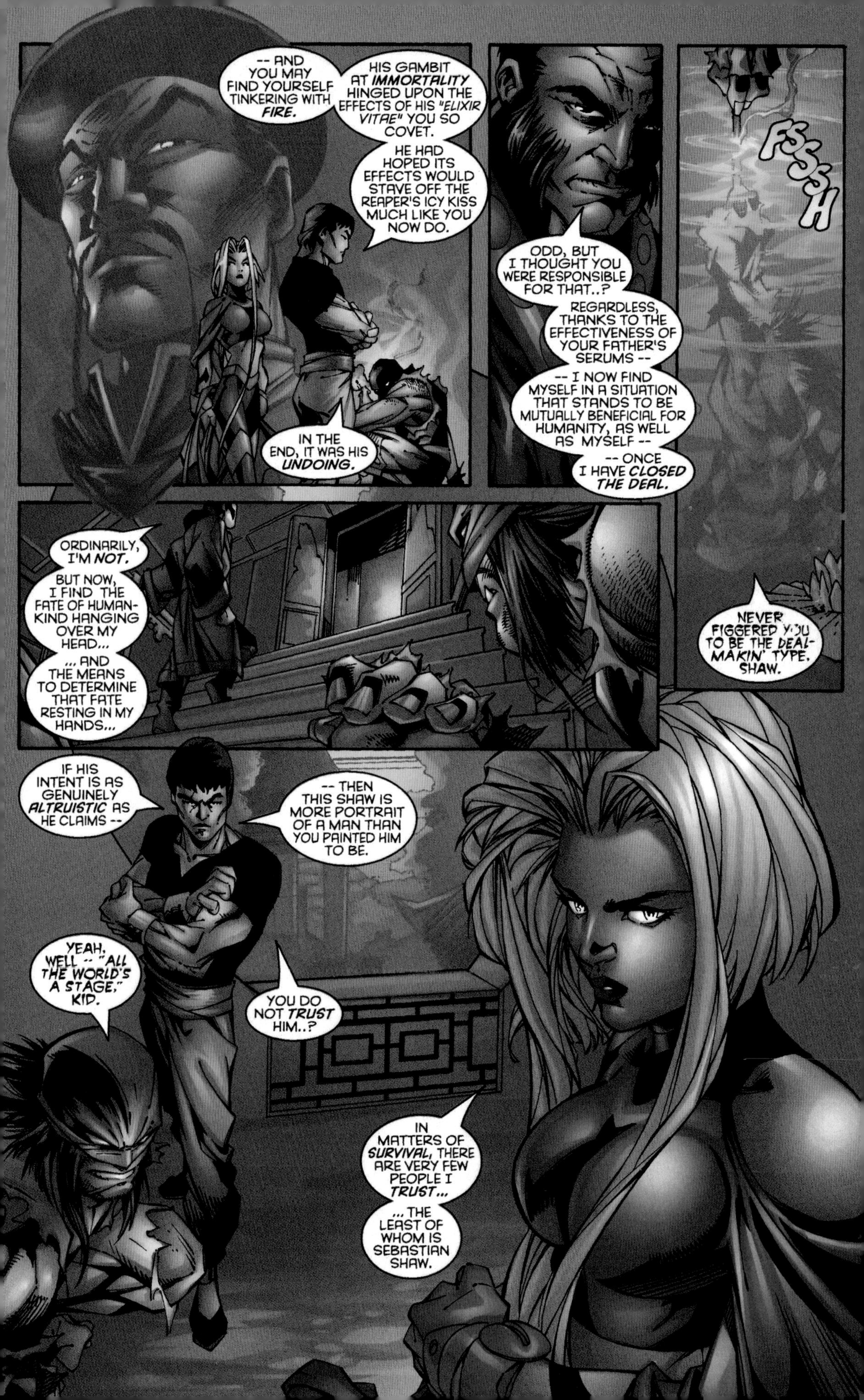
-- AND YOU MAY FIND YOURSELF TINKERING WITH FIRE.
HIS GAMBIT AT IMMORTALITY HINGED UPON THE EFFECTS OF HIS "ELIXIR VITAE" YOU SO COVET.
HE HAD HOPED ITS EFFECTS WOULD STAVE OFF THE REAPER'S ICY KISS MUCH LIKE YOU NOW DO.
IN THE END, IT WAS HIS UNDOING.
ODD, BUT I THOUGHT YOU WERE RESPONSIBLE FOR THAT..?
REGARDLESS, THANKS TO THE EFFECTIVENESS OF YOUR FATHER'S SERUMS --
-- I NOW FIND MYSELF IN A SITUATION THAT STANDS TO BE MUTUALLY BENEFICIAL FOR HUMANITY, AS WELL AS MYSELF --
-- ONCE I HAVE CLOSED THE DEAL.
FSSSH
NEVER FIGGERED YOU TO BE THE DEAL-MAKIN' TYPE, SHAW.
ORDINARILY, I'M NOT.
BUT NOW, I FIND THE FATE OF HUMAN-KIND HANGING OVER MY HEAD...
... AND THE MEANS TO DETERMINE THAT FATE RESTING IN MY HANDS...
IF HIS INTENT IS AS GENUINELY ALTRUISTIC AS HE CLAIMS --
-- THEN THIS SHAW IS MORE PORTRAIT OF A MAN THAN YOU PAINTED HIM TO BE.
YEAH, WELL -- "ALL THE WORLD'S A STAGE," KID.
YOU DO NOT TRUST HIM..?
IN MATTERS OF SURVIVAL, THERE ARE VERY FEW PEOPLE I TRUST...
... THE LEAST OF WHOM IS SEBASTIAN SHAW.

AND AS THE X-MEN PONDER THE VERACITY OF SHAW'S STATED *MOTIVES*...

YOU BROUGHT THE *CORRECT* DISK, I PRESUME?

... SHAW HIMSELF PONDERS THE BENEFITS OF A *BARGAIN* MADE IN HASTE.

BECAUSE IF YOU *DIDN'T* --

-- THEN YOU LEAVE ME NO CHOICE BUT TO *RENEGE* ON OUR AGREEMENT, DOCTOR.

MY WORD IS MY *BOND*, MR. SHAW.

I'LL *REMEMBER* THAT.

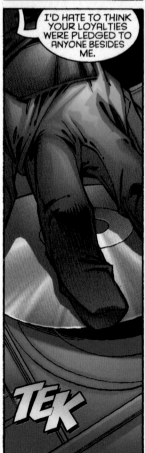

I'D HATE TO THINK YOUR LOYALTIES WERE PLEDGED TO ANYONE BESIDES ME.

TEK

Hmmm... Dr. MOIRA MacTAGGERT... MADROX, THE MULTIPLE MAN...

... POOR, OLD MASTERMIND -- NO LOSS THERE...

... INFECTIA... PRECIOUS ILLYANA RASPUTIN... AND PYRO...

... ALL VICTIMS OF THE LEGACY VIRUS IN ONE FORM OR ANOTHER.

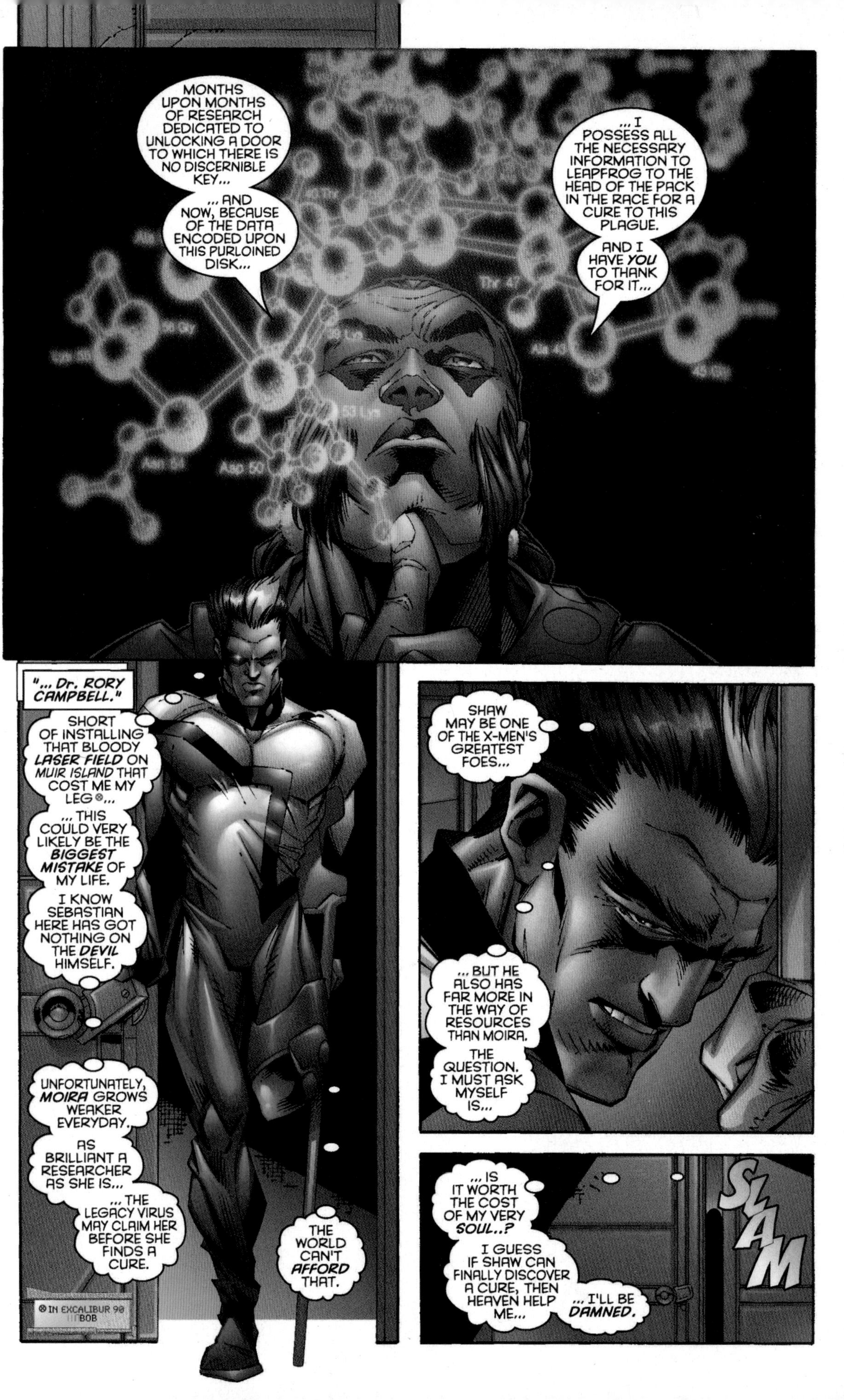
MONTHS UPON MONTHS OF RESEARCH DEDICATED TO UNLOCKING A DOOR TO WHICH THERE IS NO DISCERNIBLE KEY...
... AND NOW, BECAUSE OF THE DATA ENCODED UPON THIS PURLOINED DISK...
... I POSSESS ALL THE NECESSARY INFORMATION TO LEAPFROG TO THE HEAD OF THE PACK IN THE RACE FOR A CURE TO THIS PLAGUE.
AND I HAVE *YOU* TO THANK FOR IT...
"... Dr. RORY CAMPBELL."
SHORT OF INSTALLING THAT BLOODY *LASER FIELD* ON *MUIR ISLAND* THAT COST ME MY LEG⊗...
... THIS COULD VERY LIKELY BE THE *BIGGEST MISTAKE* OF MY LIFE.
I KNOW SEBASTIAN HERE HAS GOT NOTHING ON THE *DEVIL* HIMSELF.
UNFORTUNATELY, *MOIRA* GROWS WEAKER EVERYDAY.
AS BRILLIANT A RESEARCHER AS SHE IS...
... THE LEGACY VIRUS MAY CLAIM HER BEFORE SHE FINDS A CURE.
THE WORLD CAN'T *AFFORD* THAT.
⊗ IN EXCALIBUR 90 —BOB
SHAW MAY BE ONE OF THE X-MEN'S GREATEST FOES...
... BUT HE ALSO HAS FAR MORE IN THE WAY OF RESOURCES THAN MOIRA.
THE QUESTION. I MUST ASK MYSELF IS...
... IS IT WORTH THE COST OF MY VERY *SOUL..?*
I GUESS IF SHAW CAN FINALLY DISCOVER A CURE, THEN HEAVEN HELP ME...
... I'LL BE *DAMNED.*
SLAM

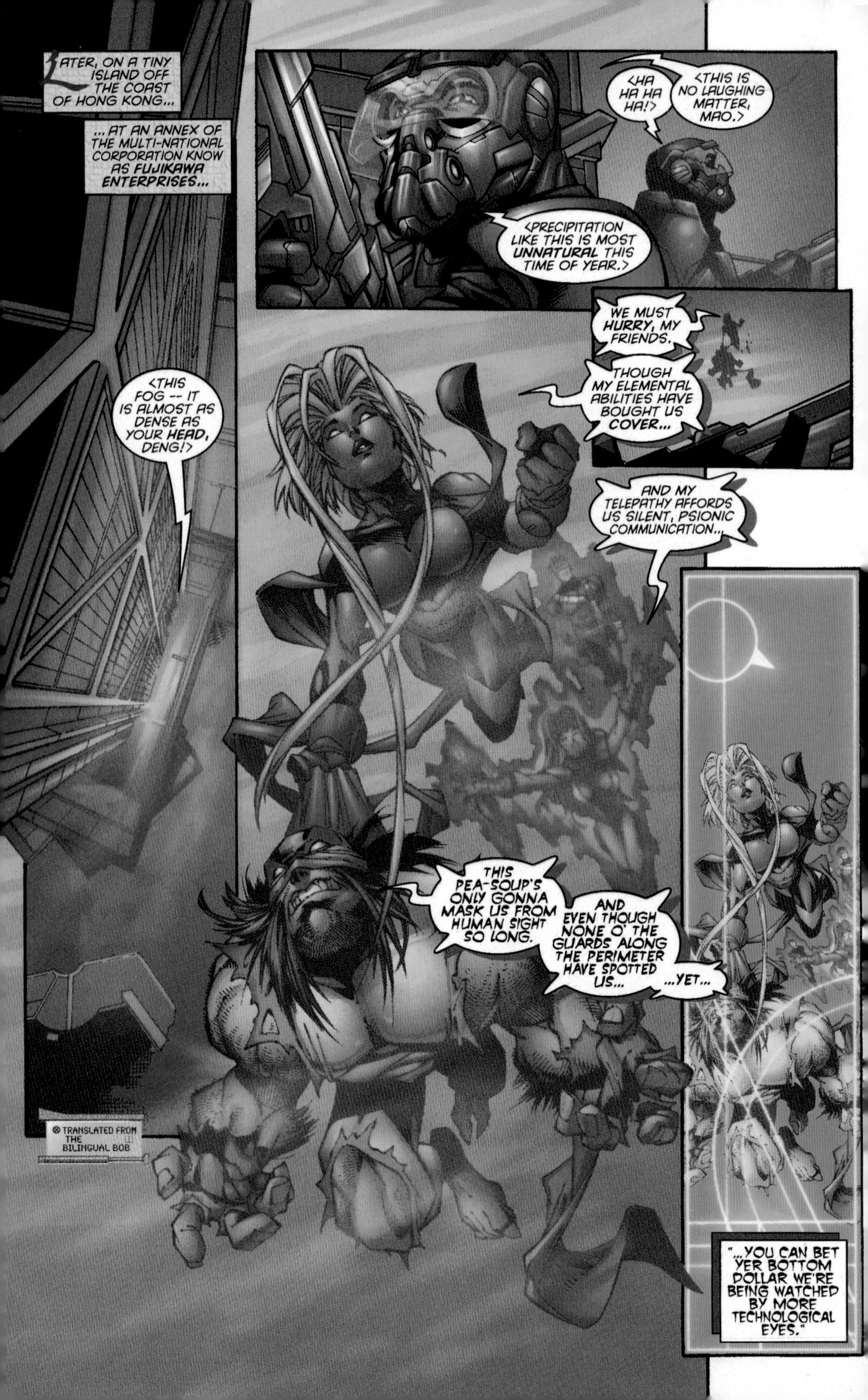
LATER, ON A TINY ISLAND OFF THE COAST OF HONG KONG...
...AT AN ANNEX OF THE MULTI-NATIONAL CORPORATION KNOW AS FUJIKAWA ENTERPRISES...
<HA HA HA HA!>
<THIS IS NO LAUGHING MATTER, MAO.>
<PRECIPITATION LIKE THIS IS MOST UNNATURAL THIS TIME OF YEAR.>
<THIS FOG -- IT IS ALMOST AS DENSE AS YOUR HEAD, DENG!>
WE MUST HURRY, MY FRIENDS.
THOUGH MY ELEMENTAL ABILITIES HAVE BOUGHT US COVER...
AND MY TELEPATHY AFFORDS US SILENT, PSIONIC COMMUNICATION...
THIS PEA-SOUP'S ONLY GONNA MASK US FROM HUMAN SIGHT SO LONG.
AND EVEN THOUGH NONE O' THE GUARDS ALONG THE PERIMETER HAVE SPOTTED US...
...YET...
"...YOU CAN BET YER BOTTOM DOLLAR WE'RE BEING WATCHED BY MORE TECHNOLOGICAL EYES."
TRANSLATED FROM THE BILINGUAL BOB

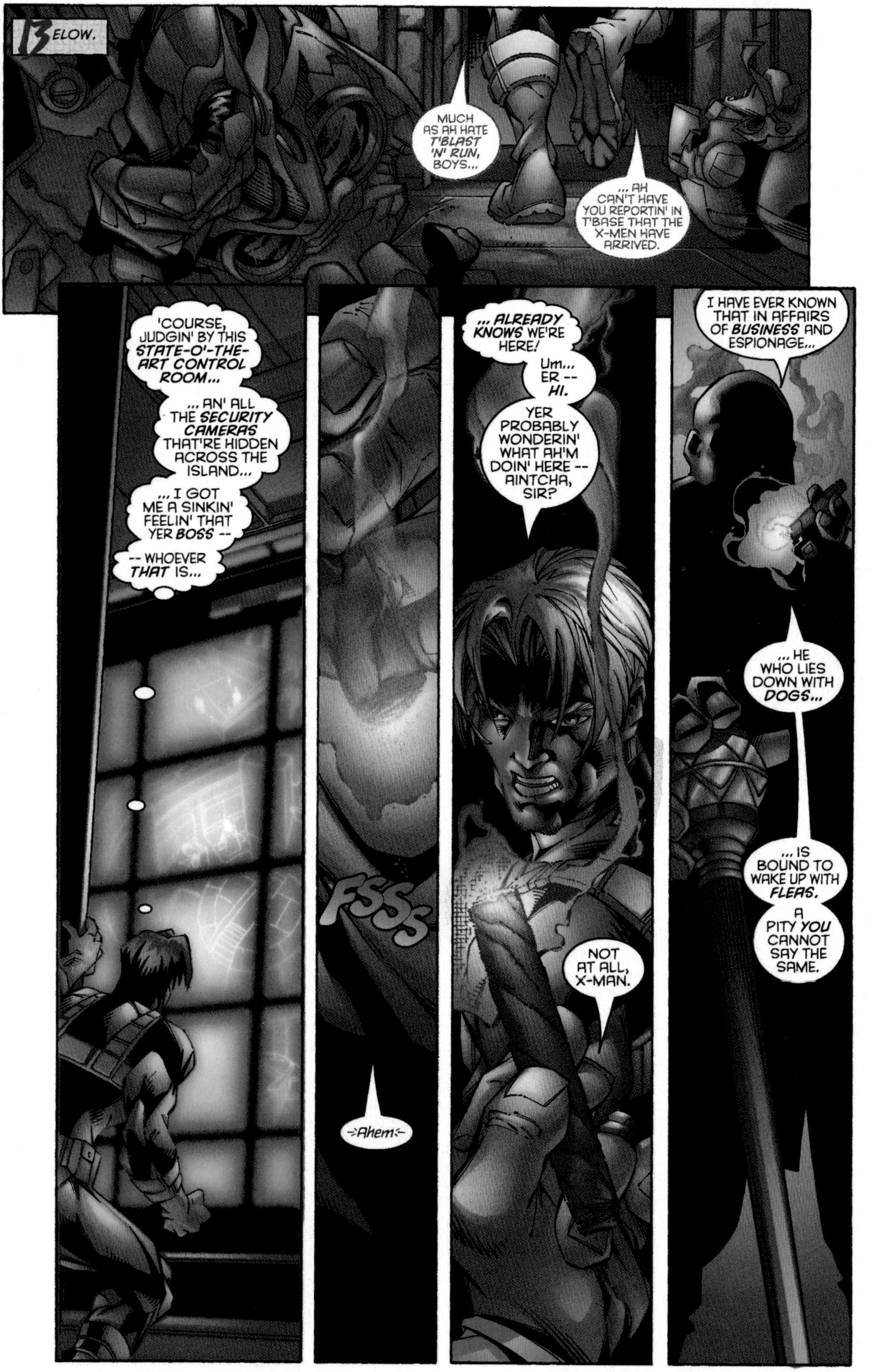
BELOW.
MUCH AS AH HATE T'BLAST 'N' RUN, BOYS...
...AH CAN'T HAVE YOU REPORTIN' IN T'BASE THAT THE X-MEN HAVE ARRIVED.
'COURSE, JUDGIN' BY THIS STATE-O'-THE-ART CONTROL ROOM...
...AN' ALL THE SECURITY CAMERAS THAT'RE HIDDEN ACROSS THE ISLAND...
...I GOT ME A SINKIN' FEELIN' THAT YER BOSS --
-- WHOEVER THAT IS...
FSSS
-Ahem-
...ALREADY KNOWS WE'RE HERE!
Um... ER -- HI.
YER PROBABLY WONDERIN' WHAT AH'M DOIN' HERE -- AINTCHA, SIR?
NOT AT ALL, X-MAN.
I HAVE EVER KNOWN THAT IN AFFAIRS OF BUSINESS AND ESPIONAGE...
...HE WHO LIES DOWN WITH DOGS...
...IS BOUND TO WAKE UP WITH FLEAS.
A PITY YOU CANNOT SAY THE SAME.

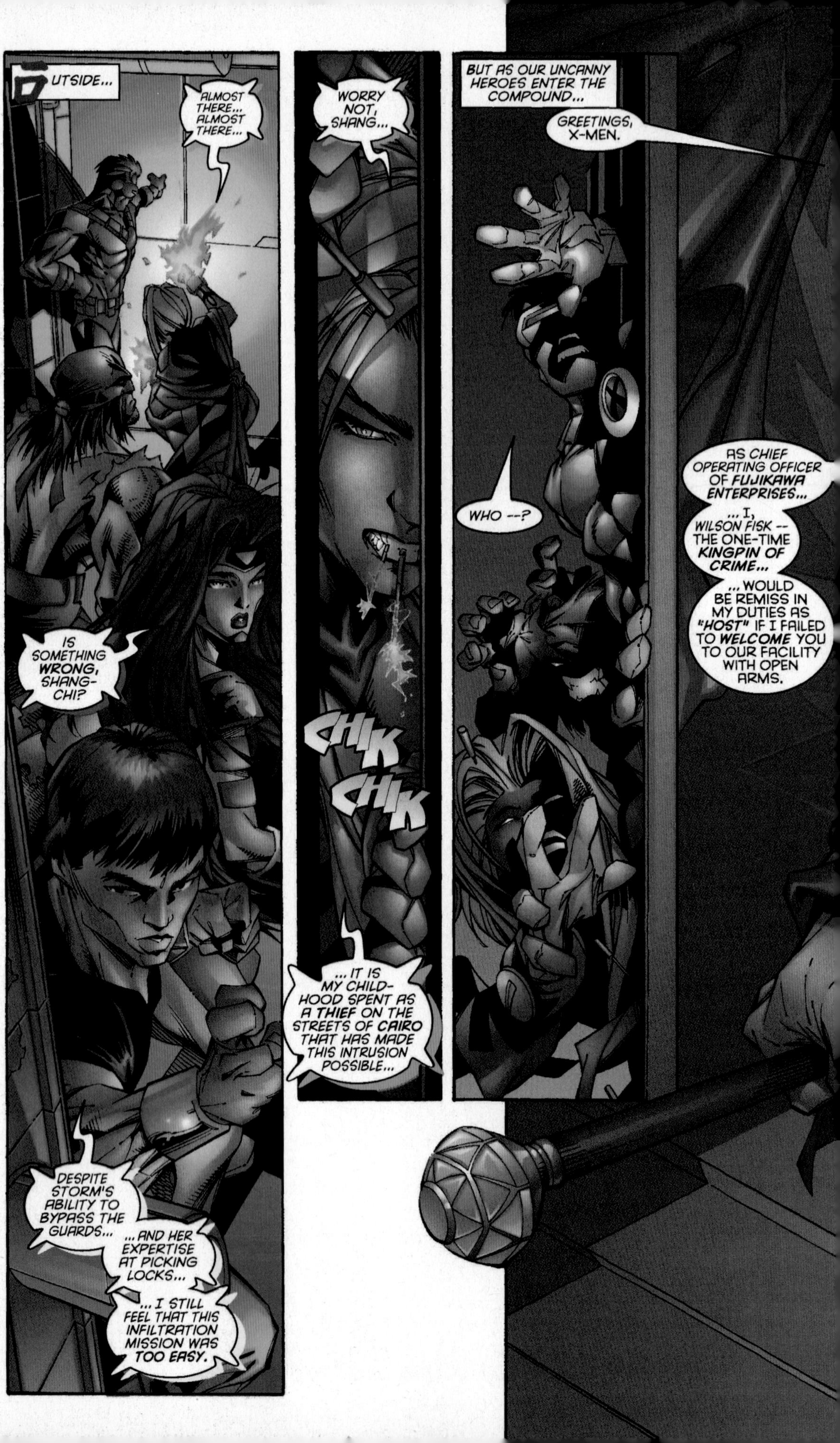
OUTSIDE...
ALMOST THERE... ALMOST THERE...
IS SOMETHING WRONG, SHANG-CHI?
DESPITE STORM'S ABILITY TO BYPASS THE GUARDS...
...AND HER EXPERTISE AT PICKING LOCKS...
...I STILL FEEL THAT THIS INFILTRATION MISSION WAS TOO EASY.
WORRY NOT, SHANG...
CHIK CHIK
...IT IS MY CHILDHOOD SPENT AS A THIEF ON THE STREETS OF CAIRO THAT HAS MADE THIS INTRUSION POSSIBLE...
BUT AS OUR UNCANNY HEROES ENTER THE COMPOUND...
GREETINGS, X-MEN.
WHO --?
AS CHIEF OPERATING OFFICER OF FUJIKAWA ENTERPRISES...
...I, WILSON FISK -- THE ONE-TIME KINGPIN OF CRIME...
...WOULD BE REMISS IN MY DUTIES AS "HOST" IF I FAILED TO WELCOME YOU TO OUR FACILITY WITH OPEN ARMS.

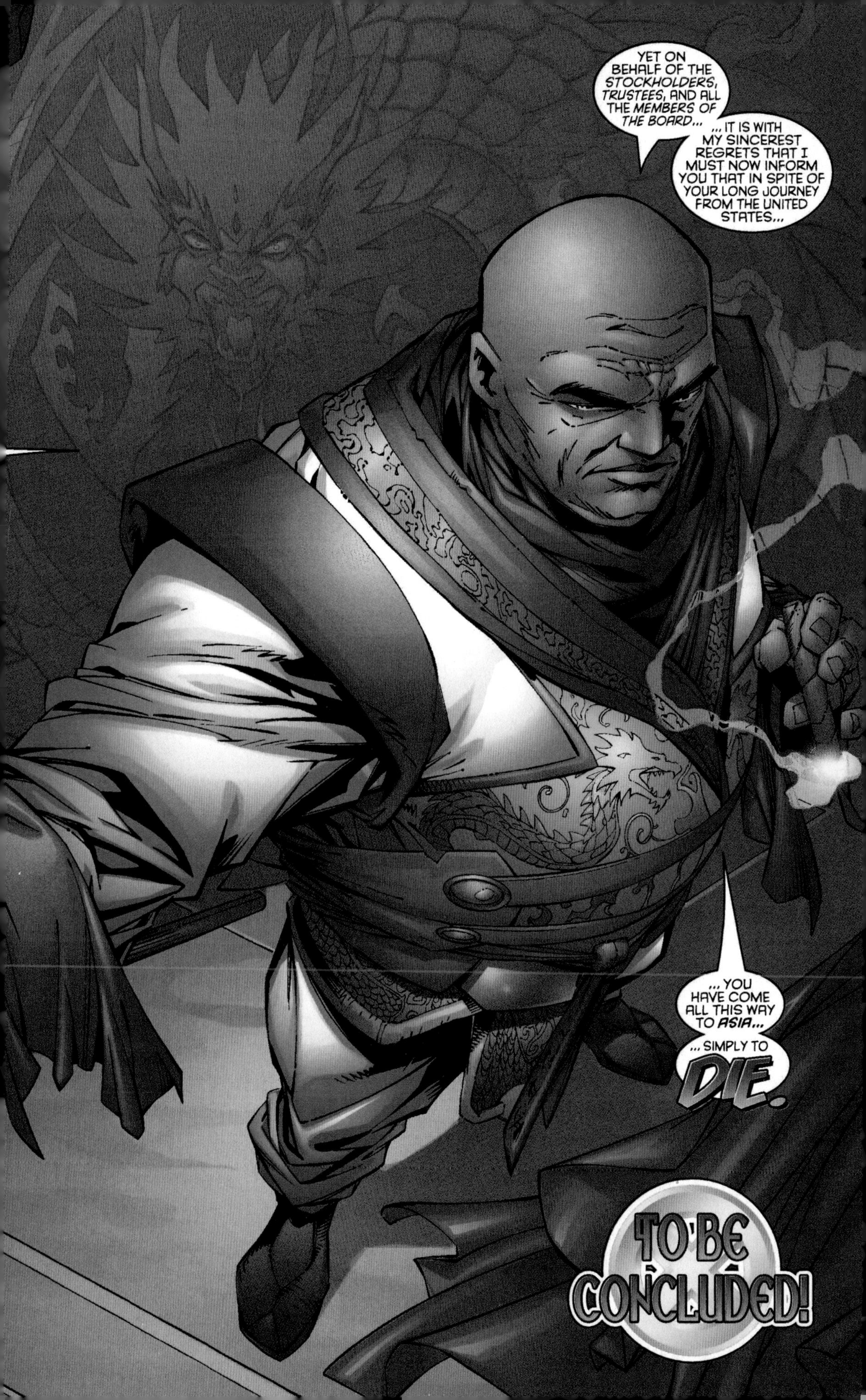
YET ON BEHALF OF THE STOCKHOLDERS, TRUSTEES, AND ALL THE MEMBERS OF THE BOARD...
...IT IS WITH MY SINCEREST REGRETS THAT I MUST NOW INFORM YOU THAT IN SPITE OF YOUR LONG JOURNEY FROM THE UNITED STATES...
...YOU HAVE COME ALL THIS WAY TO ASIA...
...SIMPLY TO DIE.
TO BE CONCLUDED!

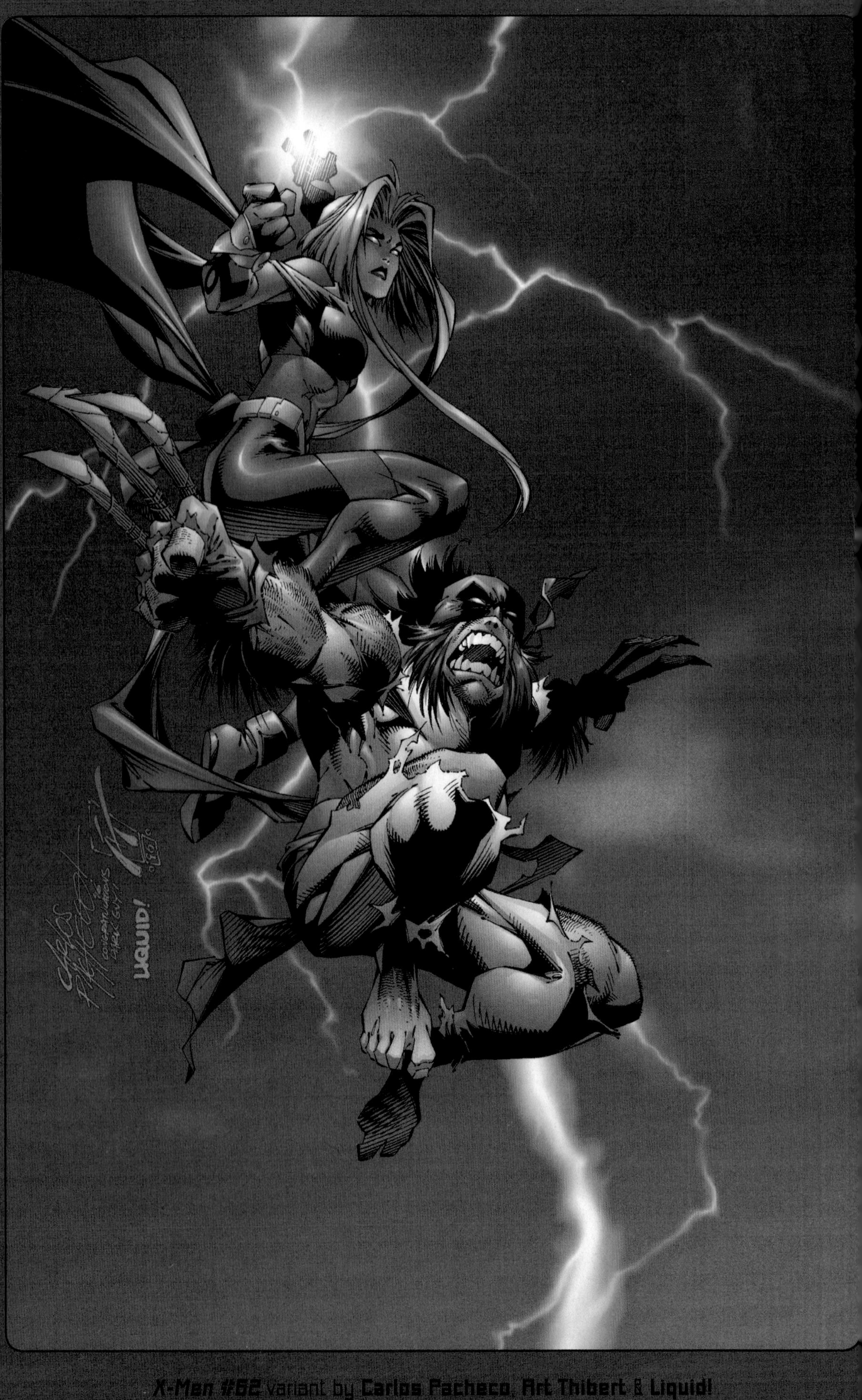
LIQUID!

X-Men #62 variant by **Carlos Pacheco, Art Thibert & Liquid!**

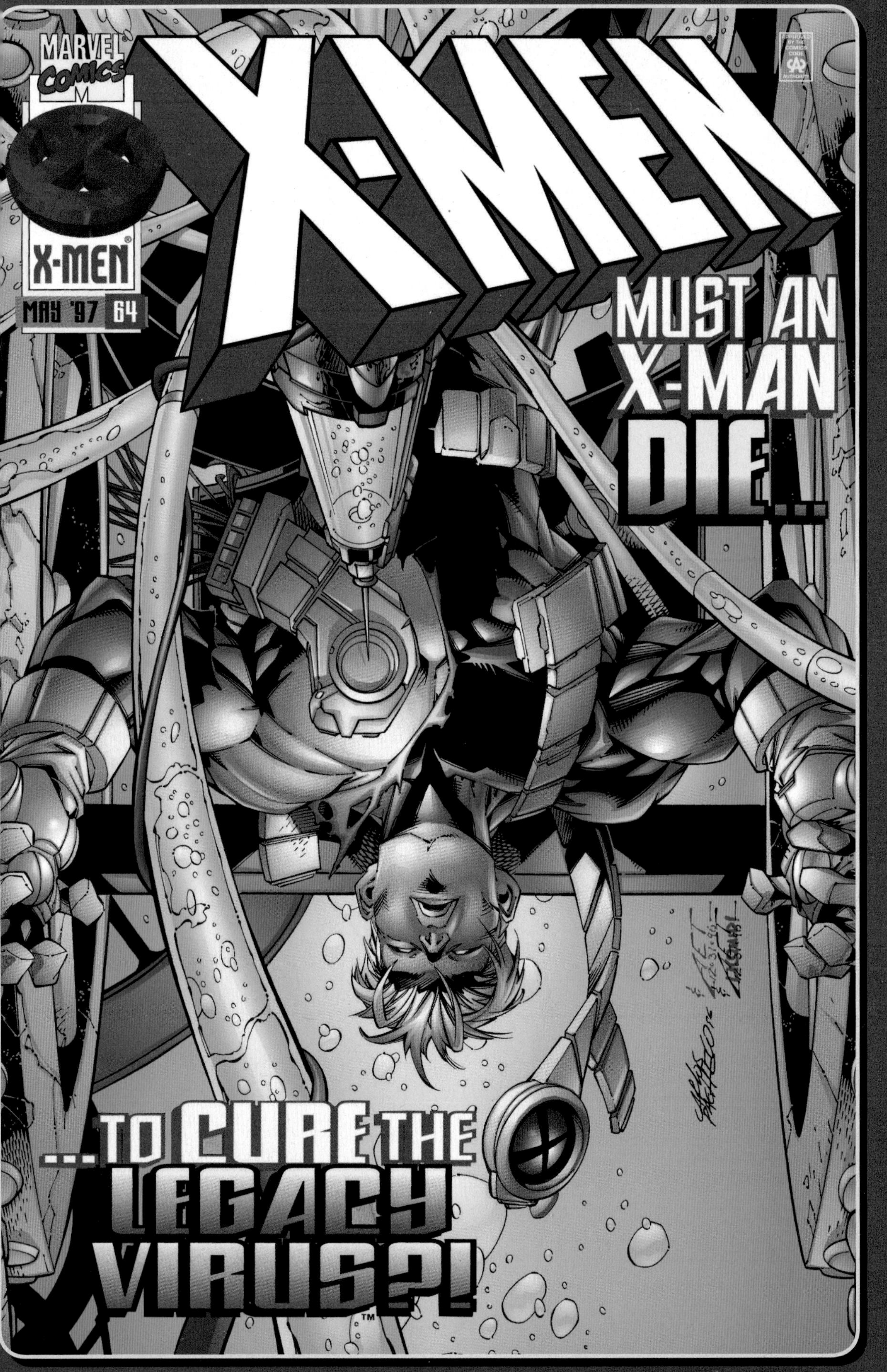
MARVEL COMICS
X-MEN
X-MEN
MAY '97 64
MUST AN X-MAN DIE...
...TO CURE THE LEGACY VIRUS?!

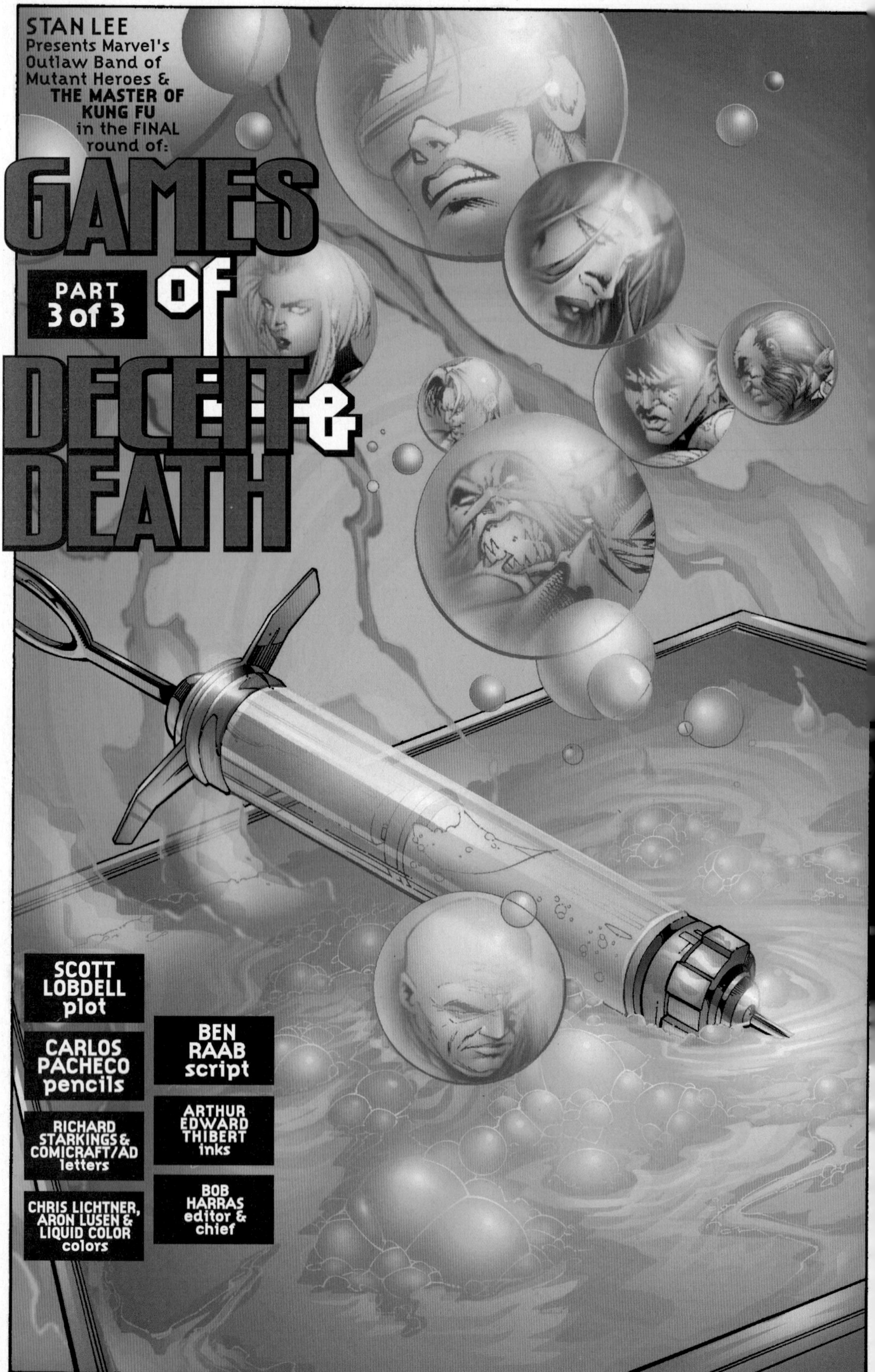

STAN LEE
Presents Marvel's Outlaw Band of Mutant Heroes & THE MASTER OF KUNG FU in the FINAL round of:
GAMES of DECEIT & DEATH
PART 3 of 3
SCOTT LOBDELL plot
CARLOS PACHECO pencils
RICHARD STARKINGS & COMICRAFT/AD letters
CHRIS LICHTNER, ARON LUSEN & LIQUID COLOR colors
BEN RAAB script
ARTHUR EDWARD THIBERT inks
BOB HARRAS editor & chief

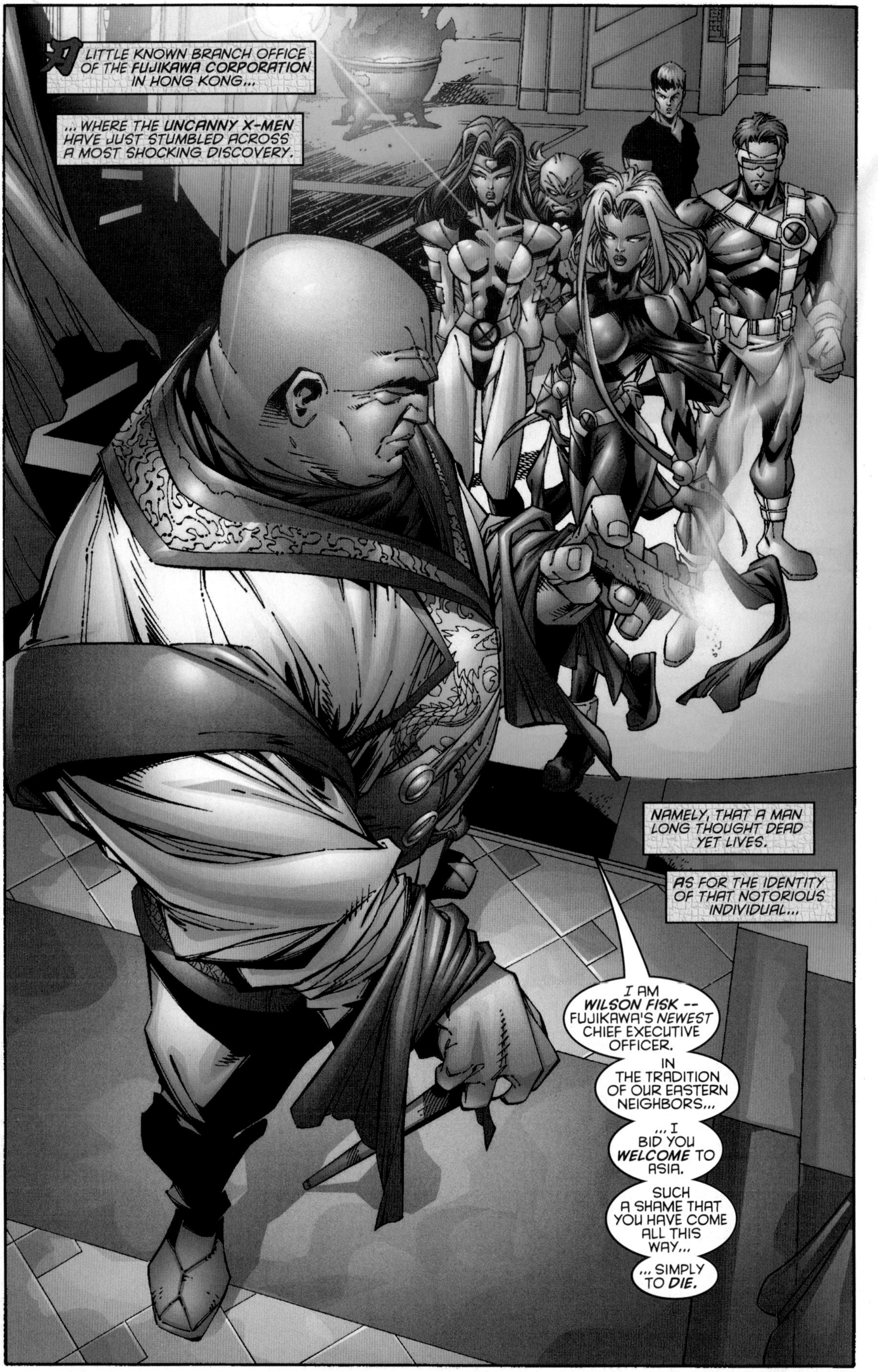
LITTLE KNOWN BRANCH OFFICE OF THE FUJIKAWA CORPORATION IN HONG KONG...
...WHERE THE UNCANNY X-MEN HAVE JUST STUMBLED ACROSS A MOST SHOCKING DISCOVERY.
NAMELY, THAT A MAN LONG THOUGHT DEAD YET LIVES.
AS FOR THE IDENTITY OF THAT NOTORIOUS INDIVIDUAL...
I AM WILSON FISK -- FUJIKAWA'S NEWEST CHIEF EXECUTIVE OFFICER.
IN THE TRADITION OF OUR EASTERN NEIGHBORS...
...I BID YOU WELCOME TO ASIA.
SUCH A SHAME THAT YOU HAVE COME ALL THIS WAY...
...SIMPLY TO DIE.

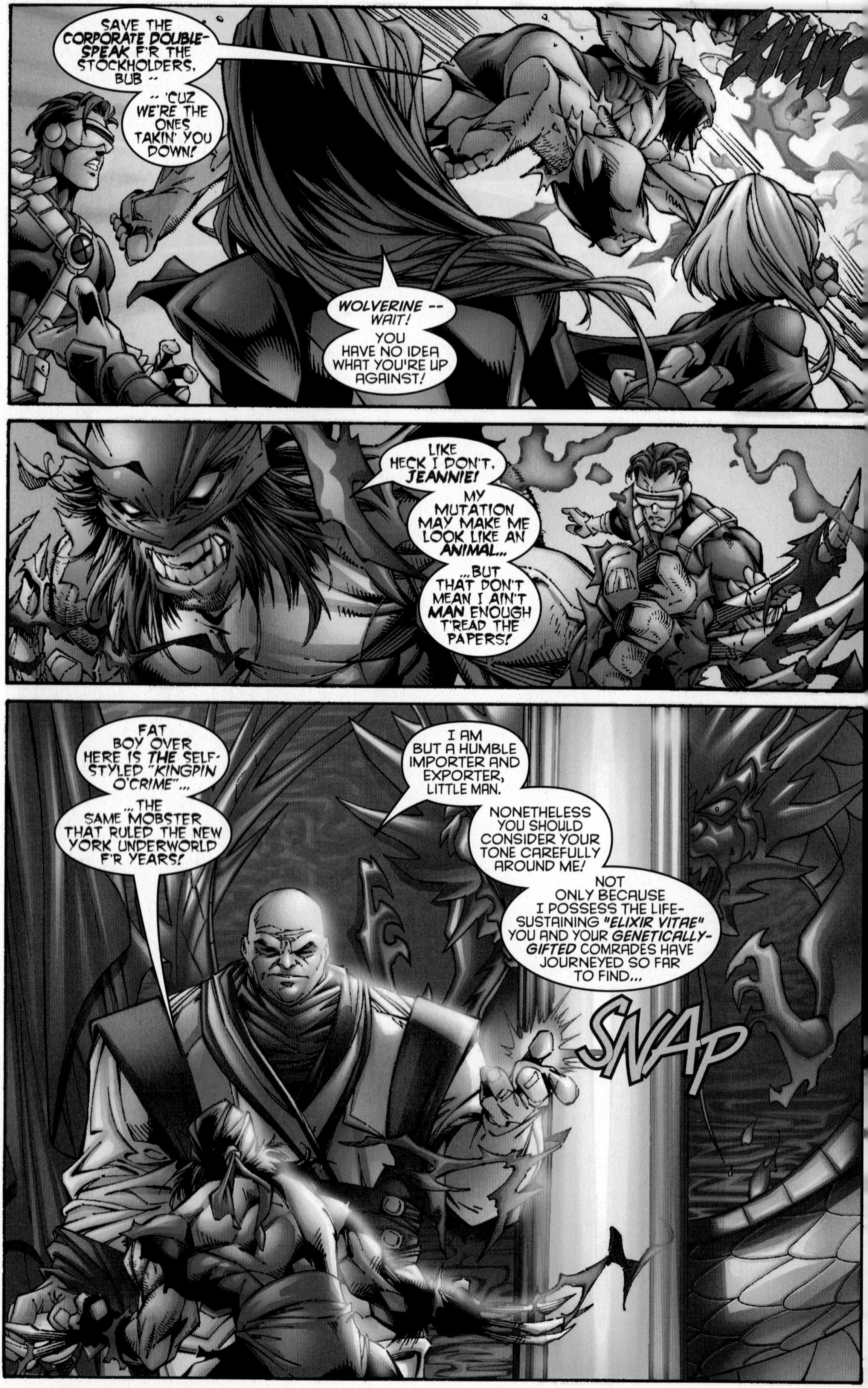
SAVE THE CORPORATE DOUBLE-SPEAK F'R THE STOCKHOLDERS, BUB --
-- 'CUZ WE'RE THE ONES TAKIN' YOU DOWN!
SCHLINK
WOLVERINE -- WAIT!
YOU HAVE NO IDEA WHAT YOU'RE UP AGAINST!
LIKE HECK I DON'T, JEANNIE!
MY MUTATION MAY MAKE ME LOOK LIKE AN ANIMAL...
...BUT THAT DON'T MEAN I AIN'T MAN ENOUGH T'READ THE PAPERS!
FAT BOY OVER HERE IS THE SELF-STYLED "KINGPIN O'CRIME"...
...THE SAME MOBSTER THAT RULED THE NEW YORK UNDERWORLD F'R YEARS!
I AM BUT A HUMBLE IMPORTER AND EXPORTER, LITTLE MAN.
NONETHELESS YOU SHOULD CONSIDER YOUR TONE CAREFULLY AROUND ME!
NOT ONLY BECAUSE I POSSESS THE LIFE-SUSTAINING "ELIXIR VITAE" YOU AND YOUR GENETICALLY-GIFTED COMRADES HAVE JOURNEYED SO FAR TO FIND...
SNAP

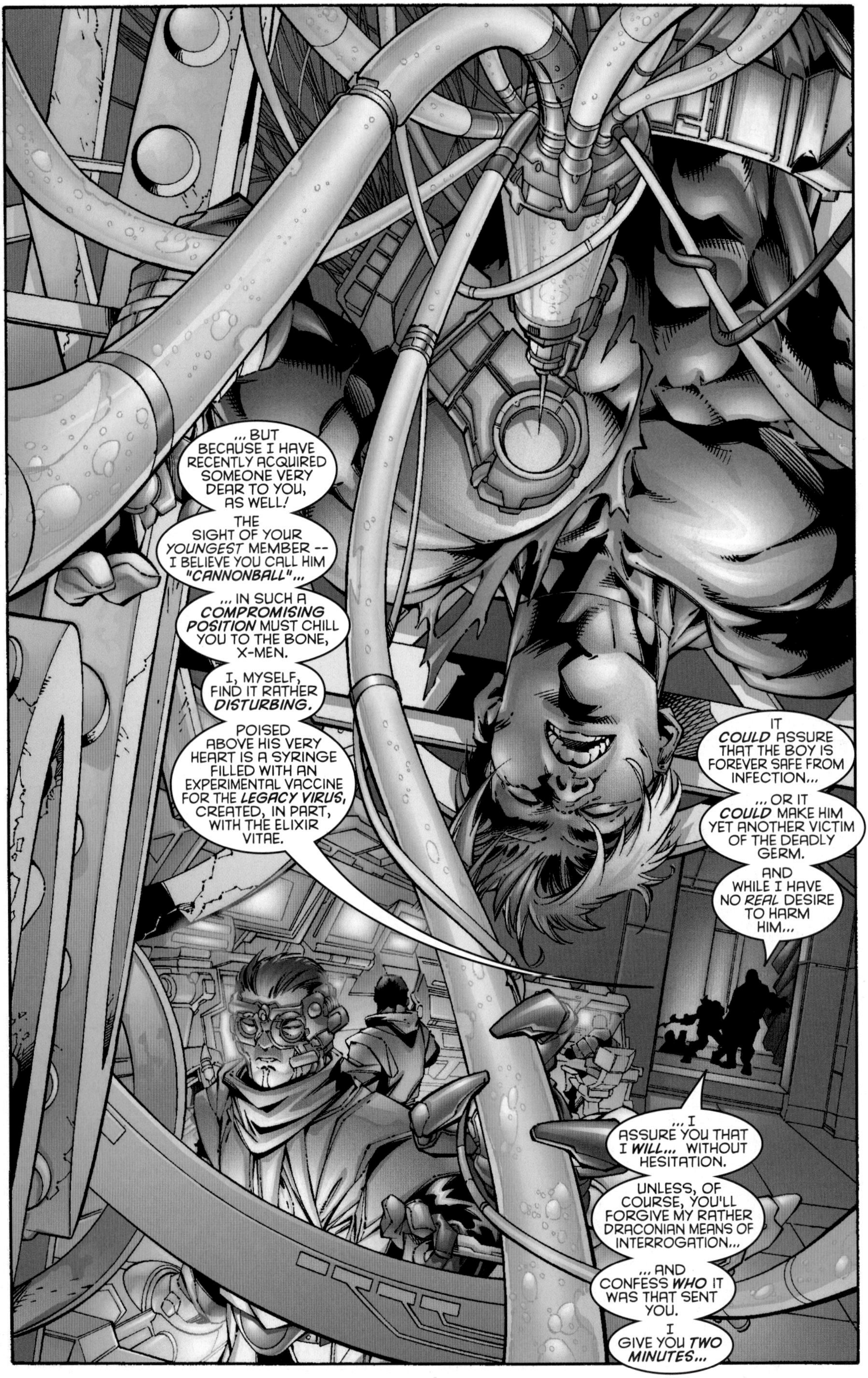
... BUT BECAUSE I HAVE RECENTLY ACQUIRED SOMEONE VERY DEAR TO YOU, AS WELL!
THE SIGHT OF YOUR *YOUNGEST* MEMBER -- I BELIEVE YOU CALL HIM *"CANNONBALL"*...
... IN SUCH A ***COMPROMISING POSITION*** MUST CHILL YOU TO THE BONE, X-MEN.
I, MYSELF, FIND IT RATHER ***DISTURBING.***
POISED ABOVE HIS VERY HEART IS A SYRINGE FILLED WITH AN EXPERIMENTAL VACCINE FOR THE ***LEGACY VIRUS,*** CREATED, IN PART, WITH THE ELIXIR VITAE.
IT ***COULD*** ASSURE THAT THE BOY IS FOREVER SAFE FROM INFECTION...
... OR IT ***COULD*** MAKE HIM YET ANOTHER VICTIM OF THE DEADLY GERM.
AND WHILE I HAVE NO *REAL* DESIRE TO HARM HIM...
... I ASSURE YOU THAT I ***WILL...*** WITHOUT HESITATION.
UNLESS, OF COURSE, YOU'LL FORGIVE MY RATHER DRACONIAN MEANS OF INTERROGATION...
... AND CONFESS ***WHO*** IT WAS THAT SENT YOU.
I GIVE YOU ***TWO MINUTES...***

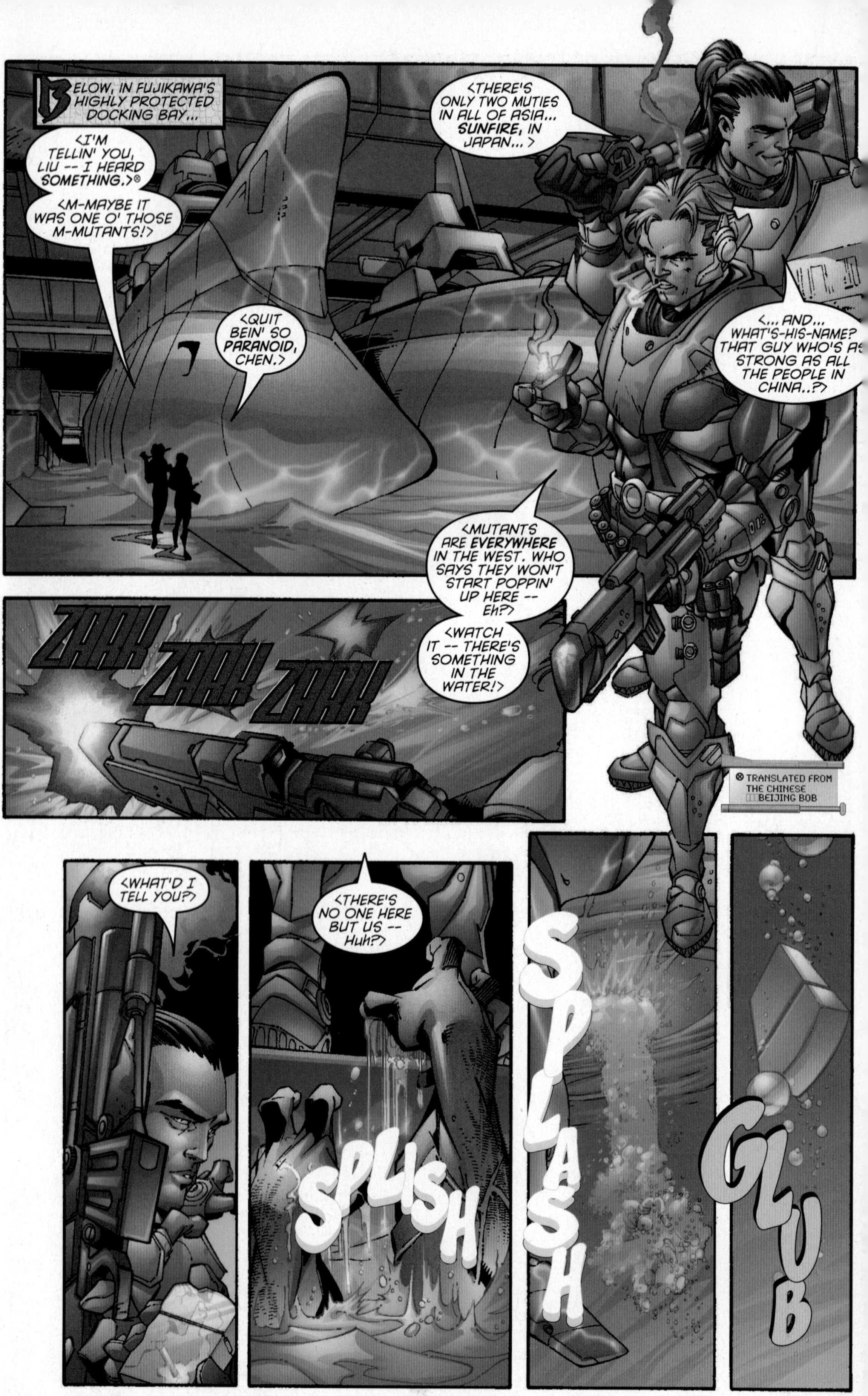
BELOW, IN FUJIKAWA'S HIGHLY PROTECTED DOCKING BAY...
<I'M TELLIN' YOU, LIU -- I HEARD SOMETHING.>
<M-MAYBE IT WAS ONE O' THOSE M-MUTANTS!>
<THERE'S ONLY TWO MUTIES IN ALL OF ASIA... SUNFIRE, IN JAPAN...>
<... AND... WHAT'S-HIS-NAME? THAT GUY WHO'S AS STRONG AS ALL THE PEOPLE IN CHINA..?>
<QUIT BEIN' SO PARANOID, CHEN.>
<MUTANTS ARE EVERYWHERE IN THE WEST. WHO SAYS THEY WON'T START POPPIN' UP HERE -- Eh?>
<WATCH IT -- THERE'S SOMETHING IN THE WATER!>
ZAKK ZAKK ZAKK
TRANSLATED FROM THE CHINESE BEIJING BOB
<WHAT'D I TELL YOU?>
<THERE'S NO ONE HERE BUT US -- Huh?>
SPLISH
SPLASH
GLUB

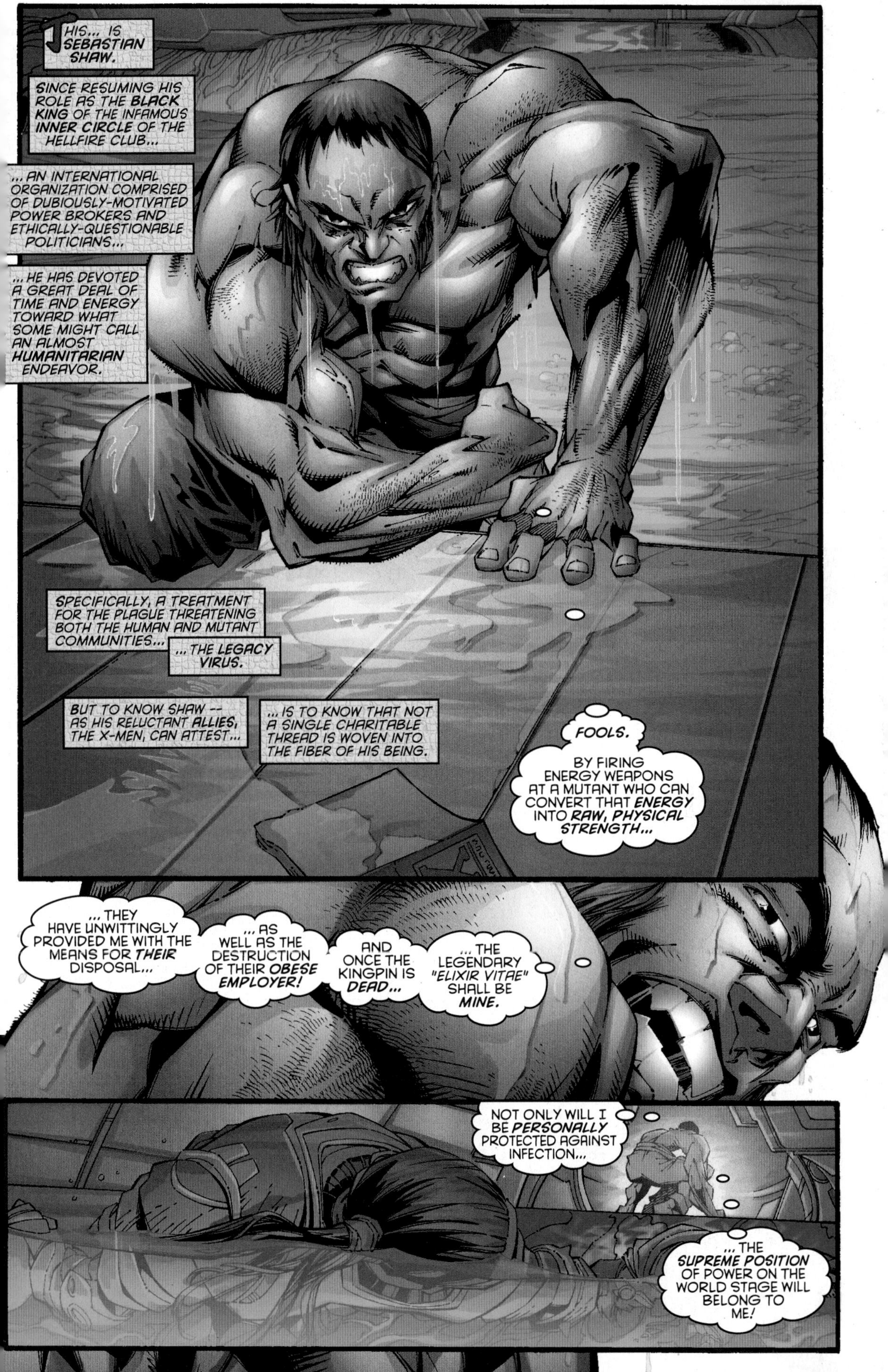
THIS... IS SEBASTIAN SHAW.
SINCE RESUMING HIS ROLE AS THE BLACK KING OF THE INFAMOUS INNER CIRCLE OF THE HELLFIRE CLUB...
...AN INTERNATIONAL ORGANIZATION COMPRISED OF DUBIOUSLY-MOTIVATED POWER BROKERS AND ETHICALLY-QUESTIONABLE POLITICIANS...
...HE HAS DEVOTED A GREAT DEAL OF TIME AND ENERGY TOWARD WHAT SOME MIGHT CALL AN ALMOST HUMANITARIAN ENDEAVOR.
SPECIFICALLY, A TREATMENT FOR THE PLAGUE THREATENING BOTH THE HUMAN AND MUTANT COMMUNITIES...
...THE LEGACY VIRUS.
BUT TO KNOW SHAW -- AS HIS RELUCTANT ALLIES, THE X-MEN, CAN ATTEST...
...IS TO KNOW THAT NOT A SINGLE CHARITABLE THREAD IS WOVEN INTO THE FIBER OF HIS BEING.
FOOLS.
BY FIRING ENERGY WEAPONS AT A MUTANT WHO CAN CONVERT THAT ENERGY INTO RAW, PHYSICAL STRENGTH...
...THEY HAVE UNWITTINGLY PROVIDED ME WITH THE MEANS FOR THEIR DISPOSAL...
...AS WELL AS THE DESTRUCTION OF THEIR OBESE EMPLOYER!
AND ONCE THE KINGPIN IS DEAD...
...THE LEGENDARY "ELIXIR VITAE" SHALL BE MINE.
NOT ONLY WILL I BE PERSONALLY PROTECTED AGAINST INFECTION...
...THE SUPREME POSITION OF POWER ON THE WORLD STAGE WILL BELONG TO ME!

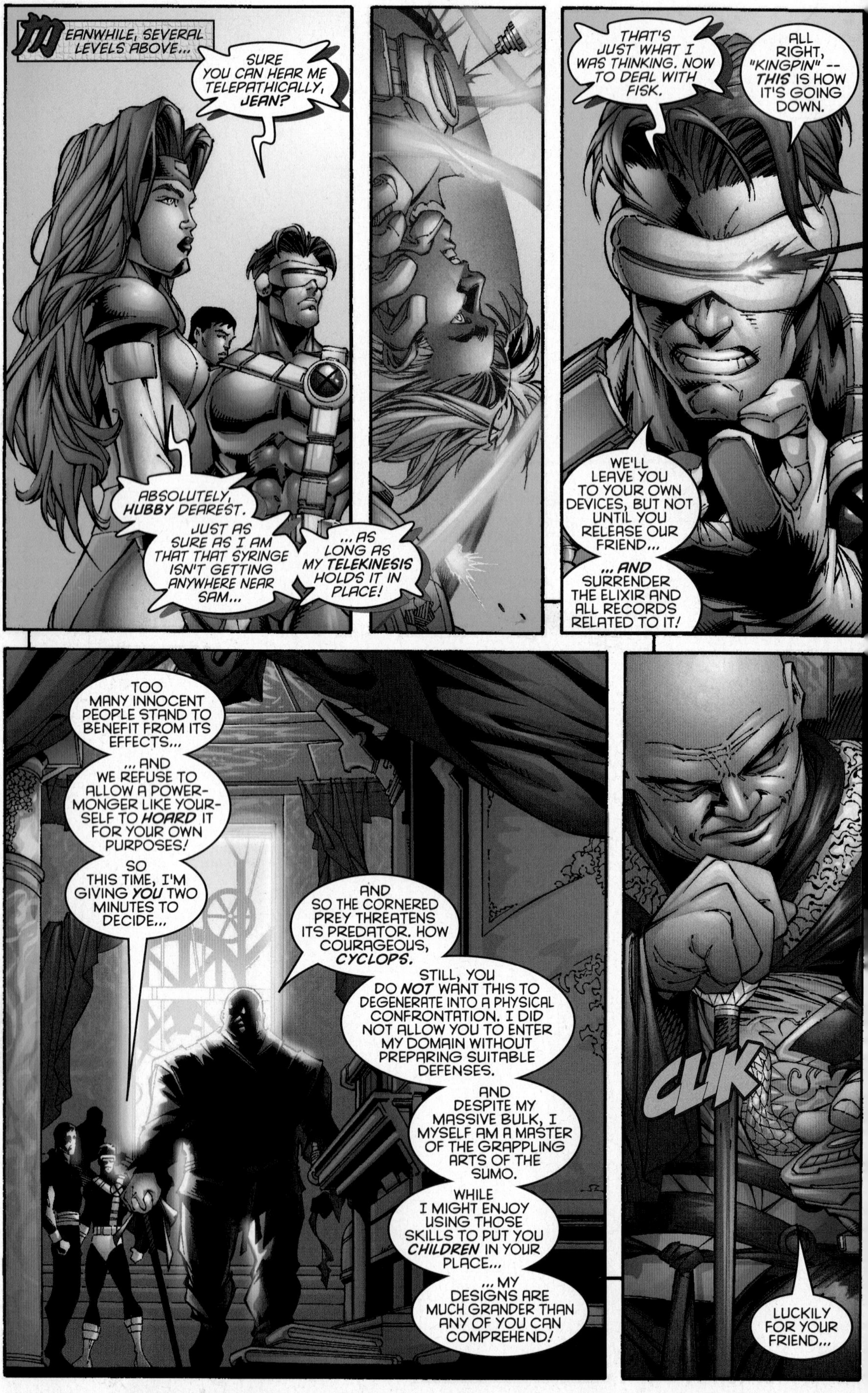
MEANWHILE, SEVERAL LEVELS ABOVE...
SURE YOU CAN HEAR ME TELEPATHICALLY, JEAN?
ABSOLUTELY, HUBBY DEAREST.
JUST AS SURE AS I AM THAT THAT SYRINGE ISN'T GETTING ANYWHERE NEAR SAM...
...AS LONG AS MY TELEKINESIS HOLDS IT IN PLACE!
THAT'S JUST WHAT I WAS THINKING. NOW TO DEAL WITH FISK.
ALL RIGHT, "KINGPIN" -- THIS IS HOW IT'S GOING DOWN.
WE'LL LEAVE YOU TO YOUR OWN DEVICES, BUT NOT UNTIL YOU RELEASE OUR FRIEND...
...AND SURRENDER THE ELIXIR AND ALL RECORDS RELATED TO IT!
TOO MANY INNOCENT PEOPLE STAND TO BENEFIT FROM ITS EFFECTS...
...AND WE REFUSE TO ALLOW A POWER-MONGER LIKE YOUR-SELF TO HOARD IT FOR YOUR OWN PURPOSES!
SO THIS TIME, I'M GIVING YOU TWO MINUTES TO DECIDE...
AND SO THE CORNERED PREY THREATENS ITS PREDATOR. HOW COURAGEOUS, CYCLOPS.
STILL, YOU DO NOT WANT THIS TO DEGENERATE INTO A PHYSICAL CONFRONTATION. I DID NOT ALLOW YOU TO ENTER MY DOMAIN WITHOUT PREPARING SUITABLE DEFENSES.
AND DESPITE MY MASSIVE BULK, I MYSELF AM A MASTER OF THE GRAPPLING ARTS OF THE SUMO.
WHILE I MIGHT ENJOY USING THOSE SKILLS TO PUT YOU CHILDREN IN YOUR PLACE...
...MY DESIGNS ARE MUCH GRANDER THAN ANY OF YOU CAN COMPREHEND!
CLIK
LUCKILY FOR YOUR FRIEND...

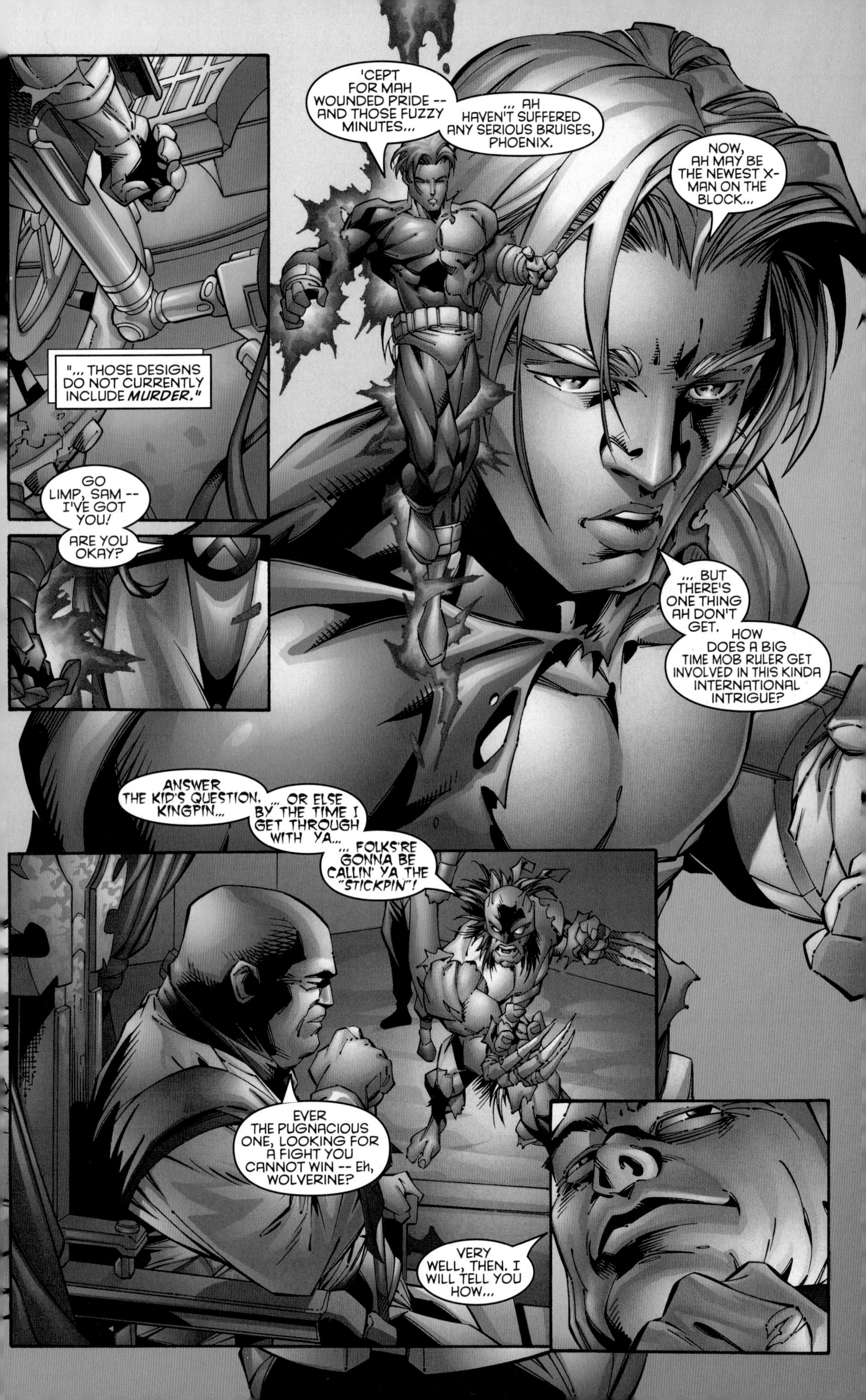
"... THOSE DESIGNS DO NOT CURRENTLY INCLUDE *MURDER*."
GO LIMP, SAM -- I'VE GOT YOU!
ARE YOU OKAY?
'CEPT FOR MAH WOUNDED PRIDE -- AND THOSE FUZZY MINUTES...
... AH HAVEN'T SUFFERED ANY SERIOUS BRUISES, PHOENIX.
NOW, AH MAY BE THE NEWEST X-MAN ON THE BLOCK...
... BUT THERE'S ONE THING AH DON'T GET.
HOW DOES A BIG TIME MOB RULER GET INVOLVED IN THIS KINDA INTERNATIONAL INTRIGUE?
ANSWER THE KID'S QUESTION, KINGPIN...
... OR ELSE BY THE TIME I GET THROUGH WITH YA...
... FOLKS'RE GONNA BE CALLIN' YA THE "STICKPIN"!
EVER THE PUGNACIOUS ONE, LOOKING FOR A FIGHT YOU CANNOT WIN -- Eh, WOLVERINE?
VERY WELL, THEN. I WILL TELL YOU HOW...

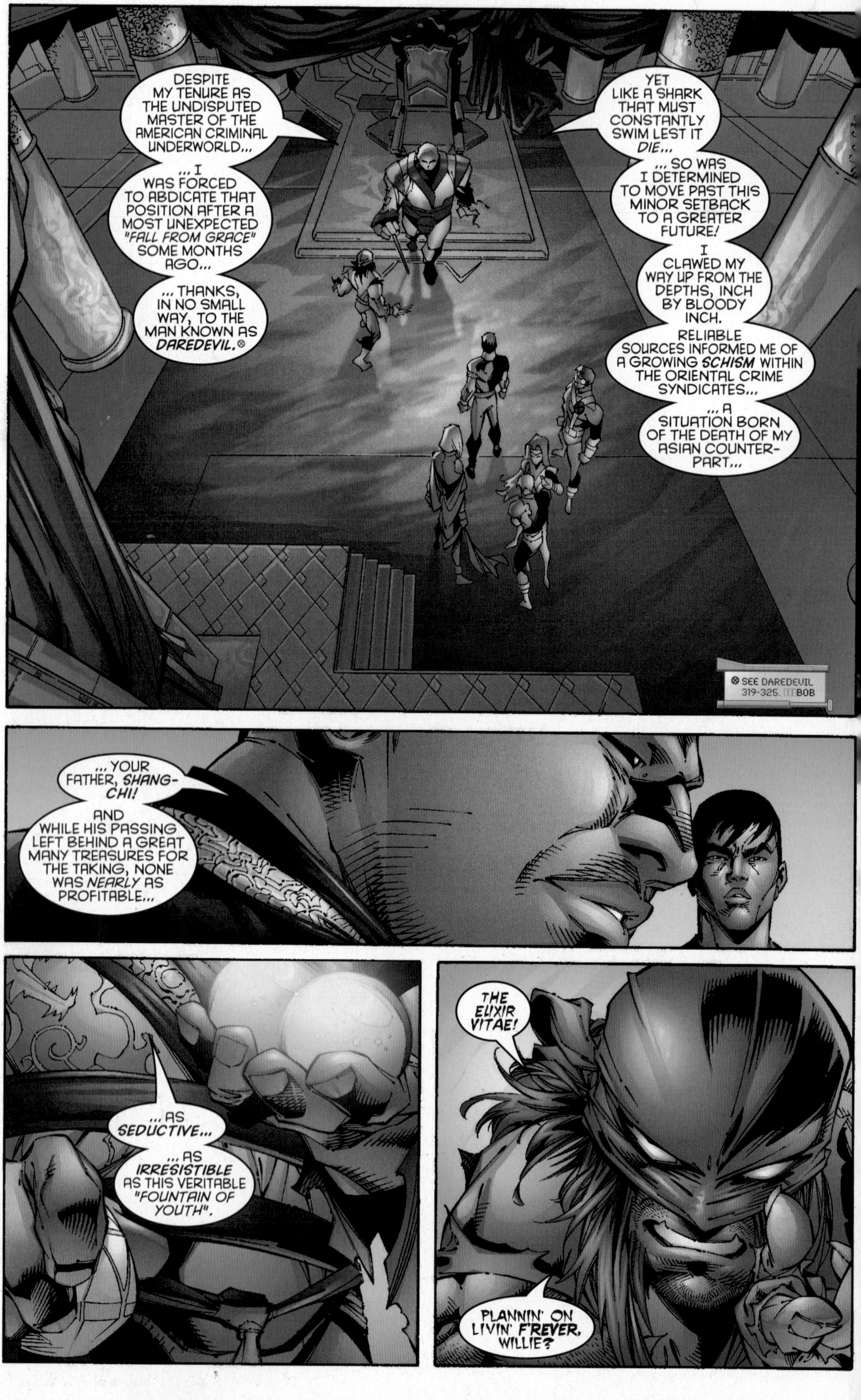

DESPITE MY TENURE AS THE UNDISPUTED MASTER OF THE AMERICAN CRIMINAL UNDERWORLD...
... I WAS FORCED TO ABDICATE THAT POSITION AFTER A MOST UNEXPECTED "FALL FROM GRACE" SOME MONTHS AGO...
... THANKS, IN NO SMALL WAY, TO THE MAN KNOWN AS DAREDEVIL.⊗
YET LIKE A SHARK THAT MUST CONSTANTLY SWIM LEST IT DIE...
... SO WAS I DETERMINED TO MOVE PAST THIS MINOR SETBACK TO A GREATER FUTURE!
I CLAWED MY WAY UP FROM THE DEPTHS, INCH BY BLOODY INCH.
RELIABLE SOURCES INFORMED ME OF A GROWING SCHISM WITHIN THE ORIENTAL CRIME SYNDICATES...
... A SITUATION BORN OF THE DEATH OF MY ASIAN COUNTER-PART...
⊗ SEE DAREDEVIL 319-325. BOB
... YOUR FATHER, SHANG-CHI!
AND WHILE HIS PASSING LEFT BEHIND A GREAT MANY TREASURES FOR THE TAKING, NONE WAS NEARLY AS PROFITABLE...
... AS SEDUCTIVE...
... AS IRRESISTIBLE AS THIS VERITABLE "FOUNTAIN OF YOUTH".
THE ELIXIR VITAE!
PLANNIN' ON LIVIN' F'REVER, WILLIE?

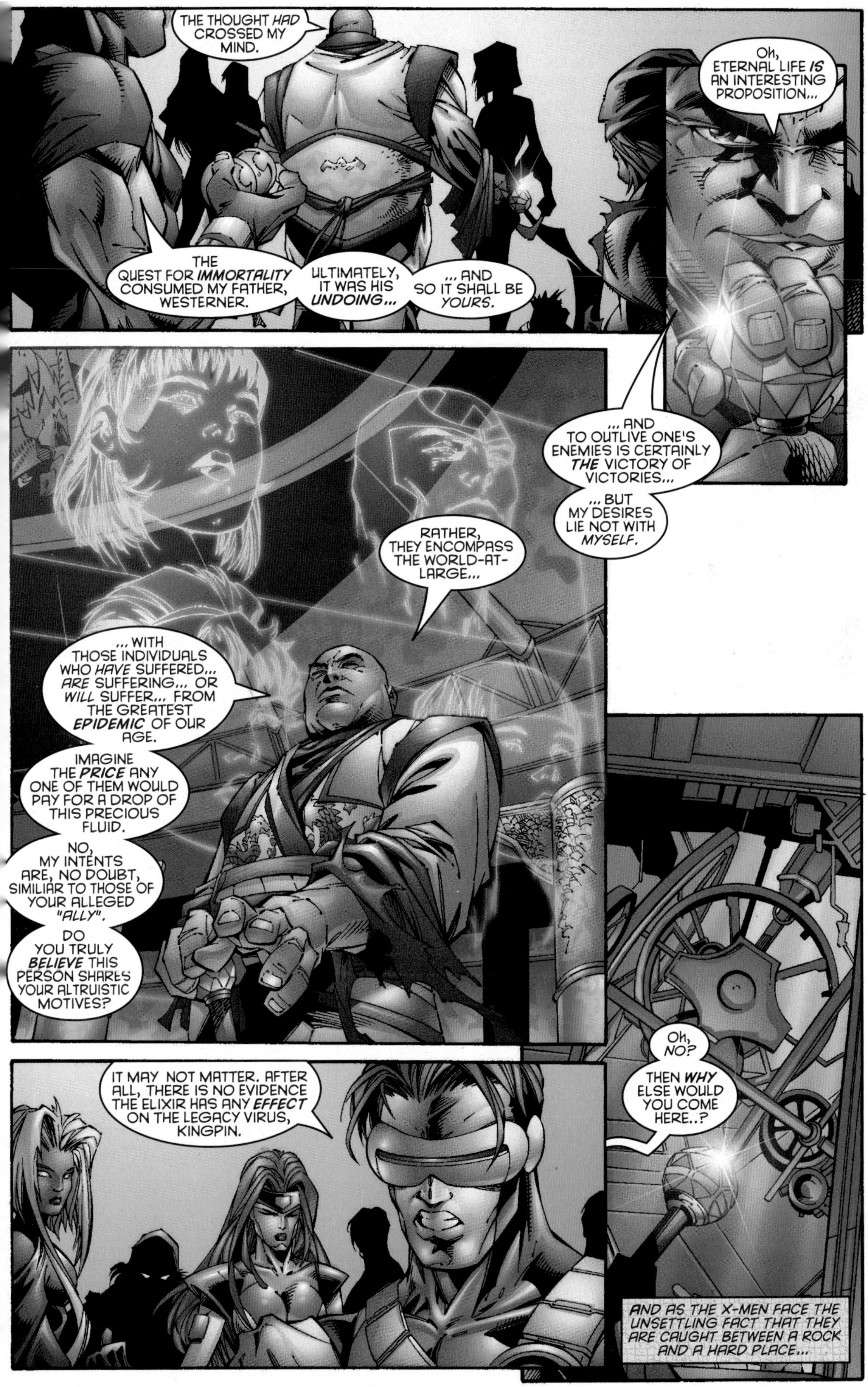
THE THOUGHT HAD CROSSED MY MIND.
Oh, ETERNAL LIFE IS AN INTERESTING PROPOSITION...
THE QUEST FOR IMMORTALITY CONSUMED MY FATHER, WESTERNER.
ULTIMATELY, IT WAS HIS UNDOING...
...AND SO IT SHALL BE YOURS.
...AND TO OUTLIVE ONE'S ENEMIES IS CERTAINLY THE VICTORY OF VICTORIES...
...BUT MY DESIRES LIE NOT WITH MYSELF.
RATHER, THEY ENCOMPASS THE WORLD-AT-LARGE...
...WITH THOSE INDIVIDUALS WHO HAVE SUFFERED... ARE SUFFERING... OR WILL SUFFER... FROM THE GREATEST EPIDEMIC OF OUR AGE.
IMAGINE THE PRICE ANY ONE OF THEM WOULD PAY FOR A DROP OF THIS PRECIOUS FLUID.
NO, MY INTENTS ARE, NO DOUBT, SIMILIAR TO THOSE OF YOUR ALLEGED "ALLY".
DO YOU TRULY BELIEVE THIS PERSON SHARES YOUR ALTRUISTIC MOTIVES?
IT MAY NOT MATTER. AFTER ALL, THERE IS NO EVIDENCE THE ELIXIR HAS ANY EFFECT ON THE LEGACY VIRUS, KINGPIN.
Oh, NO?
THEN WHY ELSE WOULD YOU COME HERE..?
AND AS THE X-MEN FACE THE UNSETTLING FACT THAT THEY ARE CAUGHT BETWEEN A ROCK AND A HARD PLACE...

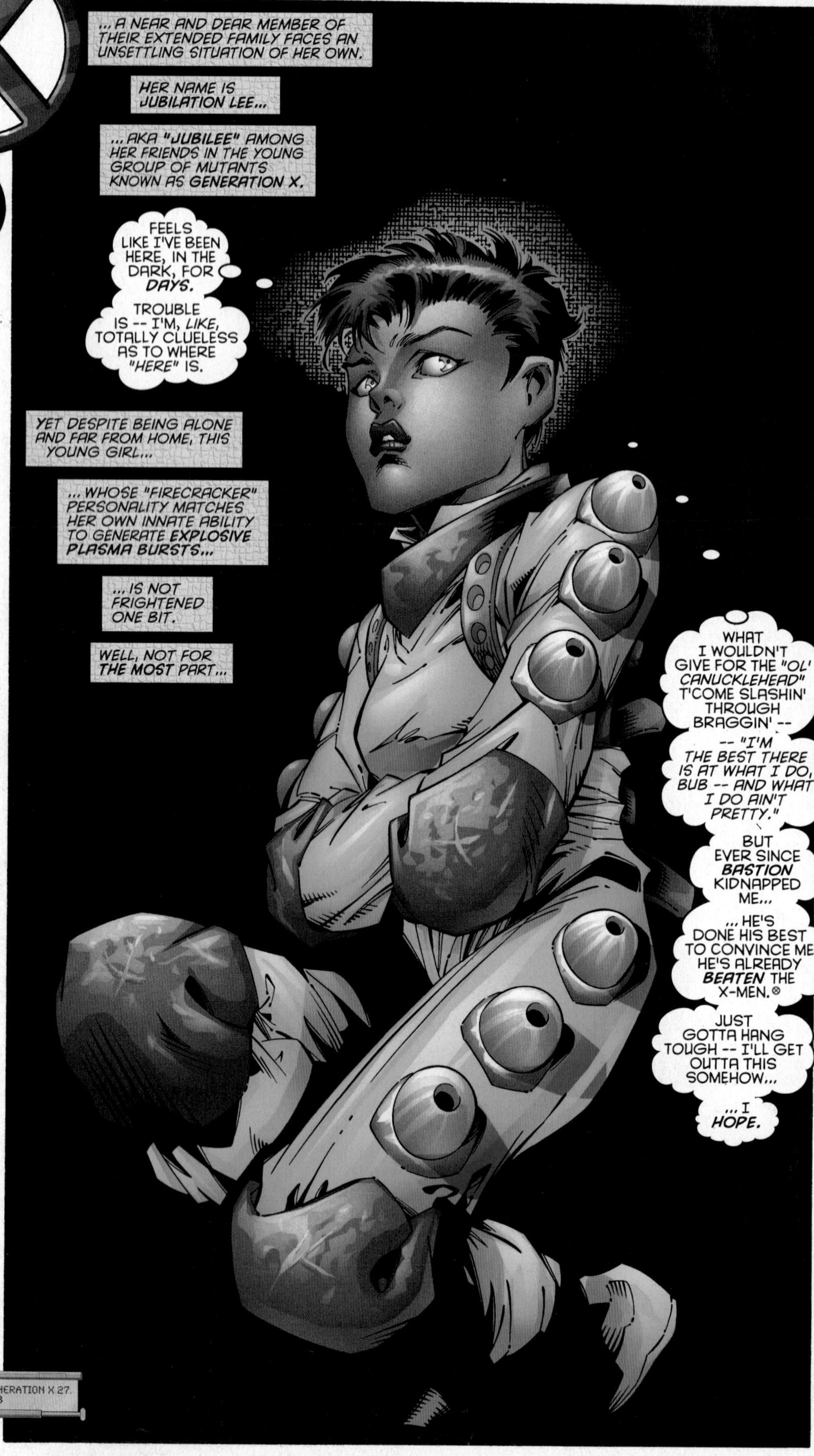

...A NEAR AND DEAR MEMBER OF THEIR EXTENDED FAMILY FACES AN UNSETTLING SITUATION OF HER OWN.
HER NAME IS JUBILATION LEE...
...AKA "JUBILEE" AMONG HER FRIENDS IN THE YOUNG GROUP OF MUTANTS KNOWN AS GENERATION X.
FEELS LIKE I'VE BEEN HERE, IN THE DARK, FOR DAYS.
TROUBLE IS -- I'M, LIKE, TOTALLY CLUELESS AS TO WHERE "HERE" IS.
YET DESPITE BEING ALONE AND FAR FROM HOME, THIS YOUNG GIRL...
...WHOSE "FIRECRACKER" PERSONALITY MATCHES HER OWN INNATE ABILITY TO GENERATE EXPLOSIVE PLASMA BURSTS...
...IS NOT FRIGHTENED ONE BIT.
WELL, NOT FOR THE MOST PART...
WHAT I WOULDN'T GIVE FOR THE "OL' CANUCKLEHEAD" T'COME SLASHIN' THROUGH BRAGGIN' --
-- "I'M THE BEST THERE IS AT WHAT I DO, BUB -- AND WHAT I DO AIN'T PRETTY."
BUT EVER SINCE BASTION KIDNAPPED ME...
...HE'S DONE HIS BEST TO CONVINCE ME HE'S ALREADY BEATEN THE X-MEN.
JUST GOTTA HANG TOUGH -- I'LL GET OUTTA THIS SOMEHOW...
...I HOPE.
IN GENERATION X 27. BOB

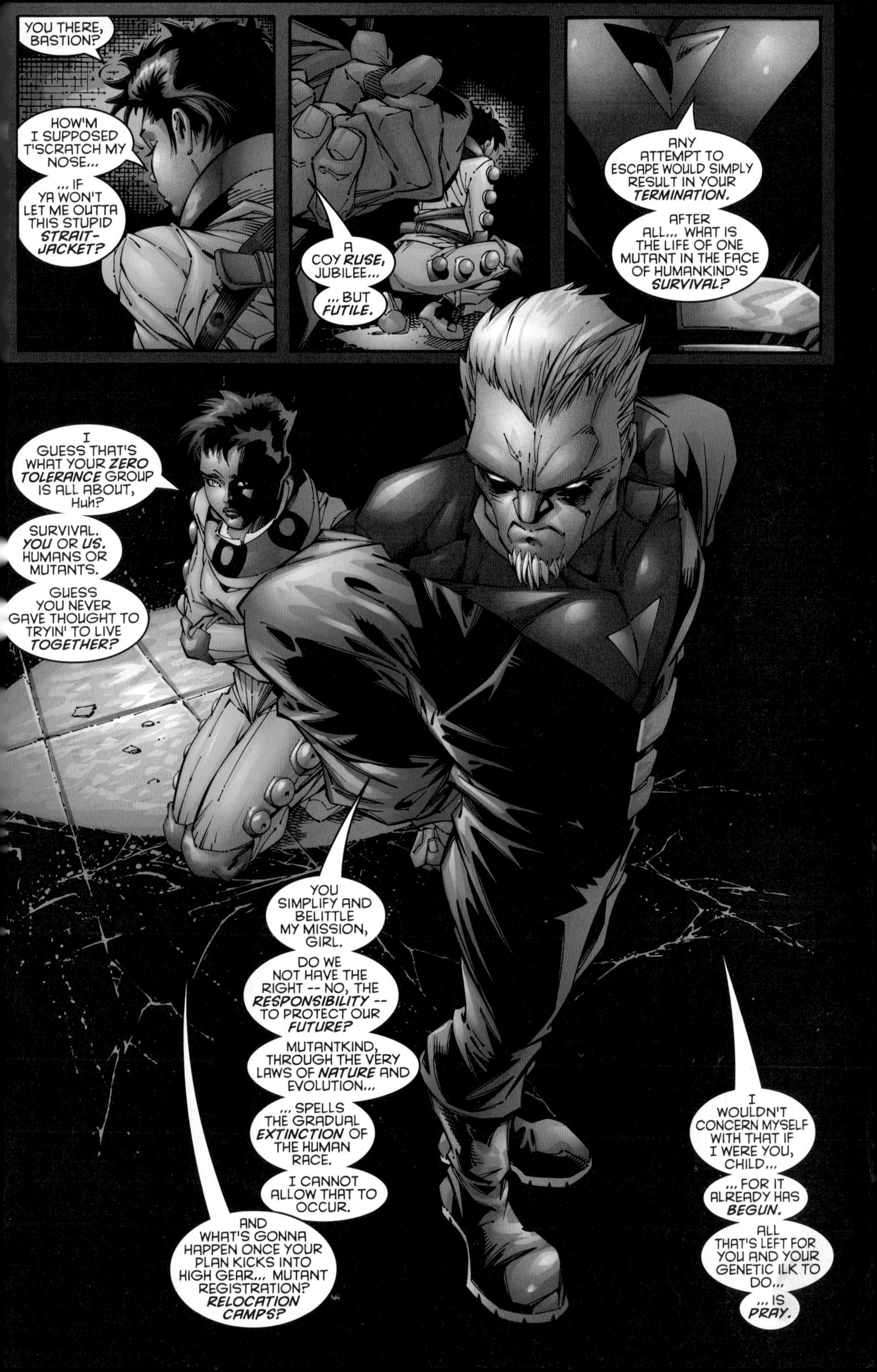
YOU THERE, BASTION?
HOW'M I SUPPOSED T'SCRATCH MY NOSE...
... IF YA WON'T LET ME OUTTA THIS STUPID STRAIT-JACKET?
A COY RUSE, JUBILEE...
... BUT FUTILE.
ANY ATTEMPT TO ESCAPE WOULD SIMPLY RESULT IN YOUR TERMINATION.
AFTER ALL... WHAT IS THE LIFE OF ONE MUTANT IN THE FACE OF HUMANKIND'S SURVIVAL?
I GUESS THAT'S WHAT YOUR ZERO TOLERANCE GROUP IS ALL ABOUT, Huh?
SURVIVAL. YOU OR US. HUMANS OR MUTANTS.
GUESS YOU NEVER GAVE THOUGHT TO TRYIN' TO LIVE TOGETHER?
YOU SIMPLIFY AND BELITTLE MY MISSION, GIRL.
DO WE NOT HAVE THE RIGHT -- NO, THE RESPONSIBILITY -- TO PROTECT OUR FUTURE?
MUTANTKIND, THROUGH THE VERY LAWS OF NATURE AND EVOLUTION...
... SPELLS THE GRADUAL EXTINCTION OF THE HUMAN RACE.
I CANNOT ALLOW THAT TO OCCUR.
AND WHAT'S GONNA HAPPEN ONCE YOUR PLAN KICKS INTO HIGH GEAR... MUTANT REGISTRATION? RELOCATION CAMPS?
I WOULDN'T CONCERN MYSELF WITH THAT IF I WERE YOU, CHILD...
... FOR IT ALREADY HAS BEGUN.
ALL THAT'S LEFT FOR YOU AND YOUR GENETIC ILK TO DO...
... IS PRAY.

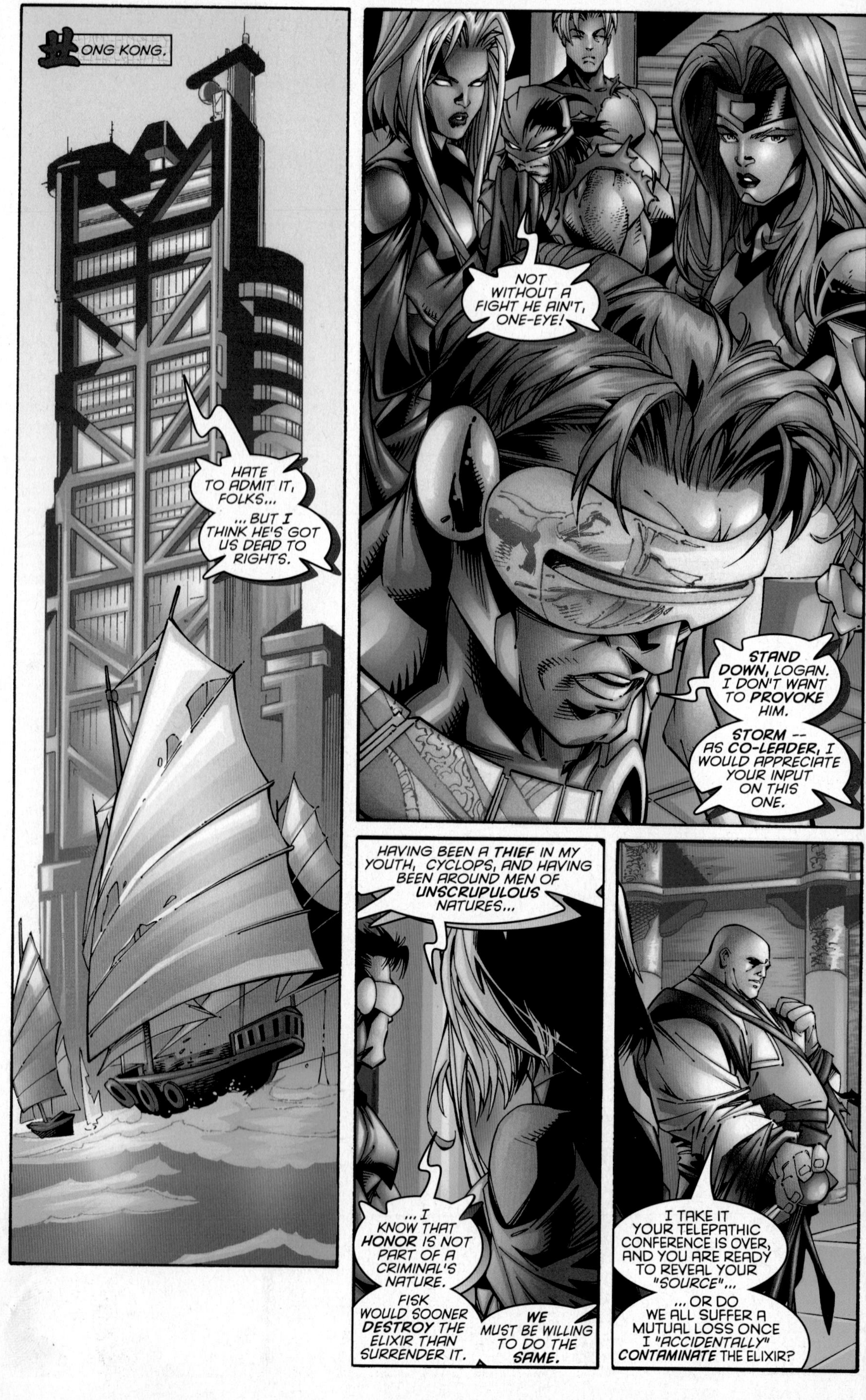
HONG KONG.
HATE TO ADMIT IT, FOLKS...
...BUT I THINK HE'S GOT US DEAD TO RIGHTS.
NOT WITHOUT A FIGHT HE AIN'T, ONE-EYE!
STAND DOWN, LOGAN. I DON'T WANT TO PROVOKE HIM.
STORM -- AS CO-LEADER, I WOULD APPRECIATE YOUR INPUT ON THIS ONE.
HAVING BEEN A THIEF IN MY YOUTH, CYCLOPS, AND HAVING BEEN AROUND MEN OF UNSCRUPULOUS NATURES...
...I KNOW THAT HONOR IS NOT PART OF A CRIMINAL'S NATURE.
FISK WOULD SOONER DESTROY THE ELIXIR THAN SURRENDER IT.
WE MUST BE WILLING TO DO THE SAME.
I TAKE IT YOUR TELEPATHIC CONFERENCE IS OVER, AND YOU ARE READY TO REVEAL YOUR "SOURCE"...
...OR DO WE ALL SUFFER A MUTUAL LOSS ONCE I "ACCIDENTALLY" CONTAMINATE THE ELIXIR?

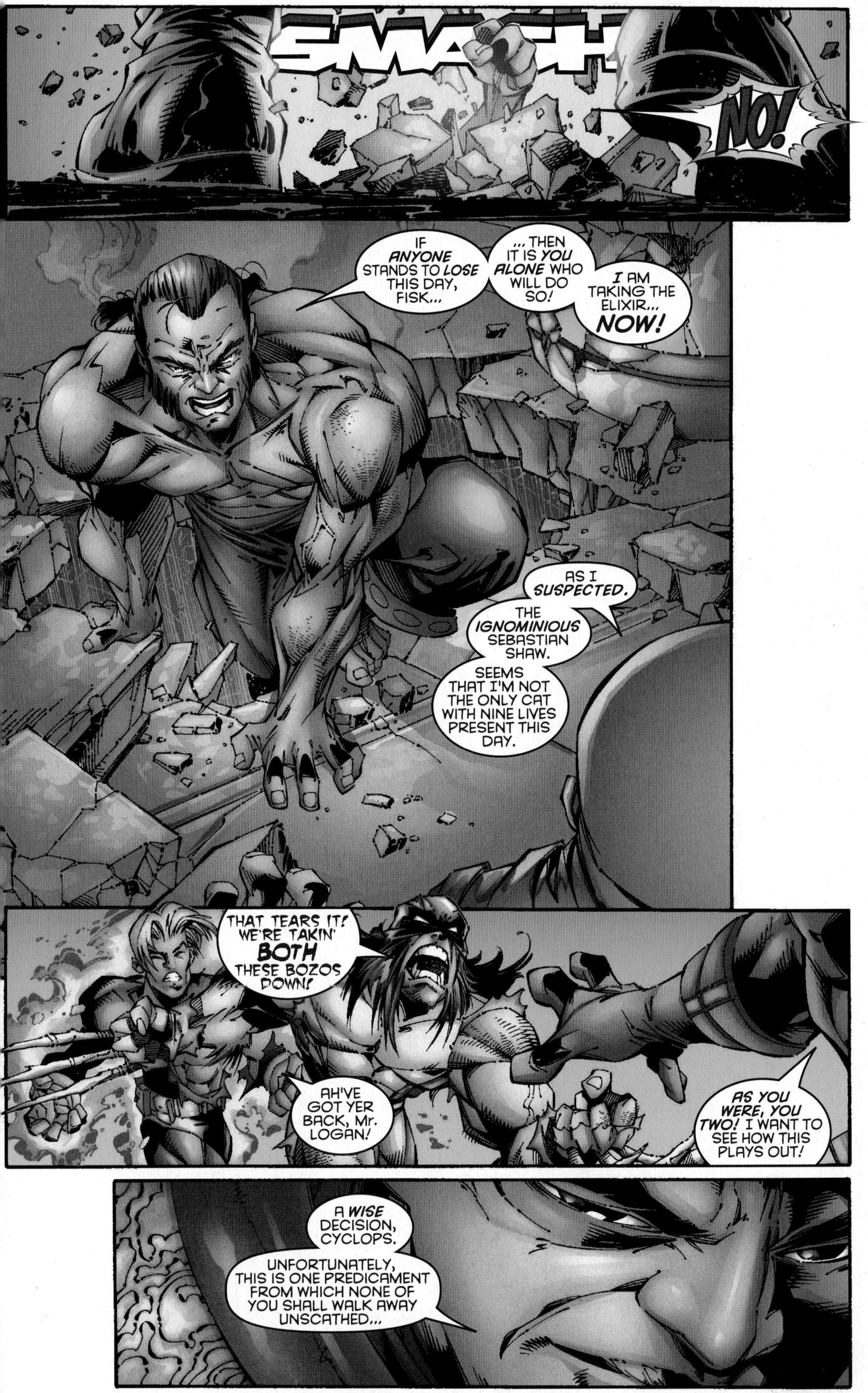
SMASH
NO!
IF ANYONE STANDS TO LOSE THIS DAY, FISK...
...THEN IT IS YOU ALONE WHO WILL DO SO!
I AM TAKING THE ELIXIR... NOW!
AS I SUSPECTED.
THE IGNOMINIOUS SEBASTIAN SHAW.
SEEMS THAT I'M NOT THE ONLY CAT WITH NINE LIVES PRESENT THIS DAY.
THAT TEARS IT! WE'RE TAKIN' BOTH THESE BOZOS DOWN!
AH'VE GOT YER BACK, Mr. LOGAN!
AS YOU WERE, YOU TWO! I WANT TO SEE HOW THIS PLAYS OUT!
A WISE DECISION, CYCLOPS.
UNFORTUNATELY, THIS IS ONE PREDICAMENT FROM WHICH NONE OF YOU SHALL WALK AWAY UNSCATHED...

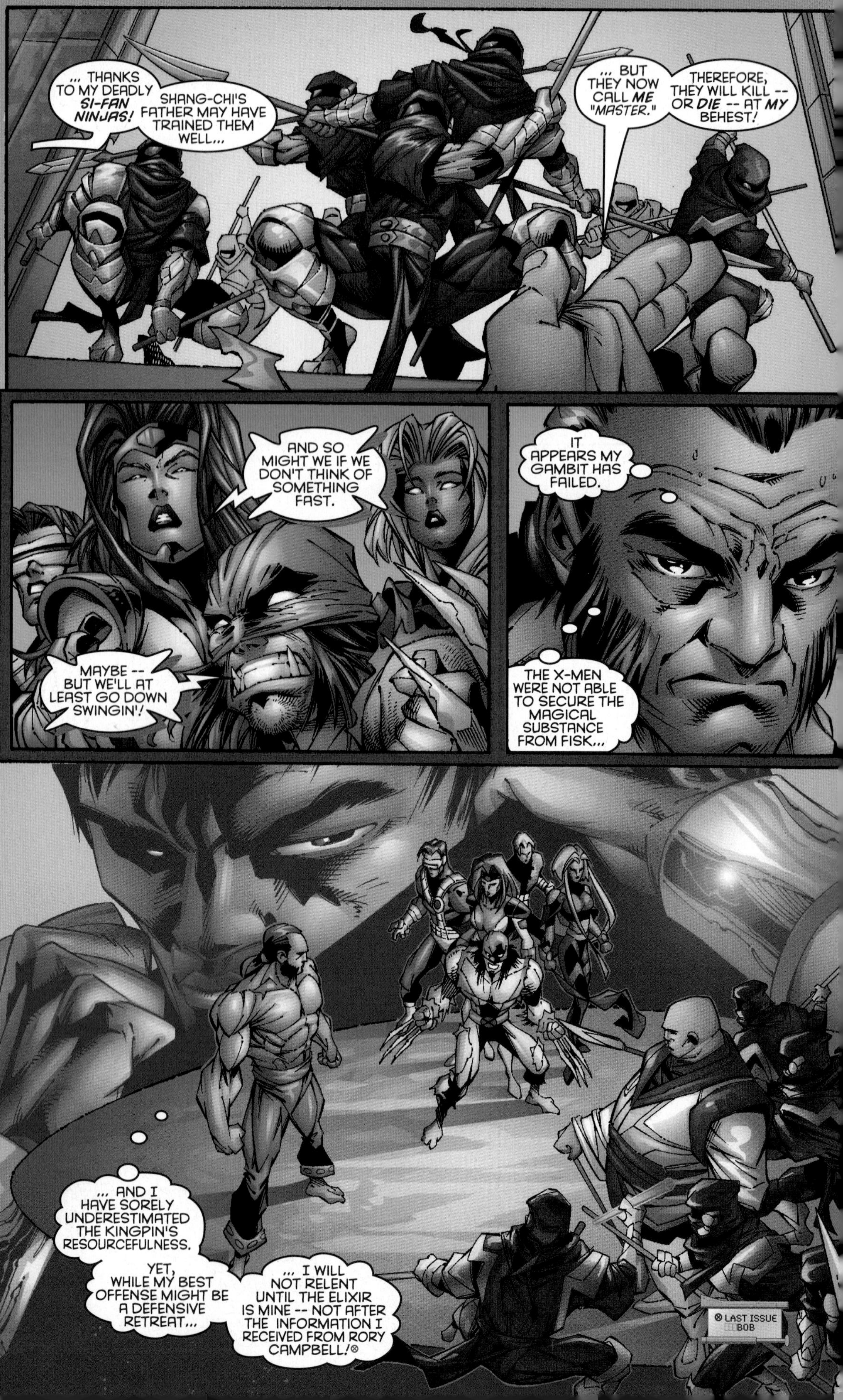

... THANKS TO MY DEADLY *SI-FAN NINJAS!*
SHANG-CHI'S FATHER MAY HAVE TRAINED THEM WELL...
... BUT THEY NOW CALL *ME* "*MASTER.*"
THEREFORE, THEY WILL KILL -- OR *DIE* -- AT *MY* BEHEST!
AND SO MIGHT WE IF WE DON'T THINK OF SOMETHING FAST.
MAYBE -- BUT WE'LL AT LEAST GO DOWN SWINGIN'!
IT APPEARS MY GAMBIT HAS FAILED.
THE X-MEN WERE NOT ABLE TO SECURE THE MAGICAL SUBSTANCE FROM FISK...
... AND I HAVE SORELY UNDERESTIMATED THE KINGPIN'S RESOURCEFULNESS.
YET, WHILE MY BEST OFFENSE MIGHT BE A DEFENSIVE RETREAT...
... I WILL NOT RELENT UNTIL THE ELIXIR IS MINE -- NOT AFTER THE INFORMATION I RECEIVED FROM RORY CAMPBELL!⊗
⊗ LAST ISSUE
BOB

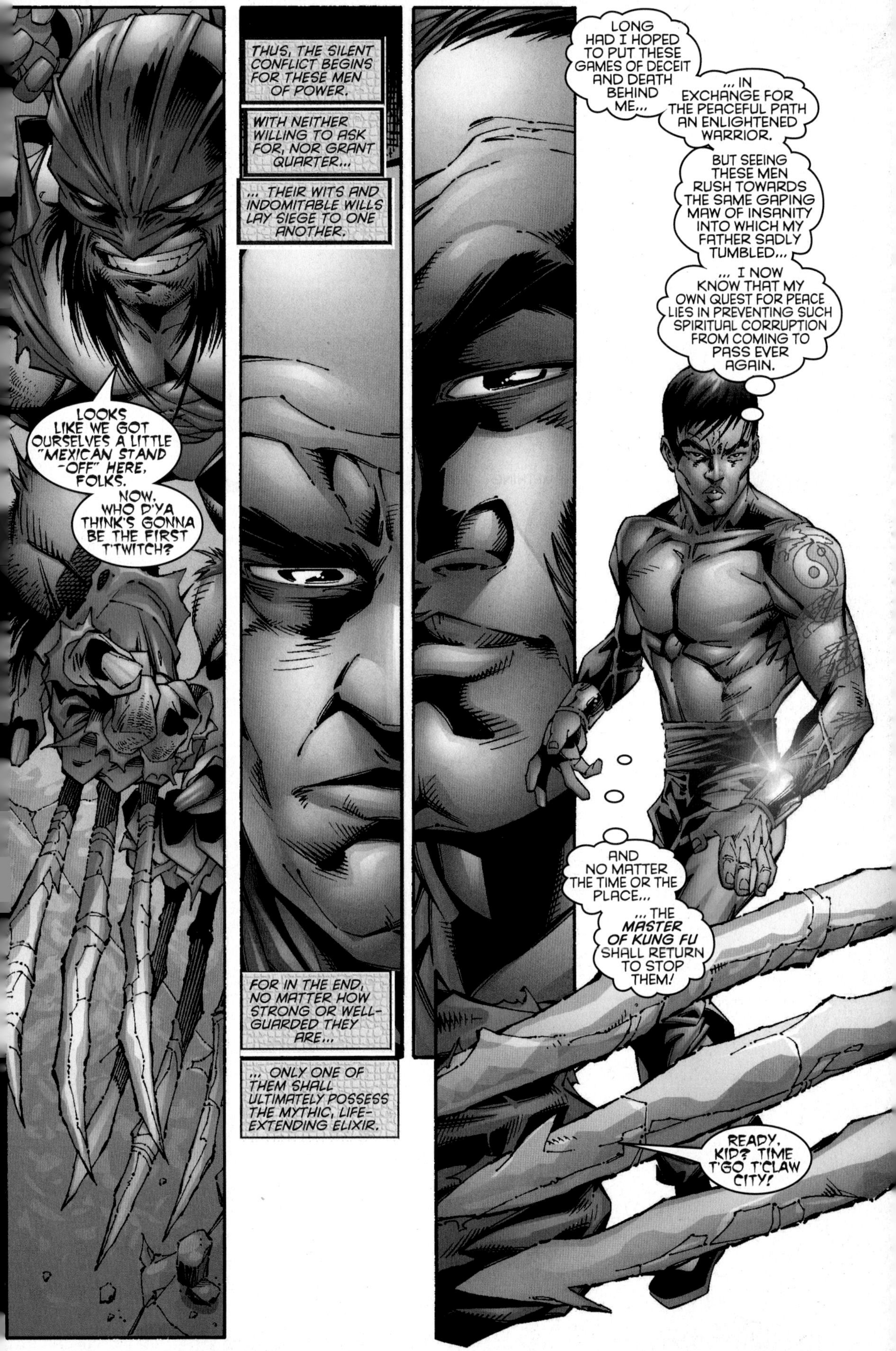
THUS, THE SILENT CONFLICT BEGINS FOR THESE MEN OF POWER.
WITH NEITHER WILLING TO ASK FOR, NOR GRANT QUARTER...
... THEIR WITS AND INDOMITABLE WILLS LAY SIEGE TO ONE ANOTHER.
LONG HAD I HOPED TO PUT THESE GAMES OF DECEIT AND DEATH BEHIND ME...
... IN EXCHANGE FOR THE PEACEFUL PATH AN ENLIGHTENED WARRIOR.
BUT SEEING THESE MEN RUSH TOWARDS THE SAME GAPING MAW OF INSANITY INTO WHICH MY FATHER SADLY TUMBLED...
... I NOW KNOW THAT MY OWN QUEST FOR PEACE LIES IN PREVENTING SUCH SPIRITUAL CORRUPTION FROM COMING TO PASS EVER AGAIN.
LOOKS LIKE WE GOT OURSELVES A LITTLE "MEXICAN STAND-OFF" HERE, FOLKS.
NOW, WHO D'YA THINK'S GONNA BE THE FIRST T'TWITCH?
AND NO MATTER THE TIME OR THE PLACE...
... THE MASTER OF KUNG FU SHALL RETURN TO STOP THEM!
FOR IN THE END, NO MATTER HOW STRONG OR WELL-GUARDED THEY ARE...
... ONLY ONE OF THEM SHALL ULTIMATELY POSSESS THE MYTHIC, LIFE-EXTENDING ELIXIR.
READY, KID? TIME T'GO T'CLAW CITY!

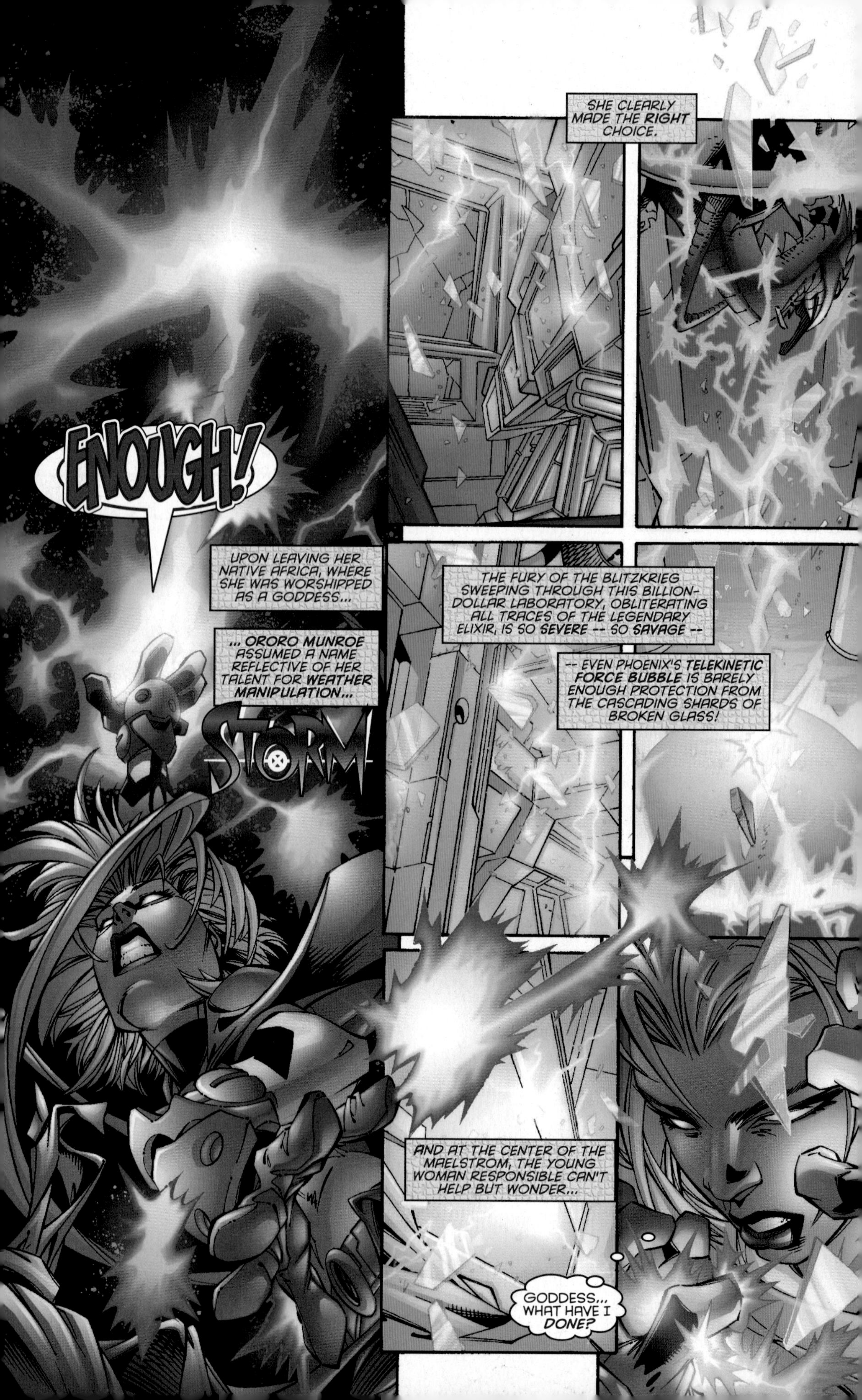
ENOUGH!
UPON LEAVING HER NATIVE AFRICA, WHERE SHE WAS WORSHIPPED AS A GODDESS...
...ORORO MUNROE ASSUMED A NAME REFLECTIVE OF HER TALENT FOR WEATHER MANIPULATION...
STORM
SHE CLEARLY MADE THE RIGHT CHOICE.
THE FURY OF THE BLITZKRIEG SWEEPING THROUGH THIS BILLION-DOLLAR LABORATORY, OBLITERATING ALL TRACES OF THE LEGENDARY ELIXIR, IS SO SEVERE -- SO SAVAGE --
-- EVEN PHOENIX'S TELEKINETIC FORCE BUBBLE IS BARELY ENOUGH PROTECTION FROM THE CASCADING SHARDS OF BROKEN GLASS!
AND AT THE CENTER OF THE MAELSTROM, THE YOUNG WOMAN RESPONSIBLE CAN'T HELP BUT WONDER...
GODDESS... WHAT HAVE I DONE?

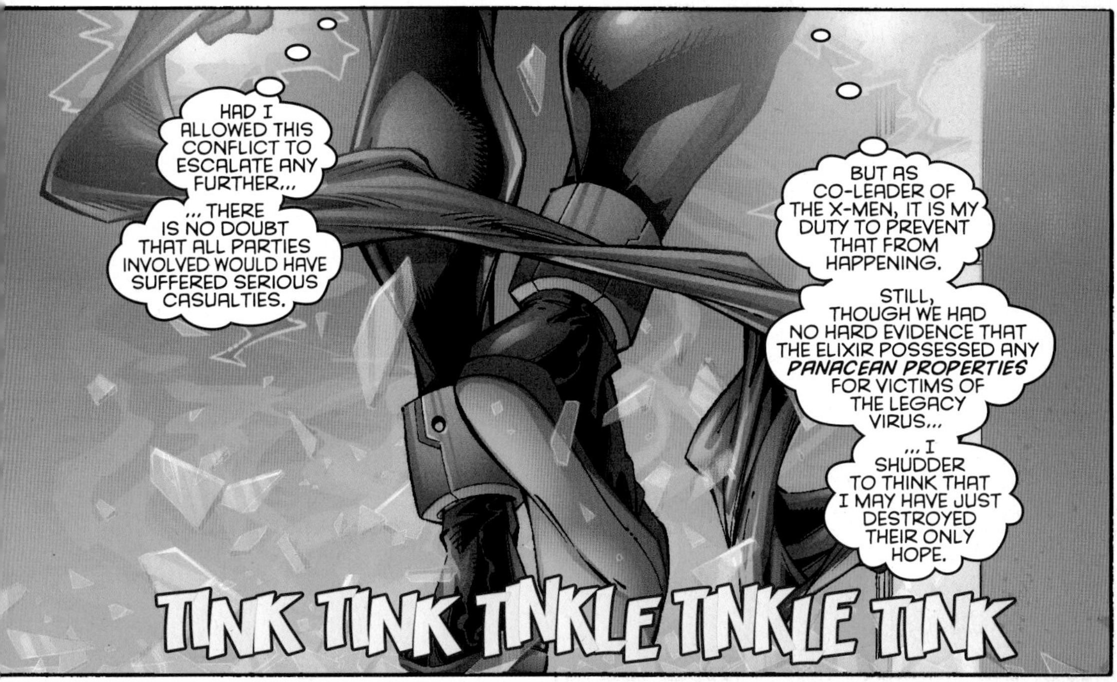
HAD I ALLOWED THIS CONFLICT TO ESCALATE ANY FURTHER...
... THERE IS NO DOUBT THAT ALL PARTIES INVOLVED WOULD HAVE SUFFERED SERIOUS CASUALTIES.
BUT AS CO-LEADER OF THE X-MEN, IT IS MY DUTY TO PREVENT THAT FROM HAPPENING.
STILL, THOUGH WE HAD NO HARD EVIDENCE THAT THE ELIXIR POSSESSED ANY *PANACEAN PROPERTIES* FOR VICTIMS OF THE LEGACY VIRUS...
... I SHUDDER TO THINK THAT I MAY HAVE JUST DESTROYED THEIR ONLY HOPE.
TINK TINK TINKLE TINKLE TINK
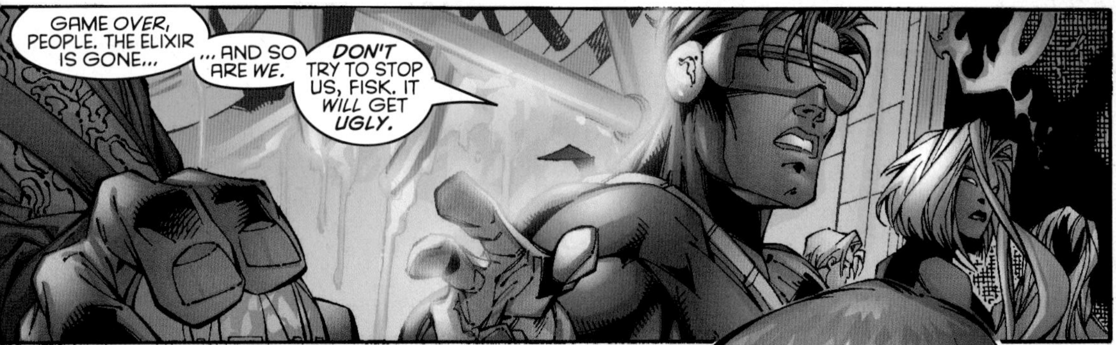
GAME *OVER*, PEOPLE. THE ELIXIR IS GONE...
... AND SO ARE *WE*.
DON'T TRY TO STOP US, FISK. IT *WILL* GET *UGLY*.
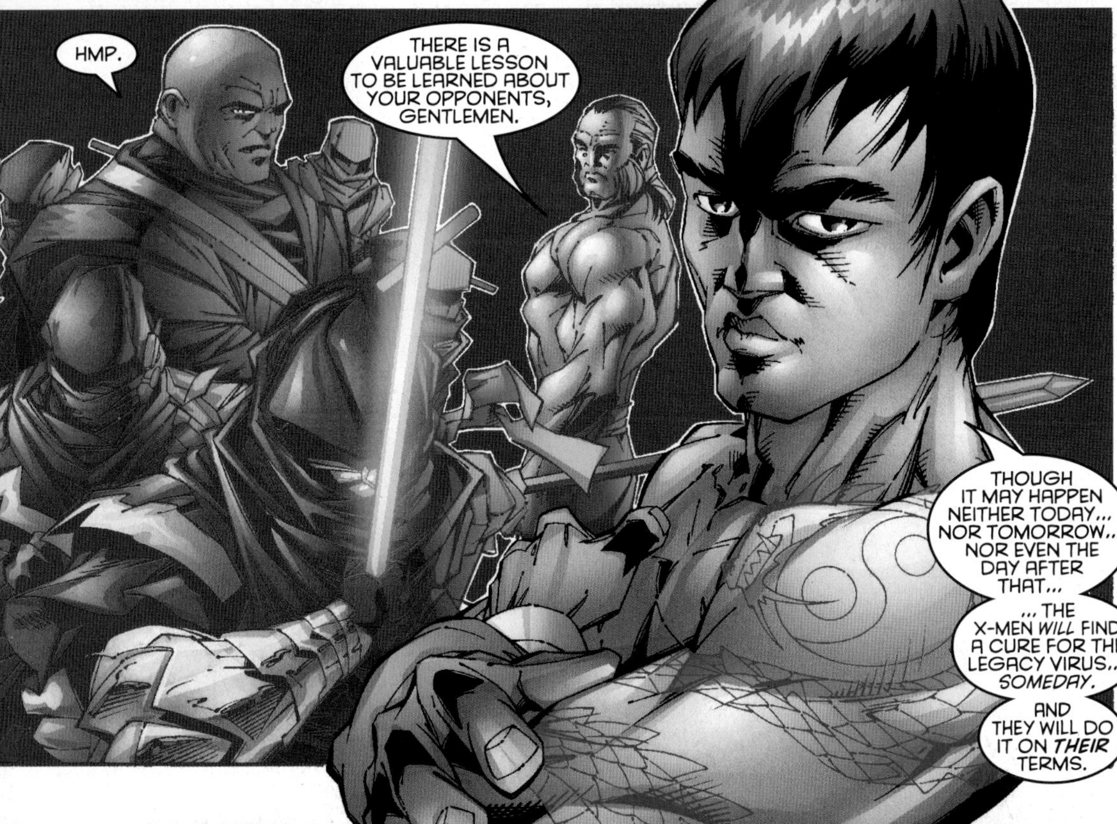
HMP.
THERE IS A VALUABLE LESSON TO BE LEARNED ABOUT YOUR OPPONENTS, GENTLEMEN.
THOUGH IT MAY HAPPEN NEITHER TODAY... NOR TOMORROW... NOR EVEN THE DAY AFTER THAT...
... THE X-MEN *WILL* FIND A CURE FOR THE LEGACY VIRUS... *SOMEDAY*.
AND THEY WILL DO IT ON *THEIR* TERMS.

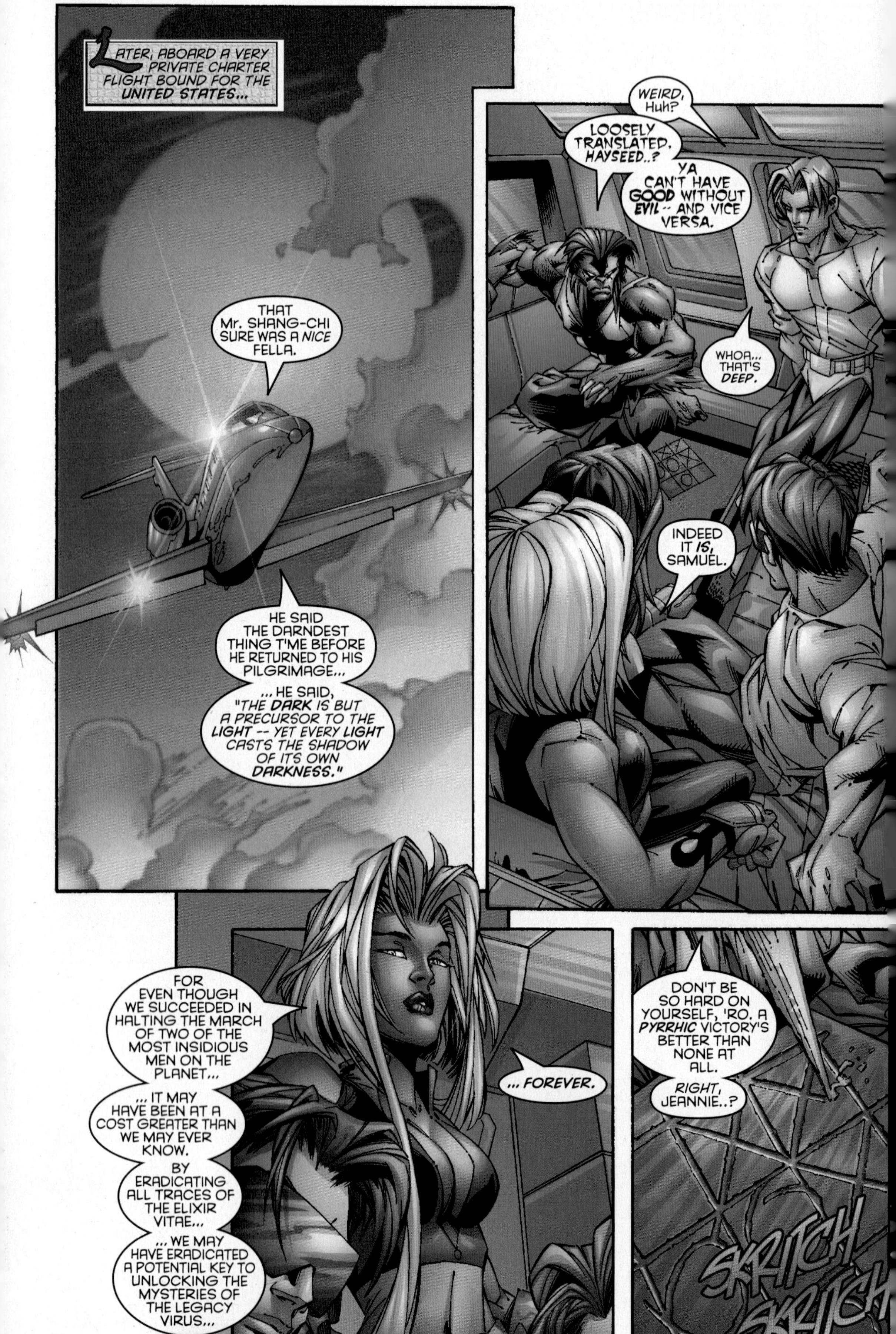
LATER, ABOARD A VERY PRIVATE CHARTER FLIGHT BOUND FOR THE UNITED STATES...
THAT Mr. SHANG-CHI SURE WAS A NICE FELLA.
HE SAID THE DARNDEST THING T'ME BEFORE HE RETURNED TO HIS PILGRIMAGE...
... HE SAID, "THE DARK IS BUT A PRECURSOR TO THE LIGHT -- YET EVERY LIGHT CASTS THE SHADOW OF ITS OWN DARKNESS."
WEIRD, Huh?
LOOSELY TRANSLATED, HAYSEED..?
YA CAN'T HAVE GOOD WITHOUT EVIL -- AND VICE VERSA.
WHOA... THAT'S DEEP.
INDEED IT IS, SAMUEL.
FOR EVEN THOUGH WE SUCCEEDED IN HALTING THE MARCH OF TWO OF THE MOST INSIDIOUS MEN ON THE PLANET...
... IT MAY HAVE BEEN AT A COST GREATER THAN WE MAY EVER KNOW.
BY ERADICATING ALL TRACES OF THE ELIXIR VITAE...
... WE MAY HAVE ERADICATED A POTENTIAL KEY TO UNLOCKING THE MYSTERIES OF THE LEGACY VIRUS...
... FOREVER.
DON'T BE SO HARD ON YOURSELF, 'RO. A PYRRHIC VICTORY'S BETTER THAN NONE AT ALL.
RIGHT, JEANNIE..?
SKRITCH
SKRITCH

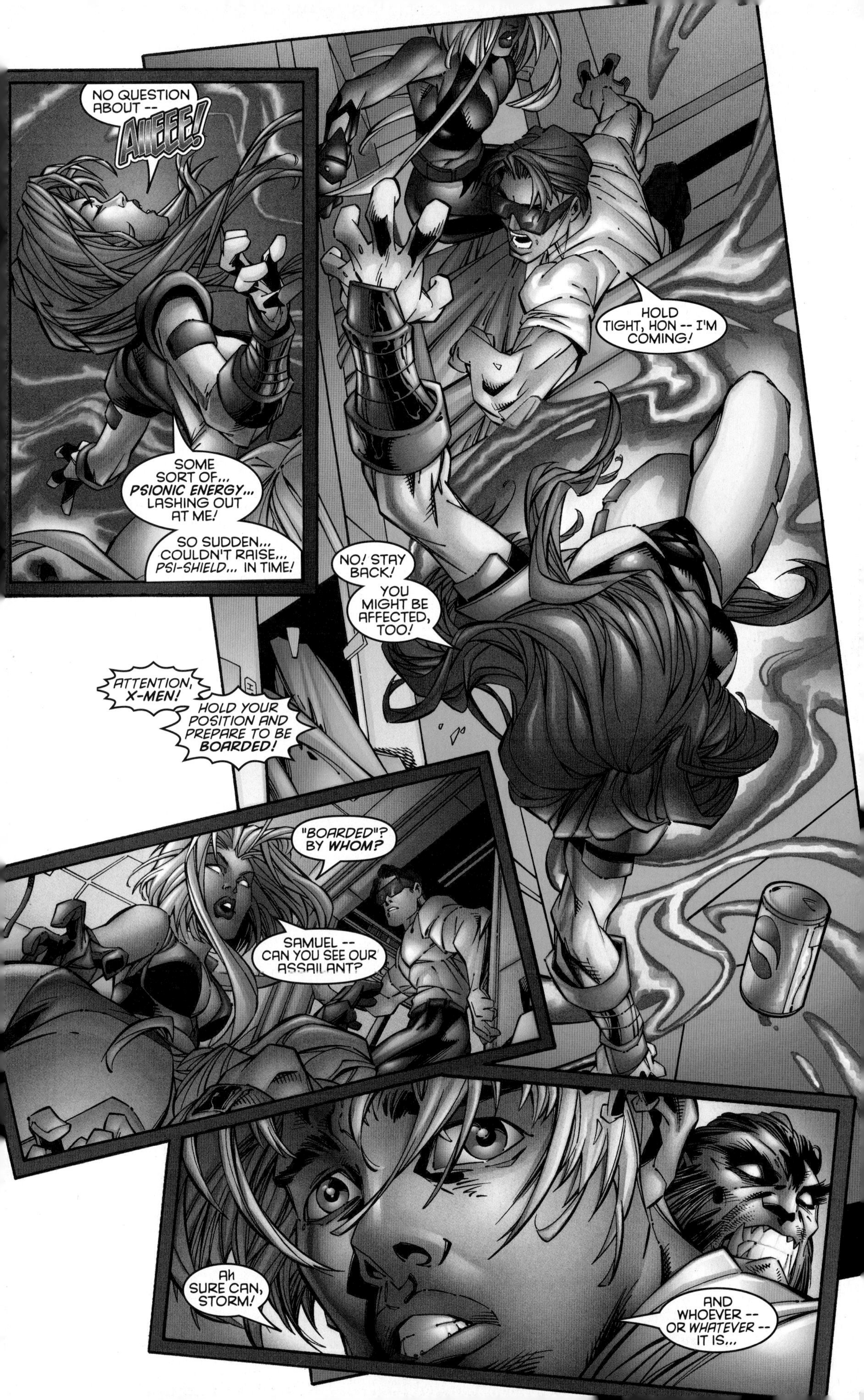
NO QUESTION ABOUT --
AIIEEE!
SOME SORT OF... PSIONIC ENERGY... LASHING OUT AT ME!
SO SUDDEN... COULDN'T RAISE... PSI-SHIELD... IN TIME!
HOLD TIGHT, HON -- I'M COMING!
NO! STAY BACK!
YOU MIGHT BE AFFECTED, TOO!
ATTENTION, X-MEN!
HOLD YOUR POSITION AND PREPARE TO BE BOARDED!
"BOARDED"? BY WHOM?
SAMUEL -- CAN YOU SEE OUR ASSAILANT?
Ah SURE CAN, STORM!
AND WHOEVER -- OR WHATEVER -- IT IS...

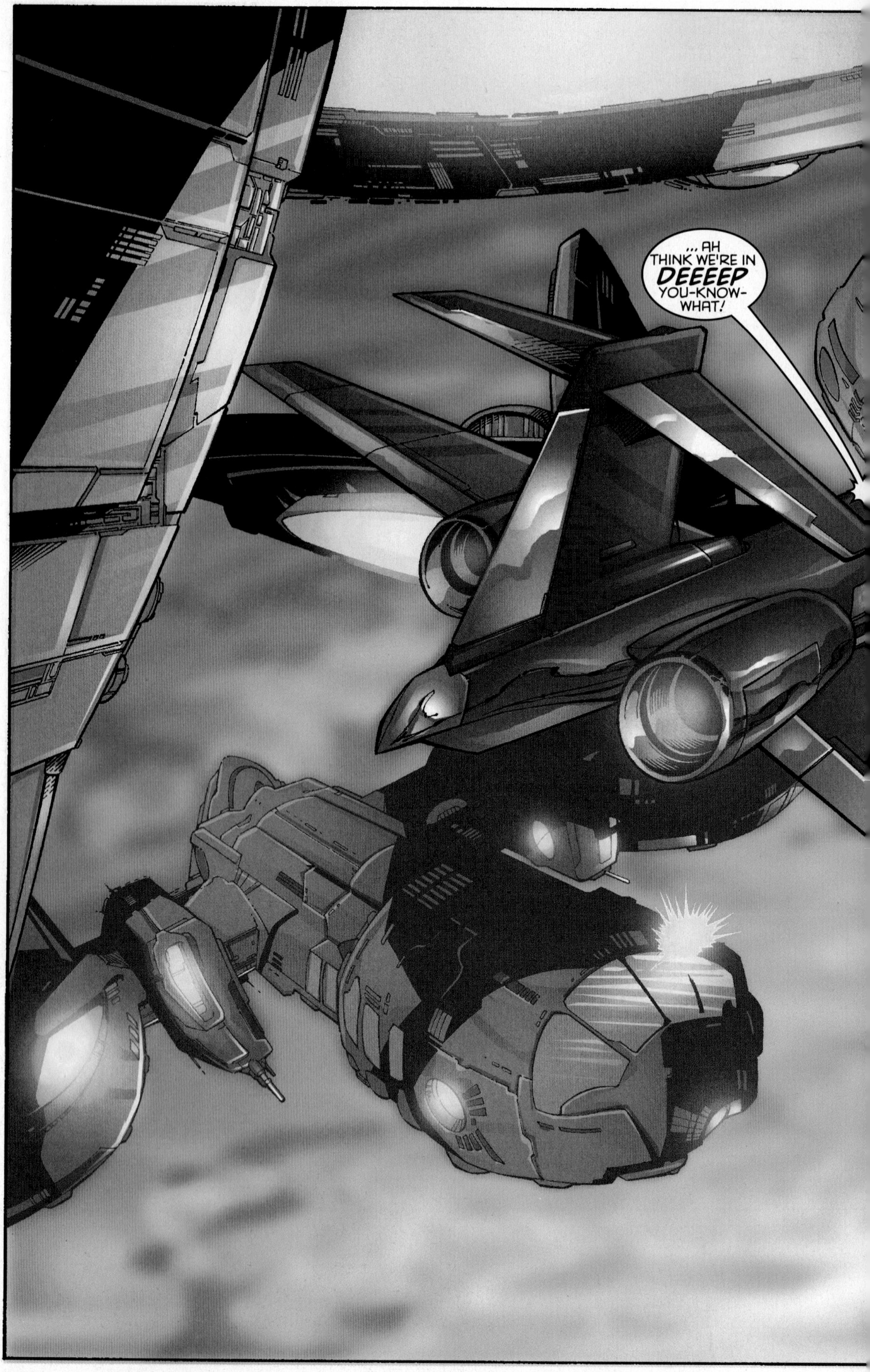
...AH THINK WE'RE IN DEEEEP YOU-KNOW-WHAT!

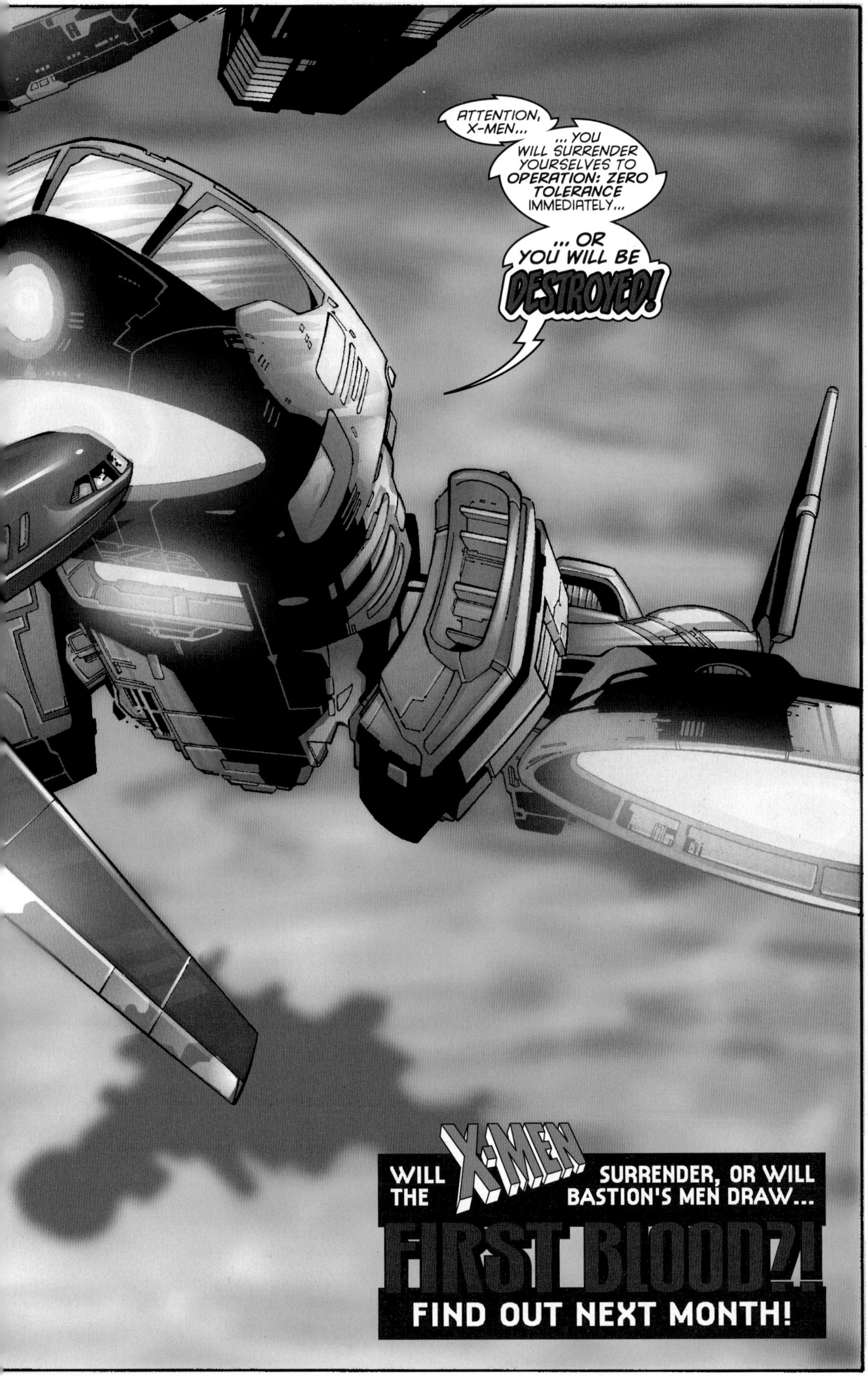
ATTENTION, X-MEN...
...YOU WILL SURRENDER YOURSELVES TO OPERATION: ZERO TOLERANCE IMMEDIATELY...
...OR YOU WILL BE DESTROYED!
WILL THE X-MEN SURRENDER, OR WILL BASTION'S MEN DRAW...
FIRST BLOOD?!
FIND OUT NEXT MONTH!

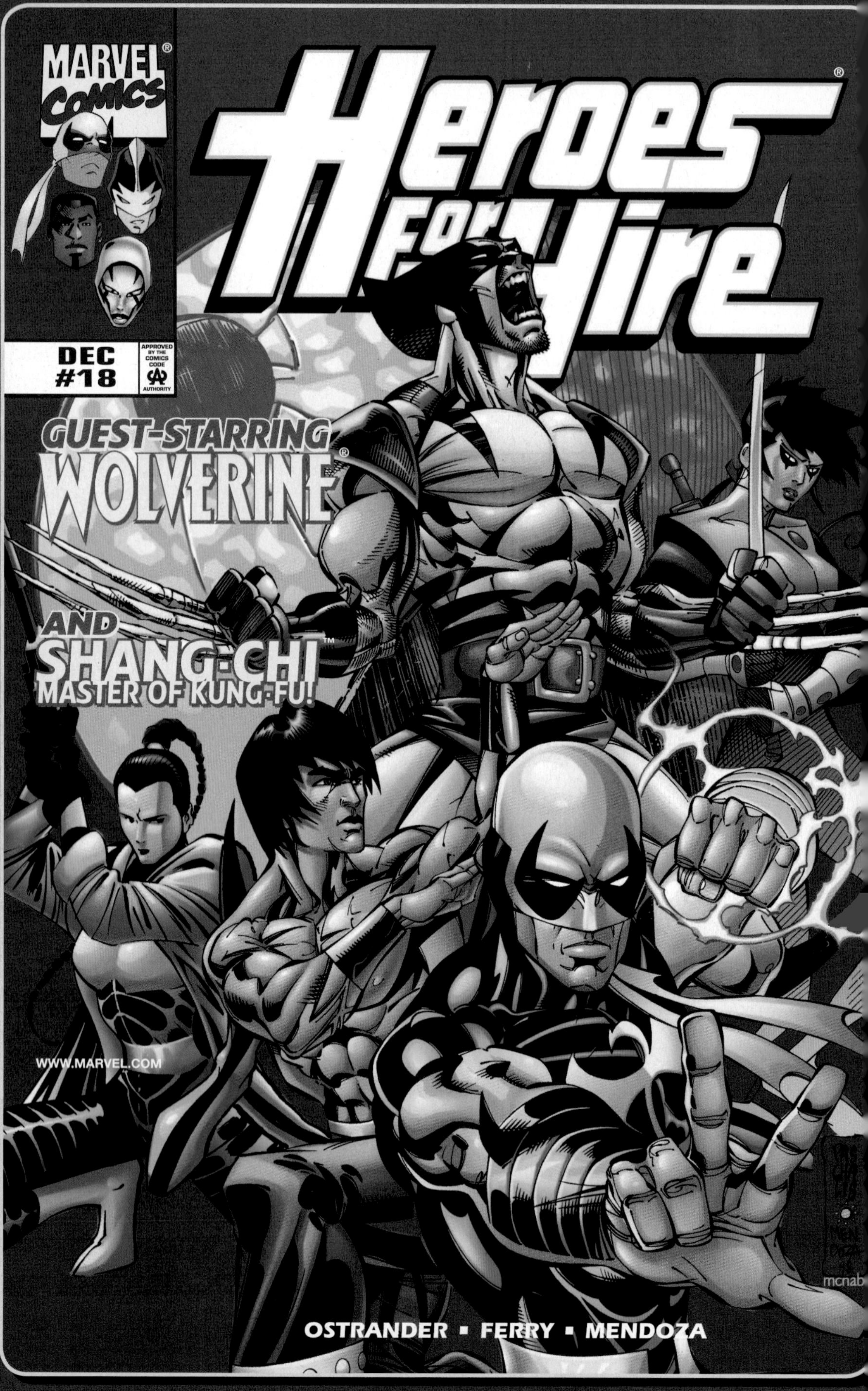
MARVEL COMICS
Heroes For Hire
DEC #18
APPROVED BY THE COMICS CODE AUTHORITY
GUEST-STARRING WOLVERINE
AND SHANG-CHI MASTER OF KUNG-FU!
WWW.MARVEL.COM
mcnab
OSTRANDER • FERRY • MENDOZA

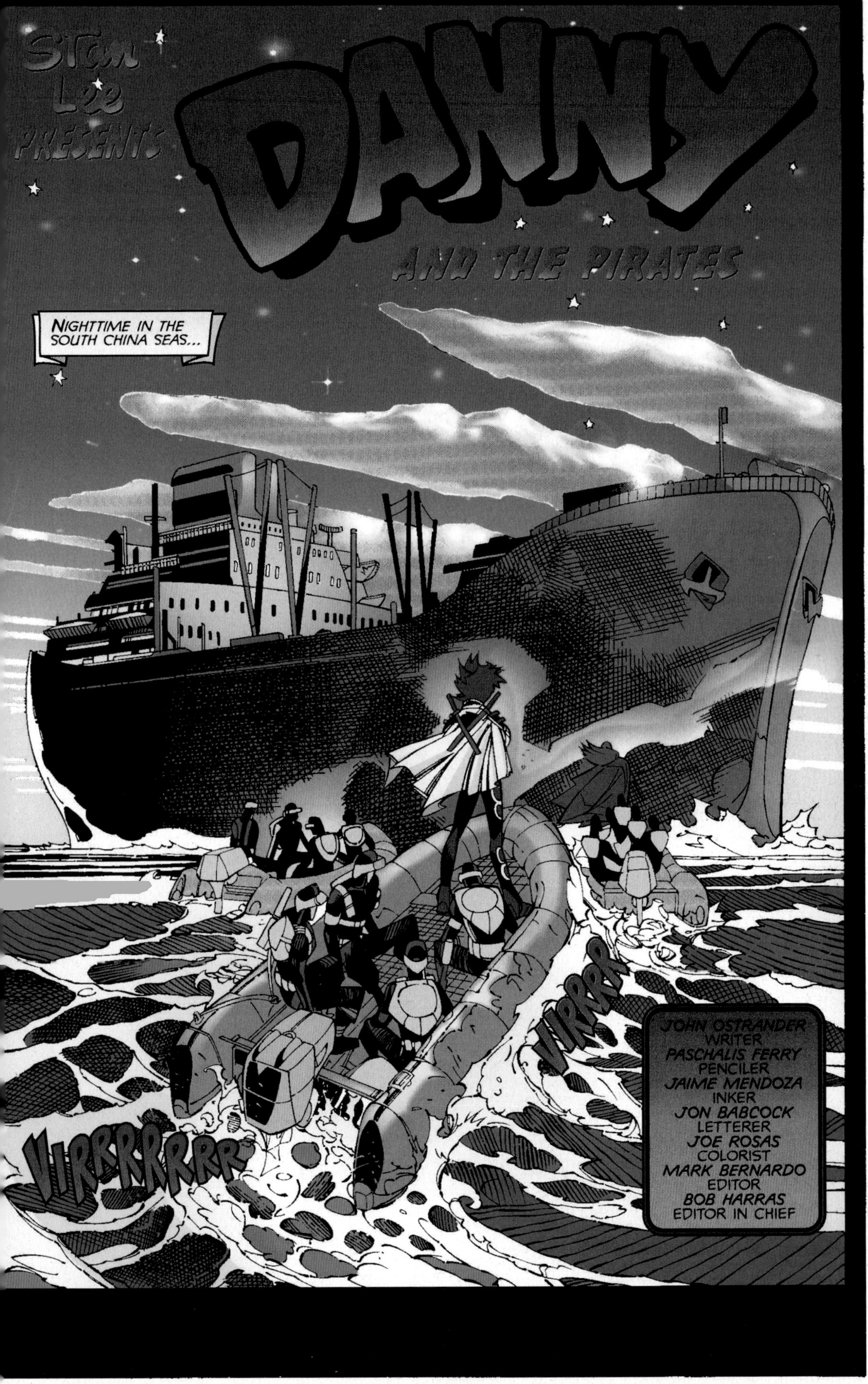

Stan Lee PRESENTS
DANNY
AND THE PIRATES
NIGHTTIME IN THE SOUTH CHINA SEAS...
VIRRR
VIRRRRRRR
JOHN OSTRANDER WRITER
PASCHALIS FERRY PENCILER
JAIME MENDOZA INKER
JON BABCOCK LETTERER
JOE ROSAS COLORIST
MARK BERNARDO EDITOR
BOB HARRAS EDITOR IN CHIEF

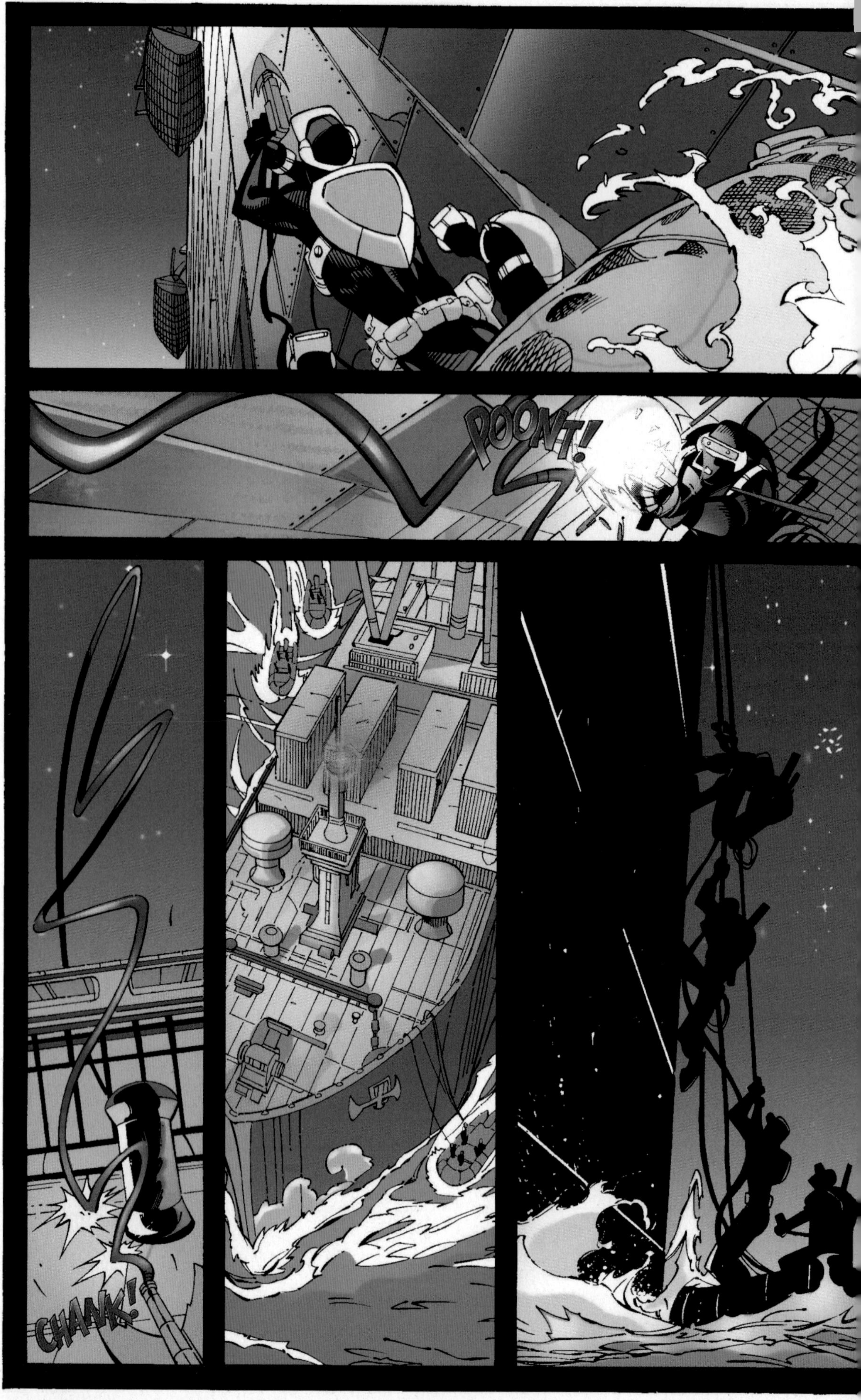
POONT!
CHANK!

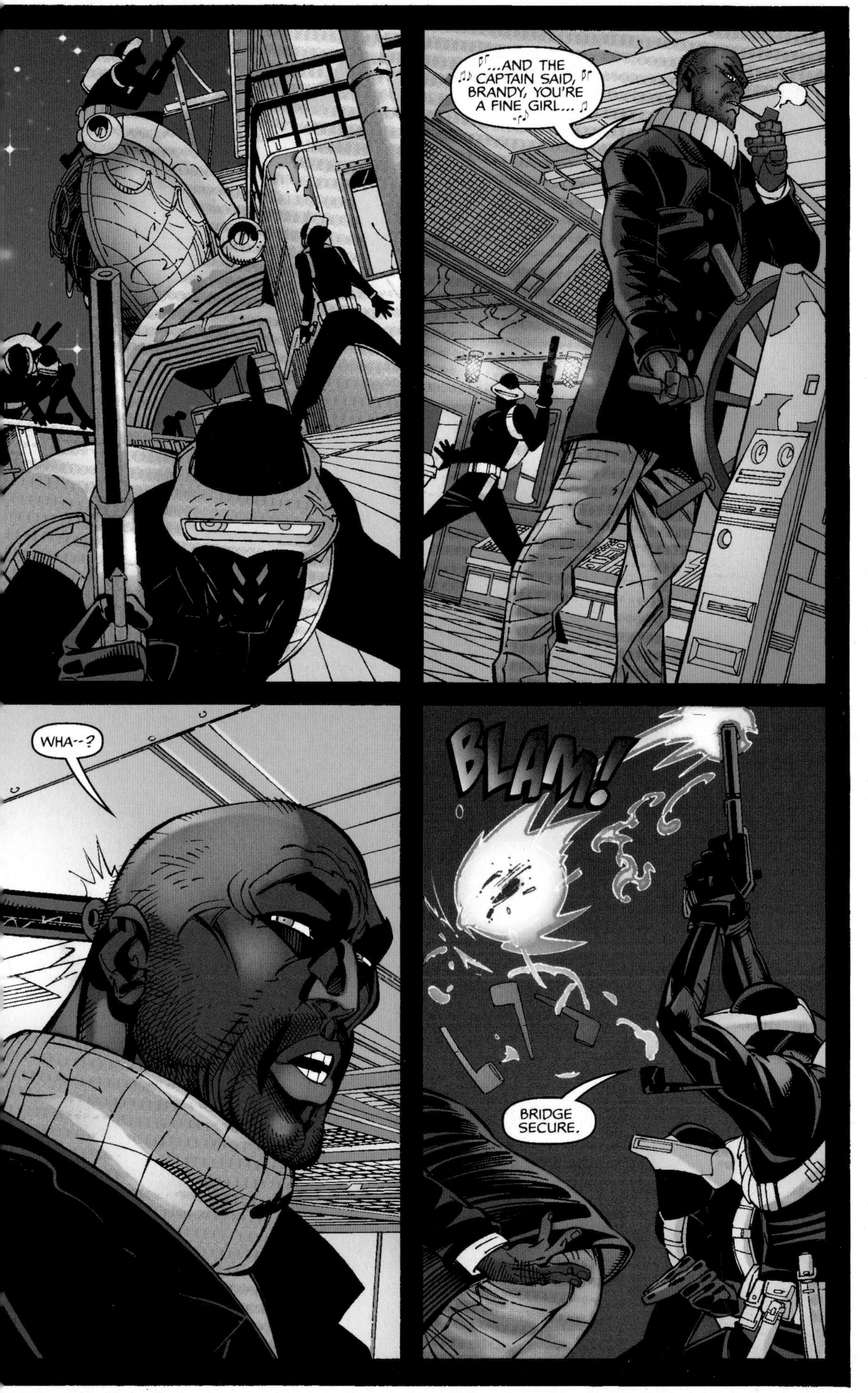
...AND THE CAPTAIN SAID, BRANDY, YOU'RE A FINE GIRL...
WHA--?
BLAM!
BRIDGE SECURE.

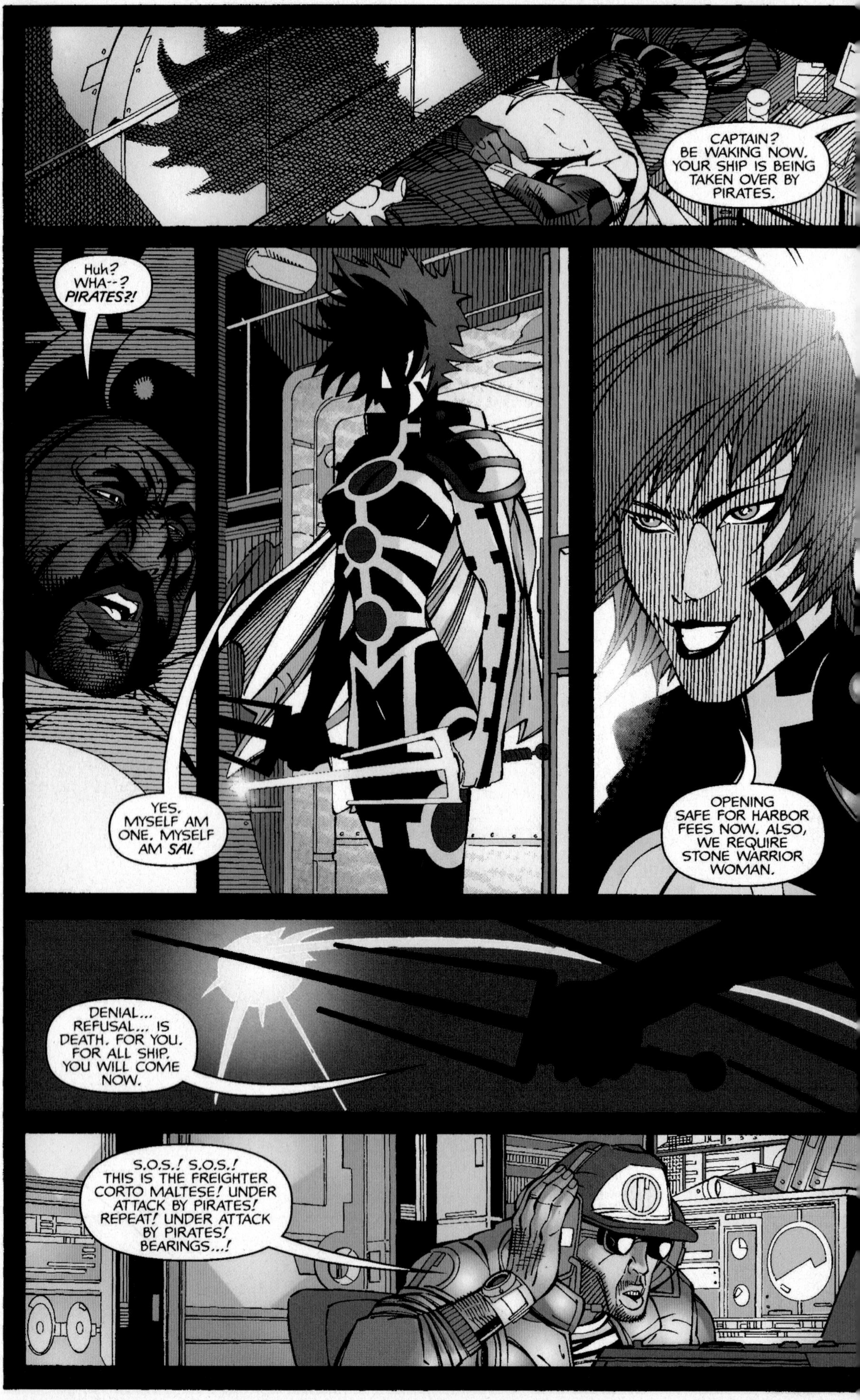
CAPTAIN? BE WAKING NOW. YOUR SHIP IS BEING TAKEN OVER BY PIRATES.
Huh? WHA--? PIRATES?!
YES. MYSELF AM ONE. MYSELF AM SAI.
OPENING SAFE FOR HARBOR FEES NOW. ALSO, WE REQUIRE STONE WARRIOR WOMAN.
DENIAL... REFUSAL... IS DEATH. FOR YOU. FOR ALL SHIP. YOU WILL COME NOW.
S.O.S.! S.O.S.! THIS IS THE FREIGHTER CORTO MALTESE! UNDER ATTACK BY PIRATES! REPEAT! UNDER ATTACK BY PIRATES! BEARINGS...!

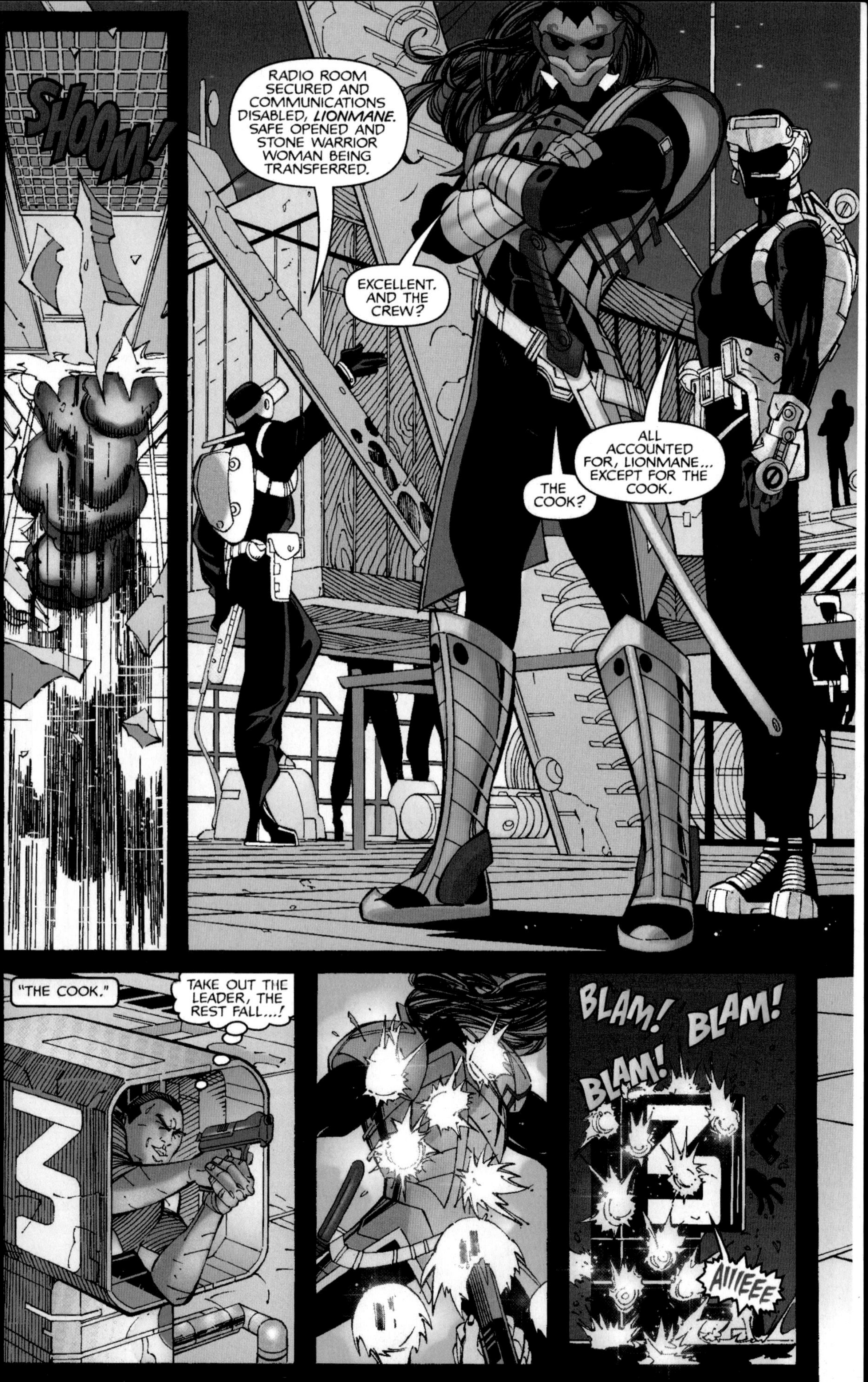
SHOOM!
RADIO ROOM SECURED AND COMMUNICATIONS DISABLED, LIONMANE. SAFE OPENED AND STONE WARRIOR WOMAN BEING TRANSFERRED.
EXCELLENT. AND THE CREW?
ALL ACCOUNTED FOR, LIONMANE... EXCEPT FOR THE COOK.
THE COOK?
"THE COOK."
TAKE OUT THE LEADER, THE REST FALL...!
BLAM!
BLAM!
BLAM!
AIIIEEE

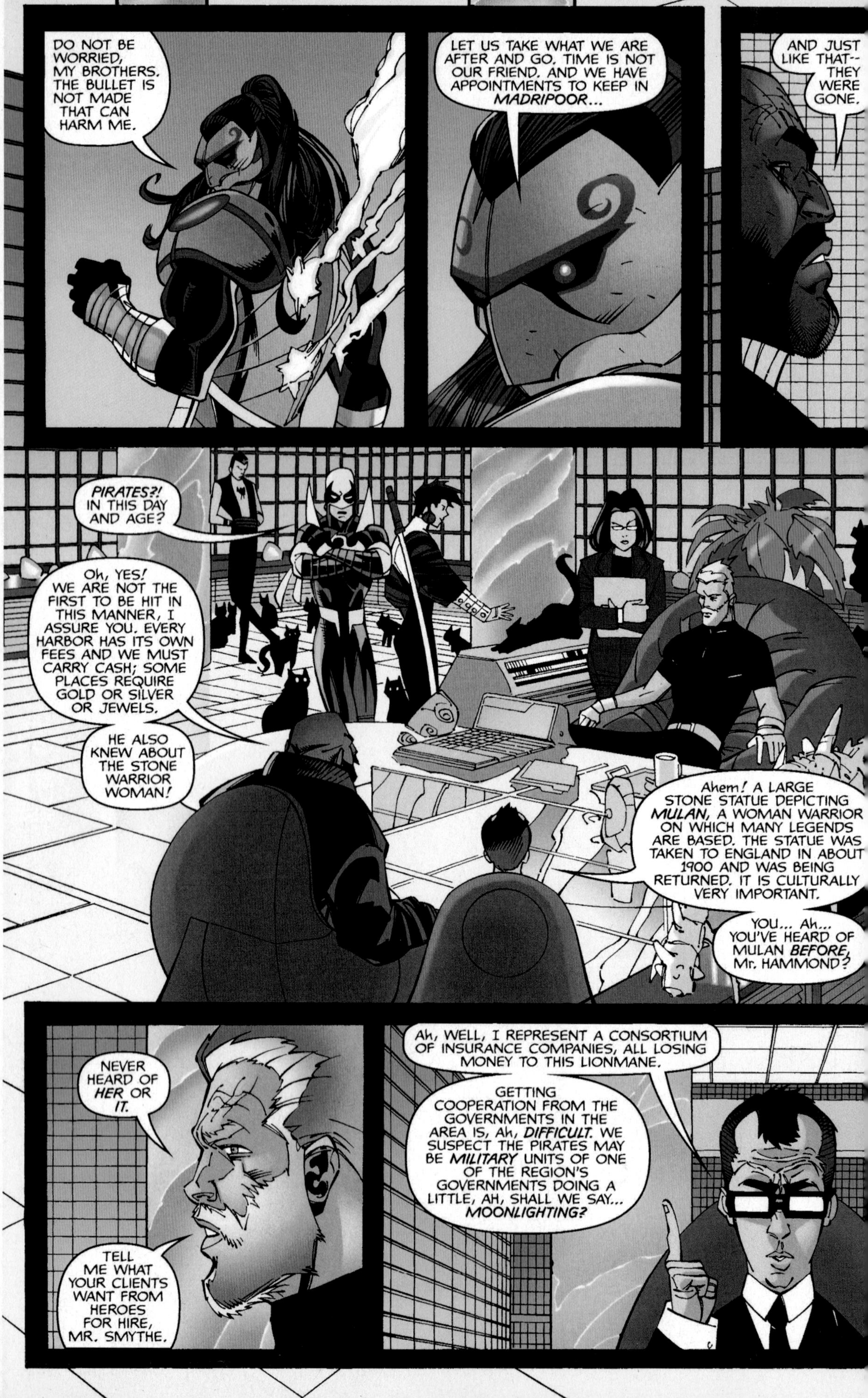
DO NOT BE WORRIED, MY BROTHERS. THE BULLET IS NOT MADE THAT CAN HARM ME.
LET US TAKE WHAT WE ARE AFTER AND GO. TIME IS NOT OUR FRIEND, AND WE HAVE APPOINTMENTS TO KEEP IN MADRIPOOR...
AND JUST LIKE THAT-- THEY WERE GONE.
PIRATES?! IN THIS DAY AND AGE?
Oh, YES! WE ARE NOT THE FIRST TO BE HIT IN THIS MANNER, I ASSURE YOU. EVERY HARBOR HAS ITS OWN FEES AND WE MUST CARRY CASH; SOME PLACES REQUIRE GOLD OR SILVER OR JEWELS.
HE ALSO KNEW ABOUT THE STONE WARRIOR WOMAN!
Ahem! A LARGE STONE STATUE DEPICTING MULAN, A WOMAN WARRIOR ON WHICH MANY LEGENDS ARE BASED. THE STATUE WAS TAKEN TO ENGLAND IN ABOUT 1900 AND WAS BEING RETURNED. IT IS CULTURALLY VERY IMPORTANT.
YOU... Ah... YOU'VE HEARD OF MULAN BEFORE, Mr. HAMMOND?
NEVER HEARD OF HER OR IT.
TELL ME WHAT YOUR CLIENTS WANT FROM HEROES FOR HIRE, MR. SMYTHE.
Ah, WELL, I REPRESENT A CONSORTIUM OF INSURANCE COMPANIES, ALL LOSING MONEY TO THIS LIONMANE.
GETTING COOPERATION FROM THE GOVERNMENTS IN THE AREA IS, Ah, DIFFICULT. WE SUSPECT THE PIRATES MAY BE MILITARY UNITS OF ONE OF THE REGION'S GOVERNMENTS DOING A LITTLE, AH, SHALL WE SAY... MOONLIGHTING?

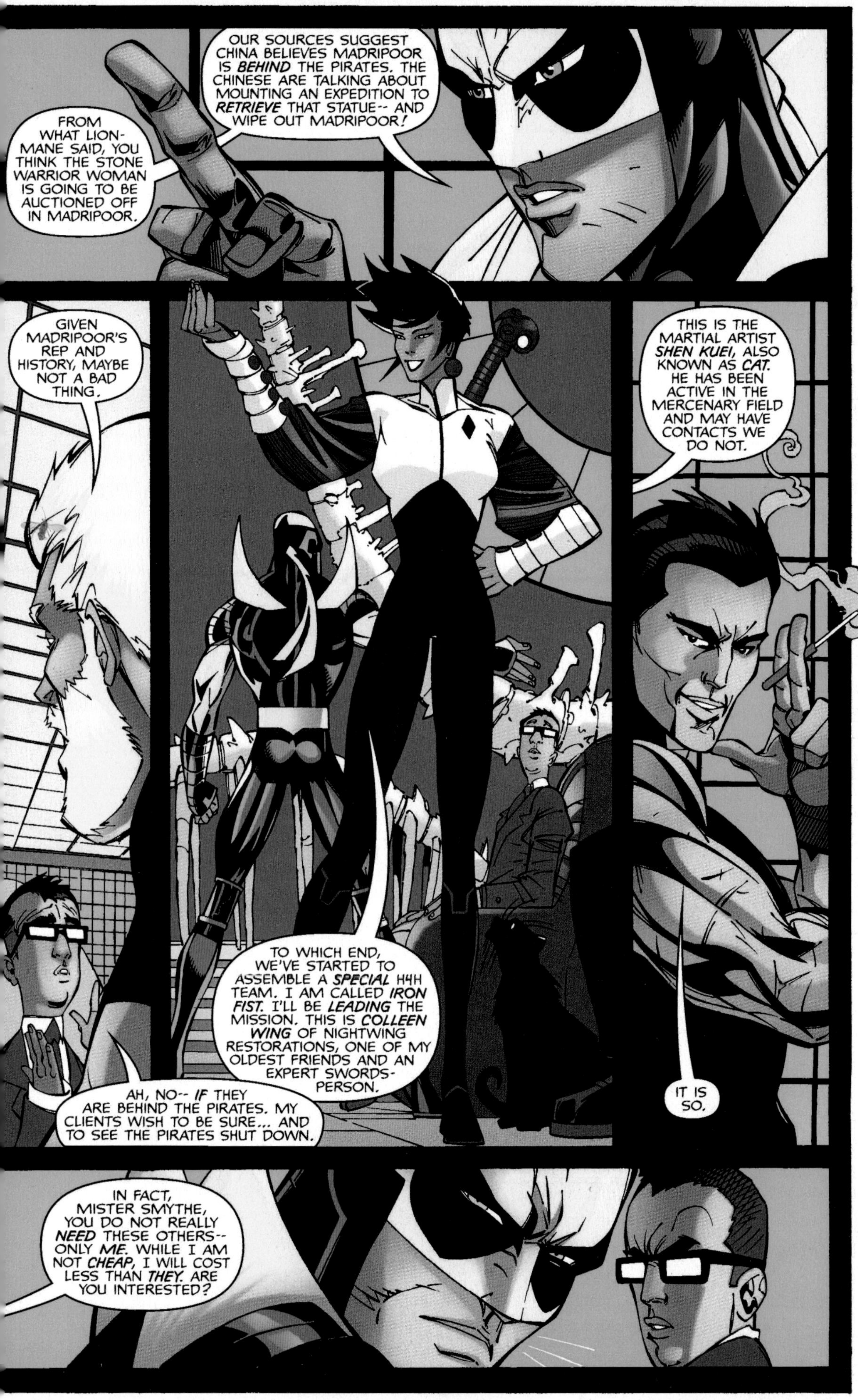
FROM WHAT LION-MANE SAID, YOU THINK THE STONE WARRIOR WOMAN IS GOING TO BE AUCTIONED OFF IN MADRIPOOR.
OUR SOURCES SUGGEST CHINA BELIEVES MADRIPOOR IS *BEHIND* THE PIRATES. THE CHINESE ARE TALKING ABOUT MOUNTING AN EXPEDITION TO *RETRIEVE* THAT STATUE-- AND WIPE OUT MADRIPOOR!
GIVEN MADRIPOOR'S REP AND HISTORY, MAYBE NOT A BAD THING.
AH, NO-- *IF* THEY ARE BEHIND THE PIRATES. MY CLIENTS WISH TO BE SURE... AND TO SEE THE PIRATES SHUT DOWN.
TO WHICH END, WE'VE STARTED TO ASSEMBLE A *SPECIAL* H4H TEAM. I AM CALLED *IRON FIST.* I'LL BE *LEADING* THE MISSION. THIS IS *COLLEEN WING* OF NIGHTWING RESTORATIONS, ONE OF MY OLDEST FRIENDS AND AN EXPERT SWORDS-PERSON.
THIS IS THE MARTIAL ARTIST *SHEN KUEI,* ALSO KNOWN AS *CAT.* HE HAS BEEN ACTIVE IN THE MERCENARY FIELD AND MAY HAVE CONTACTS WE DO NOT.
IT IS SO.
IN FACT, MISTER SMYTHE, YOU DO NOT REALLY *NEED* THESE OTHERS-- ONLY *ME.* WHILE I AM NOT *CHEAP,* I WILL COST LESS THAN *THEY.* ARE YOU INTERESTED?

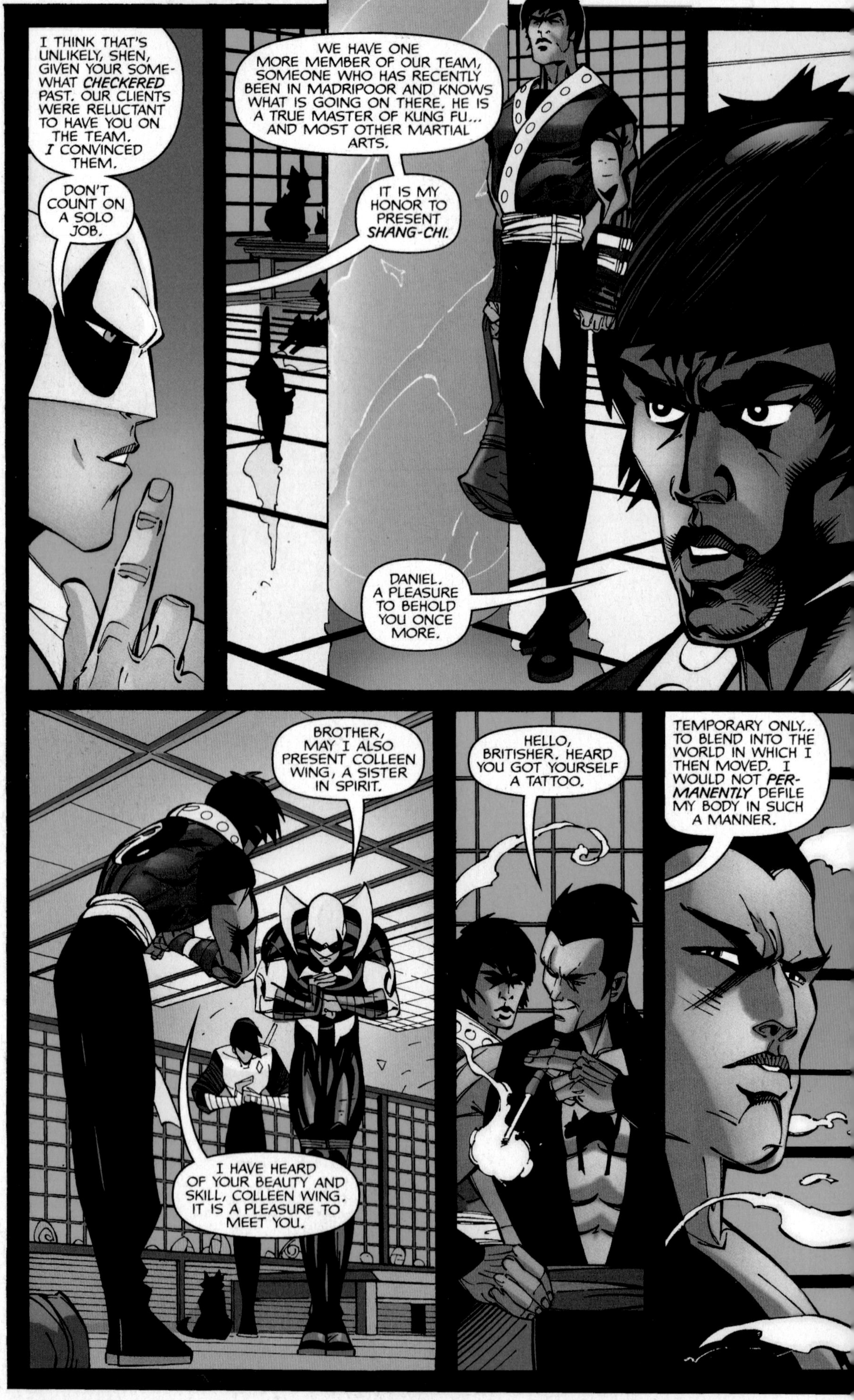
I THINK THAT'S UNLIKELY, SHEN, GIVEN YOUR SOMEWHAT *CHECKERED* PAST. OUR CLIENTS WERE RELUCTANT TO HAVE YOU ON THE TEAM. *I* CONVINCED THEM.
DON'T COUNT ON A SOLO JOB.
WE HAVE ONE MORE MEMBER OF OUR TEAM, SOMEONE WHO HAS RECENTLY BEEN IN MADRIPOOR AND KNOWS WHAT IS GOING ON THERE. HE IS A TRUE MASTER OF KUNG FU... AND MOST OTHER MARTIAL ARTS.
IT IS MY HONOR TO PRESENT *SHANG-CHI.*
DANIEL. A PLEASURE TO BEHOLD YOU ONCE MORE.
BROTHER, MAY I ALSO PRESENT COLLEEN WING, A SISTER IN SPIRIT.
I HAVE HEARD OF YOUR BEAUTY AND SKILL, COLLEEN WING. IT IS A PLEASURE TO MEET YOU.
HELLO, BRITISHER. HEARD YOU GOT YOURSELF A TATTOO.
TEMPORARY ONLY... TO BLEND INTO THE WORLD IN WHICH I THEN MOVED. I WOULD NOT *PERMANENTLY* DEFILE MY BODY IN SUCH A MANNER.

AS YOU MAY KNOW, MADRIPOOR WAS RECENTLY TAKEN OVER BY THE FORMER HEAD OF *HYDRA* KNOWN AS *VIPER*.* THE UNDER-WORLD ITSELF, HOWEVER, IS STILL RUN BY A WOMAN CALLING HERSELF TYGER TYGER.

THE STONE WARRIOR WOMAN IS TO BE AUCTIONED OFF IN MADRIPOOR IN 36 HOURS.

*IN WOLVERINE#125.
--Mark

DANNY, HOW SOON CAN YOUR TEAM GET TO MADRIPOOR?

"THIRTY-FIVE HOURS FROM NOW.

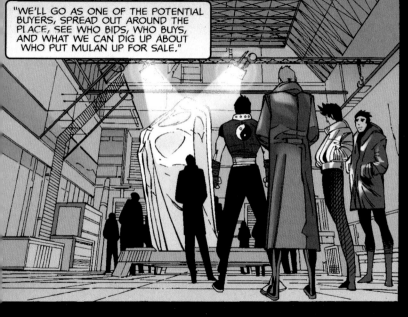

"WE'LL GO AS ONE OF THE POTENTIAL BUYERS, SPREAD OUT AROUND THE PLACE, SEE WHO BIDS, WHO BUYS, AND WHAT WE CAN DIG UP ABOUT WHO PUT MULAN UP FOR SALE."

THIS *SMELLS*, DANNY.

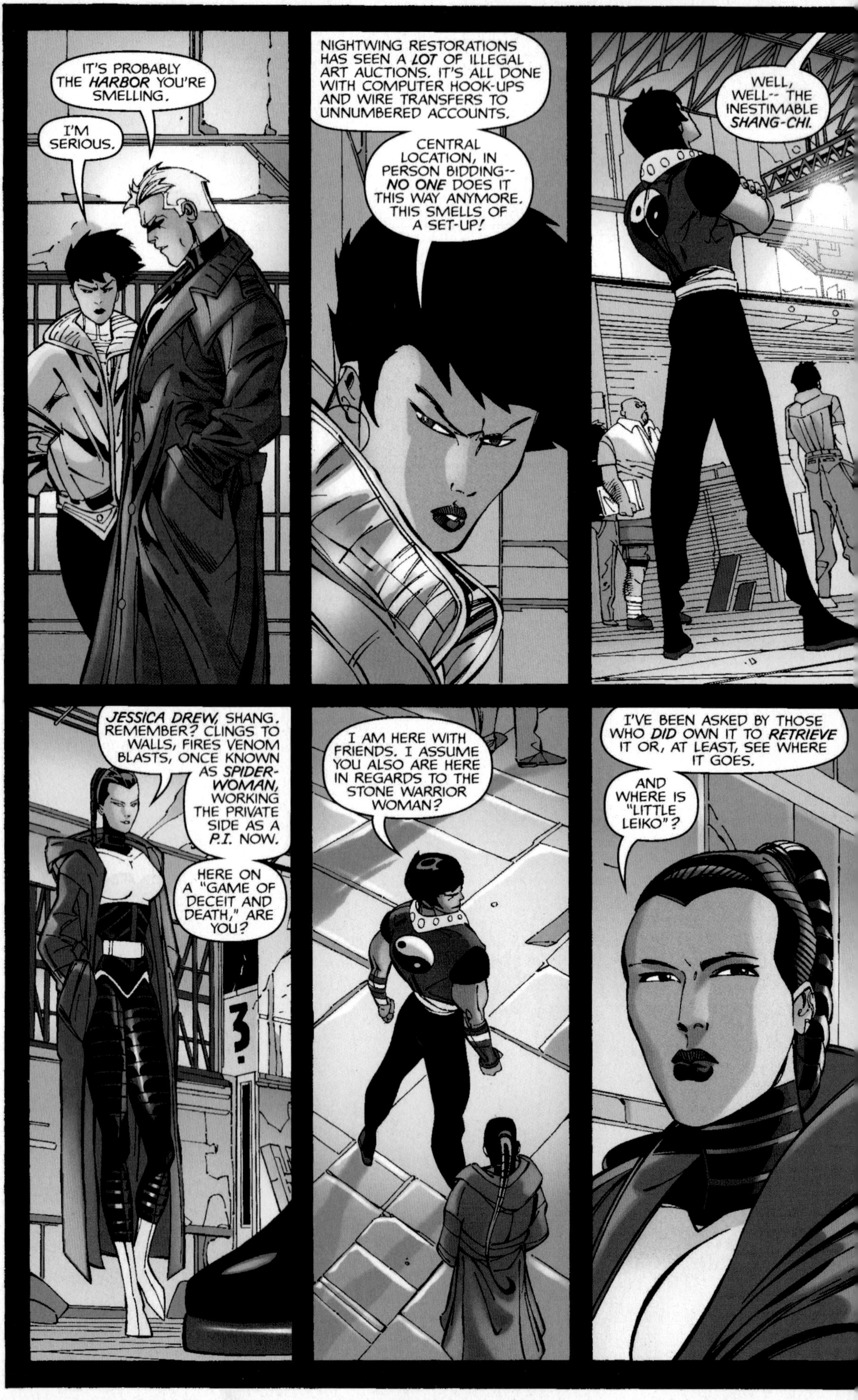
IT'S PROBABLY THE *HARBOR* YOU'RE SMELLING.
I'M SERIOUS.
NIGHTWING RESTORATIONS HAS SEEN A *LOT* OF ILLEGAL ART AUCTIONS. IT'S ALL DONE WITH COMPUTER HOOK-UPS AND WIRE TRANSFERS TO UNNUMBERED ACCOUNTS.
CENTRAL LOCATION, IN PERSON BIDDING-- *NO ONE* DOES IT THIS WAY ANYMORE. THIS SMELLS OF A SET-UP!
WELL, WELL-- THE INESTIMABLE *SHANG-CHI.*
JESSICA DREW, SHANG. REMEMBER? CLINGS TO WALLS, FIRES VENOM BLASTS, ONCE KNOWN AS *SPIDER-WOMAN,* WORKING THE PRIVATE SIDE AS A *P.I.* NOW.
HERE ON A "GAME OF DECEIT AND DEATH," ARE YOU?
I AM HERE WITH FRIENDS. I ASSUME YOU ALSO ARE HERE IN REGARDS TO THE STONE WARRIOR WOMAN?
I'VE BEEN ASKED BY THOSE WHO *DID* OWN IT TO *RETRIEVE* IT OR, AT LEAST, SEE WHERE IT GOES.
AND WHERE IS "LITTLE LEIKO"?

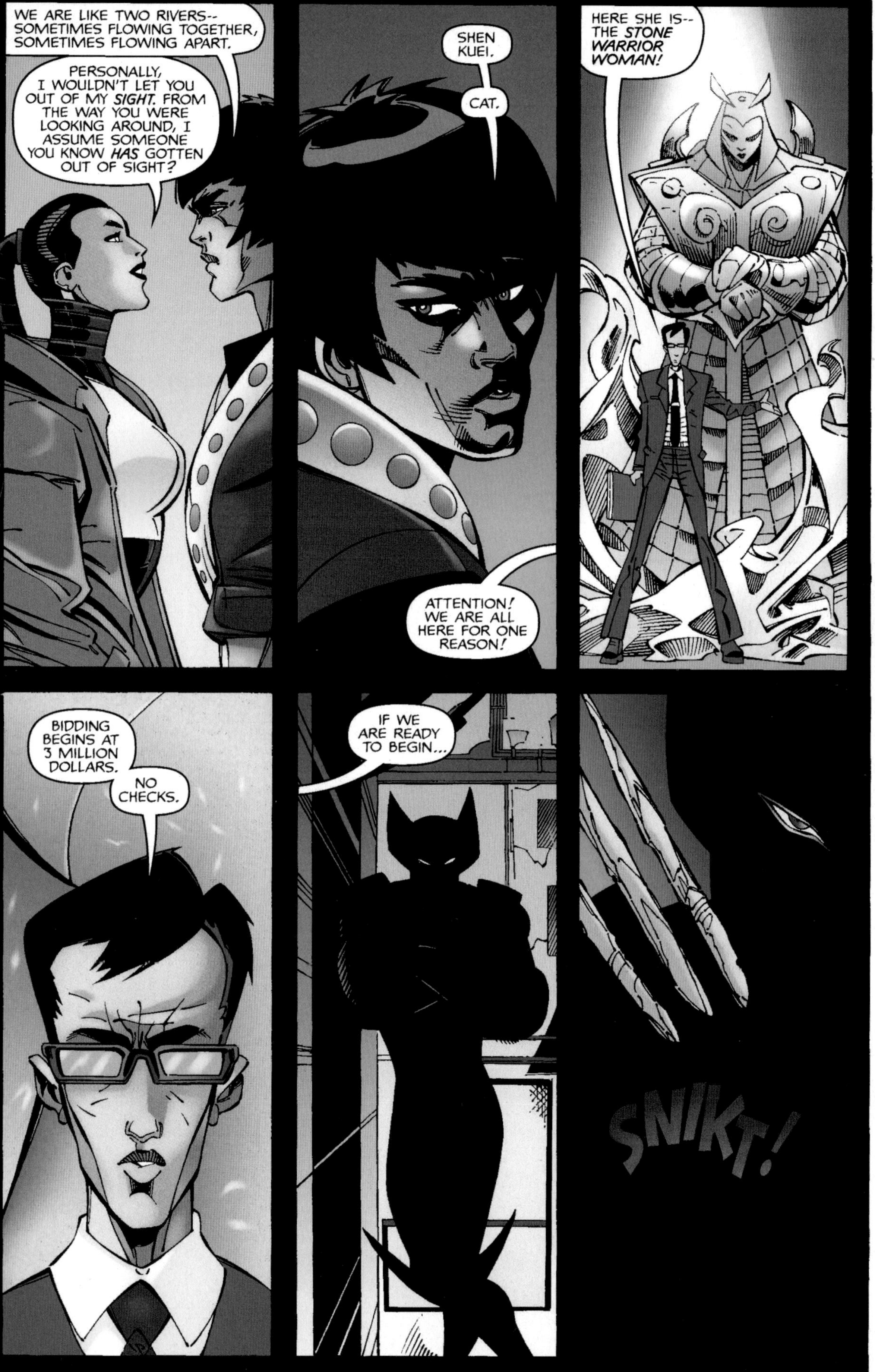
WE ARE LIKE TWO RIVERS-- SOMETIMES FLOWING TOGETHER, SOMETIMES FLOWING APART.
PERSONALLY, I WOULDN'T LET YOU OUT OF MY *SIGHT.* FROM THE WAY YOU WERE LOOKING AROUND, I ASSUME SOMEONE YOU KNOW *HAS* GOTTEN OUT OF SIGHT?
SHEN KUEI.
CAT.
ATTENTION! WE ARE ALL HERE FOR ONE REASON!
HERE SHE IS-- THE *STONE WARRIOR WOMAN!*
BIDDING BEGINS AT 3 MILLION DOLLARS.
NO CHECKS.
IF WE ARE READY TO BEGIN...
SNIKT!

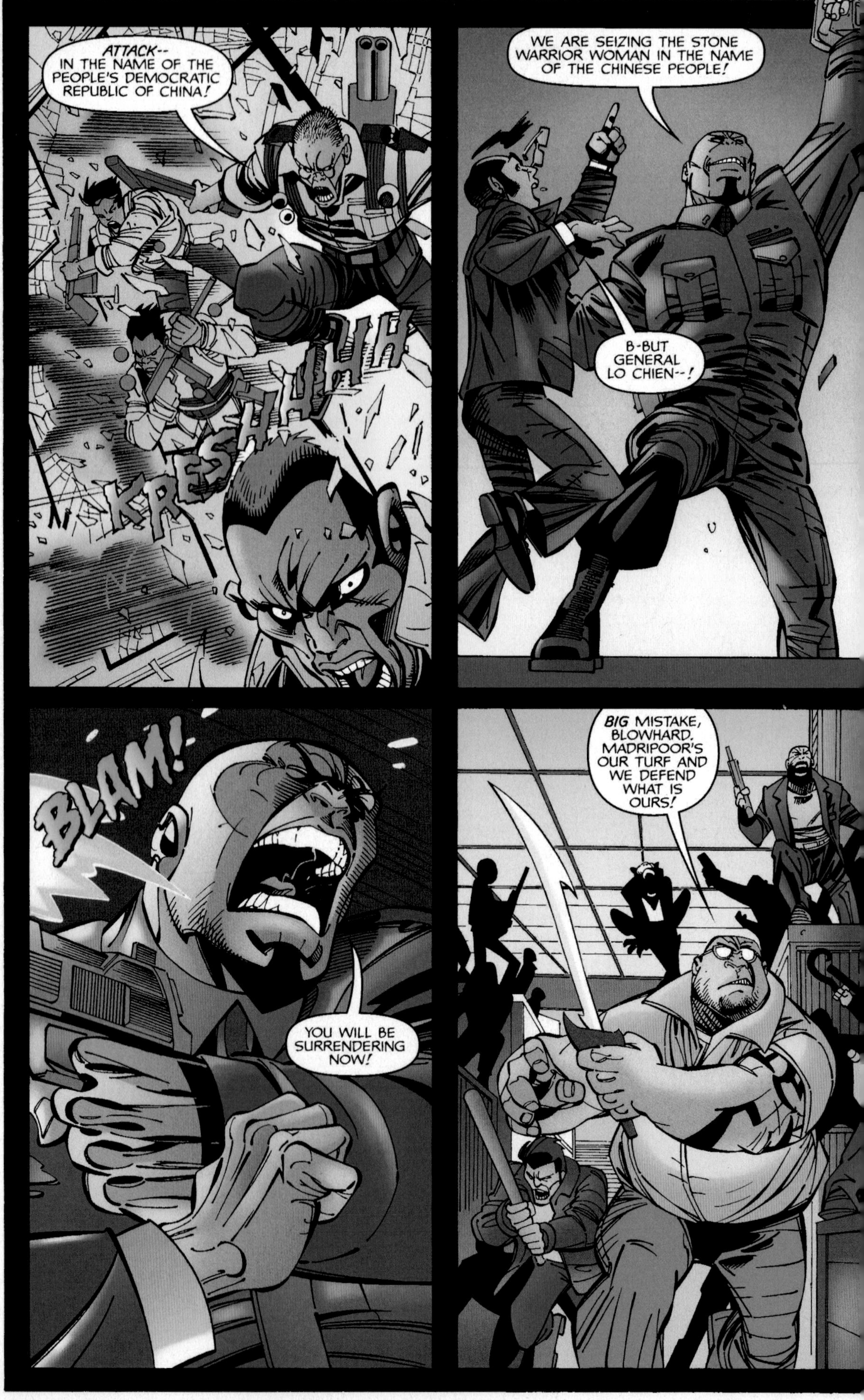
ATTACK--
IN THE NAME OF THE PEOPLE'S DEMOCRATIC REPUBLIC OF CHINA!
KRESHHHHH
WE ARE SEIZING THE STONE WARRIOR WOMAN IN THE NAME OF THE CHINESE PEOPLE!
B-BUT GENERAL LO CHIEN--!
BLAM!
YOU WILL BE SURRENDERING NOW!
BIG MISTAKE, BLOWHARD. MADRIPOOR'S OUR TURF AND WE DEFEND WHAT IS OURS!

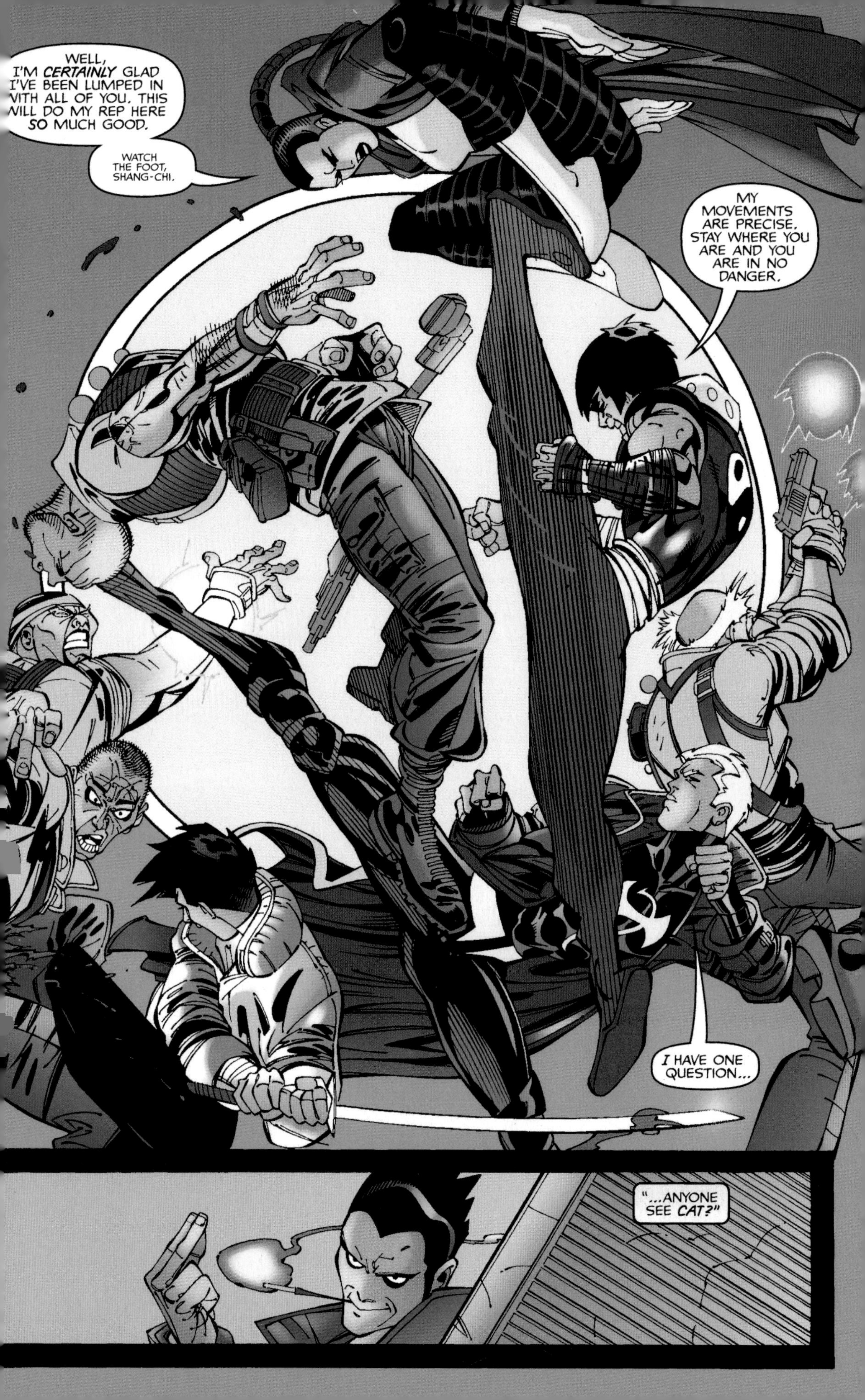
WELL, I'M *CERTAINLY* GLAD I'VE BEEN LUMPED IN WITH ALL OF YOU. THIS WILL DO MY REP HERE *SO* MUCH GOOD.
WATCH THE FOOT, SHANG-CHI.
MY MOVEMENTS ARE PRECISE. STAY WHERE YOU ARE AND YOU ARE IN NO DANGER.
I HAVE ONE QUESTION...
"...ANYONE SEE *CAT?*"

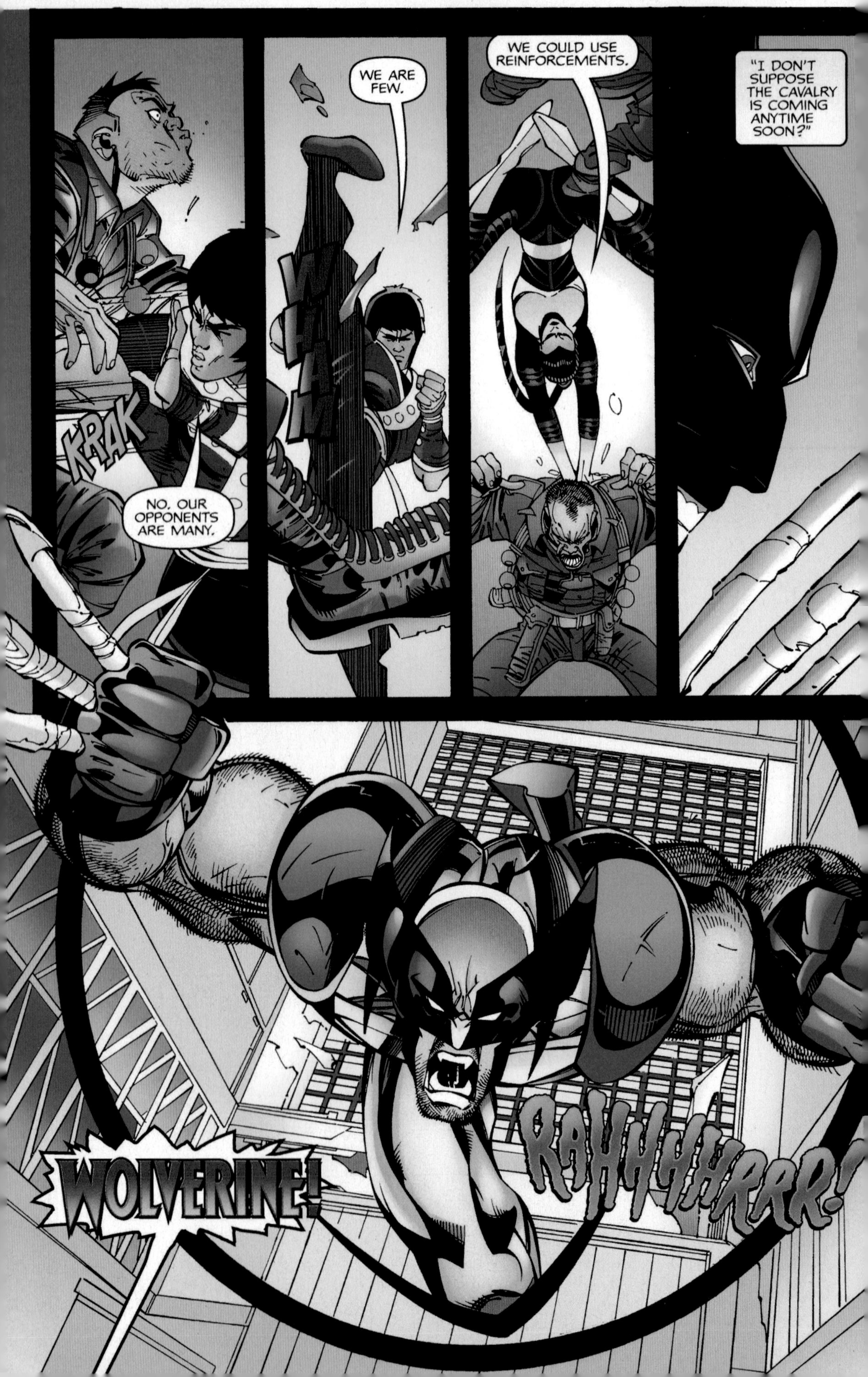
KRAK
NO. OUR OPPONENTS ARE MANY.
WE ARE FEW.
WHAM
WE COULD USE REINFORCEMENTS.
"I DON'T SUPPOSE THE CAVALRY IS COMING ANYTIME SOON?"
WOLVERINE!
RAHHHHRRR!

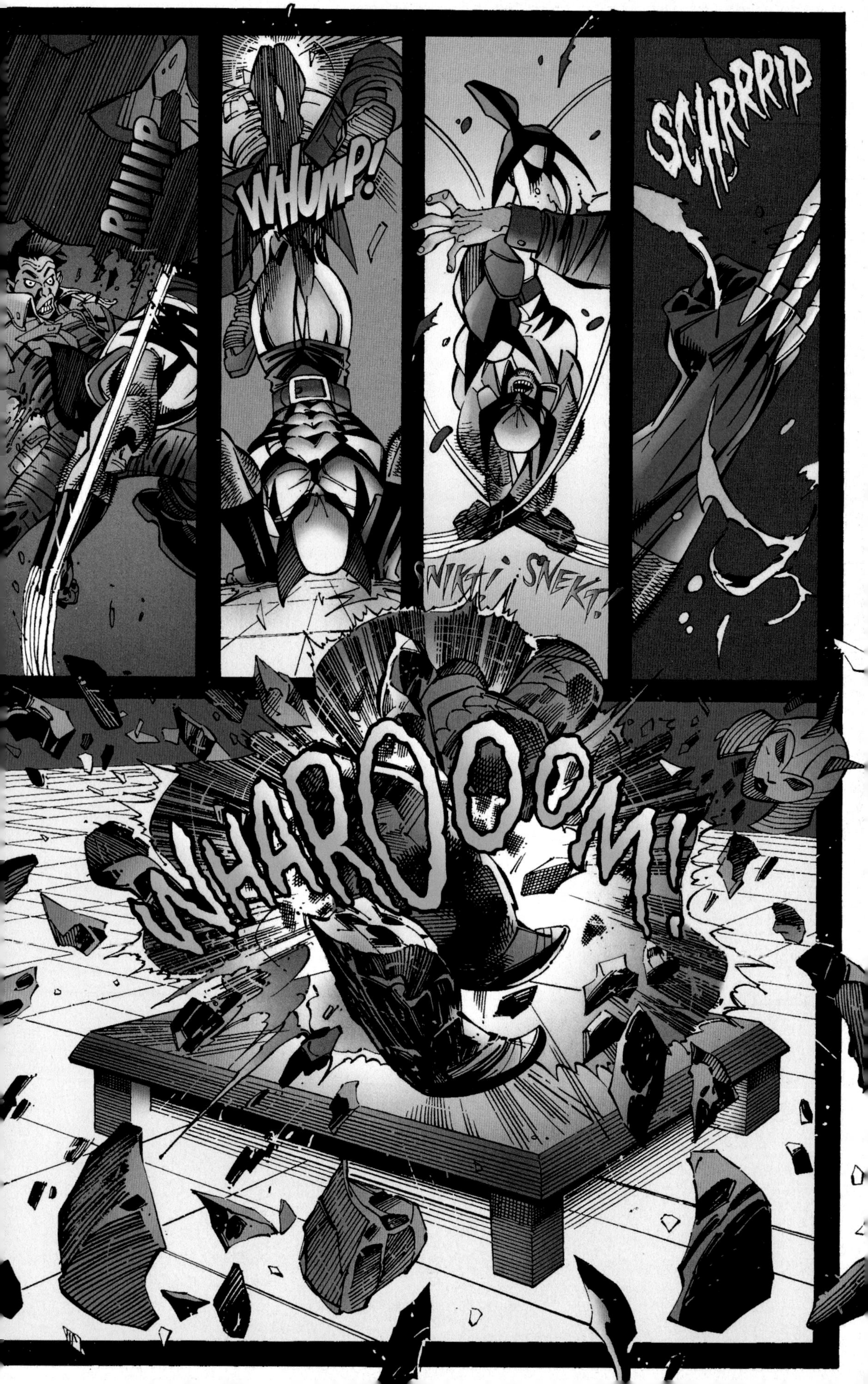
RIIIIP
WHUMP!
SNIKT!
SNEKT!
SCHRRRIP
WHAROOOM!

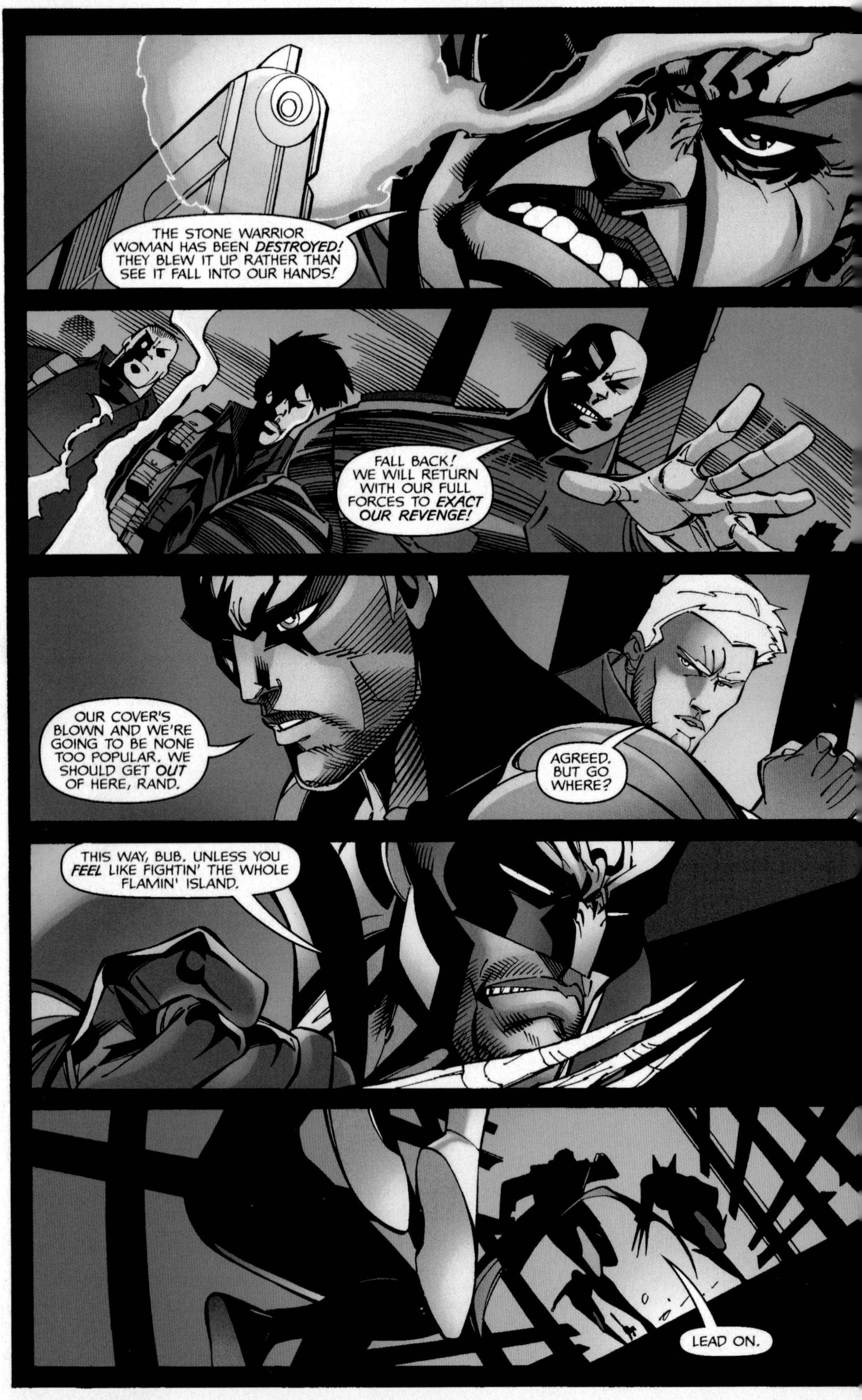
THE STONE WARRIOR WOMAN HAS BEEN DESTROYED! THEY BLEW IT UP RATHER THAN SEE IT FALL INTO OUR HANDS!
FALL BACK! WE WILL RETURN WITH OUR FULL FORCES TO EXACT OUR REVENGE!
OUR COVER'S BLOWN AND WE'RE GOING TO BE NONE TOO POPULAR. WE SHOULD GET OUT OF HERE, RAND.
AGREED. BUT GO WHERE?
THIS WAY, BUB. UNLESS YOU FEEL LIKE FIGHTIN' THE WHOLE FLAMIN' ISLAND.
LEAD ON.

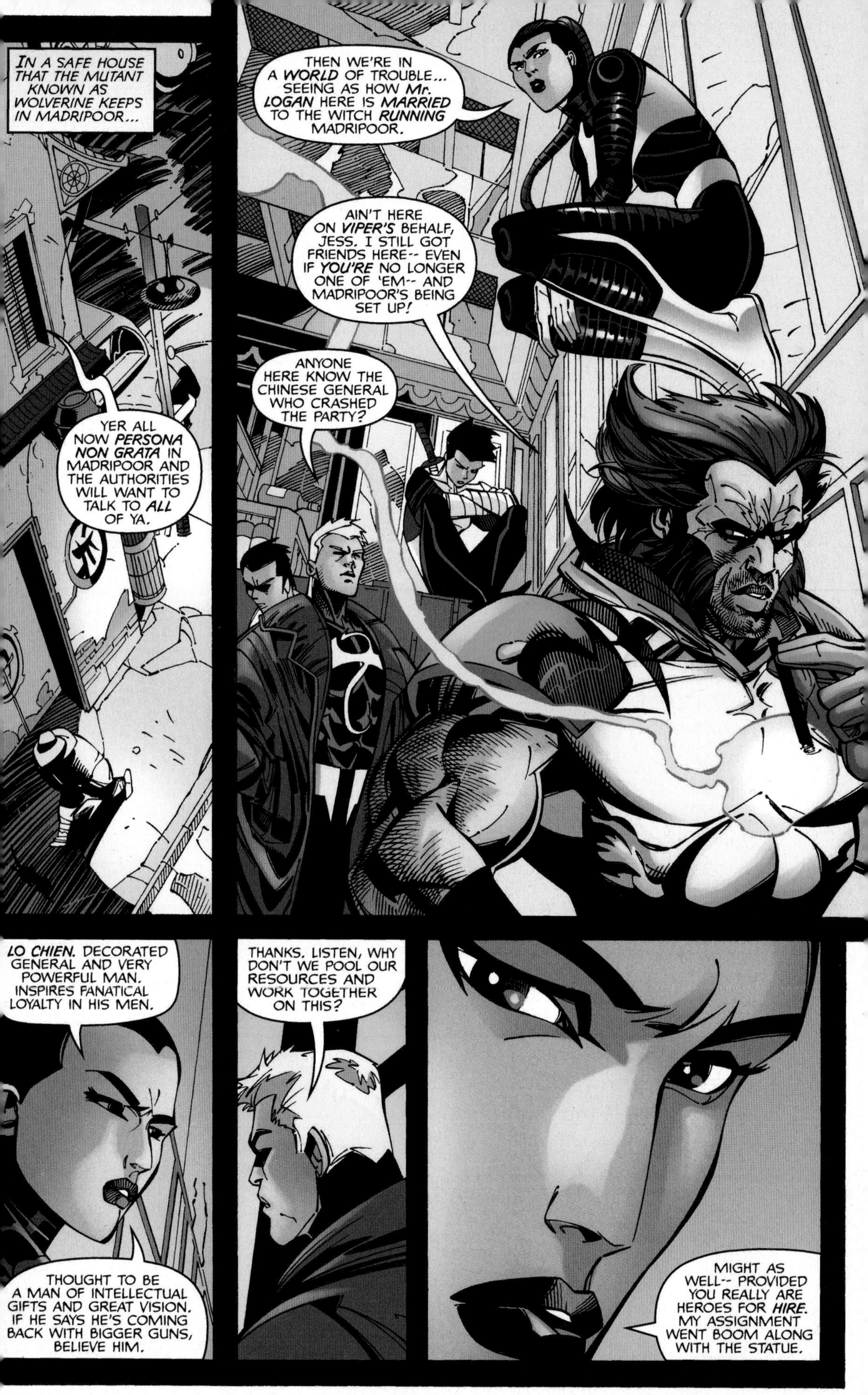
IN A SAFE HOUSE THAT THE MUTANT KNOWN AS WOLVERINE KEEPS IN MADRIPOOR...
THEN WE'RE IN A WORLD OF TROUBLE... SEEING AS HOW Mr. LOGAN HERE IS MARRIED TO THE WITCH RUNNING MADRIPOOR.
AIN'T HERE ON VIPER'S BEHALF, JESS. I STILL GOT FRIENDS HERE-- EVEN IF YOU'RE NO LONGER ONE OF 'EM-- AND MADRIPOOR'S BEING SET UP!
ANYONE HERE KNOW THE CHINESE GENERAL WHO CRASHED THE PARTY?
YER ALL NOW PERSONA NON GRATA IN MADRIPOOR AND THE AUTHORITIES WILL WANT TO TALK TO ALL OF YA.
LO CHIEN. DECORATED GENERAL AND VERY POWERFUL MAN. INSPIRES FANATICAL LOYALTY IN HIS MEN.
THOUGHT TO BE A MAN OF INTELLECTUAL GIFTS AND GREAT VISION. IF HE SAYS HE'S COMING BACK WITH BIGGER GUNS, BELIEVE HIM.
THANKS. LISTEN, WHY DON'T WE POOL OUR RESOURCES AND WORK TOGETHER ON THIS?
MIGHT AS WELL-- PROVIDED YOU REALLY ARE HEROES FOR HIRE. MY ASSIGNMENT WENT BOOM ALONG WITH THE STATUE.

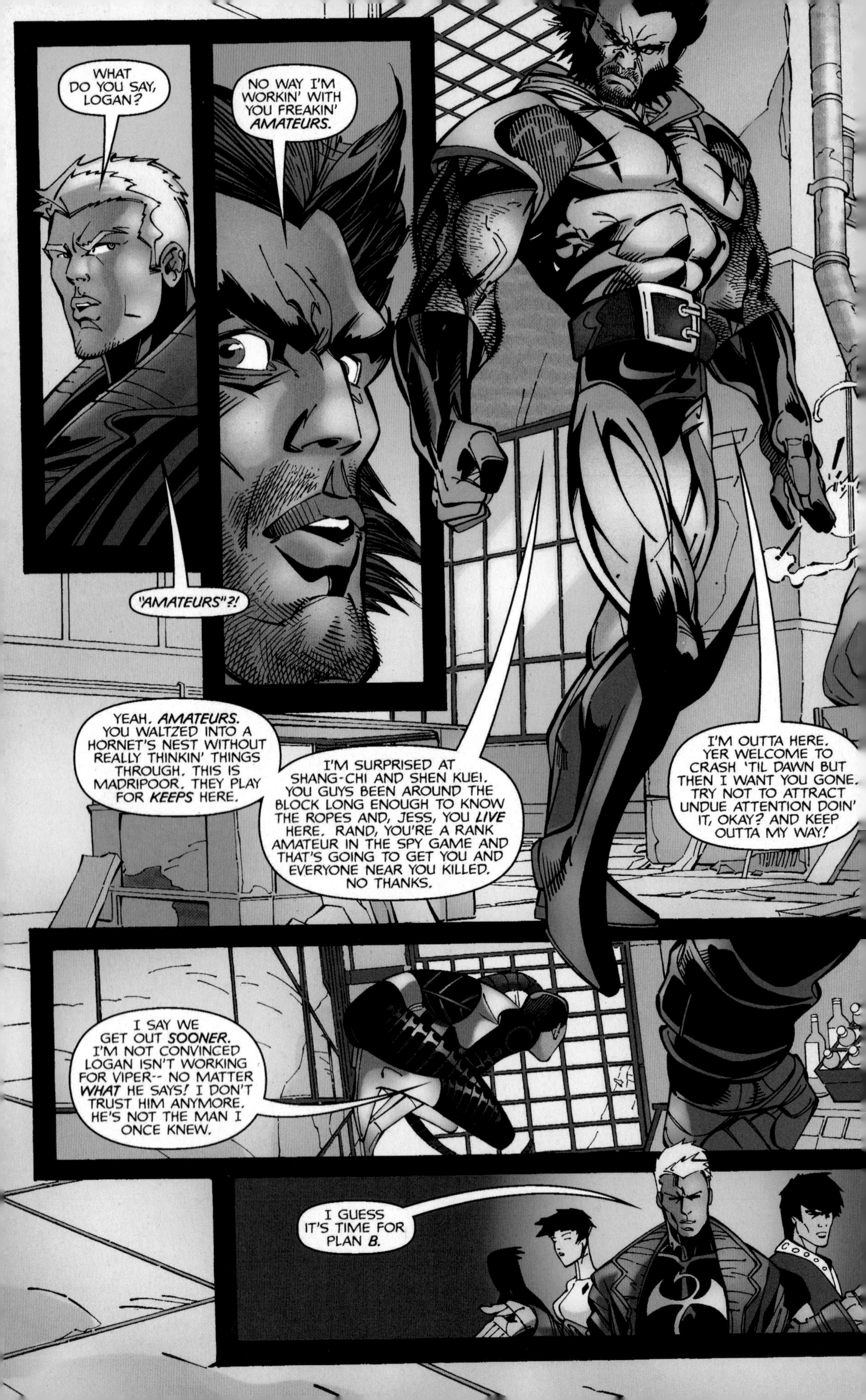
WHAT DO YOU SAY, LOGAN?
NO WAY I'M WORKIN' WITH YOU FREAKIN' *AMATEURS*.
"AMATEURS"?!
YEAH. *AMATEURS*. YOU WALTZED INTO A HORNET'S NEST WITHOUT REALLY THINKIN' THINGS THROUGH. THIS IS MADRIPOOR. THEY PLAY FOR *KEEPS* HERE.
I'M SURPRISED AT SHANG-CHI AND SHEN KUEI. YOU GUYS BEEN AROUND THE BLOCK LONG ENOUGH TO KNOW THE ROPES AND, JESS, YOU *LIVE* HERE. RAND, YOU'RE A RANK AMATEUR IN THE SPY GAME AND THAT'S GOING TO GET YOU AND EVERYONE NEAR YOU KILLED. NO THANKS.
I'M OUTTA HERE. YER WELCOME TO CRASH 'TIL DAWN BUT THEN I WANT YOU GONE. TRY NOT TO ATTRACT UNDUE ATTENTION DOIN' IT, OKAY? AND KEEP OUTTA MY WAY!
I SAY WE GET OUT *SOONER*. I'M NOT CONVINCED LOGAN ISN'T WORKING FOR VIPER-- NO MATTER *WHAT* HE SAYS! I DON'T TRUST HIM ANYMORE. HE'S NOT THE MAN I ONCE KNEW.
I GUESS IT'S TIME FOR PLAN *B*.

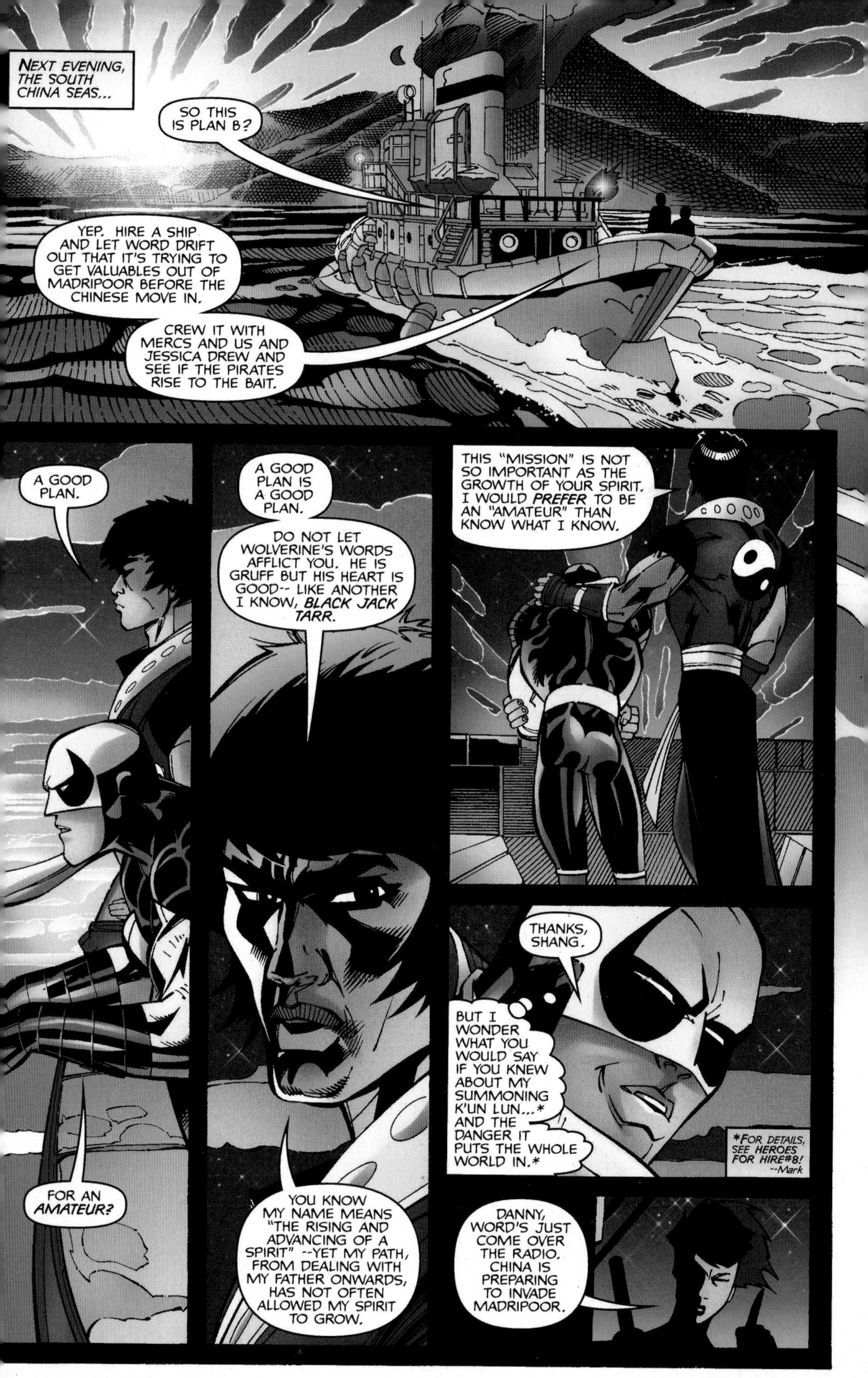
NEXT EVENING, THE SOUTH CHINA SEAS...
SO THIS IS PLAN B?
YEP. HIRE A SHIP AND LET WORD DRIFT OUT THAT IT'S TRYING TO GET VALUABLES OUT OF MADRIPOOR BEFORE THE CHINESE MOVE IN.
CREW IT WITH MERCS AND US AND JESSICA DREW AND SEE IF THE PIRATES RISE TO THE BAIT.
A GOOD PLAN.
FOR AN AMATEUR?
A GOOD PLAN IS A GOOD PLAN.
DO NOT LET WOLVERINE'S WORDS AFFLICT YOU. HE IS GRUFF BUT HIS HEART IS GOOD-- LIKE ANOTHER I KNOW, BLACK JACK TARR.
YOU KNOW MY NAME MEANS "THE RISING AND ADVANCING OF A SPIRIT" --YET MY PATH, FROM DEALING WITH MY FATHER ONWARDS, HAS NOT OFTEN ALLOWED MY SPIRIT TO GROW.
THIS "MISSION" IS NOT SO IMPORTANT AS THE GROWTH OF YOUR SPIRIT. I WOULD PREFER TO BE AN "AMATEUR" THAN KNOW WHAT I KNOW.
THANKS, SHANG.
BUT I WONDER WHAT YOU WOULD SAY IF YOU KNEW ABOUT MY SUMMONING K'UN LUN...* AND THE DANGER IT PUTS THE WHOLE WORLD IN.*
*FOR DETAILS, SEE HEROES FOR HIRE#8! --Mark
DANNY, WORD'S JUST COME OVER THE RADIO. CHINA IS PREPARING TO INVADE MADRIPOOR.

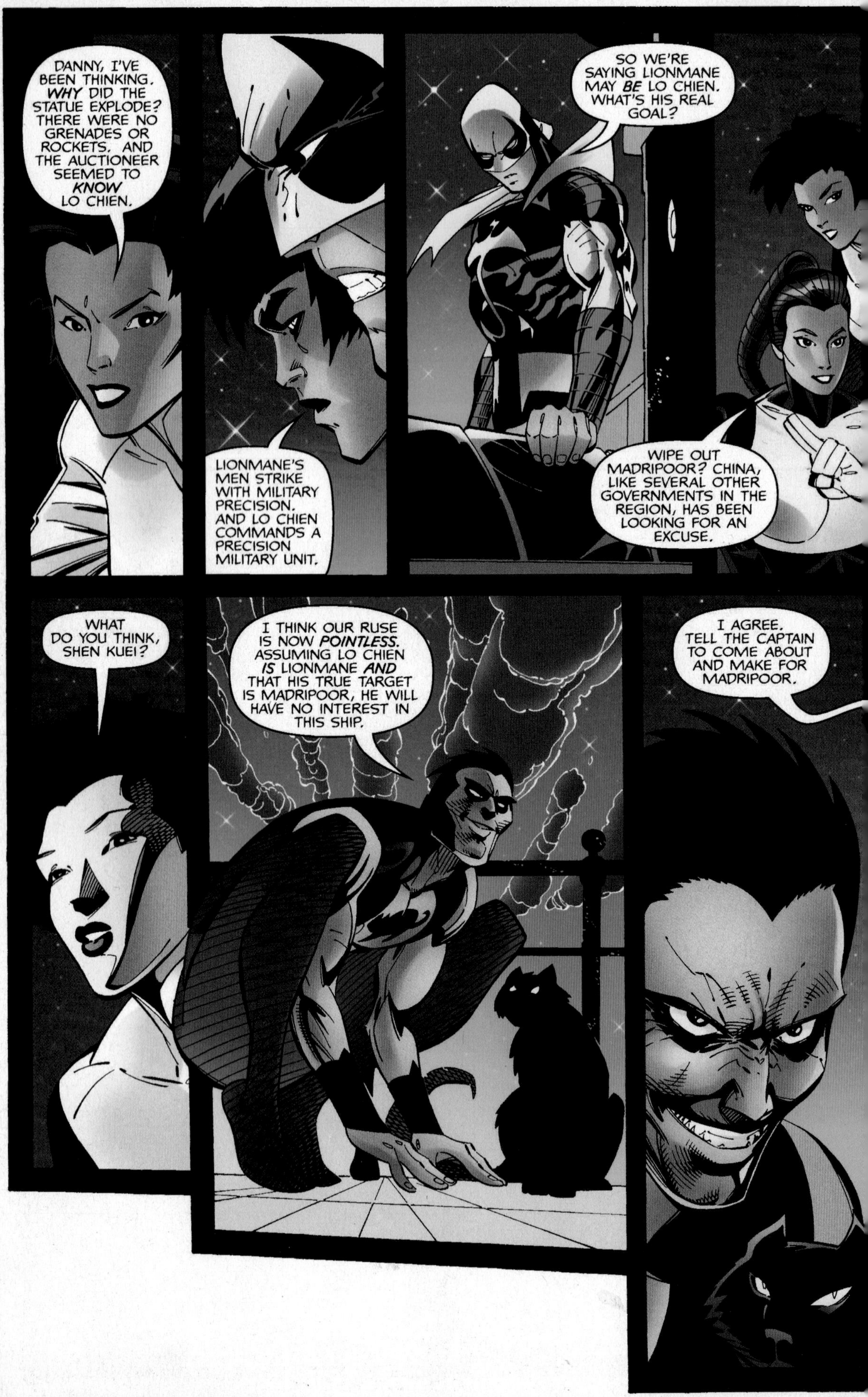
DANNY, I'VE BEEN THINKING. WHY DID THE STATUE EXPLODE? THERE WERE NO GRENADES OR ROCKETS. AND THE AUCTIONEER SEEMED TO KNOW LO CHIEN.
LIONMANE'S MEN STRIKE WITH MILITARY PRECISION. AND LO CHIEN COMMANDS A PRECISION MILITARY UNIT.
SO WE'RE SAYING LIONMANE MAY BE LO CHIEN. WHAT'S HIS REAL GOAL?
WIPE OUT MADRIPOOR? CHINA, LIKE SEVERAL OTHER GOVERNMENTS IN THE REGION, HAS BEEN LOOKING FOR AN EXCUSE.
WHAT DO YOU THINK, SHEN KUEI?
I THINK OUR RUSE IS NOW POINTLESS. ASSUMING LO CHIEN IS LIONMANE AND THAT HIS TRUE TARGET IS MADRIPOOR, HE WILL HAVE NO INTEREST IN THIS SHIP.
I AGREE. TELL THE CAPTAIN TO COME ABOUT AND MAKE FOR MADRIPOOR.

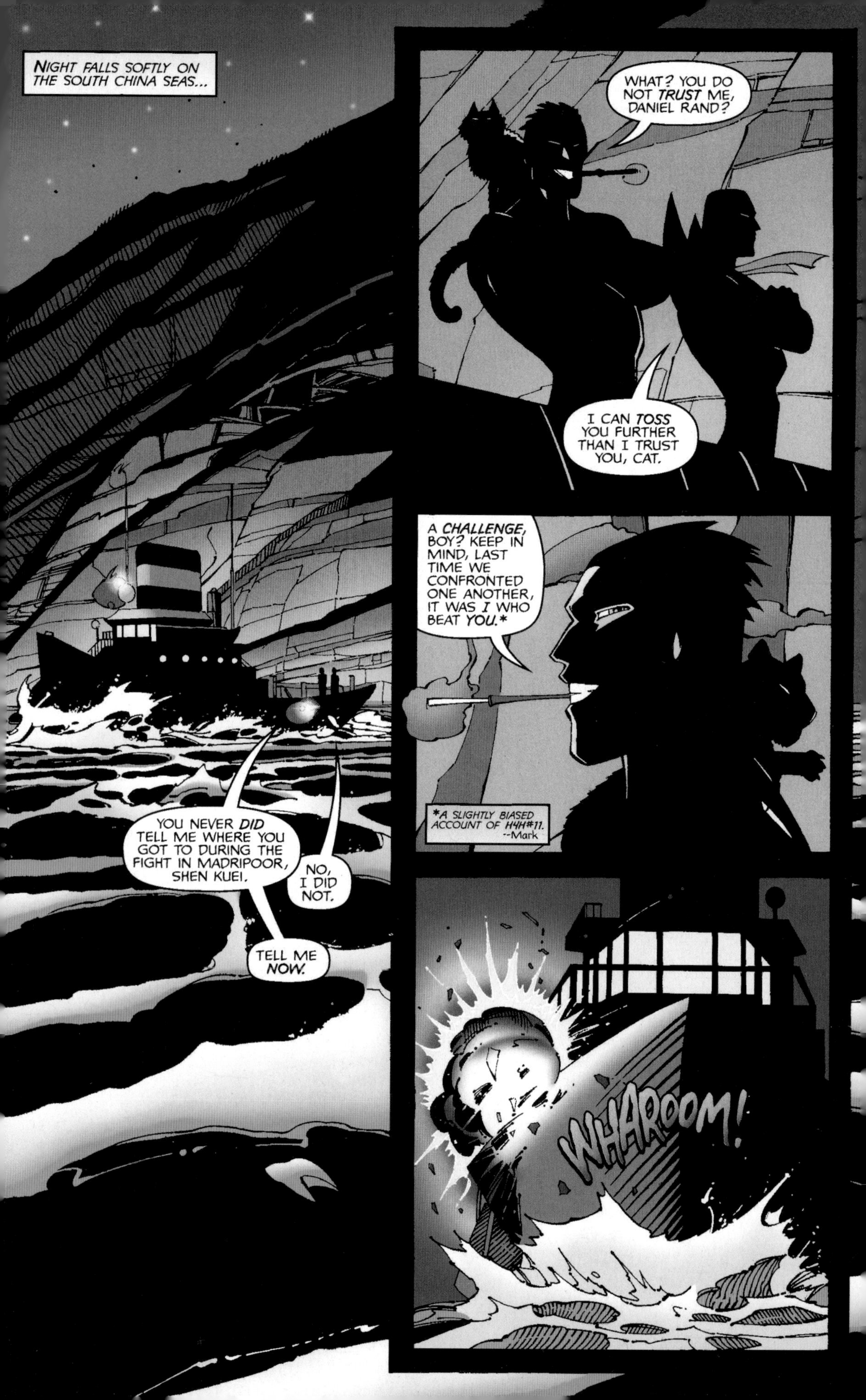
NIGHT FALLS SOFTLY ON THE SOUTH CHINA SEAS...
YOU NEVER DID TELL ME WHERE YOU GOT TO DURING THE FIGHT IN MADRIPOOR, SHEN KUEI.
NO, I DID NOT.
TELL ME NOW.
WHAT? YOU DO NOT TRUST ME, DANIEL RAND?
I CAN TOSS YOU FURTHER THAN I TRUST YOU, CAT.
A CHALLENGE, BOY? KEEP IN MIND, LAST TIME WE CONFRONTED ONE ANOTHER, IT WAS I WHO BEAT YOU.*
*A SLIGHTLY BIASED ACCOUNT OF H4H#11. --Mark
WHAROOM!

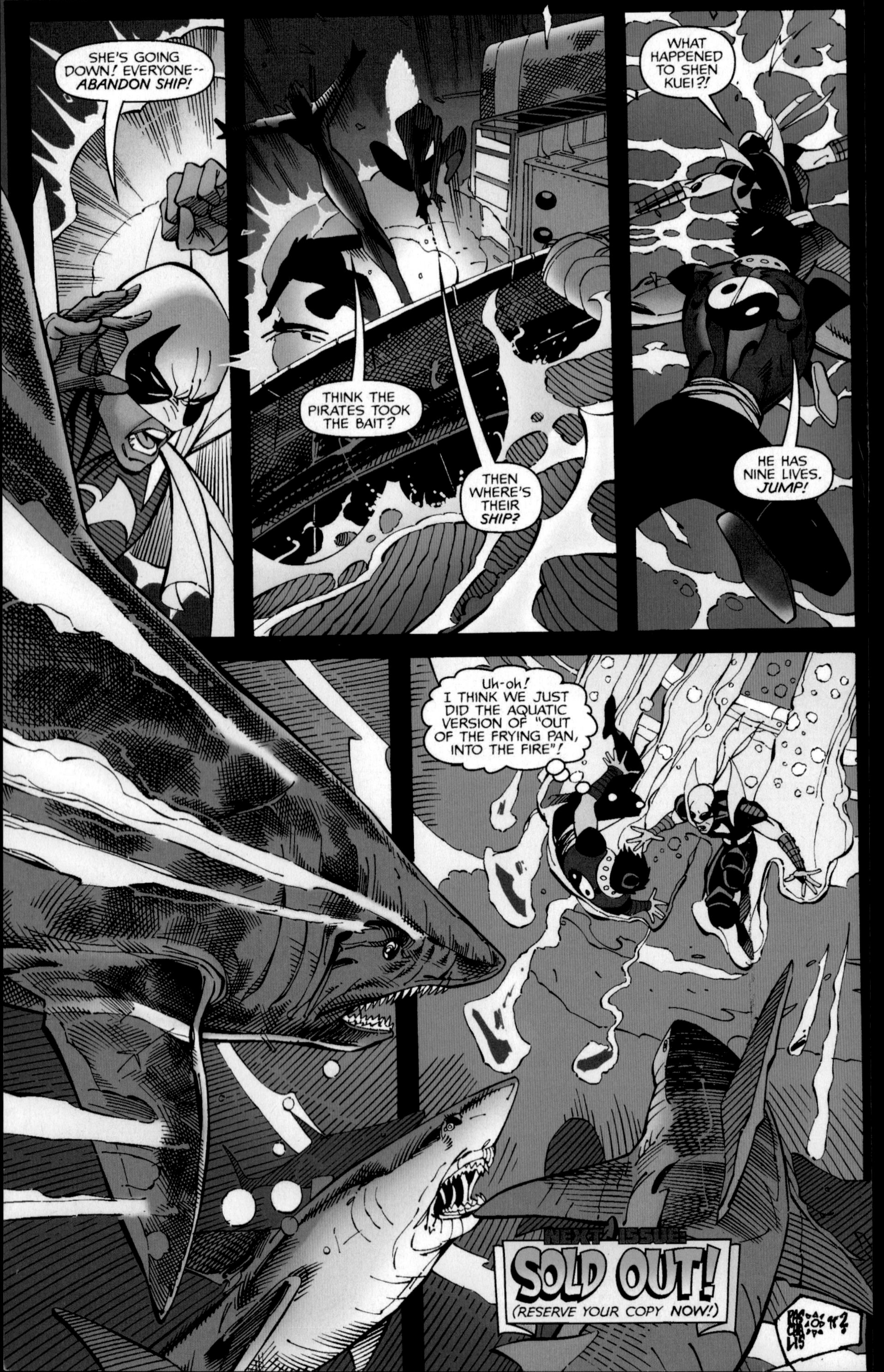
SHE'S GOING DOWN! EVERYONE-- ABANDON SHIP!
THINK THE PIRATES TOOK THE BAIT?
THEN WHERE'S THEIR SHIP?
WHAT HAPPENED TO SHEN KUEI?!
HE HAS NINE LIVES. JUMP!
Uh-oh! I THINK WE JUST DID THE AQUATIC VERSION OF "OUT OF THE FRYING PAN, INTO THE FIRE"!
NEXT ISSUE:
SOLD OUT!
(RESERVE YOUR COPY NOW!)

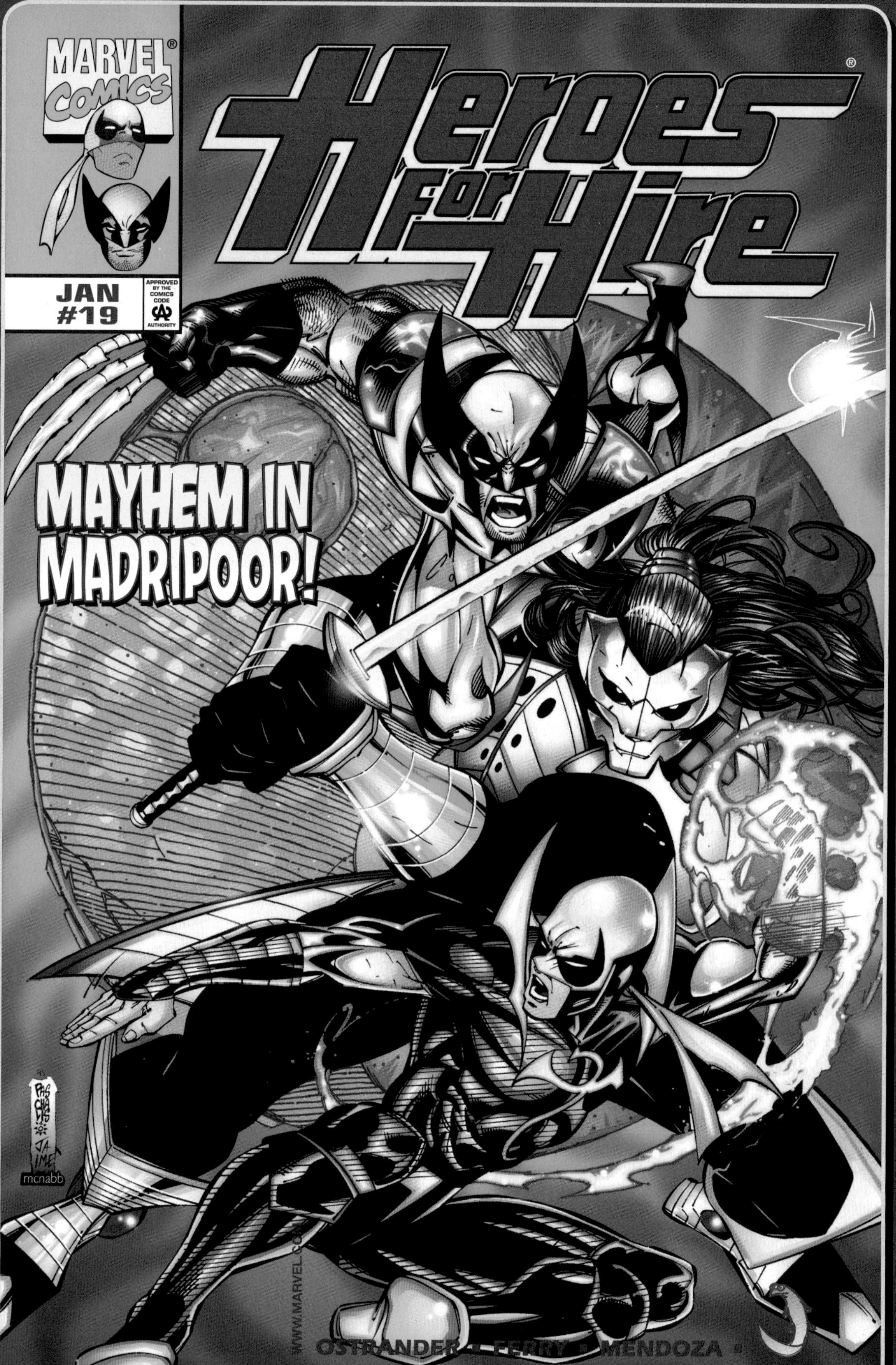
MARVEL COMICS
Heroes for Hire
JAN #19
APPROVED BY THE COMICS CODE AUTHORITY
MAYHEM IN MADRIPOOR!
WWW.MARVEL.COM
OSTRANDER • PERRY • MENDOZA

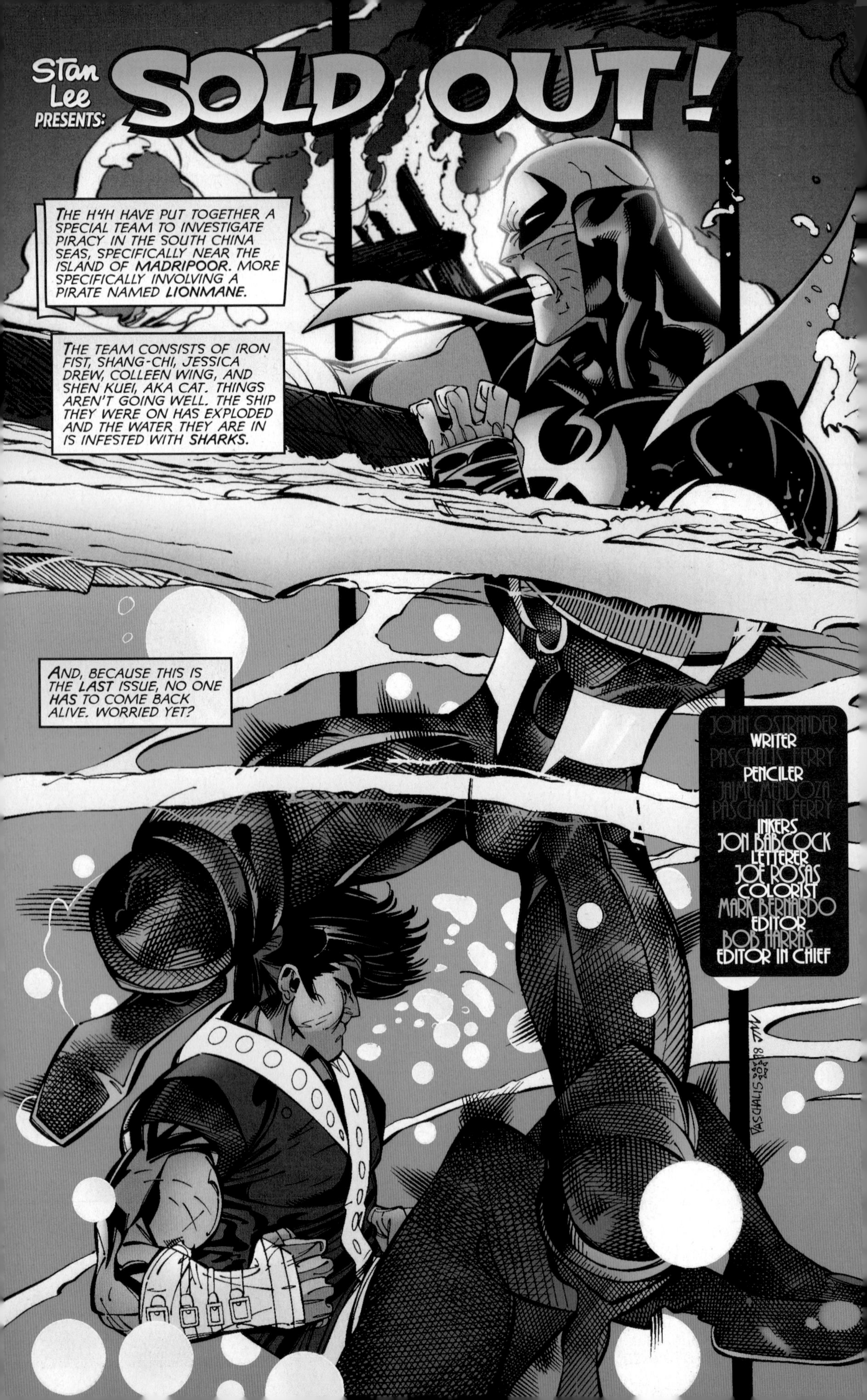

Stan Lee PRESENTS:
SOLD OUT!
THE H4H HAVE PUT TOGETHER A SPECIAL TEAM TO INVESTIGATE PIRACY IN THE SOUTH CHINA SEAS, SPECIFICALLY NEAR THE ISLAND OF MADRIPOOR. MORE SPECIFICALLY INVOLVING A PIRATE NAMED LIONMANE.
THE TEAM CONSISTS OF IRON FIST, SHANG-CHI, JESSICA DREW, COLLEEN WING, AND SHEN KUEI, AKA CAT. THINGS AREN'T GOING WELL. THE SHIP THEY WERE ON HAS EXPLODED AND THE WATER THEY ARE IN IS INFESTED WITH SHARKS.
AND, BECAUSE THIS IS THE LAST ISSUE, NO ONE HAS TO COME BACK ALIVE. WORRIED YET?
JOHN OSTRANDER
WRITER
PASCHALIS FERRY
PENCILER
JAIME MENDOZA
PASCHALIS FERRY
INKERS
JON BABCOCK
LETTERER
JOE ROSAS
COLORIST
MARK BERNARDO
EDITOR
BOB HARRAS
EDITOR IN CHIEF

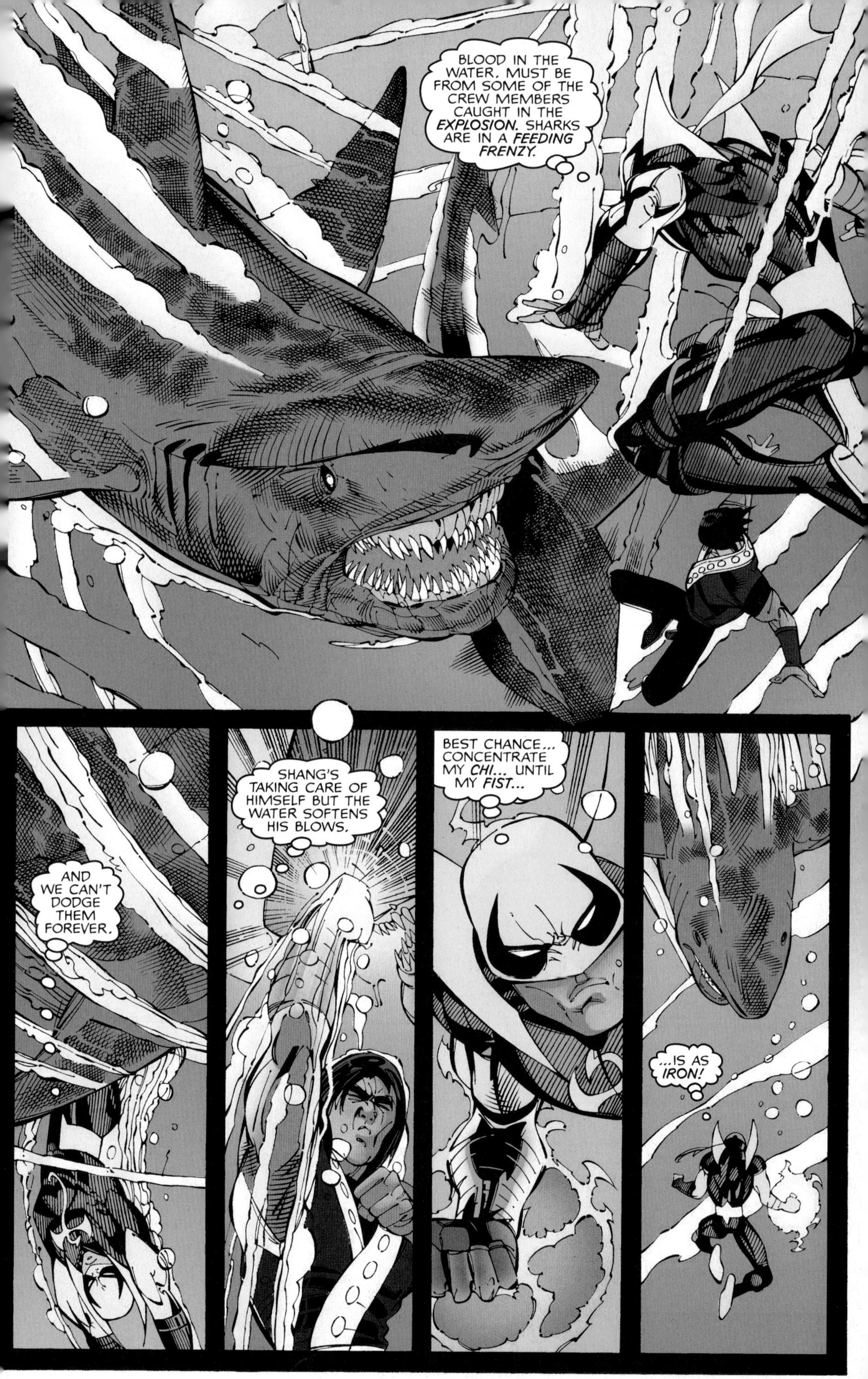
BLOOD IN THE WATER. MUST BE FROM SOME OF THE CREW MEMBERS CAUGHT IN THE *EXPLOSION.* SHARKS ARE IN A *FEEDING FRENZY.*
AND WE CAN'T DODGE THEM FOREVER.
SHANG'S TAKING CARE OF HIMSELF BUT THE WATER SOFTENS HIS BLOWS.
BEST CHANCE... CONCENTRATE MY *CHI*... UNTIL MY *FIST*...
...IS AS *IRON!*

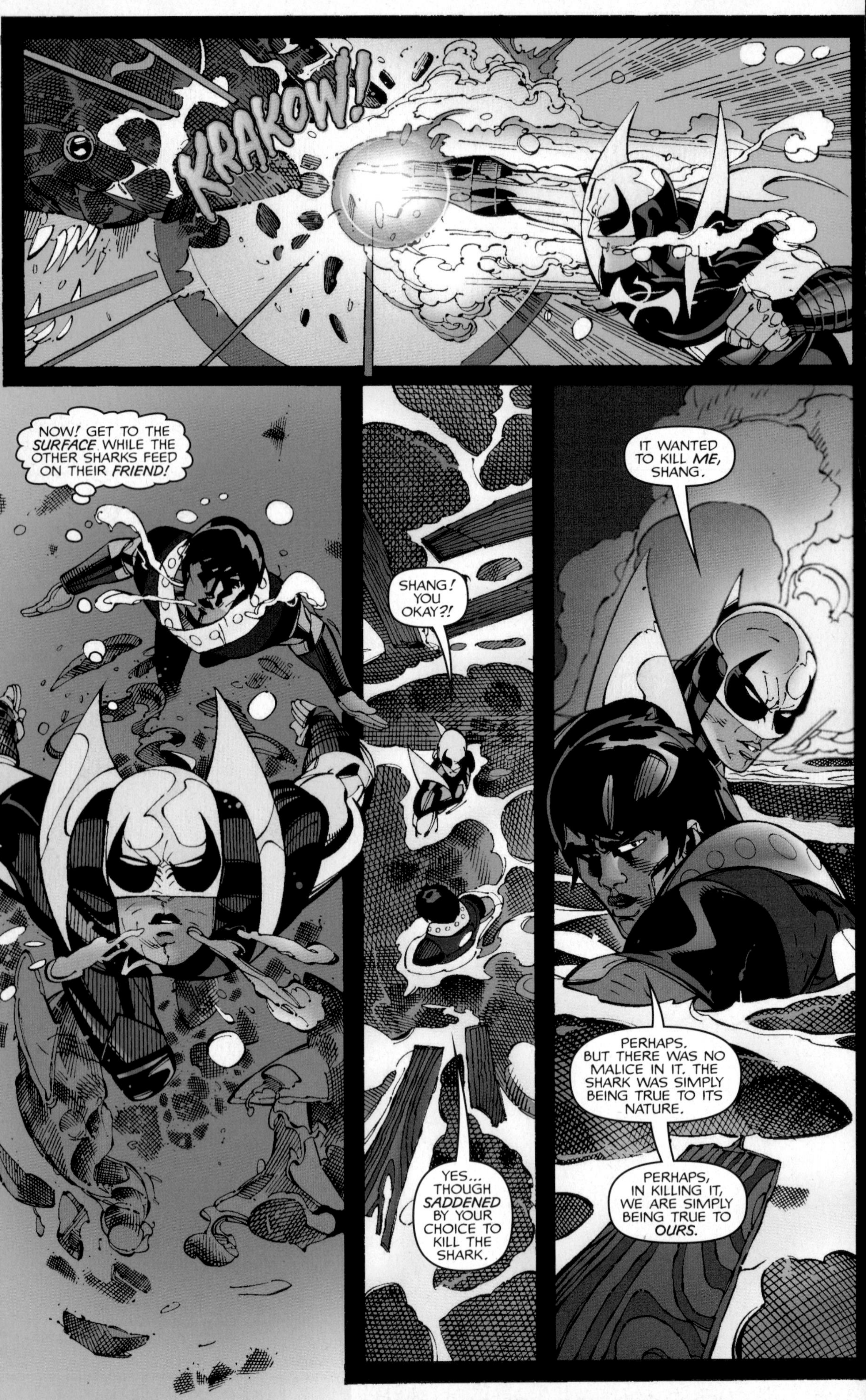
KRAKOW!!
NOW! GET TO THE SURFACE WHILE THE OTHER SHARKS FEED ON THEIR FRIEND!
SHANG! YOU OKAY?!
YES... THOUGH SADDENED BY YOUR CHOICE TO KILL THE SHARK.
IT WANTED TO KILL ME, SHANG.
PERHAPS. BUT THERE WAS NO MALICE IN IT. THE SHARK WAS SIMPLY BEING TRUE TO ITS NATURE.
PERHAPS, IN KILLING IT, WE ARE SIMPLY BEING TRUE TO OURS.

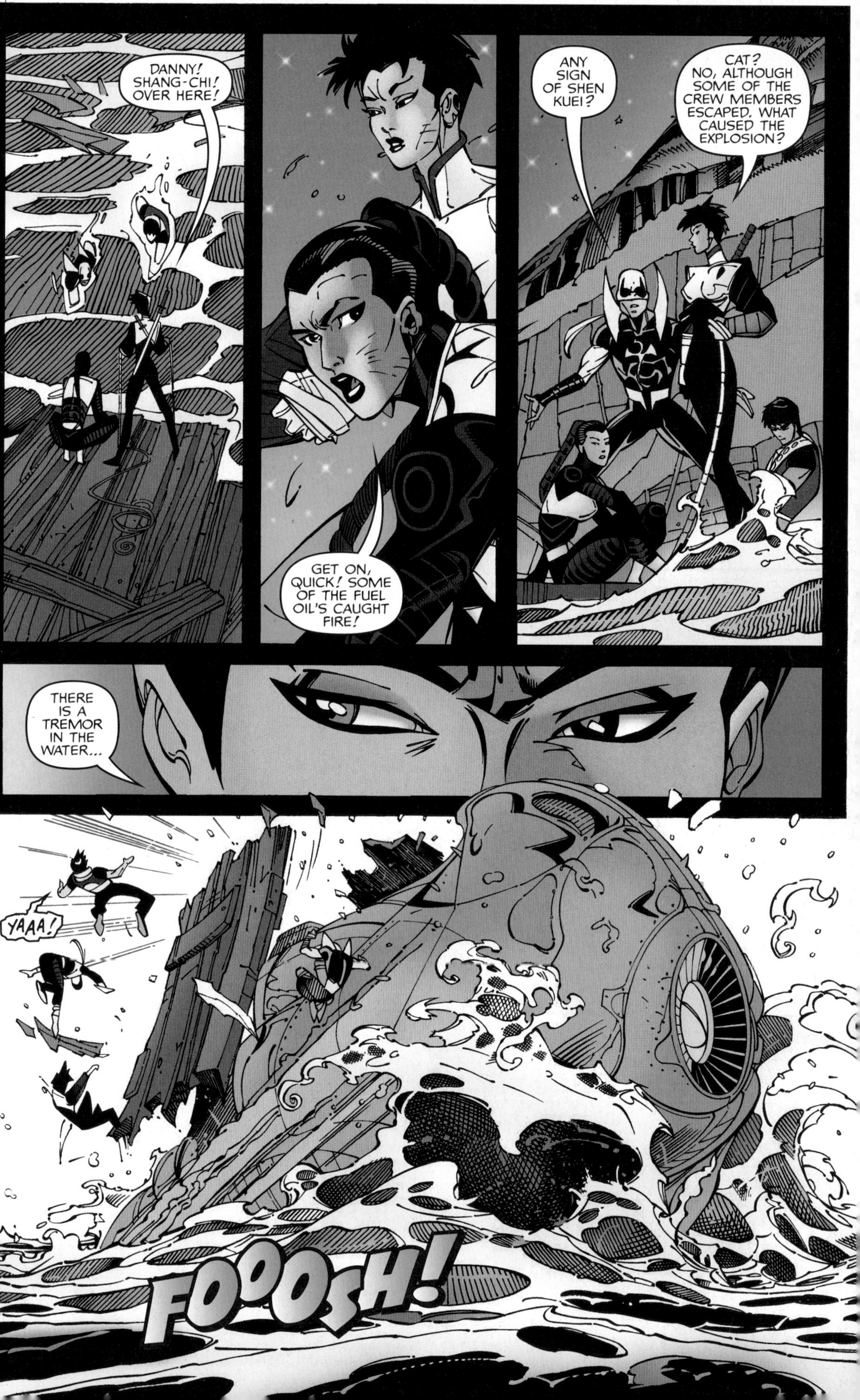
DANNY! SHANG-CHI! OVER HERE!
GET ON, QUICK! SOME OF THE FUEL OIL'S CAUGHT FIRE!
ANY SIGN OF SHEN KUEI?
CAT? NO, ALTHOUGH SOME OF THE CREW MEMBERS ESCAPED. WHAT CAUSED THE EXPLOSION?
THERE IS A TREMOR IN THE WATER...
YAAA!
FOOOSH!

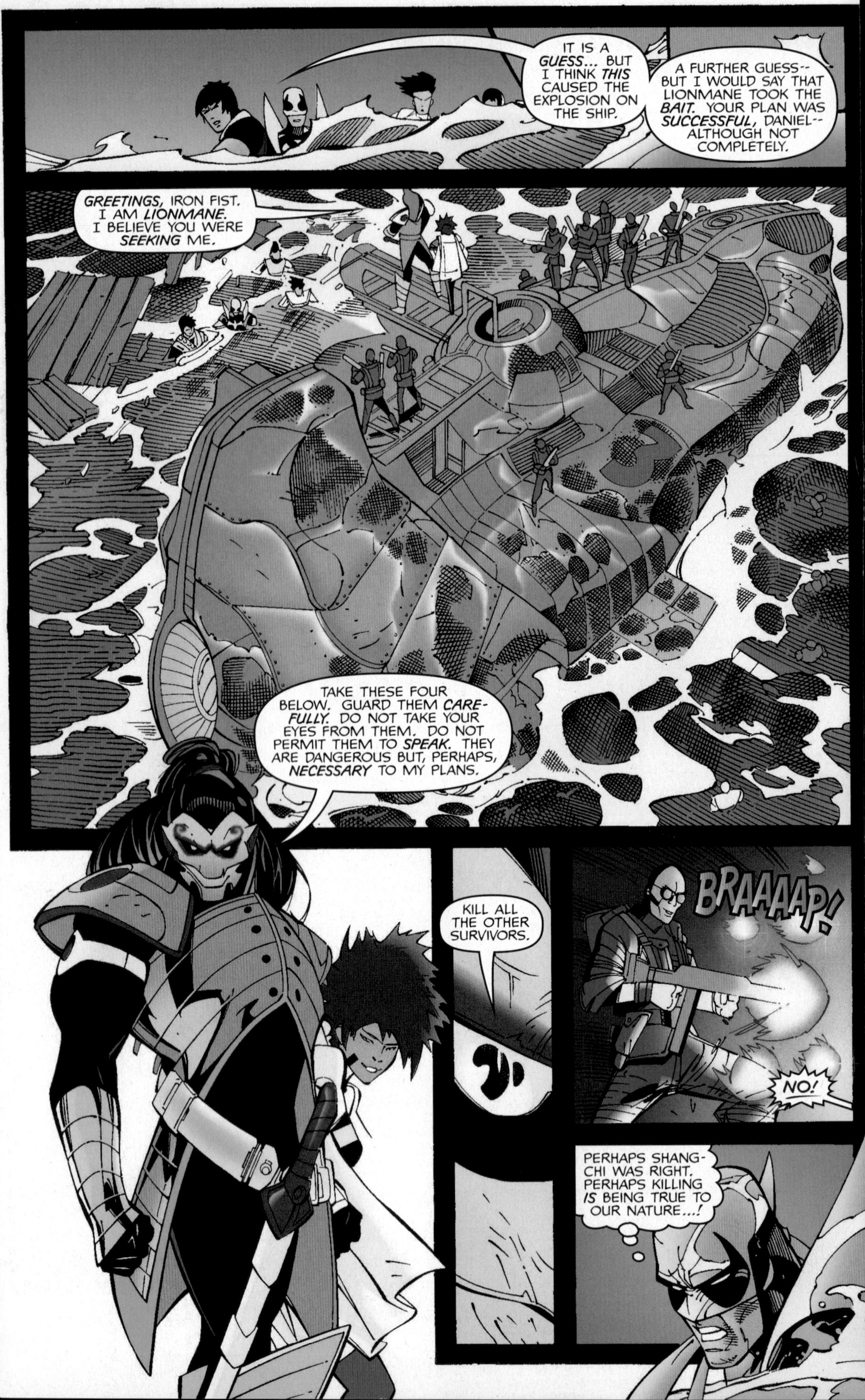
IT IS A GUESS... BUT I THINK THIS CAUSED THE EXPLOSION ON THE SHIP.
A FURTHER GUESS-- BUT I WOULD SAY THAT LIONMANE TOOK THE BAIT. YOUR PLAN WAS SUCCESSFUL, DANIEL-- ALTHOUGH NOT COMPLETELY.
GREETINGS, IRON FIST. I AM LIONMANE. I BELIEVE YOU WERE SEEKING ME.
TAKE THESE FOUR BELOW. GUARD THEM CAREFULLY. DO NOT TAKE YOUR EYES FROM THEM. DO NOT PERMIT THEM TO SPEAK. THEY ARE DANGEROUS BUT, PERHAPS, NECESSARY TO MY PLANS.
KILL ALL THE OTHER SURVIVORS.
BRAAAAP!
NO!
PERHAPS SHANG-CHI WAS RIGHT. PERHAPS KILLING IS BEING TRUE TO OUR NATURE...!

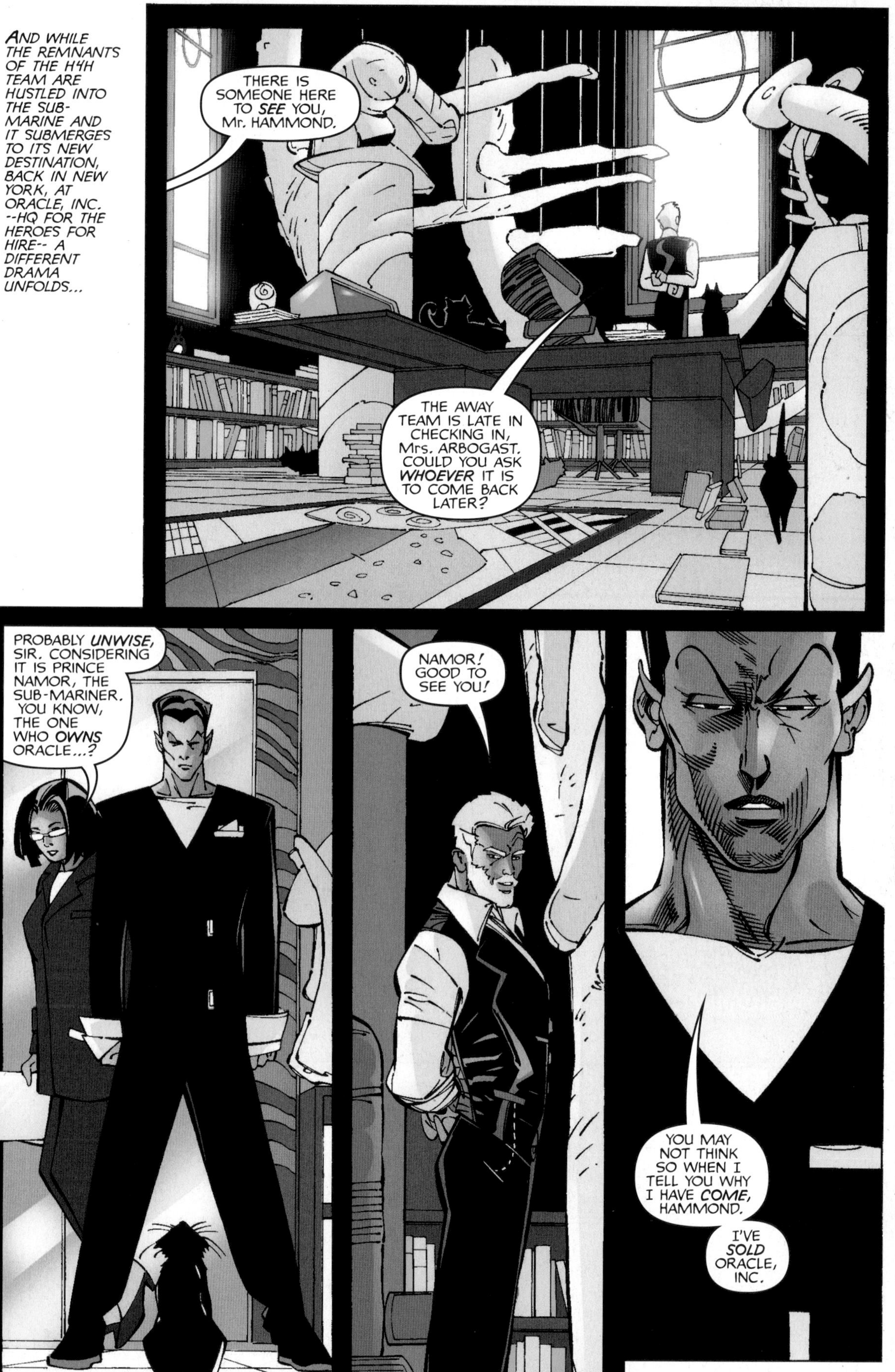
AND WHILE THE REMNANTS OF THE H4H TEAM ARE HUSTLED INTO THE SUB-MARINE AND IT SUBMERGES TO ITS NEW DESTINATION, BACK IN NEW YORK, AT ORACLE, INC. --HQ FOR THE HEROES FOR HIRE-- A DIFFERENT DRAMA UNFOLDS...
THERE IS SOMEONE HERE TO SEE YOU, Mr. HAMMOND.
THE AWAY TEAM IS LATE IN CHECKING IN, Mrs. ARBOGAST. COULD YOU ASK WHOEVER IT IS TO COME BACK LATER?
PROBABLY UNWISE, SIR. CONSIDERING IT IS PRINCE NAMOR, THE SUB-MARINER. YOU KNOW, THE ONE WHO OWNS ORACLE...?
NAMOR! GOOD TO SEE YOU!
YOU MAY NOT THINK SO WHEN I TELL YOU WHY I HAVE COME, HAMMOND.
I'VE SOLD ORACLE, INC.

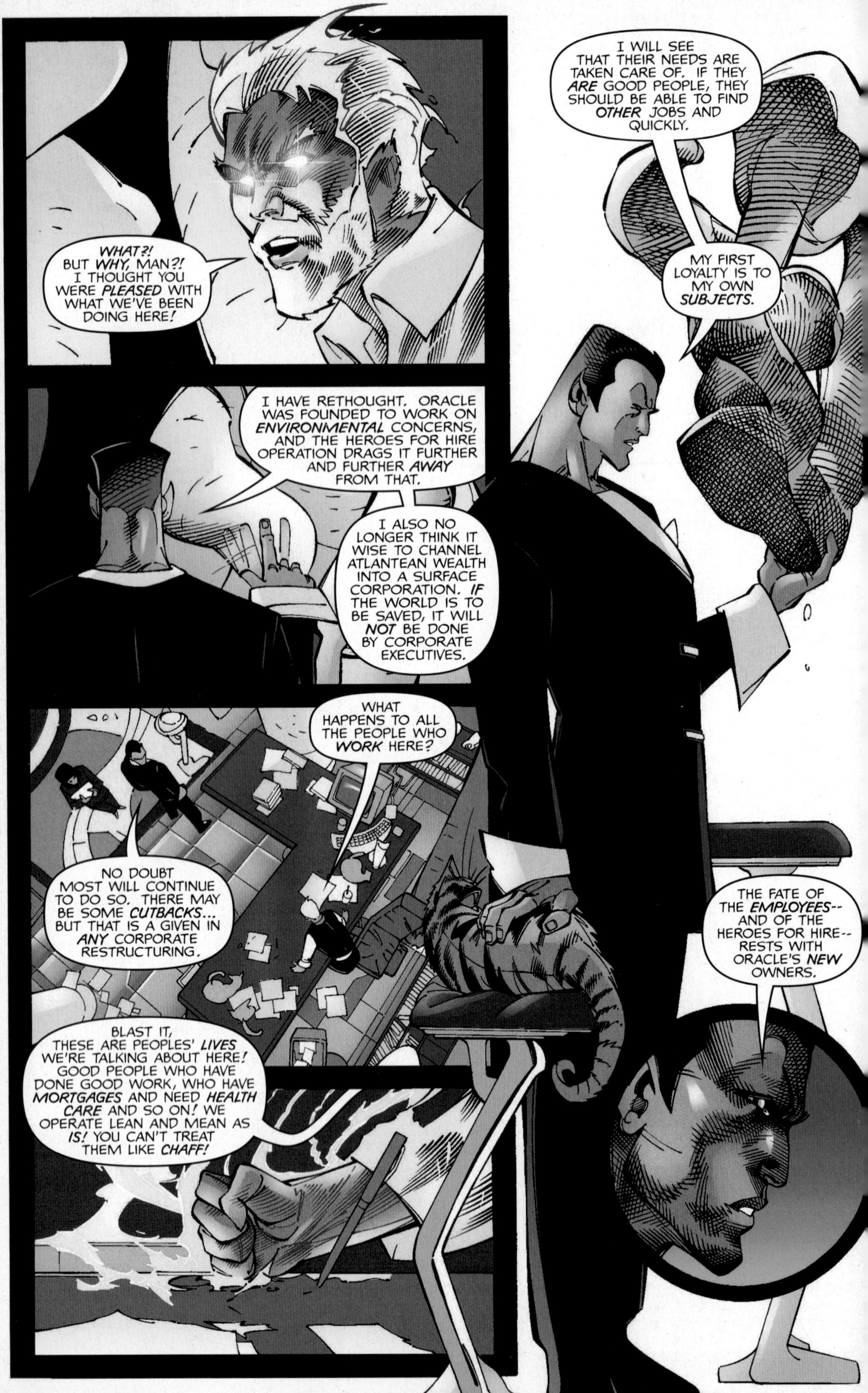
WHAT?! BUT WHY, MAN?! I THOUGHT YOU WERE PLEASED WITH WHAT WE'VE BEEN DOING HERE!
I WILL SEE THAT THEIR NEEDS ARE TAKEN CARE OF. IF THEY ARE GOOD PEOPLE, THEY SHOULD BE ABLE TO FIND OTHER JOBS AND QUICKLY.
MY FIRST LOYALTY IS TO MY OWN SUBJECTS.
I HAVE RETHOUGHT. ORACLE WAS FOUNDED TO WORK ON ENVIRONMENTAL CONCERNS, AND THE HEROES FOR HIRE OPERATION DRAGS IT FURTHER AND FURTHER AWAY FROM THAT.
I ALSO NO LONGER THINK IT WISE TO CHANNEL ATLANTEAN WEALTH INTO A SURFACE CORPORATION. IF THE WORLD IS TO BE SAVED, IT WILL NOT BE DONE BY CORPORATE EXECUTIVES.
WHAT HAPPENS TO ALL THE PEOPLE WHO WORK HERE?
NO DOUBT MOST WILL CONTINUE TO DO SO. THERE MAY BE SOME CUTBACKS... BUT THAT IS A GIVEN IN ANY CORPORATE RESTRUCTURING.
BLAST IT, THESE ARE PEOPLES' LIVES WE'RE TALKING ABOUT HERE! GOOD PEOPLE WHO HAVE DONE GOOD WORK, WHO HAVE MORTGAGES AND NEED HEALTH CARE AND SO ON! WE OPERATE LEAN AND MEAN AS IS! YOU CAN'T TREAT THEM LIKE CHAFF!
THE FATE OF THE EMPLOYEES-- AND OF THE HEROES FOR HIRE-- RESTS WITH ORACLE'S NEW OWNERS.

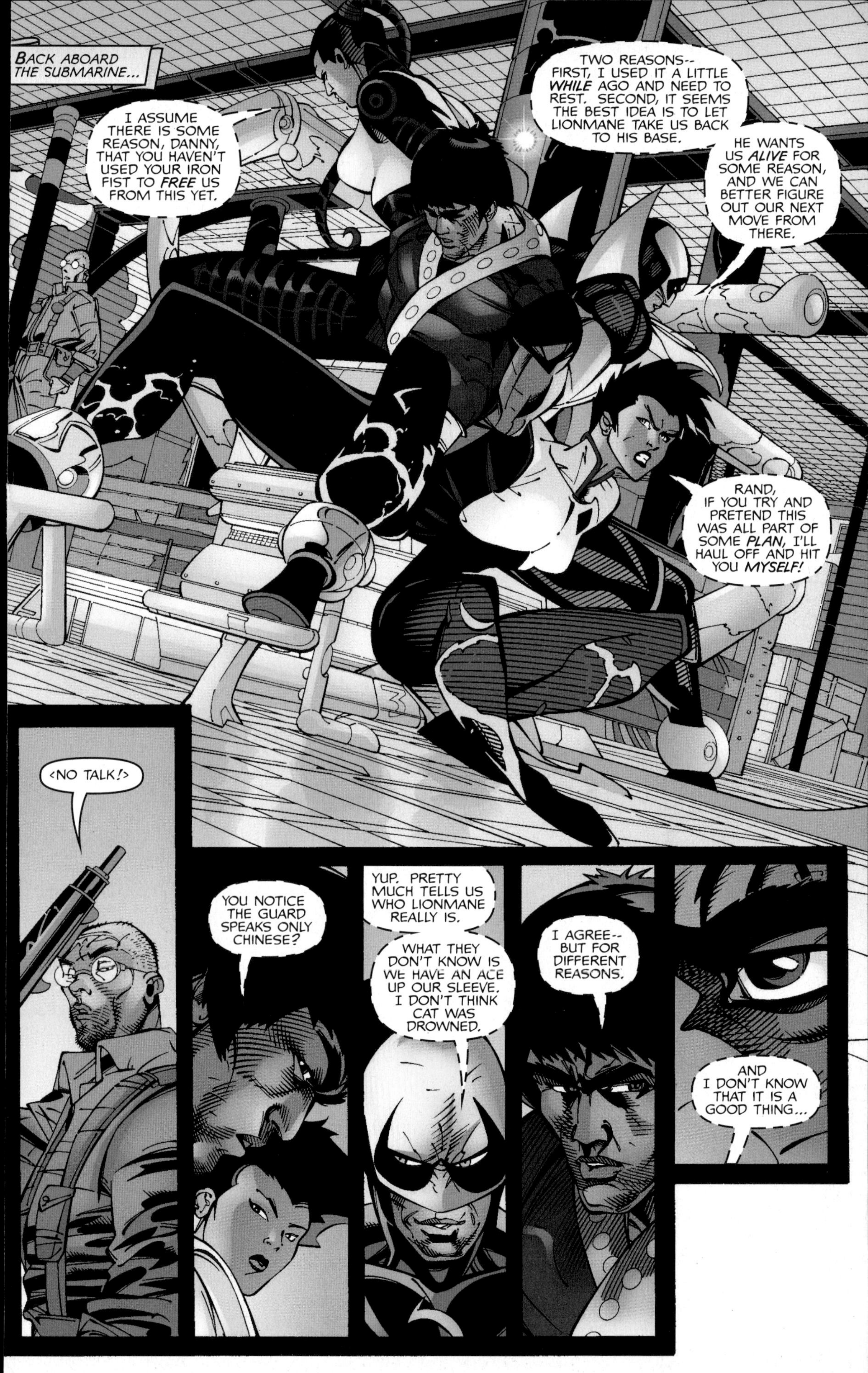
BACK ABOARD THE SUBMARINE...
I ASSUME THERE IS SOME REASON, DANNY, THAT YOU HAVEN'T USED YOUR IRON FIST TO FREE US FROM THIS YET.
TWO REASONS-- FIRST, I USED IT A LITTLE WHILE AGO AND NEED TO REST. SECOND, IT SEEMS THE BEST IDEA IS TO LET LIONMANE TAKE US BACK TO HIS BASE.
HE WANTS US ALIVE FOR SOME REASON, AND WE CAN BETTER FIGURE OUT OUR NEXT MOVE FROM THERE.
RAND, IF YOU TRY AND PRETEND THIS WAS ALL PART OF SOME PLAN, I'LL HAUL OFF AND HIT YOU MYSELF!
<NO TALK!>
YOU NOTICE THE GUARD SPEAKS ONLY CHINESE?
YUP. PRETTY MUCH TELLS US WHO LIONMANE REALLY IS.
WHAT THEY DON'T KNOW IS WE HAVE AN ACE UP OUR SLEEVE. I DON'T THINK CAT WAS DROWNED.
I AGREE-- BUT FOR DIFFERENT REASONS.
AND I DON'T KNOW THAT IT IS A GOOD THING...

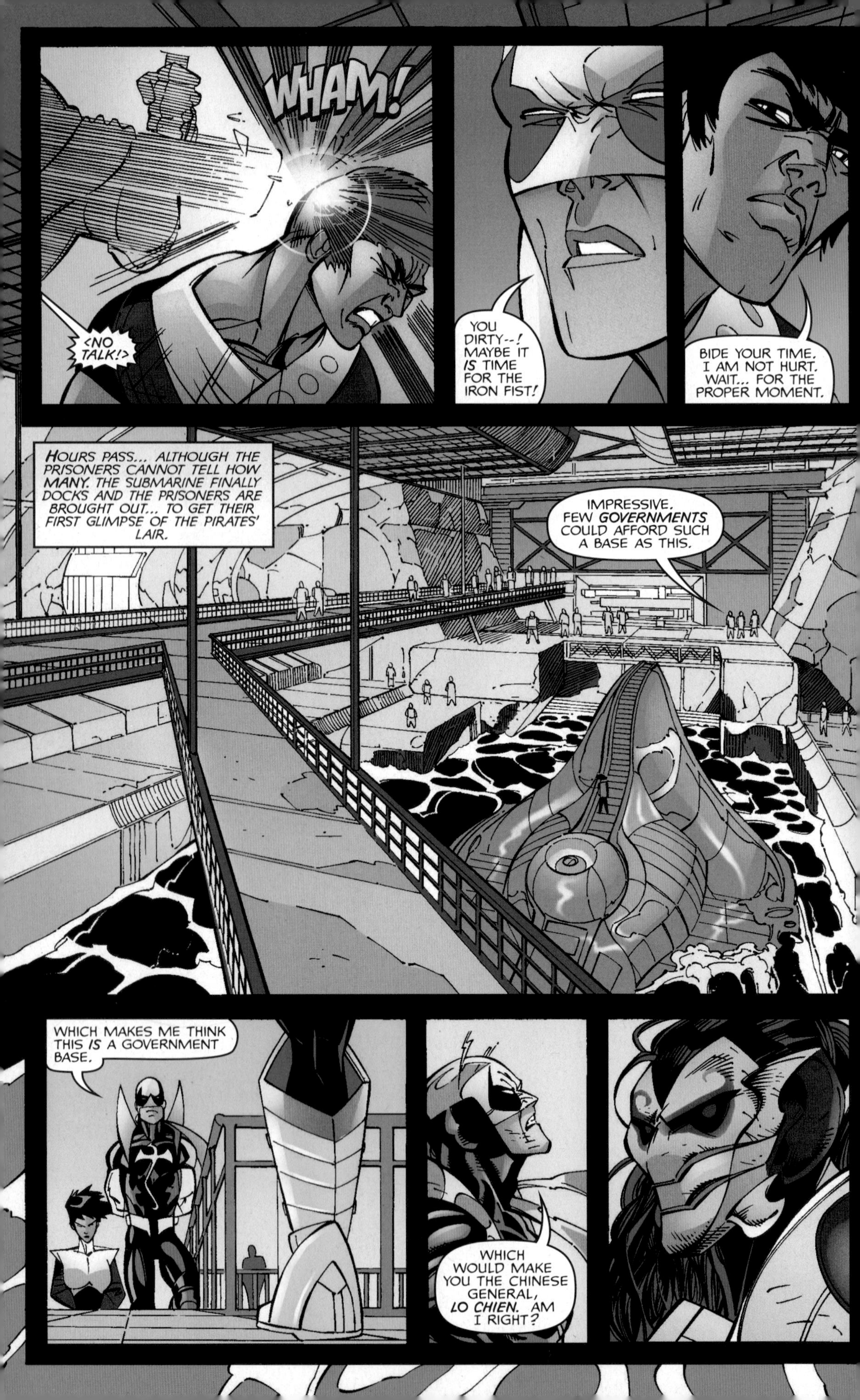

WHAM!
<NO TALK!>
YOU DIRTY--! MAYBE IT IS TIME FOR THE IRON FIST!
BIDE YOUR TIME. I AM NOT HURT. WAIT... FOR THE PROPER MOMENT.
HOURS PASS... ALTHOUGH THE PRISONERS CANNOT TELL HOW MANY. THE SUBMARINE FINALLY DOCKS AND THE PRISONERS ARE BROUGHT OUT... TO GET THEIR FIRST GLIMPSE OF THE PIRATES' LAIR.
IMPRESSIVE. FEW GOVERNMENTS COULD AFFORD SUCH A BASE AS THIS.
WHICH MAKES ME THINK THIS IS A GOVERNMENT BASE.
WHICH WOULD MAKE YOU THE CHINESE GENERAL, LO CHIEN. AM I RIGHT?

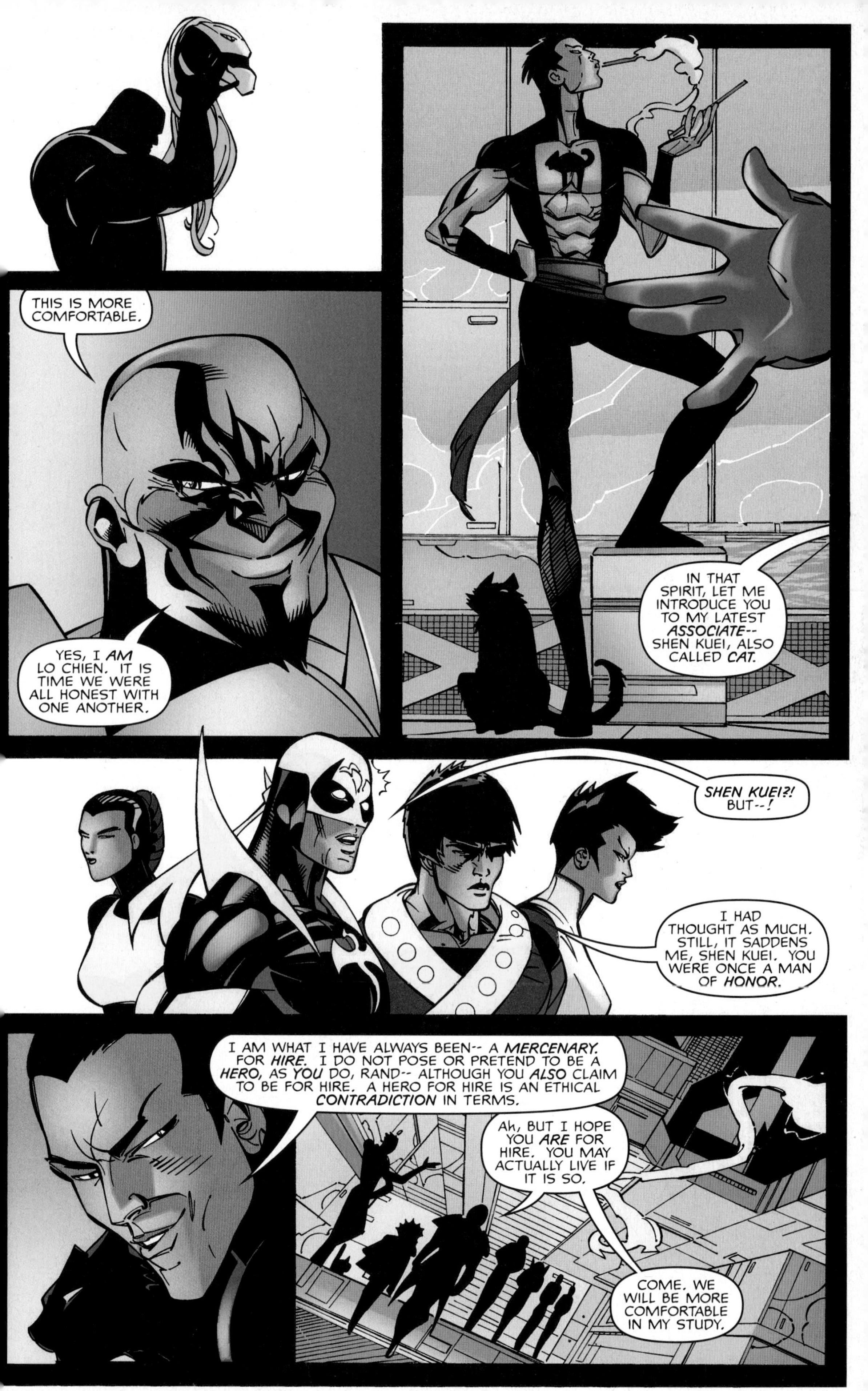
THIS IS MORE COMFORTABLE.
YES, I AM LO CHIEN. IT IS TIME WE WERE ALL HONEST WITH ONE ANOTHER.
IN THAT SPIRIT, LET ME INTRODUCE YOU TO MY LATEST ASSOCIATE-- SHEN KUEI, ALSO CALLED CAT.
SHEN KUEI?! BUT--!
I HAD THOUGHT AS MUCH. STILL, IT SADDENS ME, SHEN KUEI. YOU WERE ONCE A MAN OF HONOR.
I AM WHAT I HAVE ALWAYS BEEN-- A MERCENARY. FOR HIRE. I DO NOT POSE OR PRETEND TO BE A HERO, AS YOU DO, RAND-- ALTHOUGH YOU ALSO CLAIM TO BE FOR HIRE. A HERO FOR HIRE IS AN ETHICAL CONTRADICTION IN TERMS.
Ah, BUT I HOPE YOU ARE FOR HIRE. YOU MAY ACTUALLY LIVE IF IT IS SO.
COME. WE WILL BE MORE COMFORTABLE IN MY STUDY.

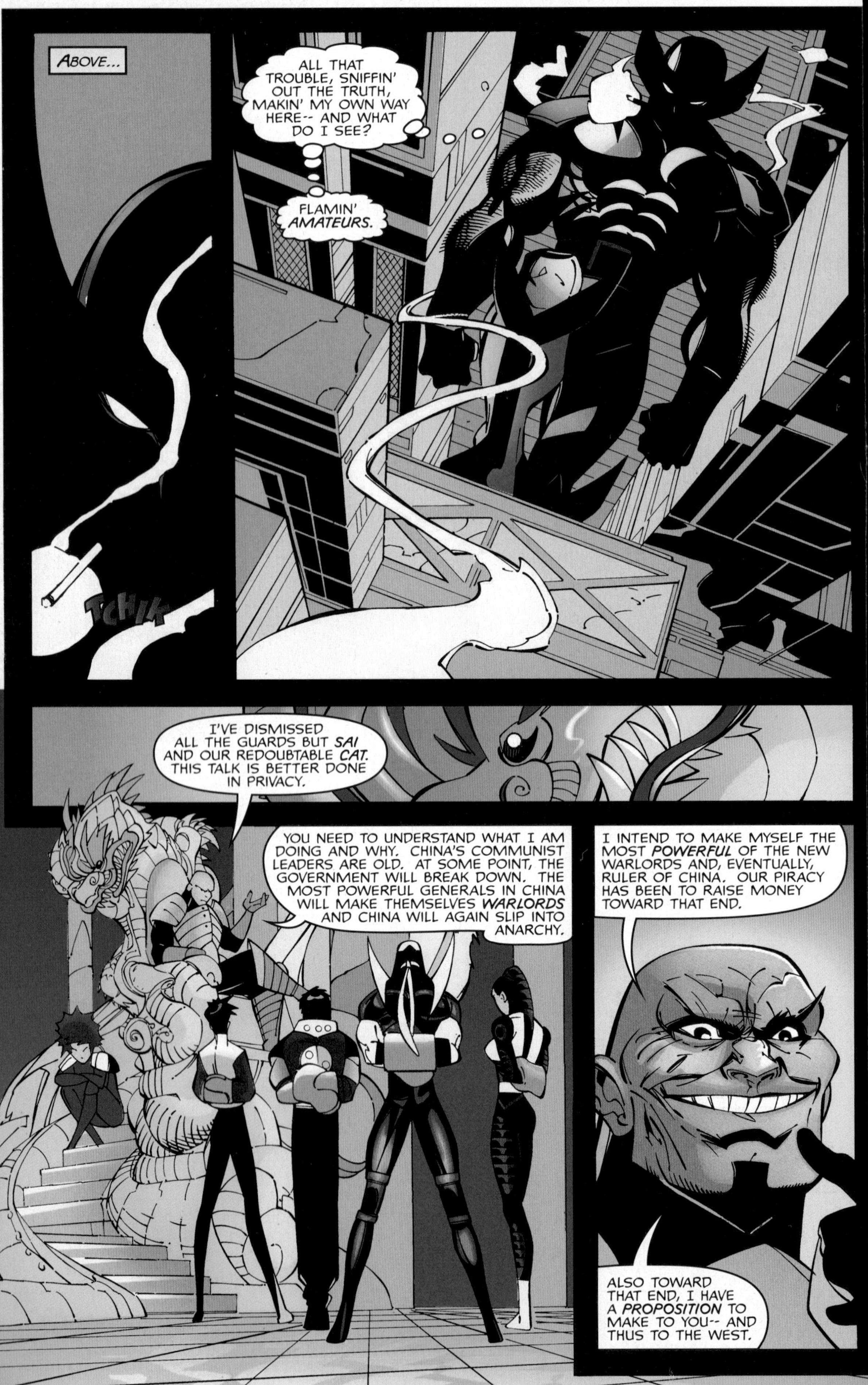
ABOVE...
ALL THAT TROUBLE, SNIFFIN' OUT THE TRUTH, MAKIN' MY OWN WAY HERE-- AND WHAT DO I SEE?
FLAMIN' AMATEURS.
TCHIK
I'VE DISMISSED ALL THE GUARDS BUT SAI AND OUR REDOUBTABLE CAT. THIS TALK IS BETTER DONE IN PRIVACY.
YOU NEED TO UNDERSTAND WHAT I AM DOING AND WHY. CHINA'S COMMUNIST LEADERS ARE OLD. AT SOME POINT, THE GOVERNMENT WILL BREAK DOWN. THE MOST POWERFUL GENERALS IN CHINA WILL MAKE THEMSELVES WARLORDS AND CHINA WILL AGAIN SLIP INTO ANARCHY.
I INTEND TO MAKE MYSELF THE MOST POWERFUL OF THE NEW WARLORDS AND, EVENTUALLY, RULER OF CHINA. OUR PIRACY HAS BEEN TO RAISE MONEY TOWARD THAT END.
ALSO TOWARD THAT END, I HAVE A PROPOSITION TO MAKE TO YOU-- AND THUS TO THE WEST.

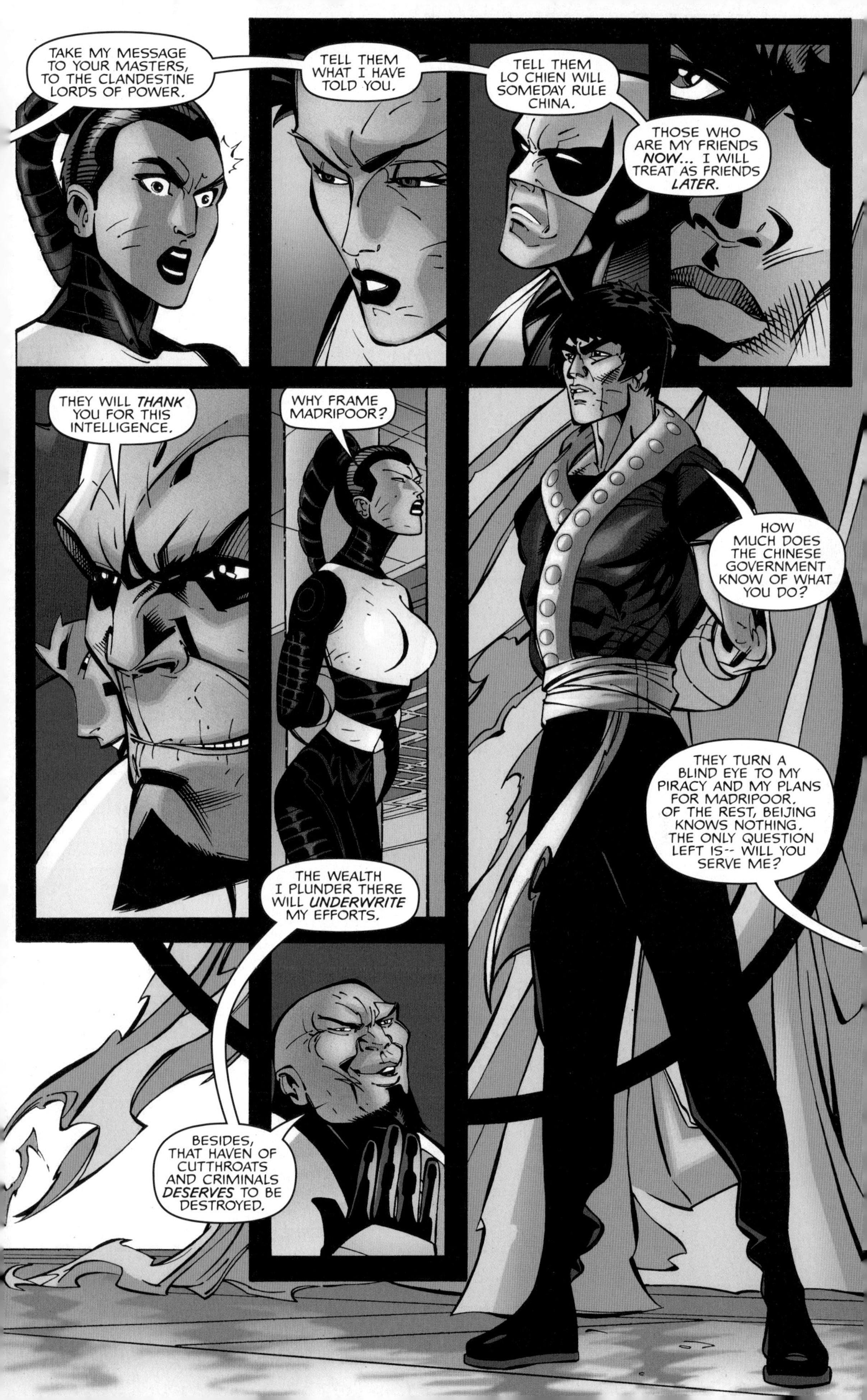
TAKE MY MESSAGE TO YOUR MASTERS, TO THE CLANDESTINE LORDS OF POWER.
TELL THEM WHAT I HAVE TOLD YOU.
TELL THEM LO CHIEN WILL SOMEDAY RULE CHINA.
THOSE WHO ARE MY FRIENDS *NOW*... I WILL TREAT AS FRIENDS *LATER*.
THEY WILL *THANK* YOU FOR THIS INTELLIGENCE.
WHY FRAME MADRIPOOR?
HOW MUCH DOES THE CHINESE GOVERNMENT KNOW OF WHAT YOU DO?
THEY TURN A BLIND EYE TO MY PIRACY AND MY PLANS FOR MADRIPOOR. OF THE REST, BEIJING KNOWS NOTHING. THE ONLY QUESTION LEFT IS-- WILL YOU SERVE ME?
THE WEALTH I PLUNDER THERE WILL *UNDERWRITE* MY EFFORTS.
BESIDES, THAT HAVEN OF CUTTHROATS AND CRIMINALS *DESERVES* TO BE DESTROYED.

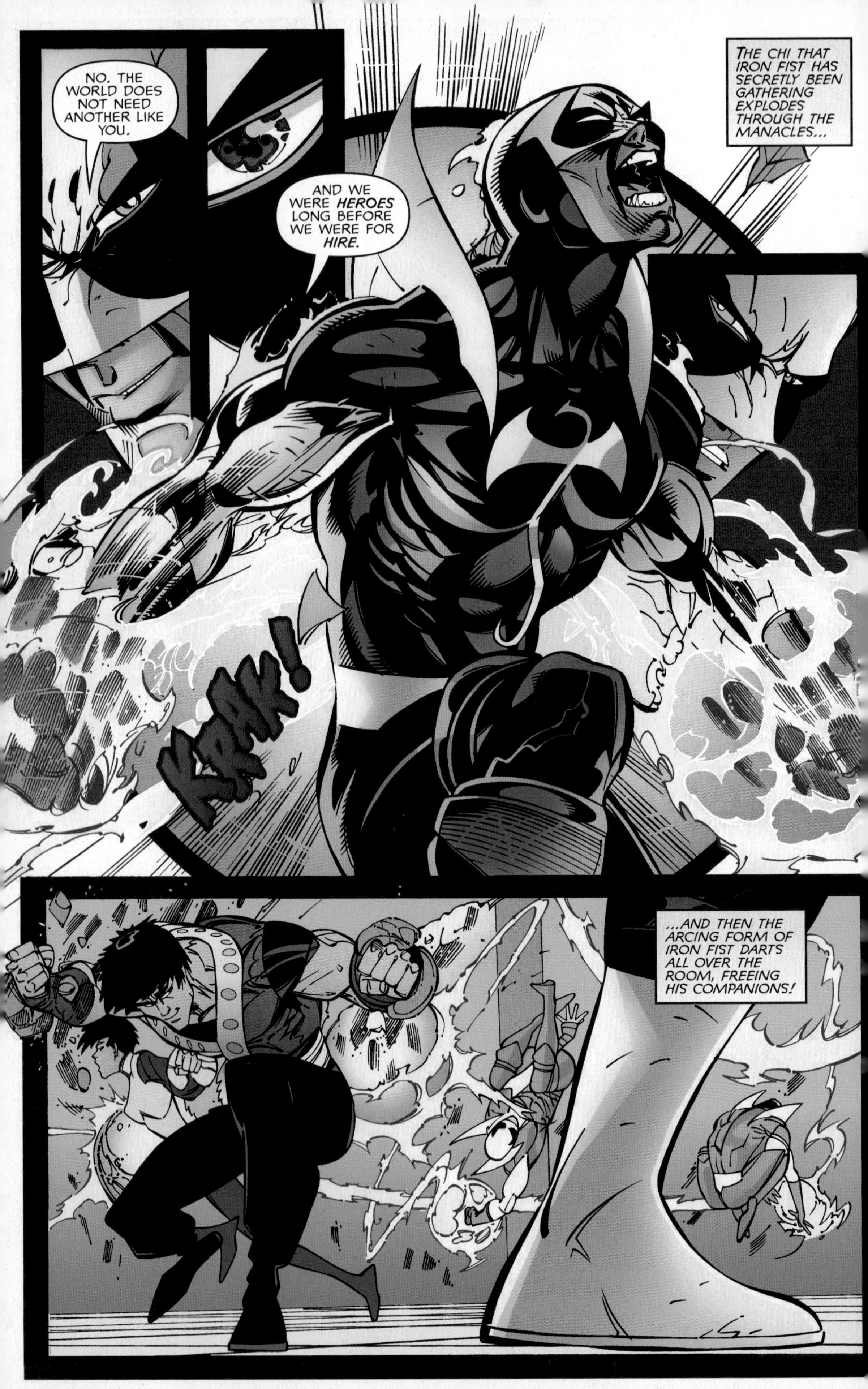
NO, THE WORLD DOES NOT NEED ANOTHER LIKE YOU.
AND WE WERE HEROES LONG BEFORE WE WERE FOR HIRE.
THE CHI THAT IRON FIST HAS SECRETLY BEEN GATHERING EXPLODES THROUGH THE MANACLES...
KRAAK!
...AND THEN THE ARCING FORM OF IRON FIST DARTS ALL OVER THE ROOM, FREEING HIS COMPANIONS!

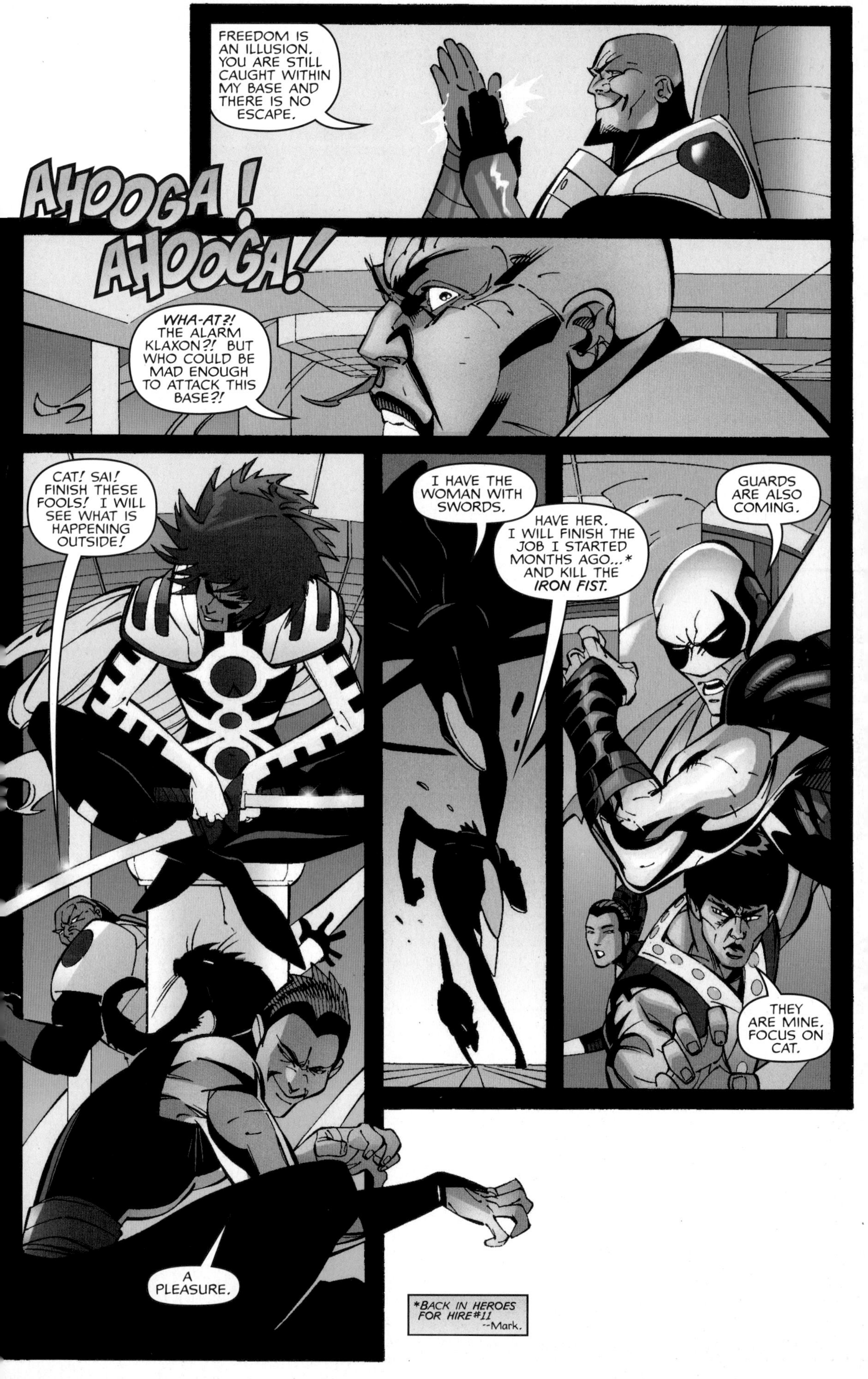
FREEDOM IS AN ILLUSION. YOU ARE STILL CAUGHT WITHIN MY BASE AND THERE IS NO ESCAPE.
AHOOGA! AHOOGA!
WHA-AT?! THE ALARM KLAXON?! BUT WHO COULD BE MAD ENOUGH TO ATTACK THIS BASE?!
CAT! SAI! FINISH THESE FOOLS! I WILL SEE WHAT IS HAPPENING OUTSIDE!
A PLEASURE.
I HAVE THE WOMAN WITH SWORDS.
HAVE HER. I WILL FINISH THE JOB I STARTED MONTHS AGO...* AND KILL THE IRON FIST.
GUARDS ARE ALSO COMING.
THEY ARE MINE. FOCUS ON CAT.
*BACK IN HEROES FOR HIRE #11 --Mark.

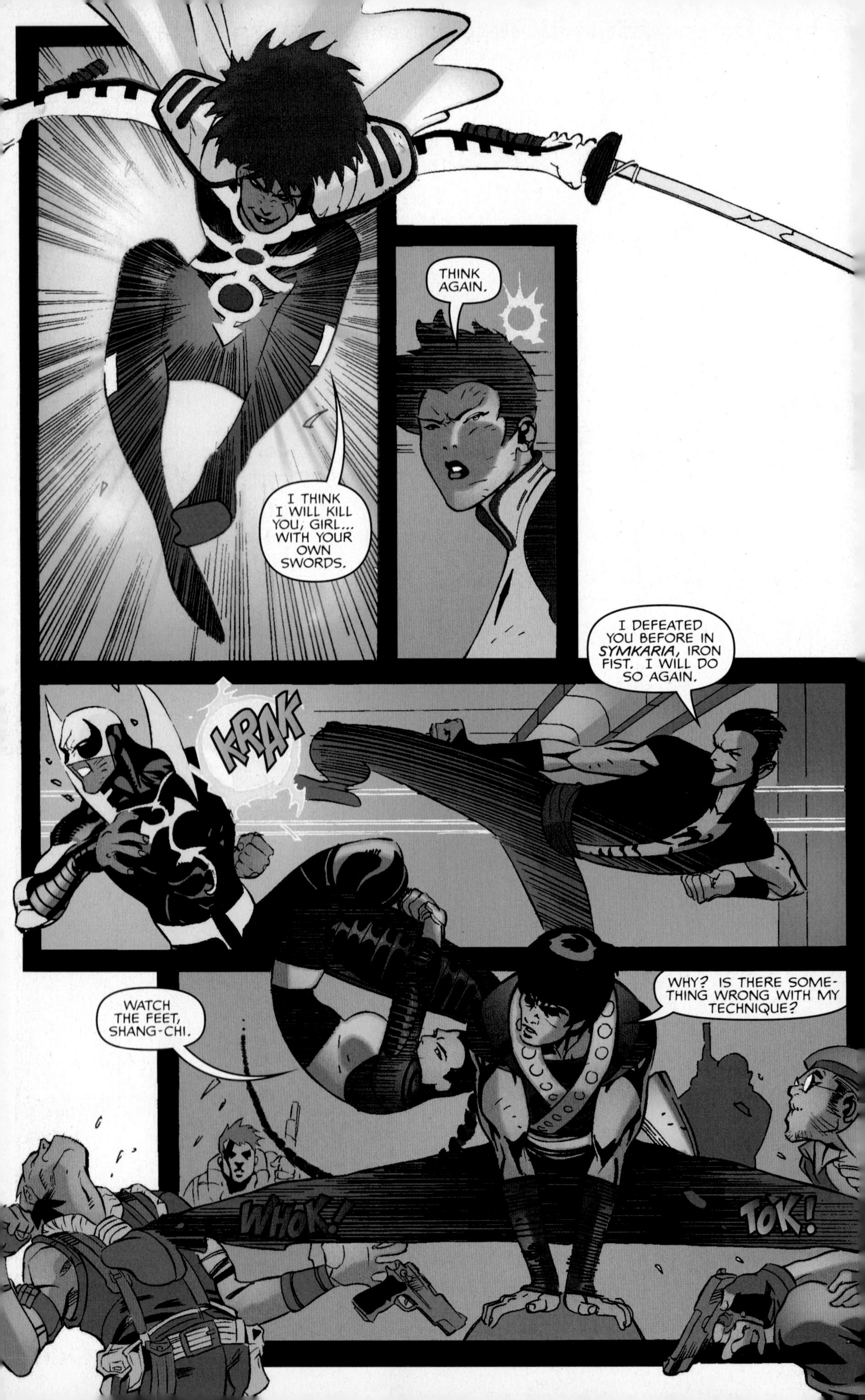
THINK AGAIN.
I THINK I WILL KILL YOU, GIRL... WITH YOUR OWN SWORDS.
I DEFEATED YOU BEFORE IN SYMKARIA, IRON FIST. I WILL DO SO AGAIN.
KRAK
WATCH THE FEET, SHANG-CHI.
WHY? IS THERE SOMETHING WRONG WITH MY TECHNIQUE?
WHOK!
TOK!

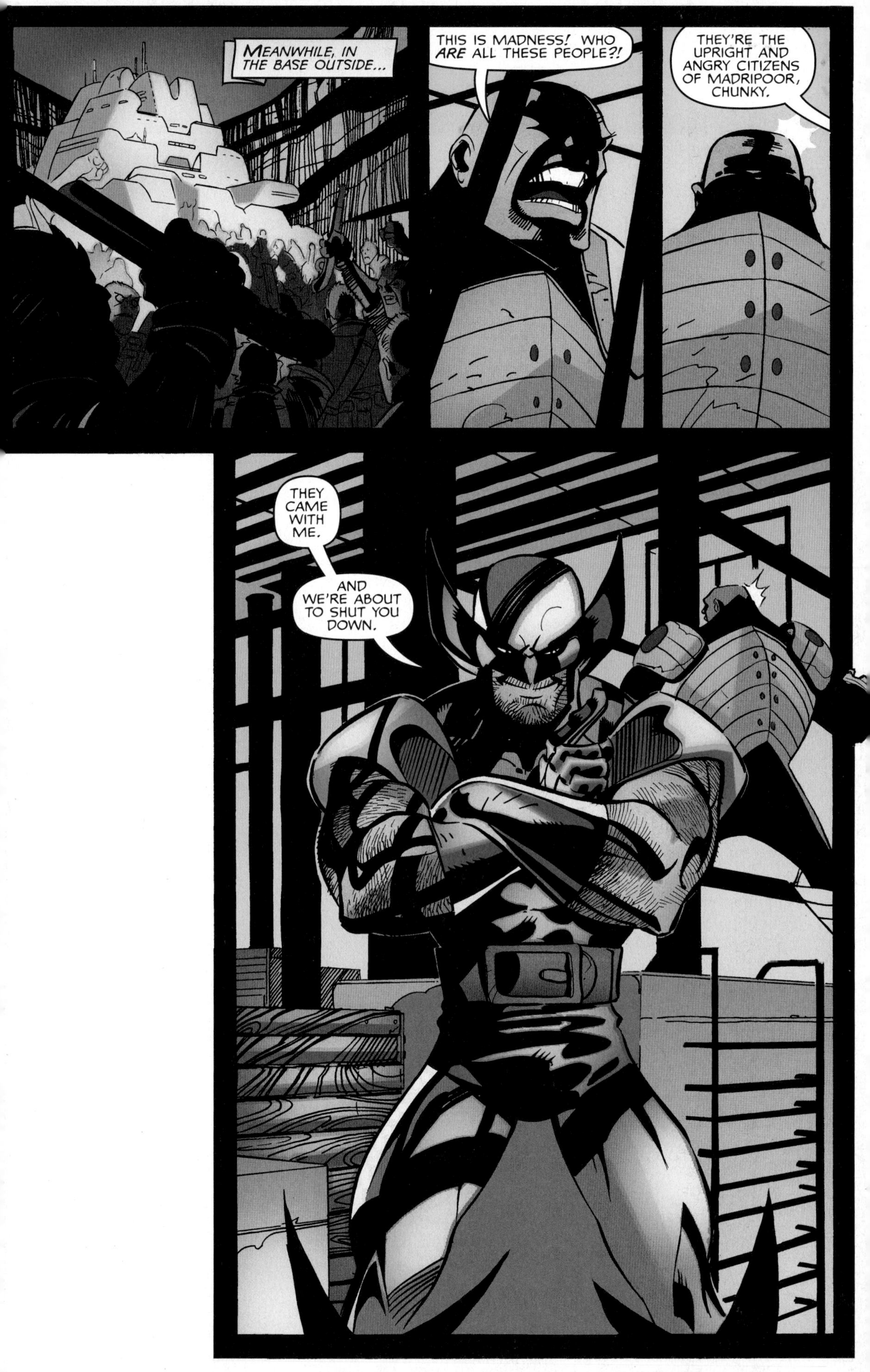
MEANWHILE, IN THE BASE OUTSIDE...
THIS IS MADNESS! WHO *ARE* ALL THESE PEOPLE?!
THEY'RE THE UPRIGHT AND ANGRY CITIZENS OF MADRIPOOR, CHUNKY.
THEY CAME WITH ME.
AND WE'RE ABOUT TO SHUT YOU DOWN.

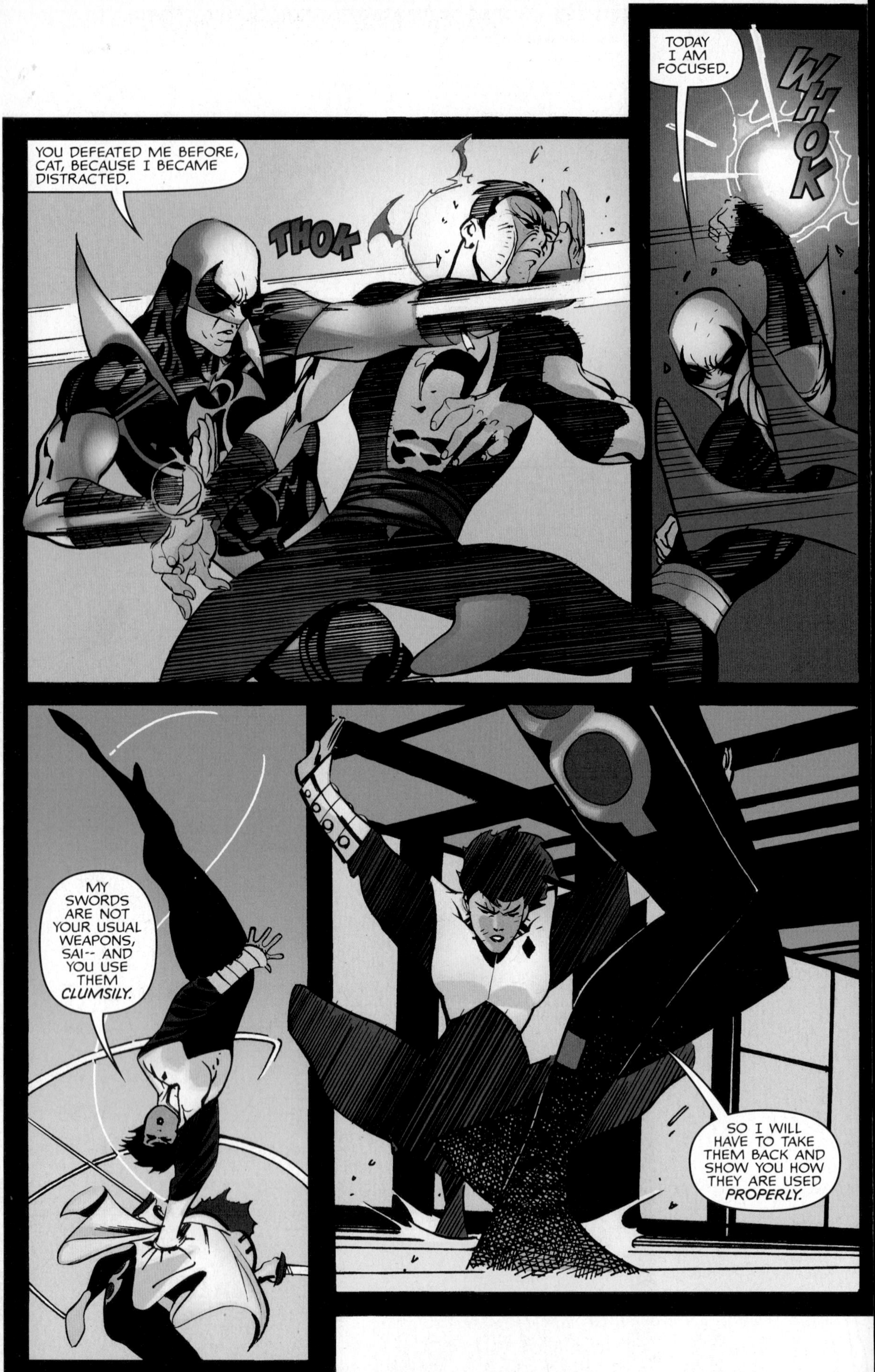
YOU DEFEATED ME BEFORE, CAT, BECAUSE I BECAME DISTRACTED.
THOK
TODAY I AM FOCUSED.
WHOK
MY SWORDS ARE NOT YOUR USUAL WEAPONS, SAI-- AND YOU USE THEM CLUMSILY.
SO I WILL HAVE TO TAKE THEM BACK AND SHOW YOU HOW THEY ARE USED PROPERLY.

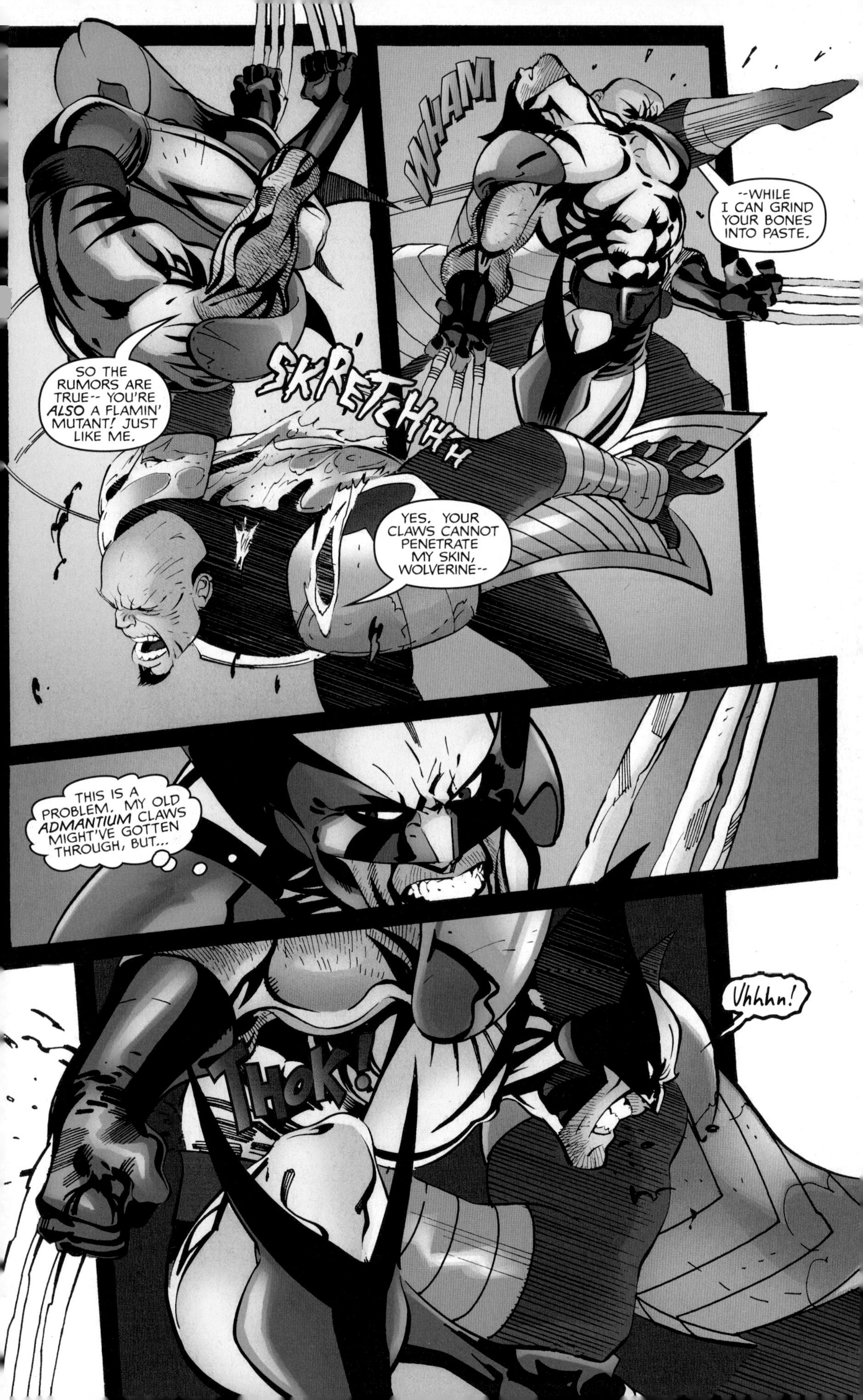
WHAM
--WHILE I CAN GRIND YOUR BONES INTO PASTE.
SO THE RUMORS ARE TRUE-- YOU'RE *ALSO* A FLAMIN' MUTANT! JUST LIKE ME.
SKRETCHHHH
YES. YOUR CLAWS CANNOT PENETRATE MY SKIN, WOLVERINE--
THIS IS A PROBLEM. MY OLD *ADMANTIUM* CLAWS MIGHT'VE GOTTEN THROUGH, BUT...
Uhhhn!
THOK!

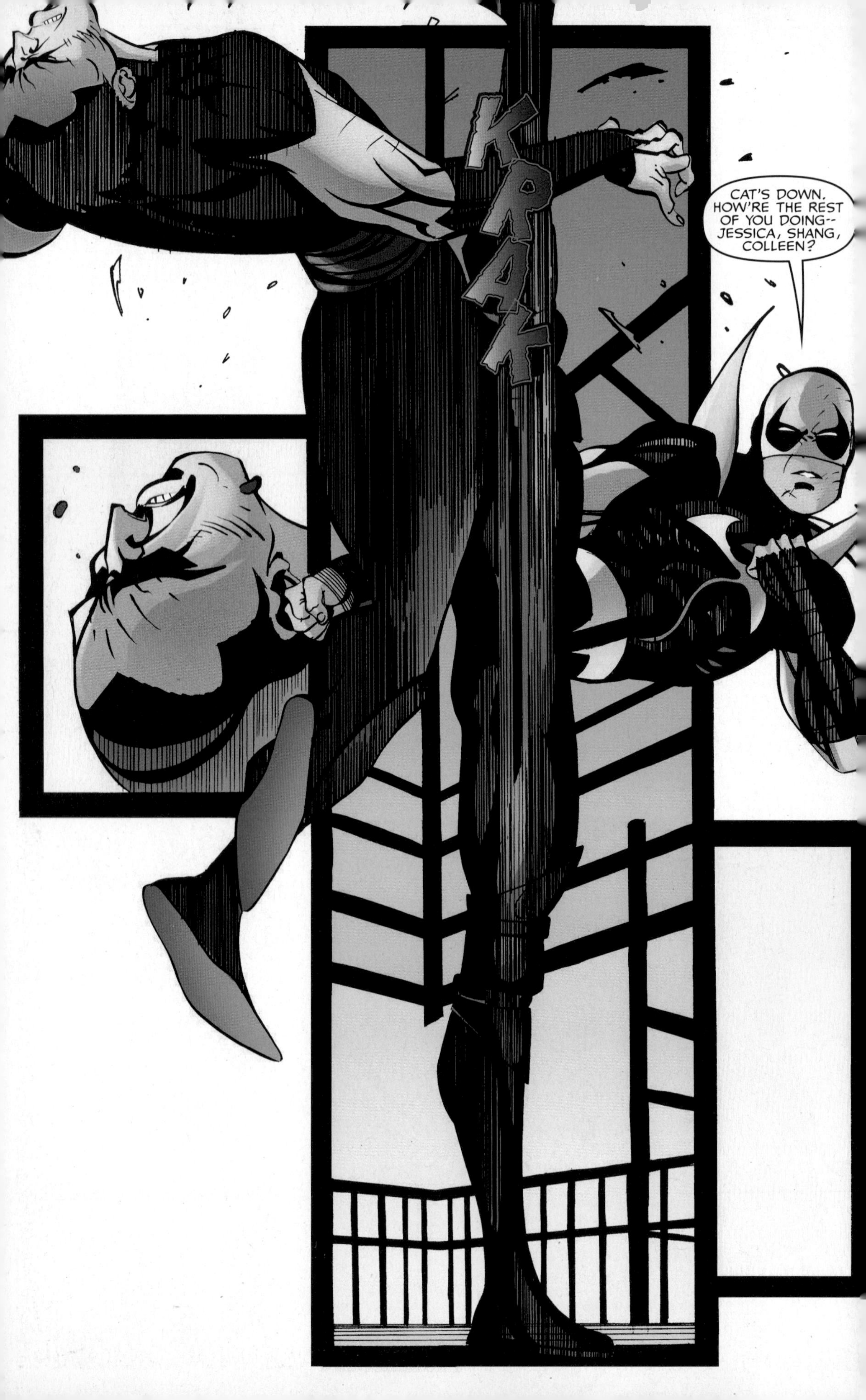
KRAAK
CAT'S DOWN. HOW'RE THE REST OF YOU DOING-- JESSICA, SHANG, COLLEEN?

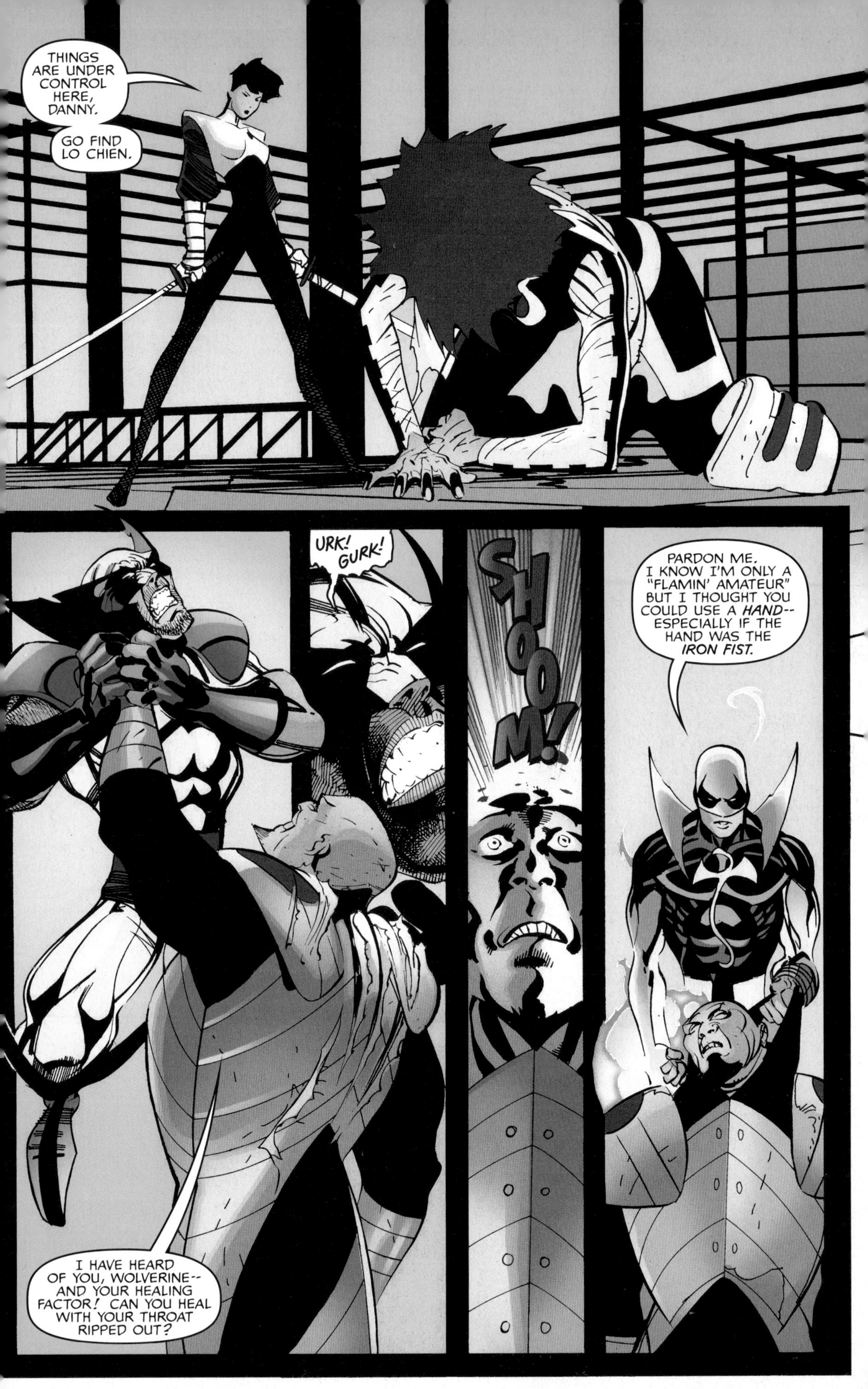
THINGS ARE UNDER CONTROL HERE, DANNY.
GO FIND LO CHIEN.
URK! GURK!
I HAVE HEARD OF YOU, WOLVERINE-- AND YOUR HEALING FACTOR! CAN YOU HEAL WITH YOUR THROAT RIPPED OUT?
SHOOOM!
PARDON ME. I KNOW I'M ONLY A "FLAMIN' AMATEUR" BUT I THOUGHT YOU COULD USE A HAND-- ESPECIALLY IF THE HAND WAS THE IRON FIST.

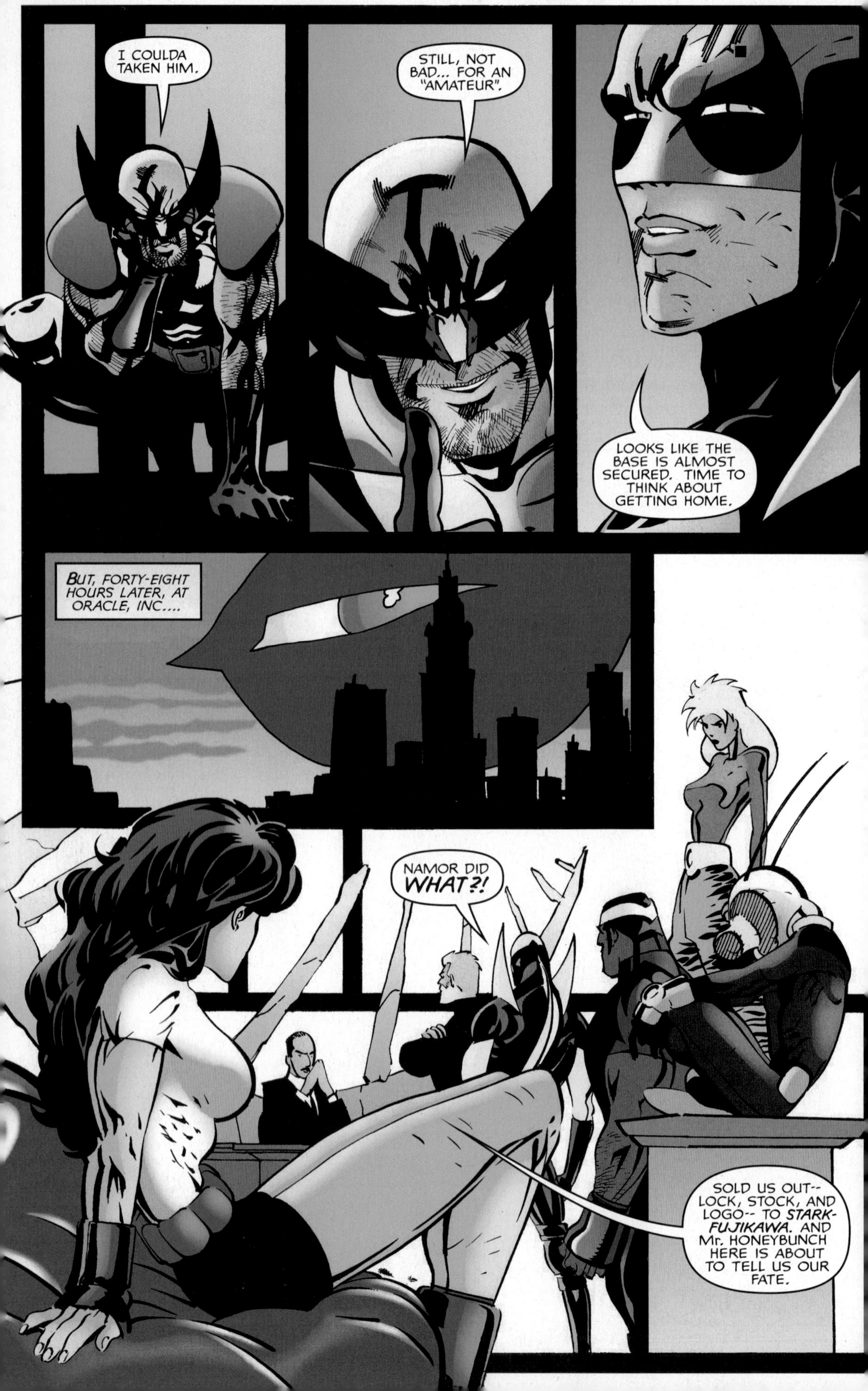
I COULDA TAKEN HIM.
STILL, NOT BAD... FOR AN "AMATEUR".
LOOKS LIKE THE BASE IS ALMOST SECURED. TIME TO THINK ABOUT GETTING HOME.
BUT, FORTY-EIGHT HOURS LATER, AT ORACLE, INC....
NAMOR DID WHAT?!
SOLD US OUT-- LOCK, STOCK, AND LOGO-- TO STARK-FUJIKAWA. AND Mr. HONEYBUNCH HERE IS ABOUT TO TELL US OUR FATE.

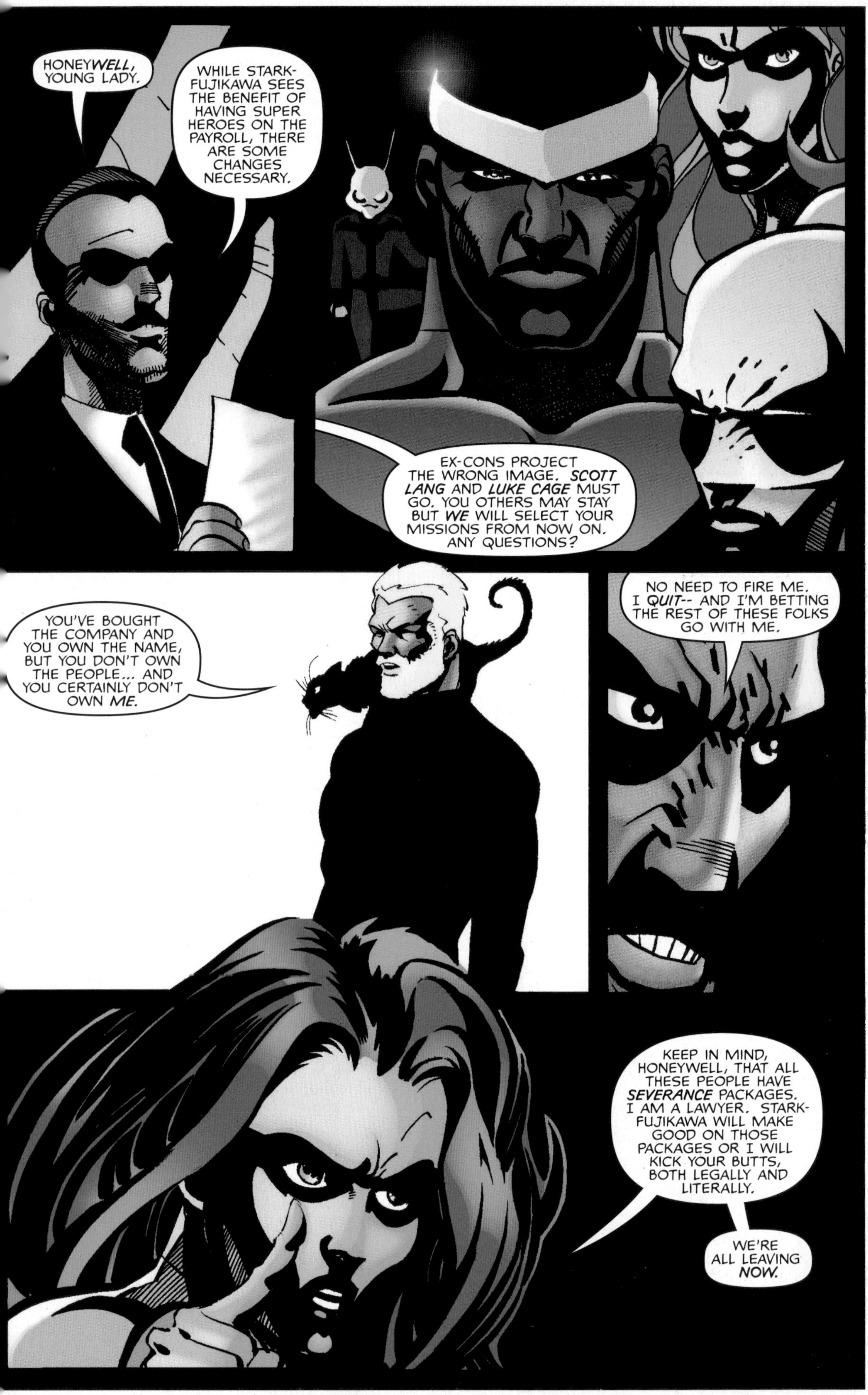
HONEYWELL, YOUNG LADY.
WHILE STARK-FUJIKAWA SEES THE BENEFIT OF HAVING SUPER HEROES ON THE PAYROLL, THERE ARE SOME CHANGES NECESSARY.
EX-CONS PROJECT THE WRONG IMAGE. SCOTT LANG AND LUKE CAGE MUST GO. YOU OTHERS MAY STAY BUT WE WILL SELECT YOUR MISSIONS FROM NOW ON. ANY QUESTIONS?
YOU'VE BOUGHT THE COMPANY AND YOU OWN THE NAME, BUT YOU DON'T OWN THE PEOPLE... AND YOU CERTAINLY DON'T OWN ME.
NO NEED TO FIRE ME. I QUIT-- AND I'M BETTING THE REST OF THESE FOLKS GO WITH ME.
KEEP IN MIND, HONEYWELL, THAT ALL THESE PEOPLE HAVE SEVERANCE PACKAGES. I AM A LAWYER. STARK-FUJIKAWA WILL MAKE GOOD ON THOSE PACKAGES OR I WILL KICK YOUR BUTTS, BOTH LEGALLY AND LITERALLY.
WE'RE ALL LEAVING NOW.

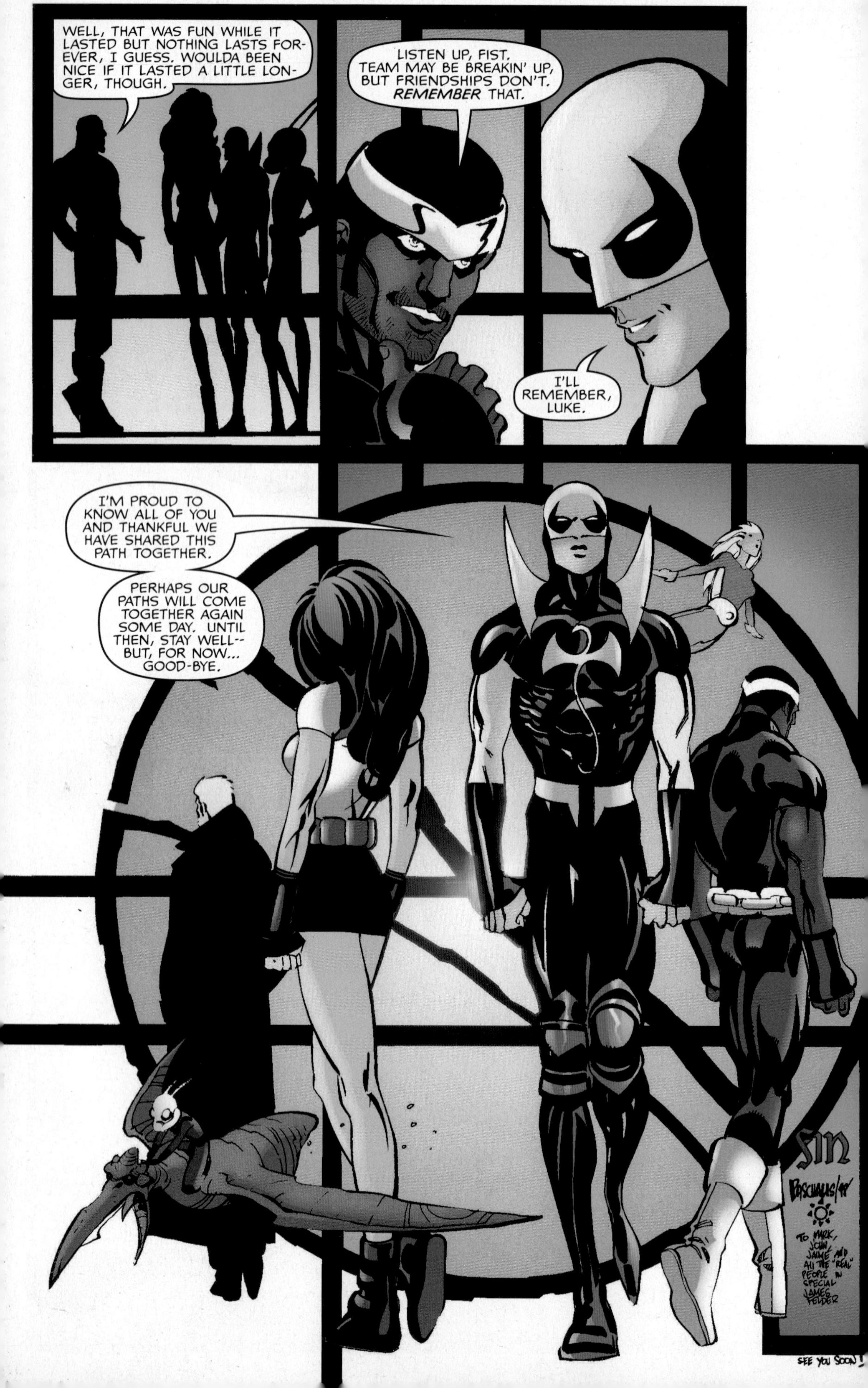
WELL, THAT WAS FUN WHILE IT LASTED BUT NOTHING LASTS FOREVER, I GUESS. WOULDA BEEN NICE IF IT LASTED A LITTLE LONGER, THOUGH.
LISTEN UP, FIST. TEAM MAY BE BREAKIN' UP, BUT FRIENDSHIPS DON'T. *REMEMBER* THAT.
I'LL REMEMBER, LUKE.
I'M PROUD TO KNOW ALL OF YOU AND THANKFUL WE HAVE SHARED THIS PATH TOGETHER.
PERHAPS OUR PATHS WILL COME TOGETHER AGAIN SOME DAY. UNTIL THEN, STAY WELL-- BUT, FOR NOW... GOOD-BYE.
FIN
TO MARK, JOHN, JAIME AND ALL THE "REAL" PEOPLE IN SPECIAL JAMES FELDER
SEE YOU SOON!

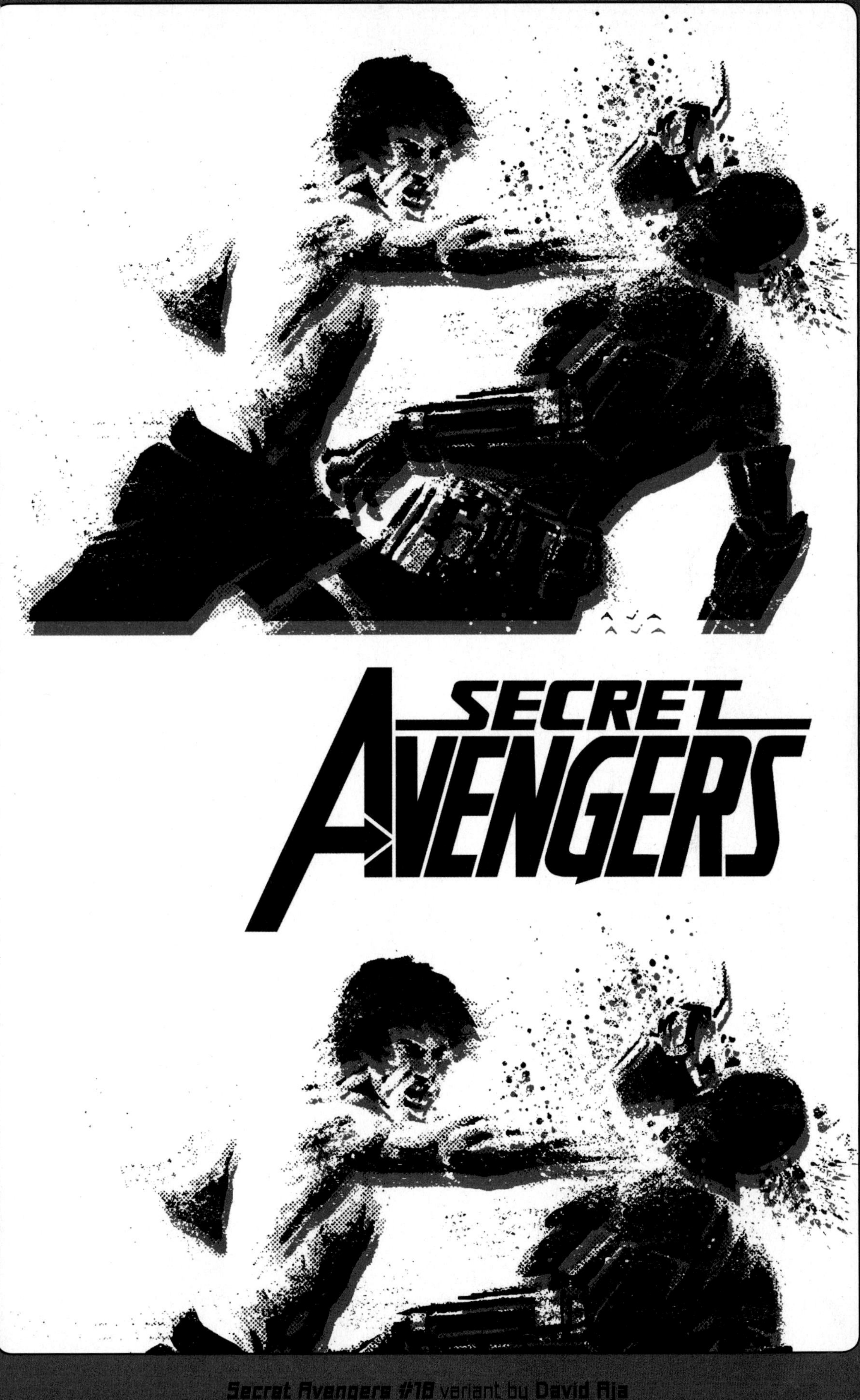
AJA
SECRET
AVENGERS

Secret Avengers #18 variant by **David Aja**

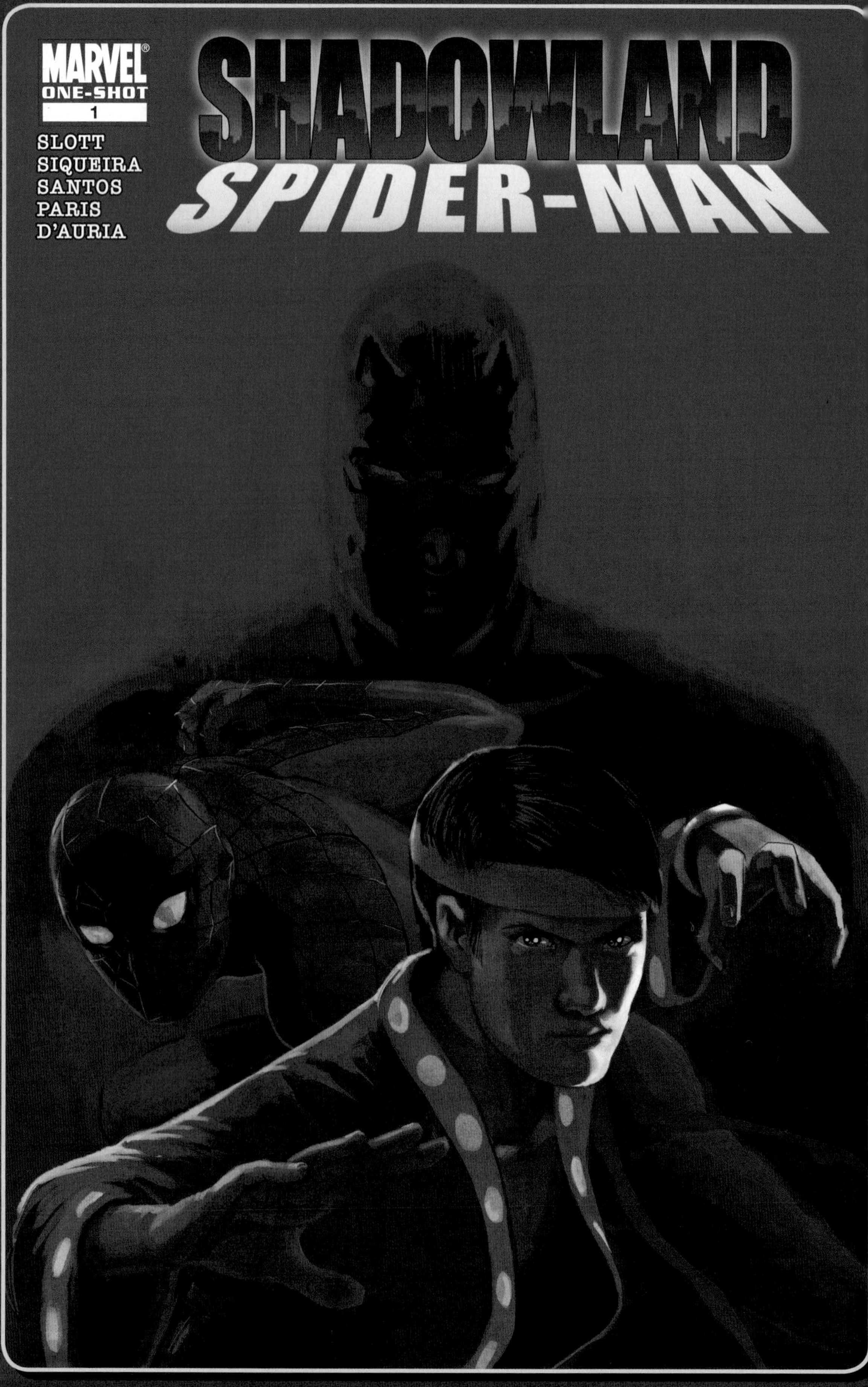
MARVEL
ONE-SHOT
1
SLOTT
SIQUEIRA
SANTOS
PARIS
D'AURIA
SHADOWLAND
SPIDER-MAN

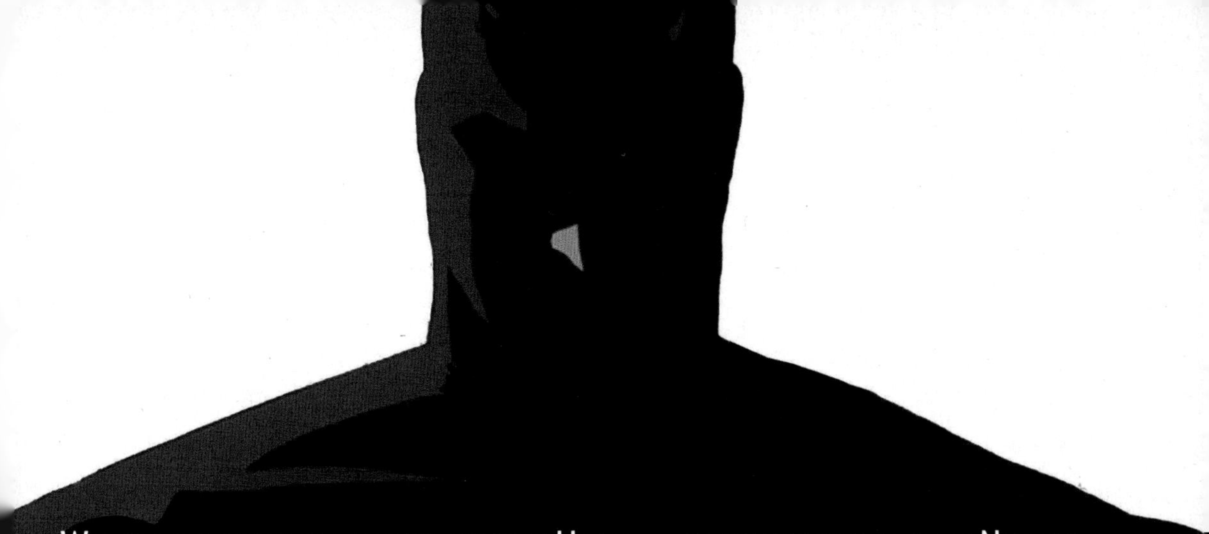

When the ancient order of the Hand — an organization of Ninjas, thieves and assassins — sought Daredevil out to become their new leader, he plotted to use the organization as a force for good. When his archenemy Bullseye destroyed a city block — and killed 107 people in the process — Murdock was pushed over the edge. He killed Bullseye, and on the site of the decimated city block, built his fortress, Shadowland.

A handful of his oldest friends, including the high-flying super hero known as the Amazing Spider-Man and the noble Shang Chi, master of Kung-Fu, attempted to appeal to whatever humanity might remain in the Man Without Fear. they discovered that the Daredevil they knew was possessed by something evil, powerful and unflinching — something even the superhuman Spider-Man wasn't tough enough to fight. He is not their ally anymore, and it may take drastic measures to stop him.

In recent months, Spider-Man has fought Mr. Negative, crime lord of Chinatown. Negative has sought to take control of the city's criminal underworld — a plan that Daredevil's new power base has greatly impeded...

SHADOWLAND
SPIDER-MAN

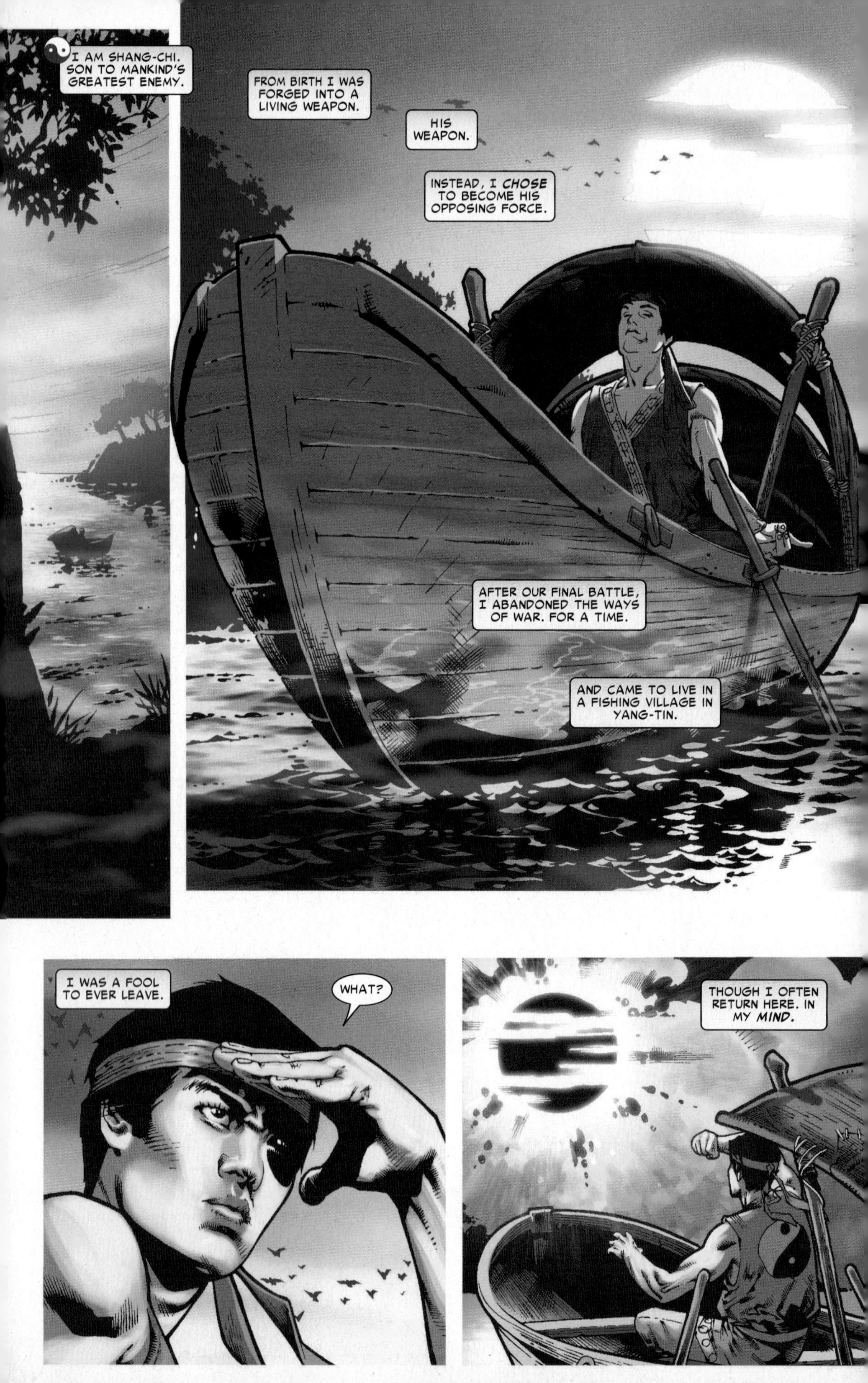
I AM SHANG-CHI. SON TO MANKIND'S GREATEST ENEMY.
FROM BIRTH I WAS FORGED INTO A LIVING WEAPON.
HIS WEAPON.
INSTEAD, I *CHOSE* TO BECOME HIS OPPOSING FORCE.
AFTER OUR FINAL BATTLE, I ABANDONED THE WAYS OF WAR. FOR A TIME.
AND CAME TO LIVE IN A FISHING VILLAGE IN YANG-TIN.
I WAS A FOOL TO EVER LEAVE.
WHAT?
THOUGH I OFTEN RETURN HERE. IN MY ***MIND.***

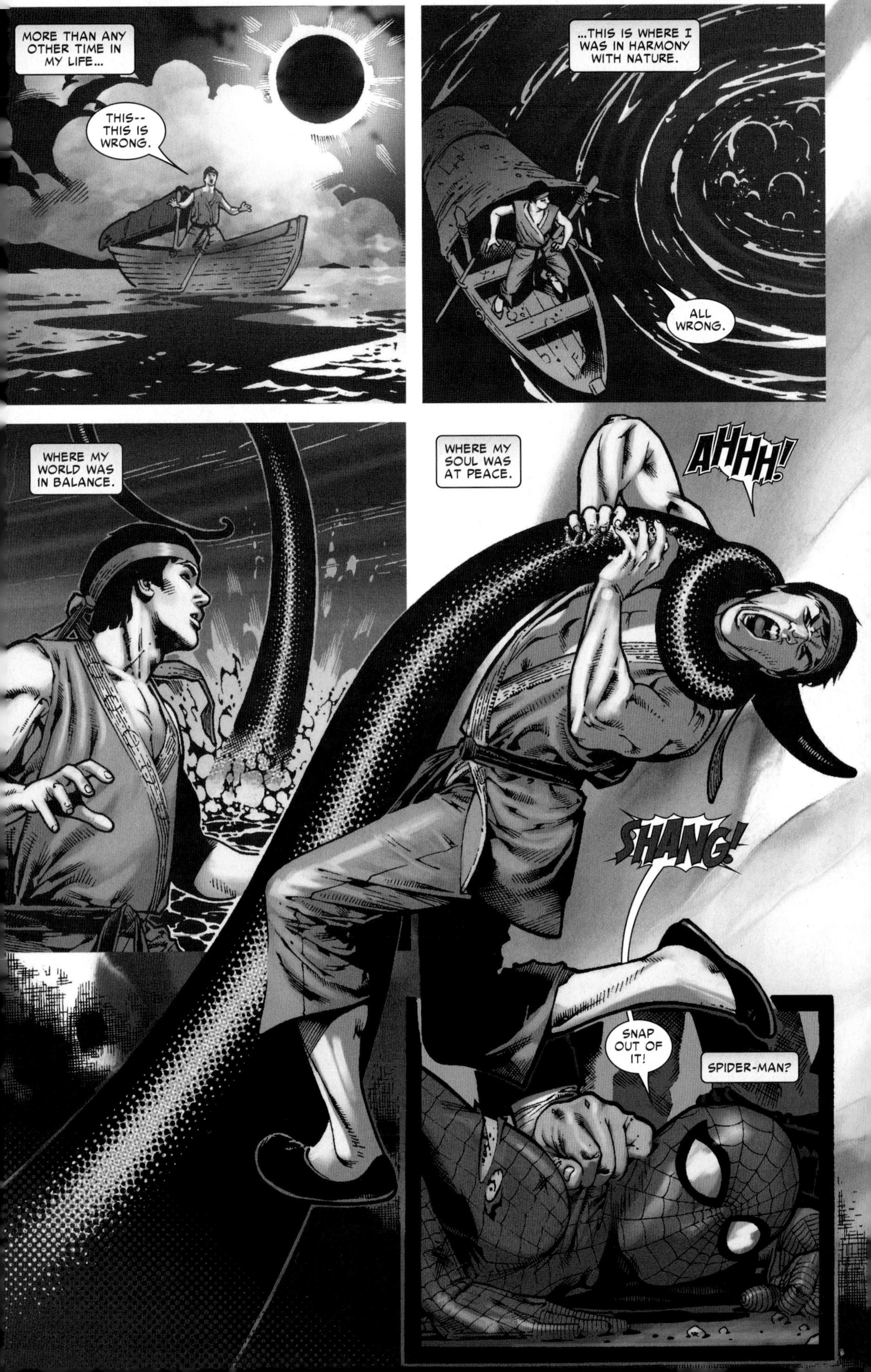
MORE THAN ANY OTHER TIME IN MY LIFE...
THIS-- THIS IS WRONG.
...THIS IS WHERE I WAS IN HARMONY WITH NATURE.
ALL WRONG.
WHERE MY WORLD WAS IN BALANCE.
WHERE MY SOUL WAS AT PEACE.
AHHH!
SHANG!
SNAP OUT OF IT!
SPIDER-MAN?

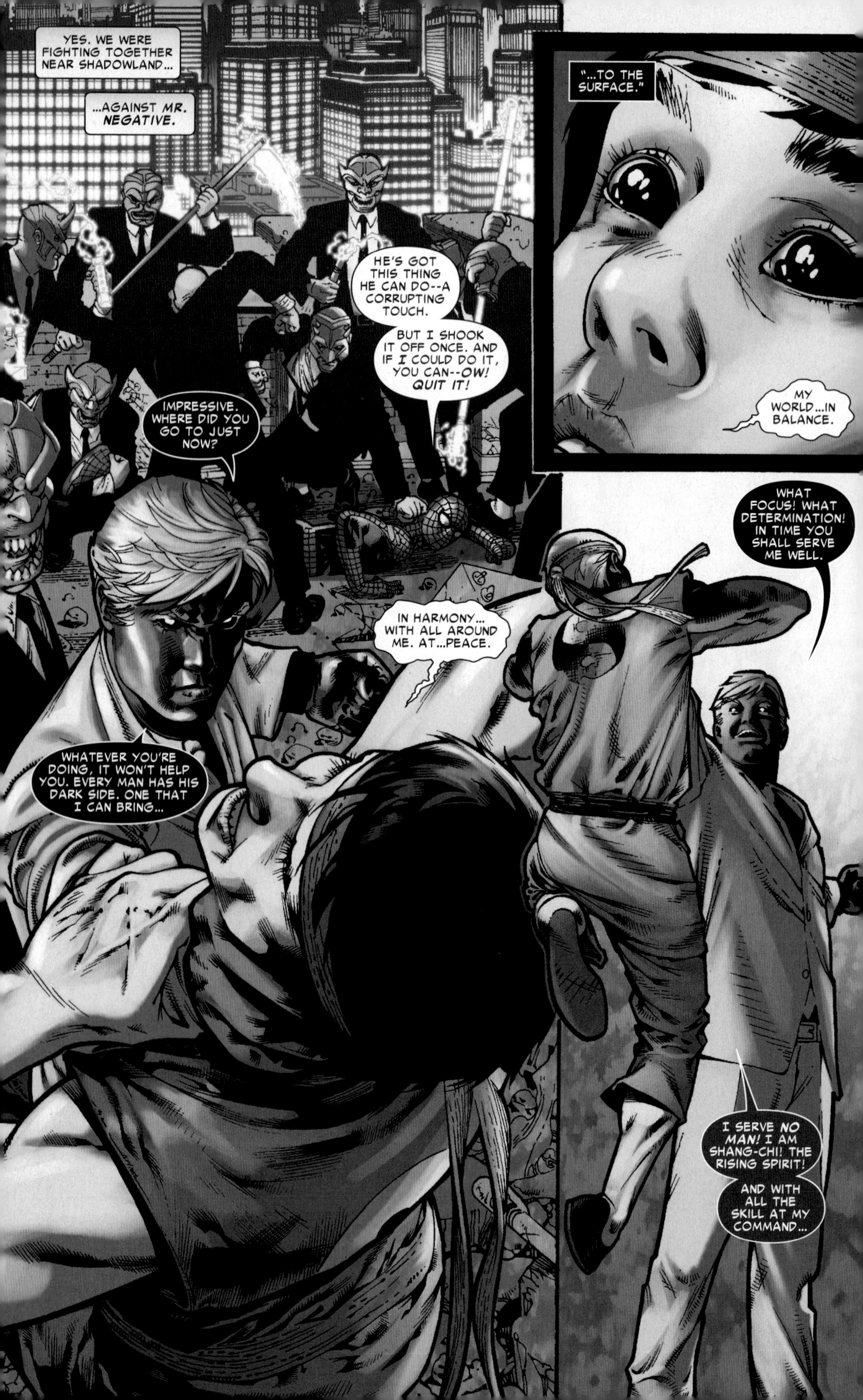
YES. WE WERE FIGHTING TOGETHER NEAR SHADOWLAND...
...AGAINST MR. NEGATIVE.
HE'S GOT THIS THING HE CAN DO--A CORRUPTING TOUCH.
BUT I SHOOK IT OFF ONCE. AND IF I COULD DO IT, YOU CAN--OW! QUIT IT!
IMPRESSIVE. WHERE DID YOU GO TO JUST NOW?
IN HARMONY... WITH ALL AROUND ME. AT...PEACE.
WHATEVER YOU'RE DOING, IT WON'T HELP YOU. EVERY MAN HAS HIS DARK SIDE. ONE THAT I CAN BRING...
"...TO THE SURFACE."
MY WORLD...IN BALANCE.
WHAT FOCUS! WHAT DETERMINATION! IN TIME YOU SHALL SERVE ME WELL.
I SERVE NO MAN! I AM SHANG-CHI! THE RISING SPIRIT!
AND WITH ALL THE SKILL AT MY COMMAND...

MBALANCED

DAN SLOTT WRITER | PAULO SIQUEIRA PENCILS | SANTOS, PARIS & SIQUEIRA INKS

FABIO D'AURIA COLORS | VC'S JOE SABINO LETTERS | STEPHANIE HANS COVER

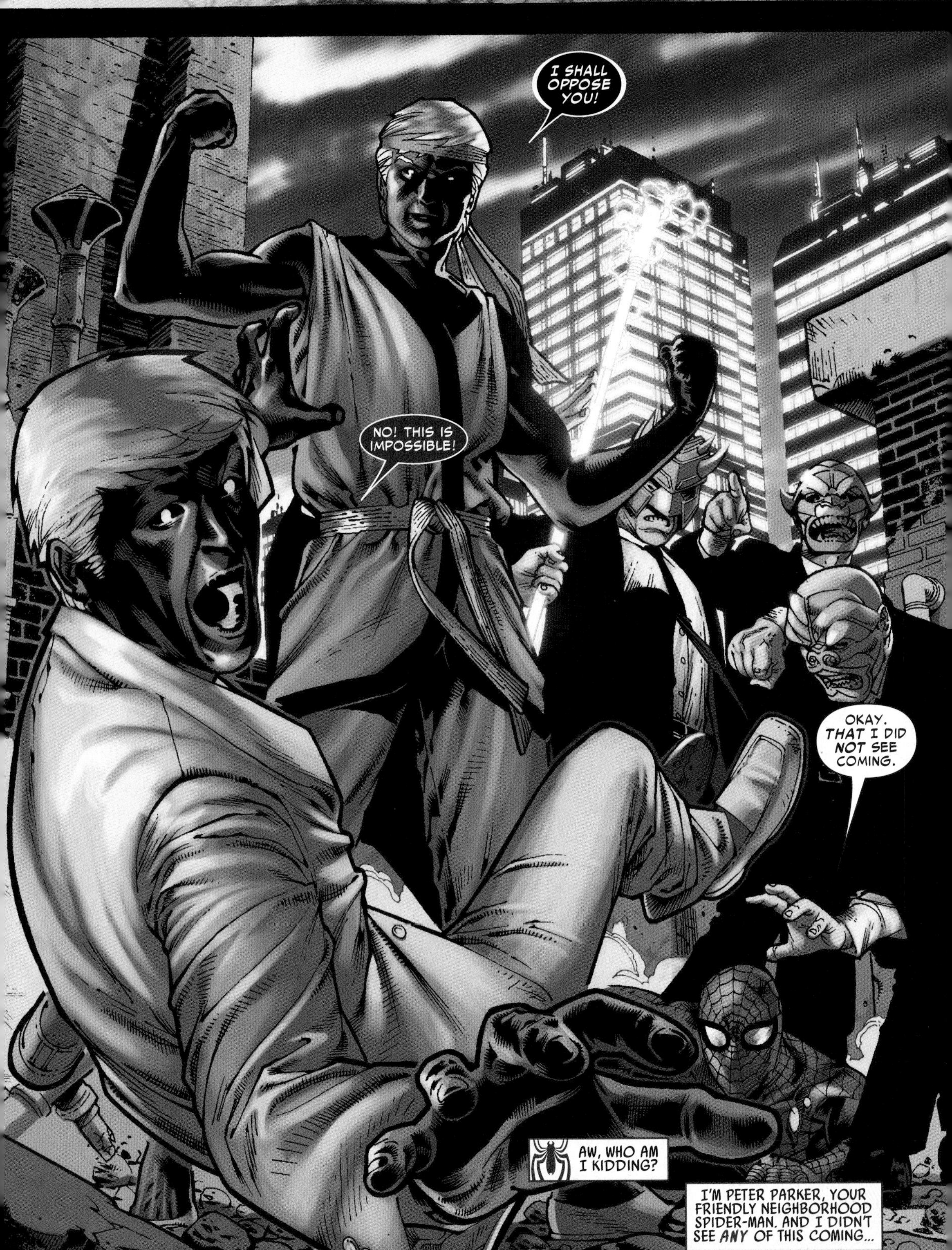
I SHALL OPPOSE YOU!
NO! THIS IS IMPOSSIBLE!
OKAY. *THAT* I DID *NOT* SEE COMING.
AW, WHO AM I KIDDING?
I'M PETER PARKER, YOUR FRIENDLY NEIGHBORHOOD SPIDER-MAN. AND I DIDN'T SEE *ANY* OF THIS COMING...

OM BRENNAN ASST. EDITOR | STEPHEN WACKER EDITOR | TOM BREVOORT EXEC. EDITOR | JOE QUESADA EDITOR IN CHIEF | DAN BUCKLEY PUBLISHER | ALAN FINE EXEC. PRODUCER

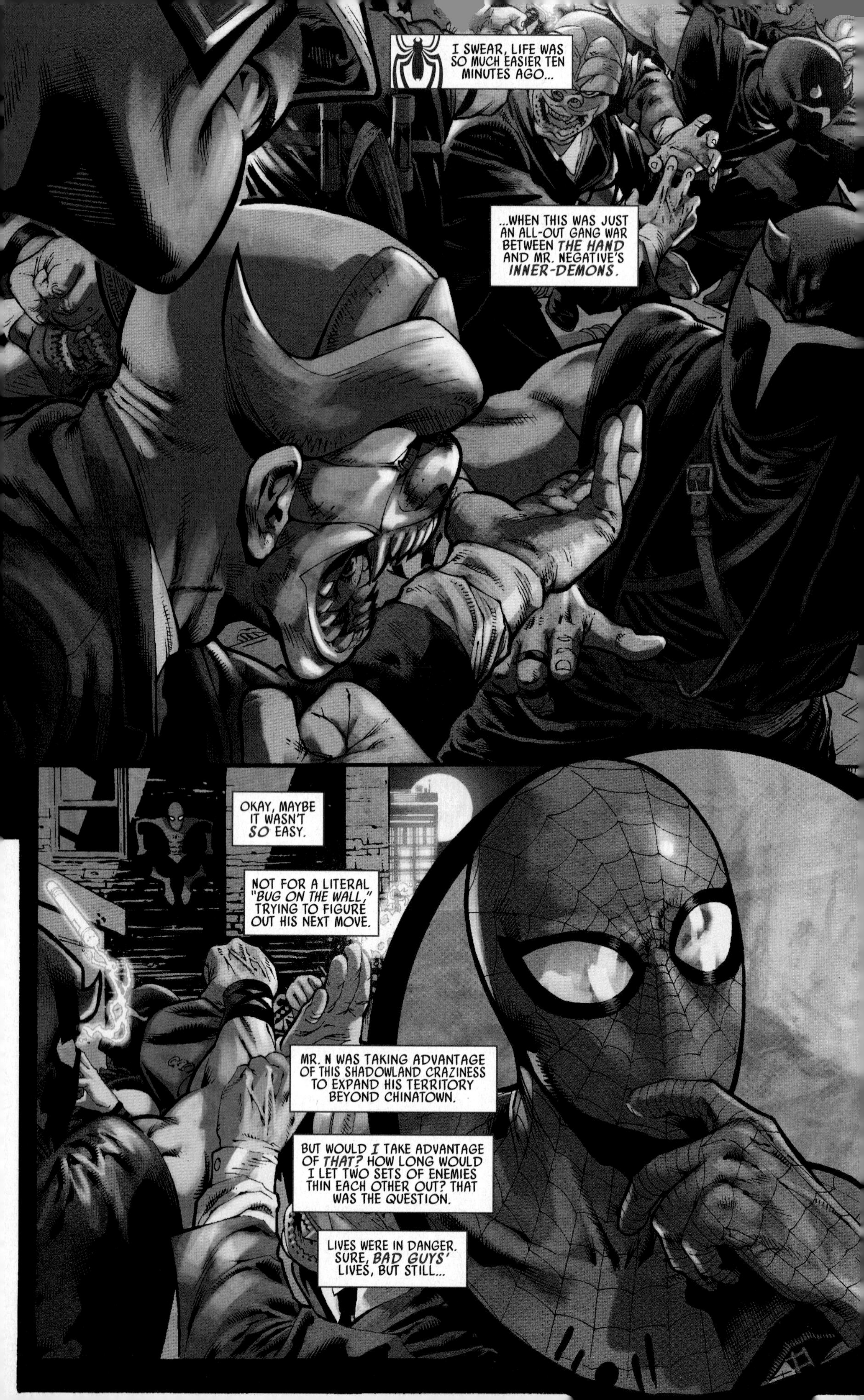
I SWEAR, LIFE WAS SO MUCH EASIER TEN MINUTES AGO...
...WHEN THIS WAS JUST AN ALL-OUT GANG WAR BETWEEN THE HAND AND MR. NEGATIVE'S INNER-DEMONS.
OKAY, MAYBE IT WASN'T SO EASY.
NOT FOR A LITERAL "BUG ON THE WALL," TRYING TO FIGURE OUT HIS NEXT MOVE.
MR. N WAS TAKING ADVANTAGE OF THIS SHADOWLAND CRAZINESS TO EXPAND HIS TERRITORY BEYOND CHINATOWN.
BUT WOULD I TAKE ADVANTAGE OF THAT? HOW LONG WOULD I LET TWO SETS OF ENEMIES THIN EACH OTHER OUT? THAT WAS THE QUESTION.
LIVES WERE IN DANGER. SURE, BAD GUYS' LIVES, BUT STILL...

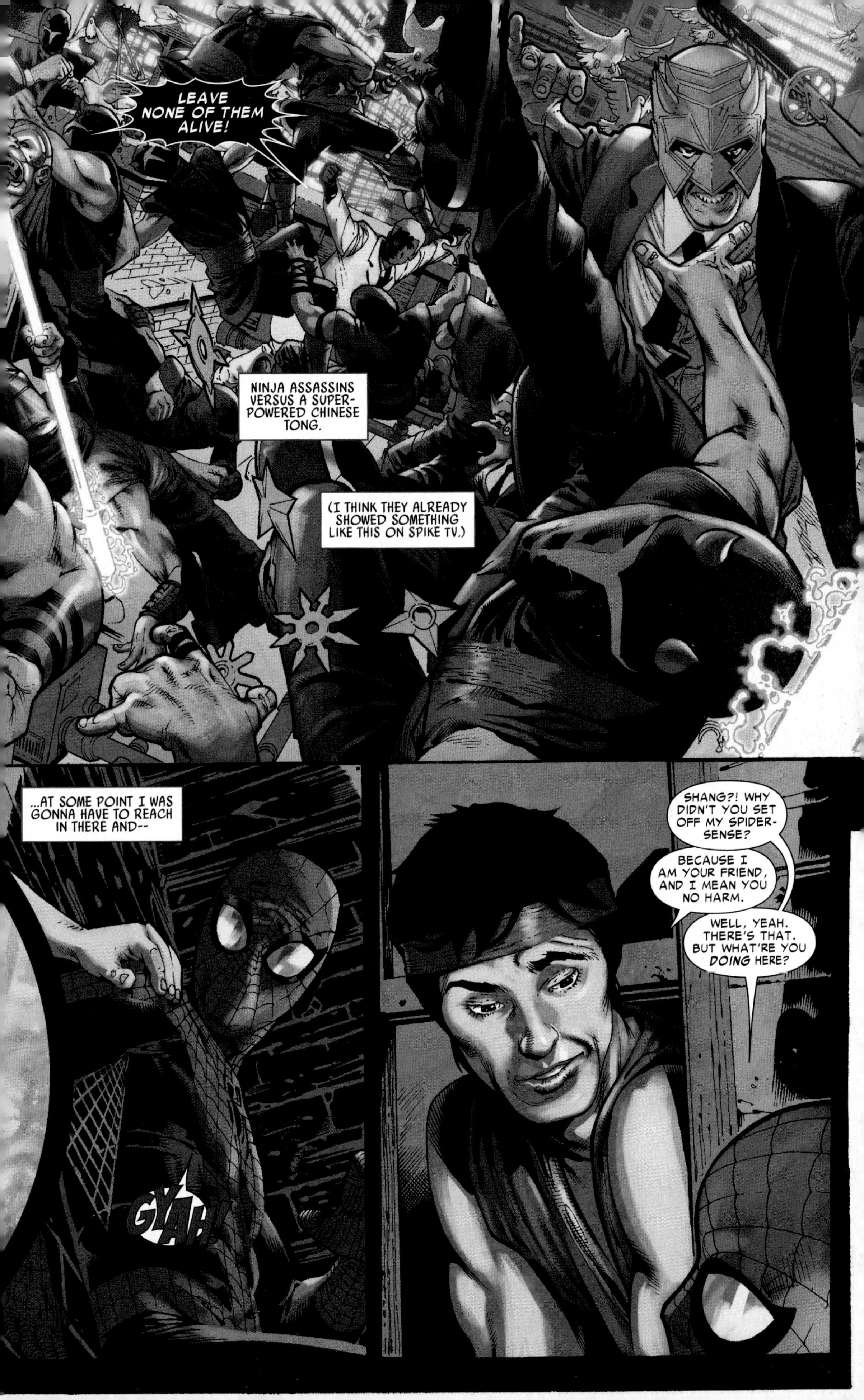
LEAVE NONE OF THEM ALIVE!
NINJA ASSASSINS VERSUS A SUPER-POWERED CHINESE TONG.
(I THINK THEY ALREADY SHOWED SOMETHING LIKE THIS ON SPIKE TV.)
...AT SOME POINT I WAS GONNA HAVE TO REACH IN THERE AND--
GYAH!
SHANG?! WHY DIDN'T YOU SET OFF MY SPIDER-SENSE?
BECAUSE I AM YOUR FRIEND, AND I MEAN YOU NO HARM.
WELL, YEAH. THERE'S THAT. BUT WHAT'RE YOU *DOING* HERE?

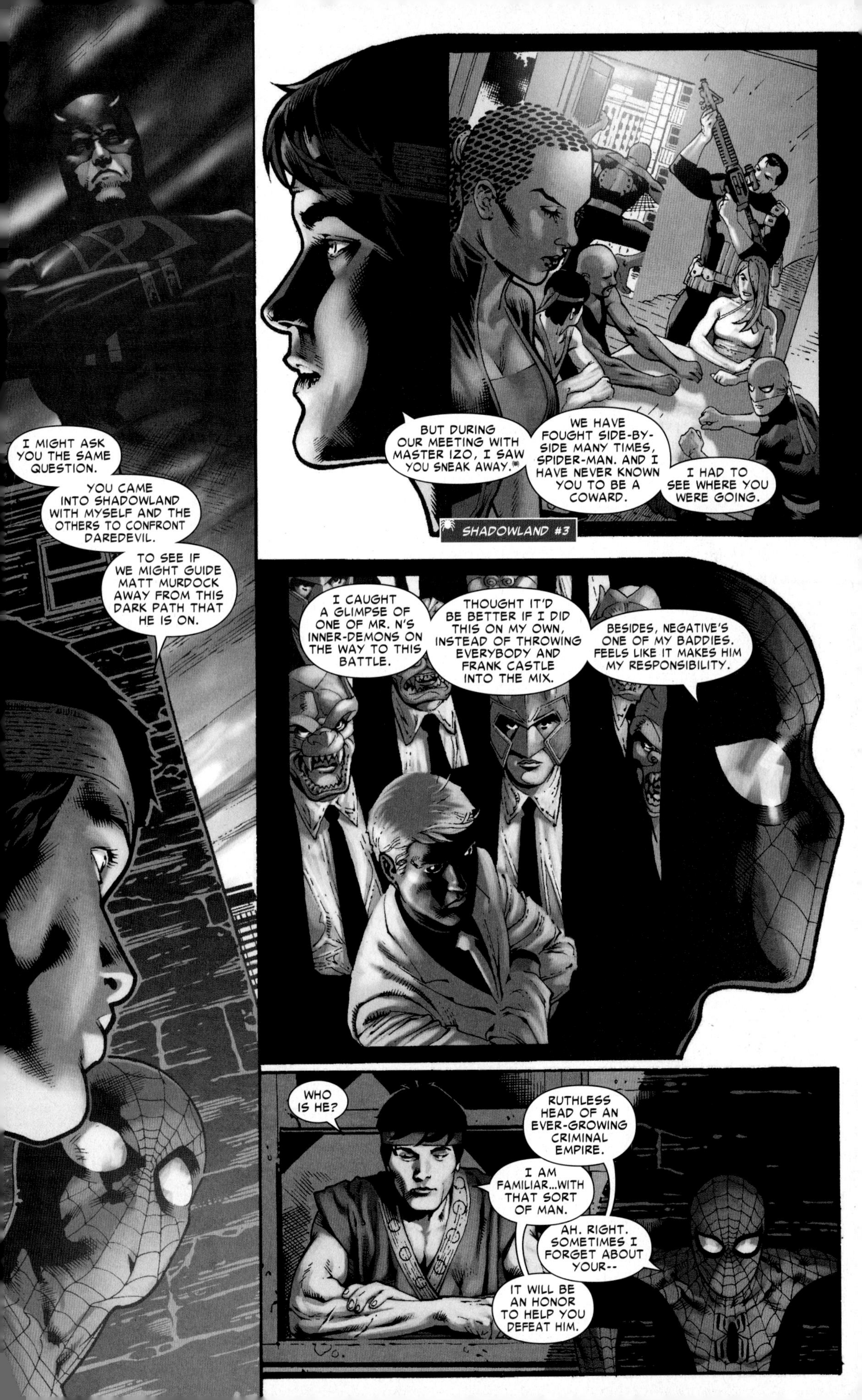
BUT DURING OUR MEETING WITH MASTER IZO, I SAW YOU SNEAK AWAY.
WE HAVE FOUGHT SIDE-BY-SIDE MANY TIMES, SPIDER-MAN. AND I HAVE NEVER KNOWN YOU TO BE A COWARD.
I HAD TO SEE WHERE YOU WERE GOING.
SHADOWLAND #3
I MIGHT ASK YOU THE SAME QUESTION.
YOU CAME INTO SHADOWLAND WITH MYSELF AND THE OTHERS TO CONFRONT DAREDEVIL.
TO SEE IF WE MIGHT GUIDE MATT MURDOCK AWAY FROM THIS DARK PATH THAT HE IS ON.
I CAUGHT A GLIMPSE OF ONE OF MR. N'S INNER-DEMONS ON THE WAY TO THIS BATTLE.
THOUGHT IT'D BE BETTER IF I DID THIS ON MY OWN, INSTEAD OF THROWING EVERYBODY AND FRANK CASTLE INTO THE MIX.
BESIDES, NEGATIVE'S ONE OF MY BADDIES. FEELS LIKE IT MAKES HIM MY RESPONSIBILITY.
WHO IS HE?
RUTHLESS HEAD OF AN EVER-GROWING CRIMINAL EMPIRE.
I AM FAMILIAR...WITH THAT SORT OF MAN.
AH. RIGHT. SOMETIMES I FORGET ABOUT YOUR--
IT WILL BE AN HONOR TO HELP YOU DEFEAT HIM.

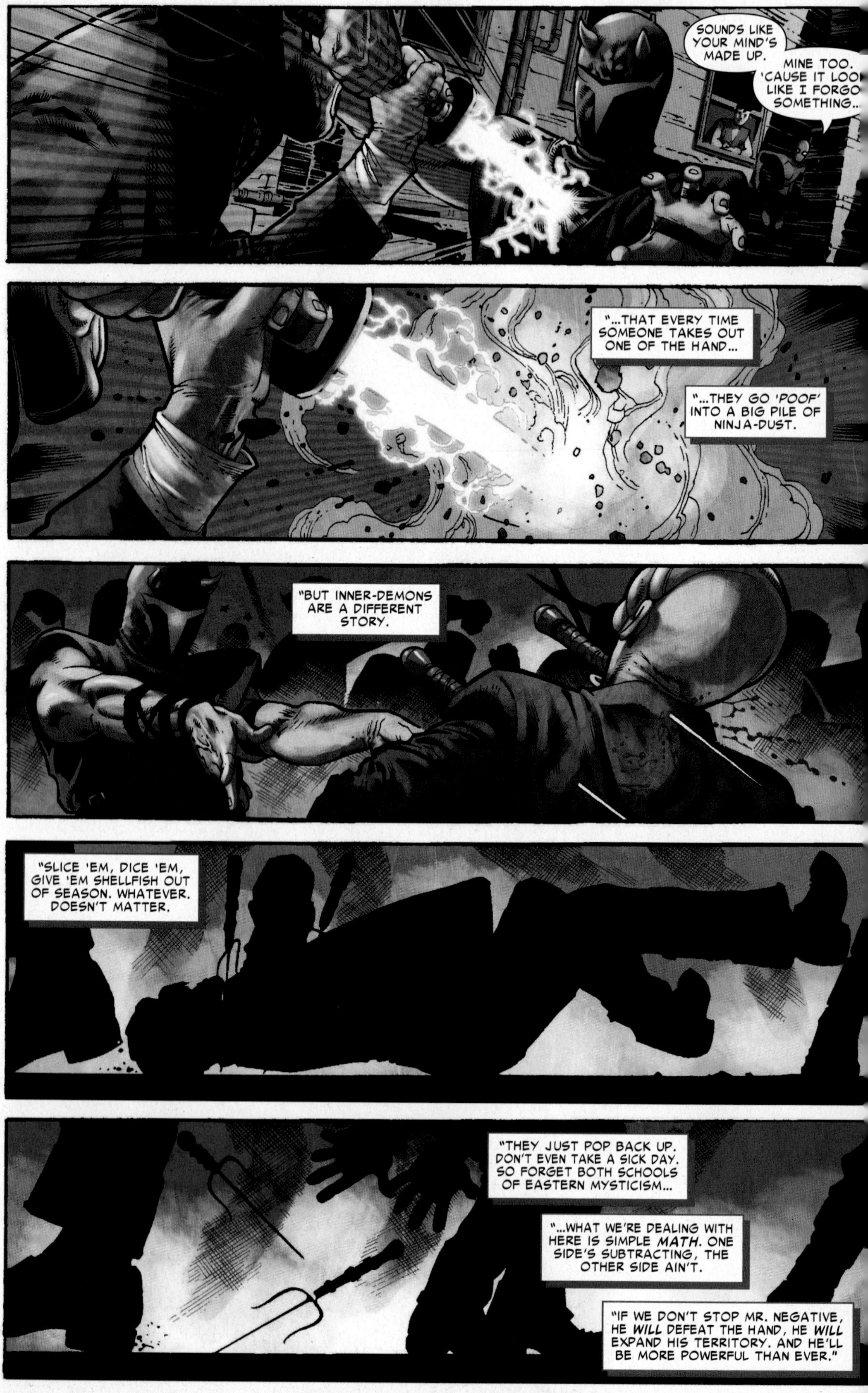
SOUNDS LIKE YOUR MIND'S MADE UP.
MINE TOO. 'CAUSE IT LOO LIKE I FORGO SOMETHING...
"...THAT EVERY TIME SOMEONE TAKES OUT ONE OF THE HAND...
"...THEY GO 'POOF' INTO A BIG PILE OF NINJA-DUST.
"BUT INNER-DEMONS ARE A DIFFERENT STORY.
"SLICE 'EM, DICE 'EM, GIVE 'EM SHELLFISH OUT OF SEASON. WHATEVER. DOESN'T MATTER.
"THEY JUST POP BACK UP. DON'T EVEN TAKE A SICK DAY. SO FORGET BOTH SCHOOLS OF EASTERN MYSTICISM...
"...WHAT WE'RE DEALING WITH HERE IS SIMPLE MATH. ONE SIDE'S SUBTRACTING, THE OTHER SIDE AIN'T.
"IF WE DON'T STOP MR. NEGATIVE, HE WILL DEFEAT THE HAND, HE WILL EXPAND HIS TERRITORY. AND HE'LL BE MORE POWERFUL THAN EVER."

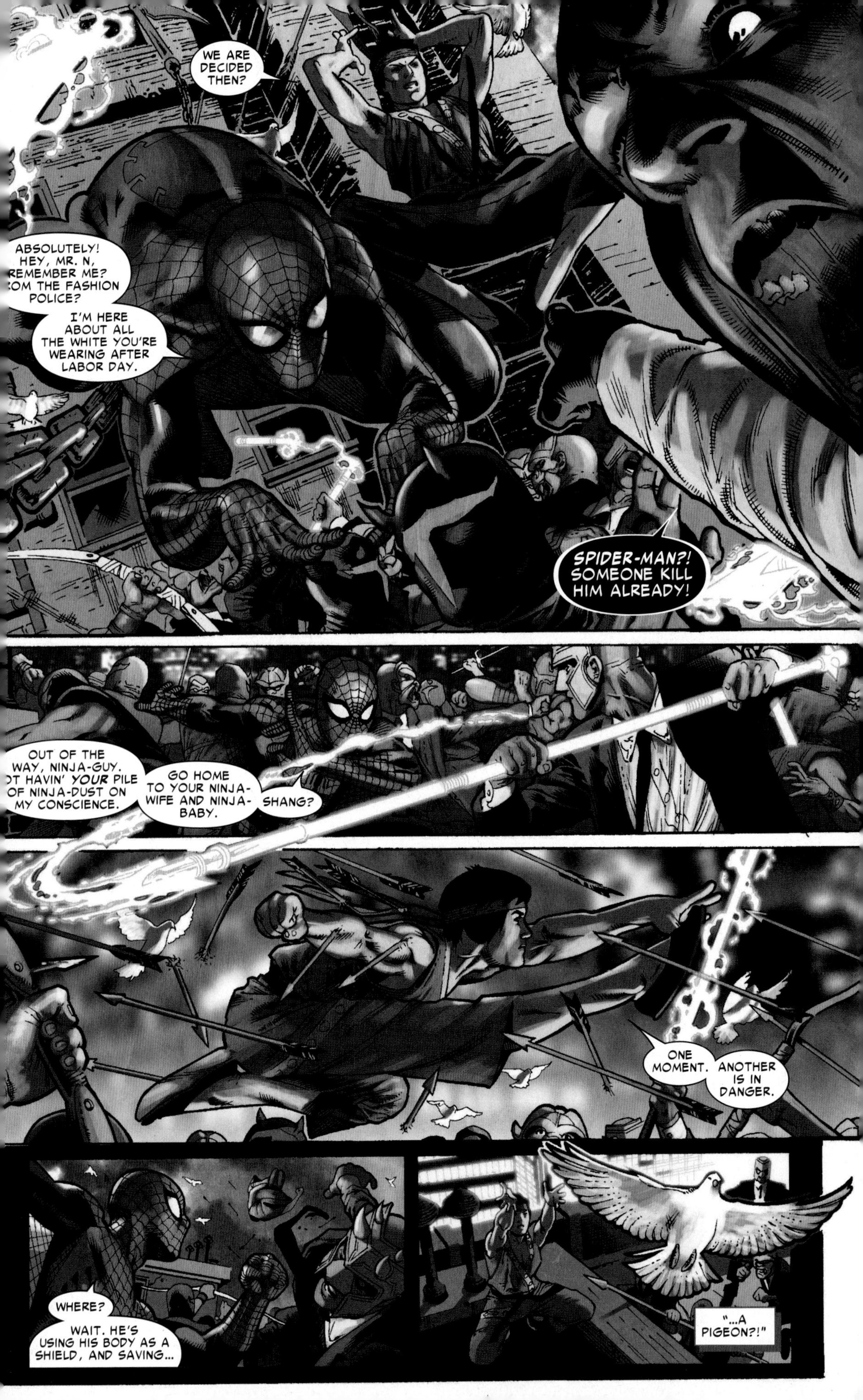
WE ARE DECIDED THEN?
ABSOLUTELY! HEY, MR. N, REMEMBER ME? OM THE FASHION POLICE?
I'M HERE ABOUT ALL THE WHITE YOU'RE WEARING AFTER LABOR DAY.
SPIDER-MAN?! SOMEONE KILL HIM ALREADY!
OUT OF THE WAY, NINJA-GUY. OT HAVIN' YOUR PILE OF NINJA-DUST ON MY CONSCIENCE.
GO HOME TO YOUR NINJA-WIFE AND NINJA-BABY.
SHANG?
ONE MOMENT.
ANOTHER IS IN DANGER.
WHERE?
WAIT. HE'S USING HIS BODY AS A SHIELD, AND SAVING...
"...A PIGEON?!"

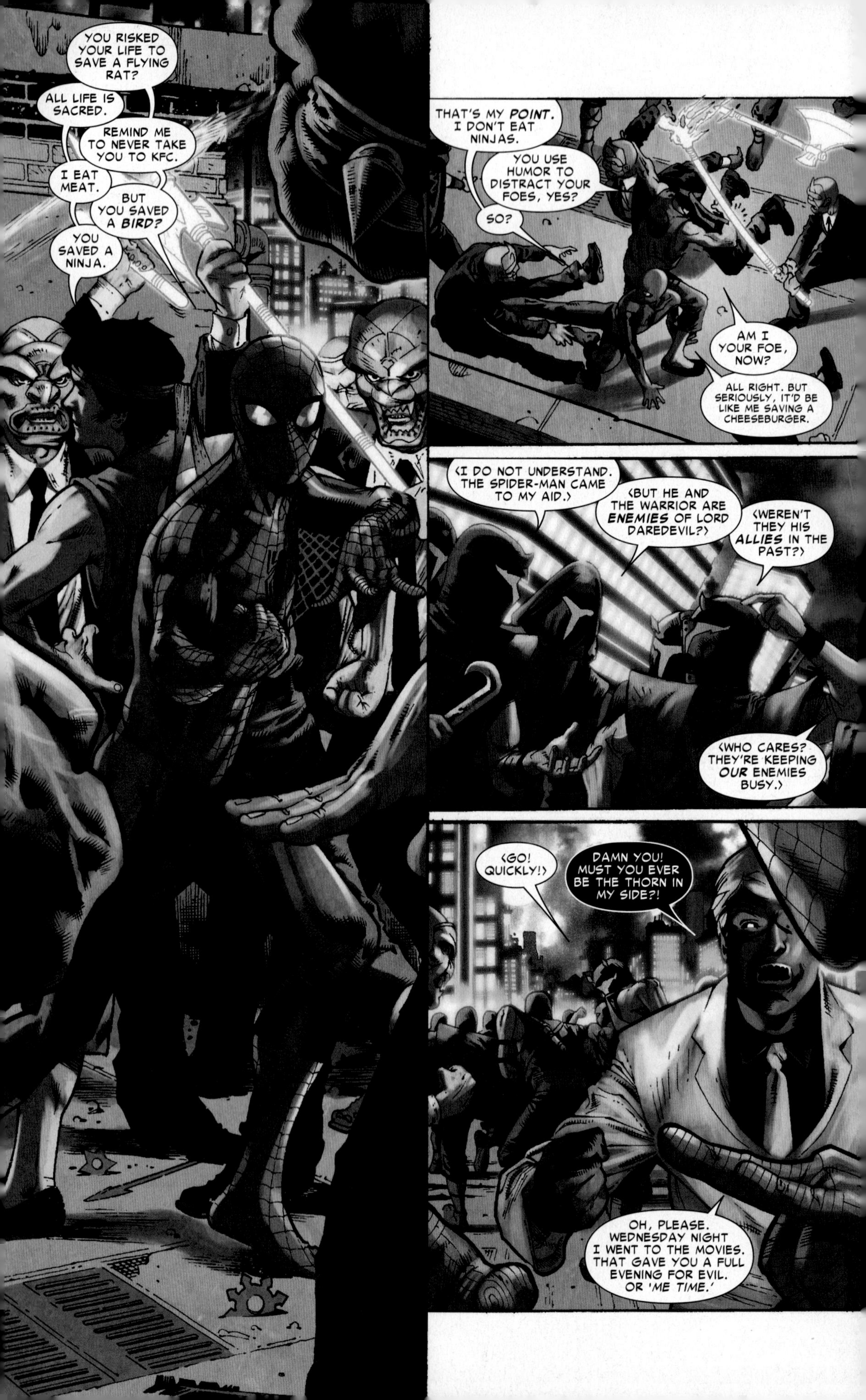
YOU RISKED YOUR LIFE TO SAVE A FLYING RAT?
ALL LIFE IS SACRED.
REMIND ME TO NEVER TAKE YOU TO KFC.
I EAT MEAT.
BUT YOU SAVED A *BIRD?*
YOU SAVED A NINJA.
THAT'S MY *POINT.* I DON'T EAT NINJAS.
YOU USE HUMOR TO DISTRACT YOUR FOES, YES?
SO?
AM I YOUR FOE, NOW?
ALL RIGHT. BUT SERIOUSLY, IT'D BE LIKE ME SAVING A CHEESEBURGER.
‹I DO NOT UNDERSTAND. THE SPIDER-MAN CAME TO MY AID.›
‹BUT HE AND THE WARRIOR ARE *ENEMIES* OF LORD DAREDEVIL?›
‹WEREN'T THEY HIS *ALLIES* IN THE PAST?›
‹WHO CARES? THEY'RE KEEPING *OUR* ENEMIES BUSY.›
‹GO! QUICKLY!›
DAMN YOU! MUST YOU EVER BE THE THORN IN MY SIDE?!
OH, PLEASE. WEDNESDAY NIGHT I WENT TO THE MOVIES. THAT GAVE YOU A FULL EVENING FOR EVIL. OR '*ME TIME.*'

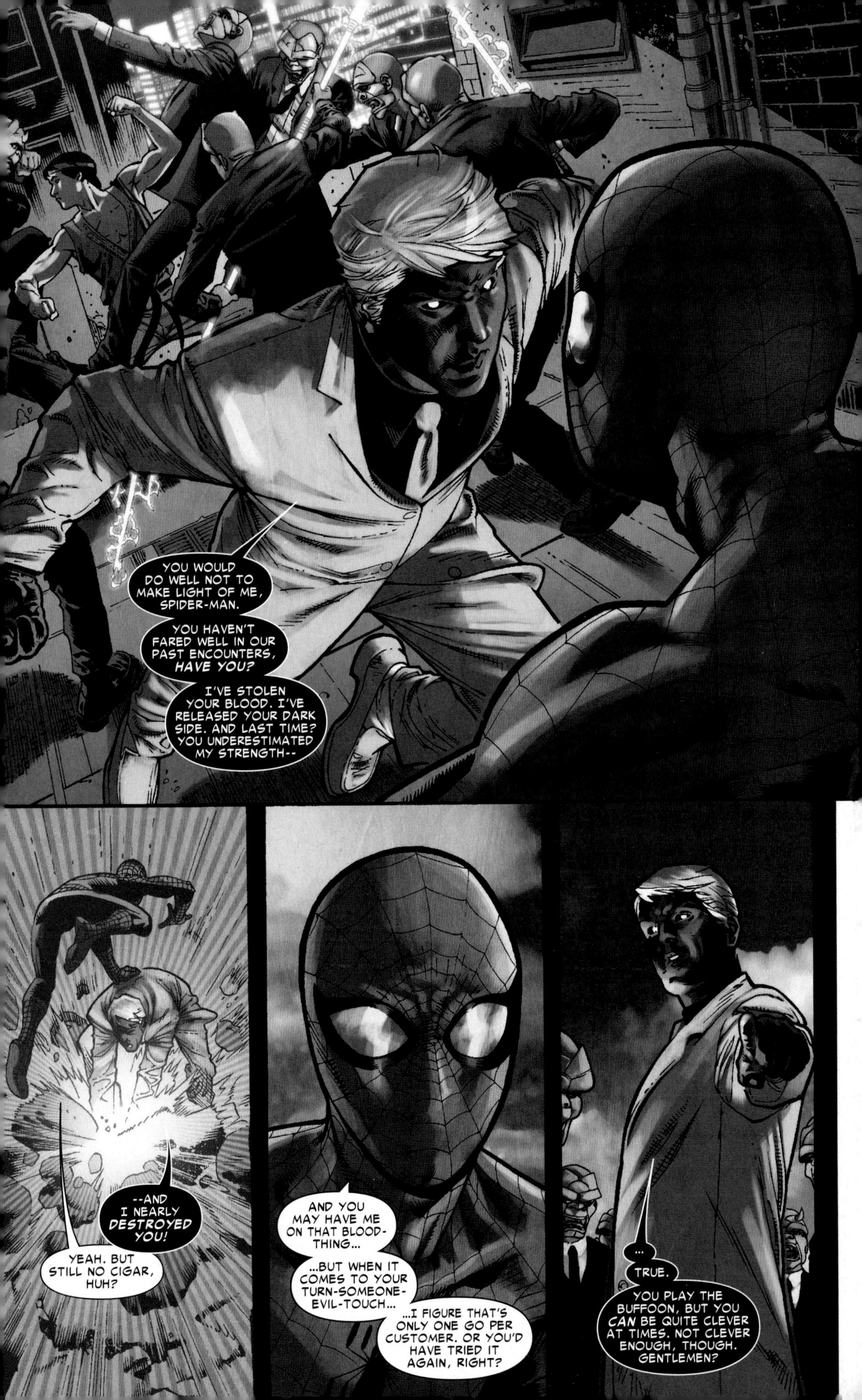
YOU WOULD DO WELL NOT TO MAKE LIGHT OF ME, SPIDER-MAN.
YOU HAVEN'T FARED WELL IN OUR PAST ENCOUNTERS, *HAVE YOU?*
I'VE STOLEN YOUR BLOOD. I'VE RELEASED YOUR DARK SIDE. AND LAST TIME? YOU UNDERESTIMATED MY STRENGTH--
--AND I NEARLY *DESTROYED* YOU!
YEAH. BUT STILL NO CIGAR, HUH?
AND YOU MAY HAVE ME ON THAT BLOOD-THING...
...BUT WHEN IT COMES TO YOUR TURN-SOMEONE-EVIL-TOUCH...
...I FIGURE THAT'S ONLY ONE GO PER CUSTOMER. OR YOU'D HAVE TRIED IT AGAIN, RIGHT?
...
TRUE.
YOU PLAY THE BUFFOON, BUT YOU *CAN* BE QUITE CLEVER AT TIMES. NOT CLEVER ENOUGH, THOUGH. GENTLEMEN?

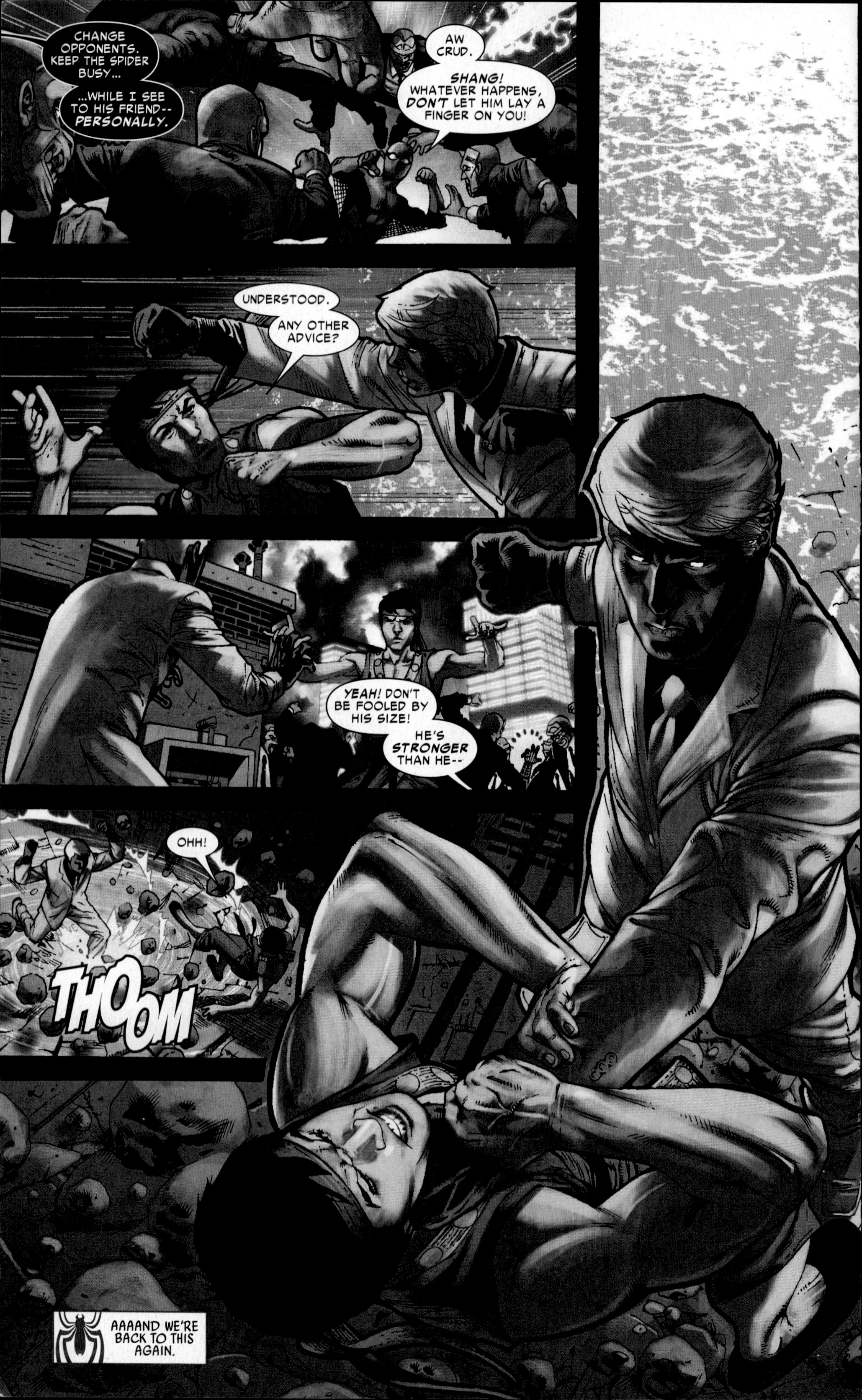
CHANGE OPPONENTS. KEEP THE SPIDER BUSY...
...WHILE I SEE TO HIS FRIEND-- PERSONALLY.
AW CRUD.
SHANG! WHATEVER HAPPENS, DON'T LET HIM LAY A FINGER ON YOU!
UNDERSTOOD.
ANY OTHER ADVICE?
YEAH! DON'T BE FOOLED BY HIS SIZE!
HE'S STRONGER THAN HE--
OHH!
THOOOM
AAAAND WE'RE BACK TO THIS AGAIN.

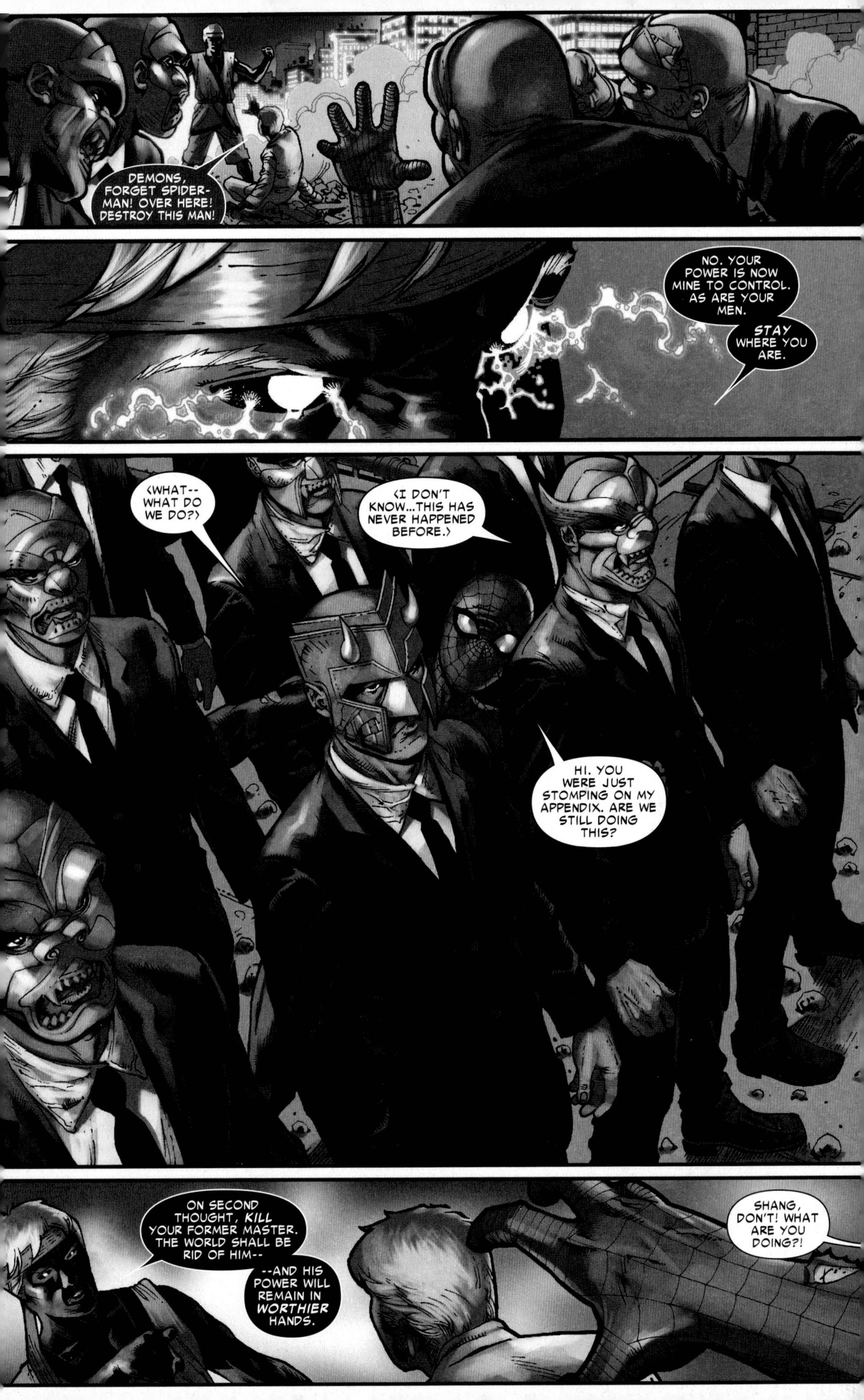
DEMONS, FORGET SPIDER-MAN! OVER HERE! DESTROY THIS MAN!
NO. YOUR POWER IS NOW MINE TO CONTROL. AS ARE YOUR MEN.
STAY WHERE YOU ARE.
<WHAT--WHAT DO WE DO?>
<I DON'T KNOW...THIS HAS NEVER HAPPENED BEFORE.>
HI. YOU WERE JUST STOMPING ON MY APPENDIX. ARE WE STILL DOING THIS?
ON SECOND THOUGHT, KILL YOUR FORMER MASTER. THE WORLD SHALL BE RID OF HIM--
--AND HIS POWER WILL REMAIN IN WORTHIER HANDS.
SHANG, DON'T! WHAT ARE YOU DOING?!

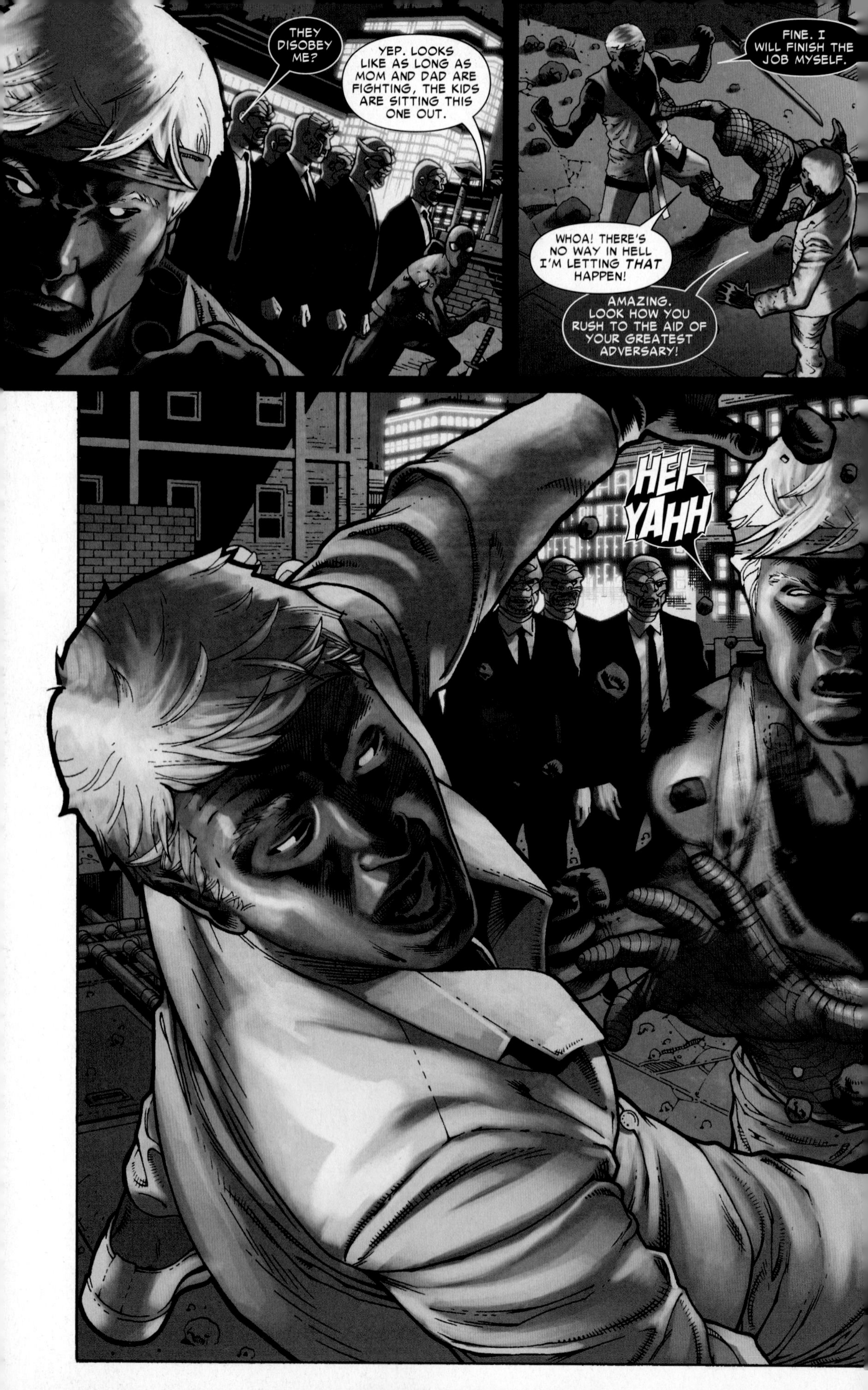
THEY DISOBEY ME?
YEP. LOOKS LIKE AS LONG AS MOM AND DAD ARE FIGHTING, THE KIDS ARE SITTING THIS ONE OUT.
FINE. I WILL FINISH THE JOB MYSELF.
WHOA! THERE'S NO WAY IN HELL I'M LETTING THAT HAPPEN!
AMAZING. LOOK HOW YOU RUSH TO THE AID OF YOUR GREATEST ADVERSARY!
HEI-YAHH

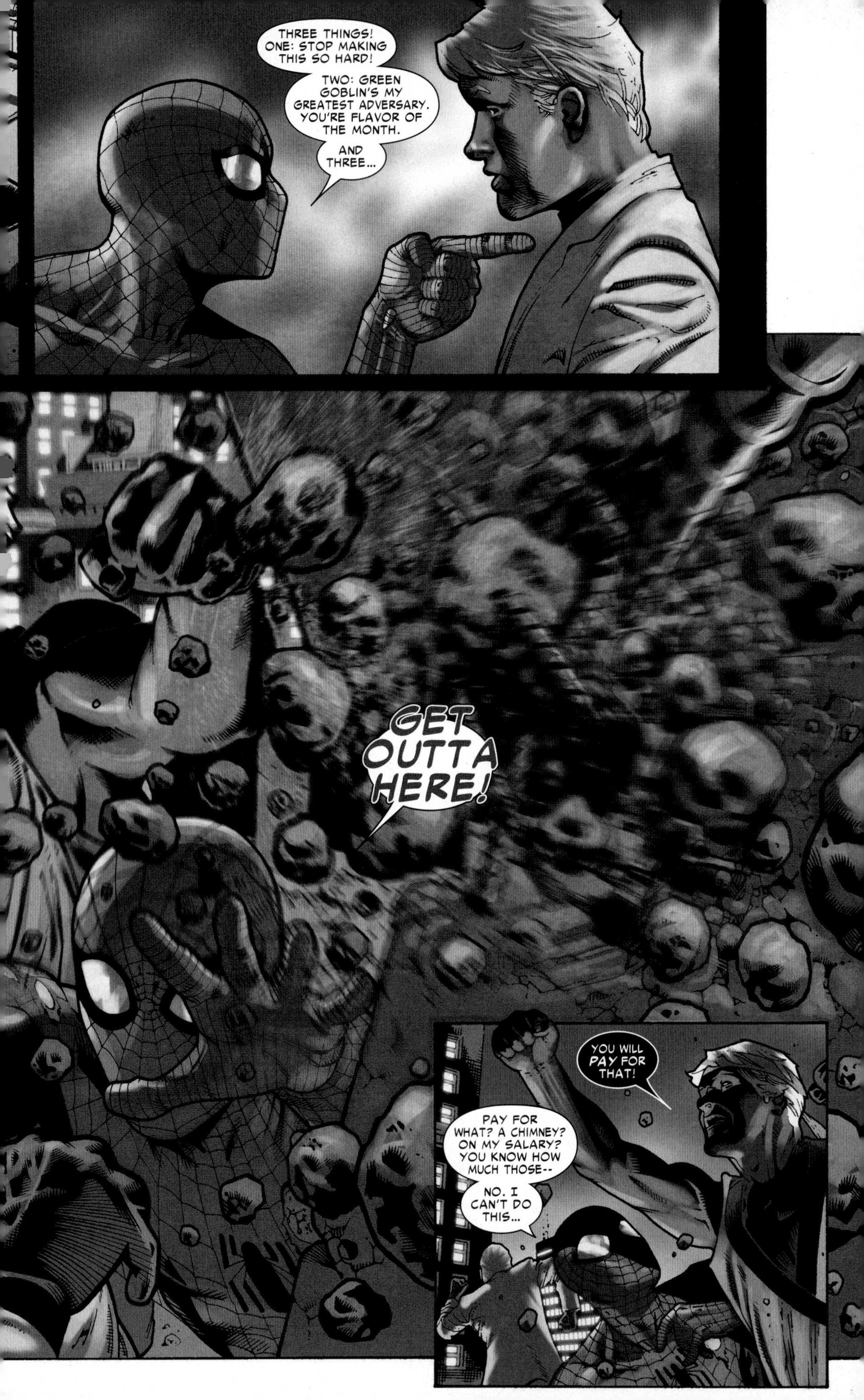
THREE THINGS! ONE: STOP MAKING THIS SO HARD!
TWO: GREEN GOBLIN'S MY GREATEST ADVERSARY. YOU'RE FLAVOR OF THE MONTH.
AND THREE...
GET OUTTA HERE!
YOU WILL PAY FOR THAT!
PAY FOR WHAT? A CHIMNEY? ON MY SALARY? YOU KNOW HOW MUCH THOSE--
NO. I CAN'T DO THIS...

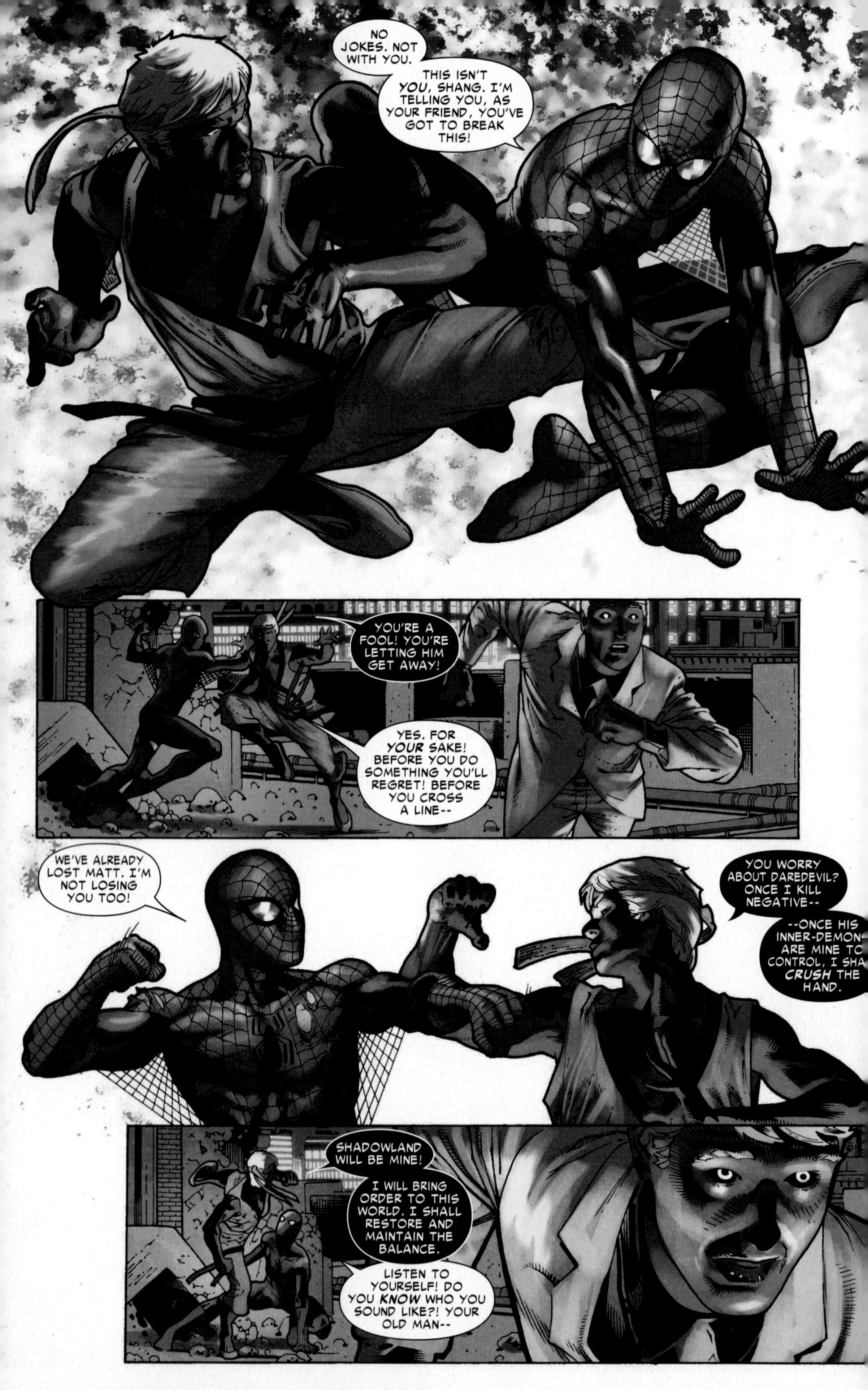
NO JOKES. NOT WITH YOU.
THIS ISN'T YOU, SHANG. I'M TELLING YOU, AS YOUR FRIEND, YOU'VE GOT TO BREAK THIS!
YOU'RE A FOOL! YOU'RE LETTING HIM GET AWAY!
YES. FOR YOUR SAKE! BEFORE YOU DO SOMETHING YOU'LL REGRET! BEFORE YOU CROSS A LINE--
WE'VE ALREADY LOST MATT. I'M NOT LOSING YOU TOO!
YOU WORRY ABOUT DAREDEVIL? ONCE I KILL NEGATIVE--
--ONCE HIS INNER-DEMON ARE MINE TO CONTROL, I SHA CRUSH THE HAND.
SHADOWLAND WILL BE MINE!
I WILL BRING ORDER TO THIS WORLD. I SHALL RESTORE AND MAINTAIN THE BALANCE.
LISTEN TO YOURSELF! DO YOU KNOW WHO YOU SOUND LIKE?! YOUR OLD MAN--

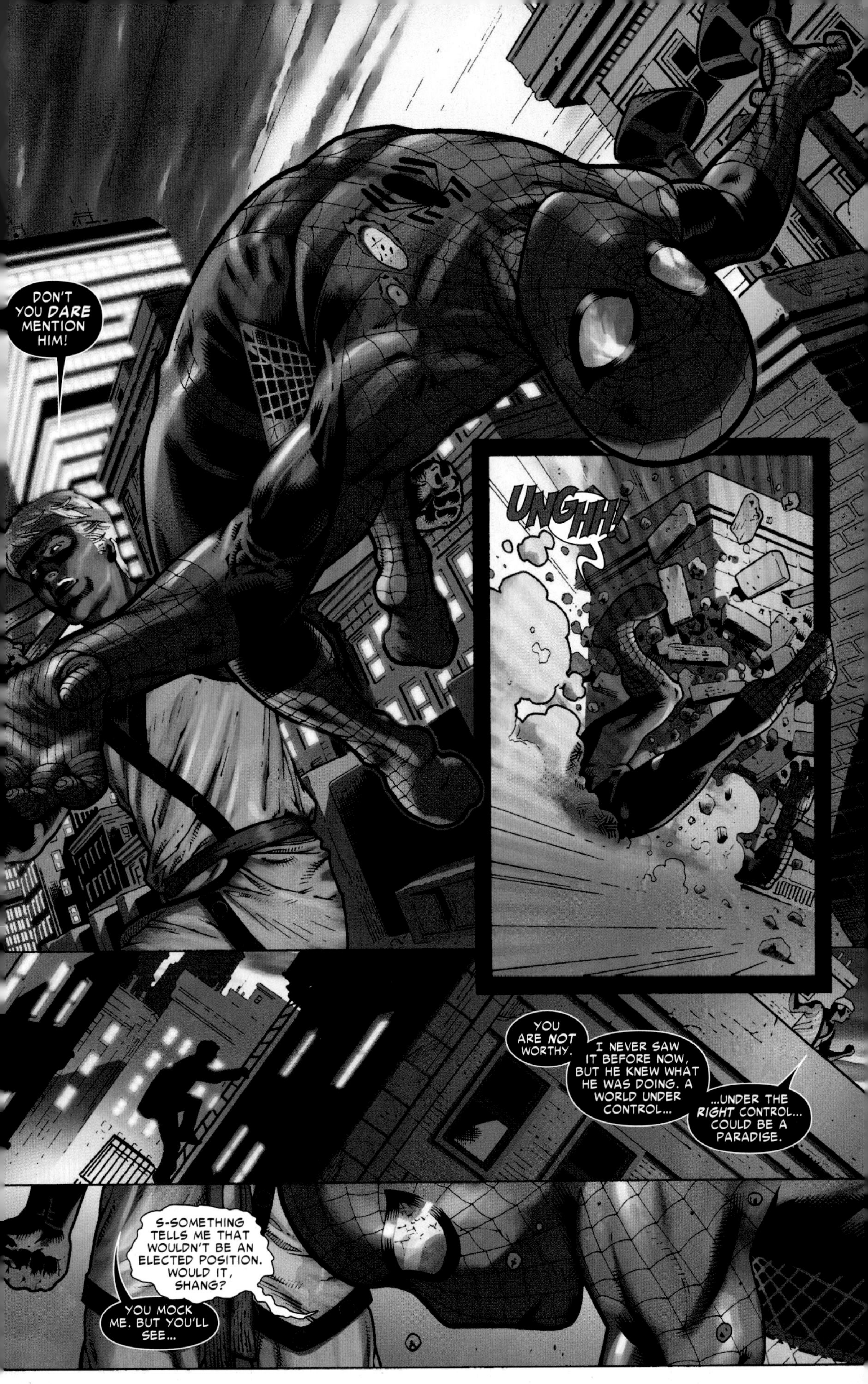
DON'T YOU DARE MENTION HIM!
UNGHH!
YOU ARE NOT WORTHY.
I NEVER SAW IT BEFORE NOW, BUT HE KNEW WHAT HE WAS DOING. A WORLD UNDER CONTROL...
...UNDER THE RIGHT CONTROL... COULD BE A PARADISE.
S-SOMETHING TELLS ME THAT WOULDN'T BE AN ELECTED POSITION. WOULD IT, SHANG?
YOU MOCK ME. BUT YOU'LL SEE...

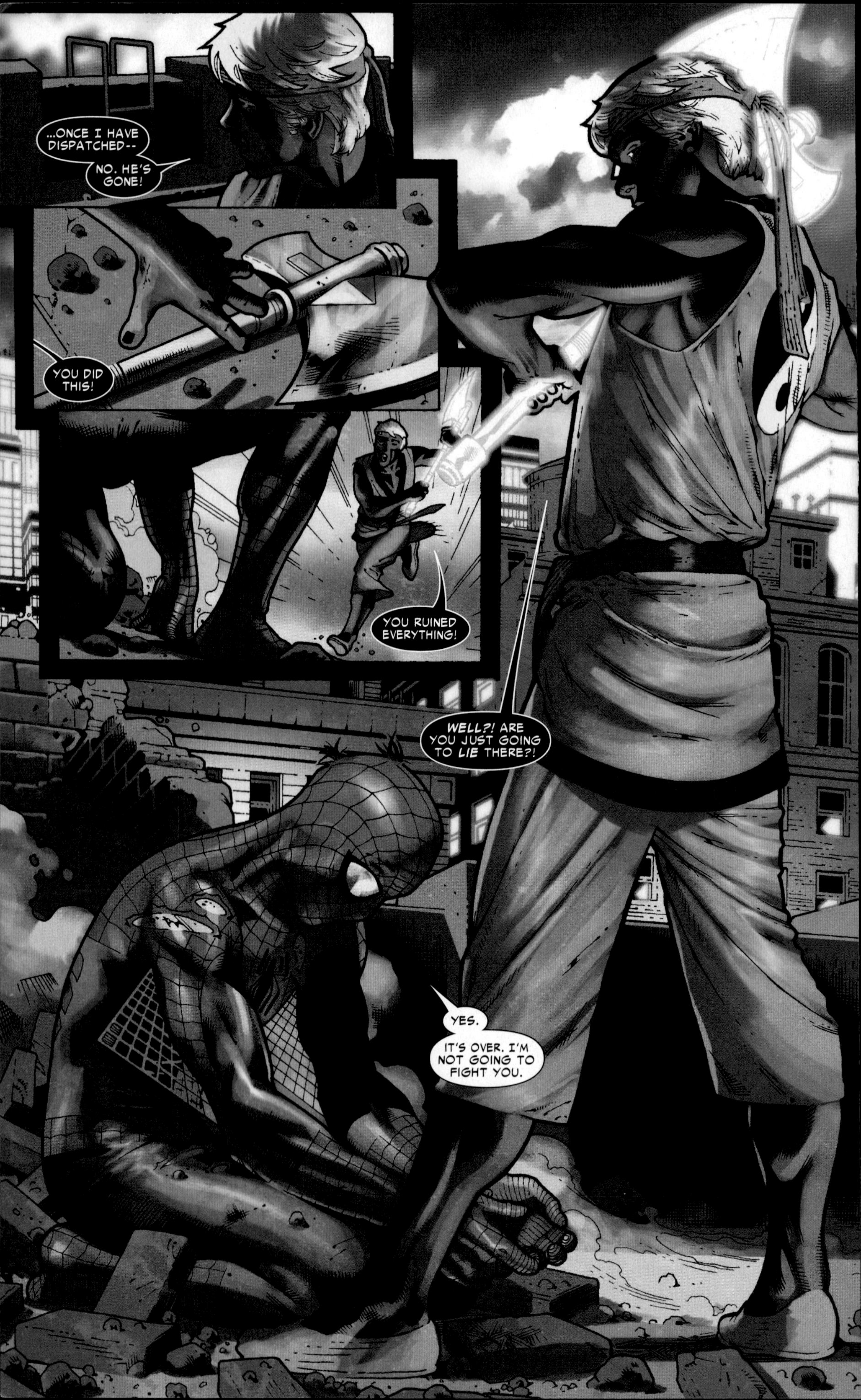
...ONCE I HAVE DISPATCHED--
NO. HE'S GONE!
YOU DID THIS!
YOU RUINED EVERYTHING!
WELL?! ARE YOU JUST GOING TO LIE THERE?!
YES.
IT'S OVER. I'M NOT GOING TO FIGHT YOU.

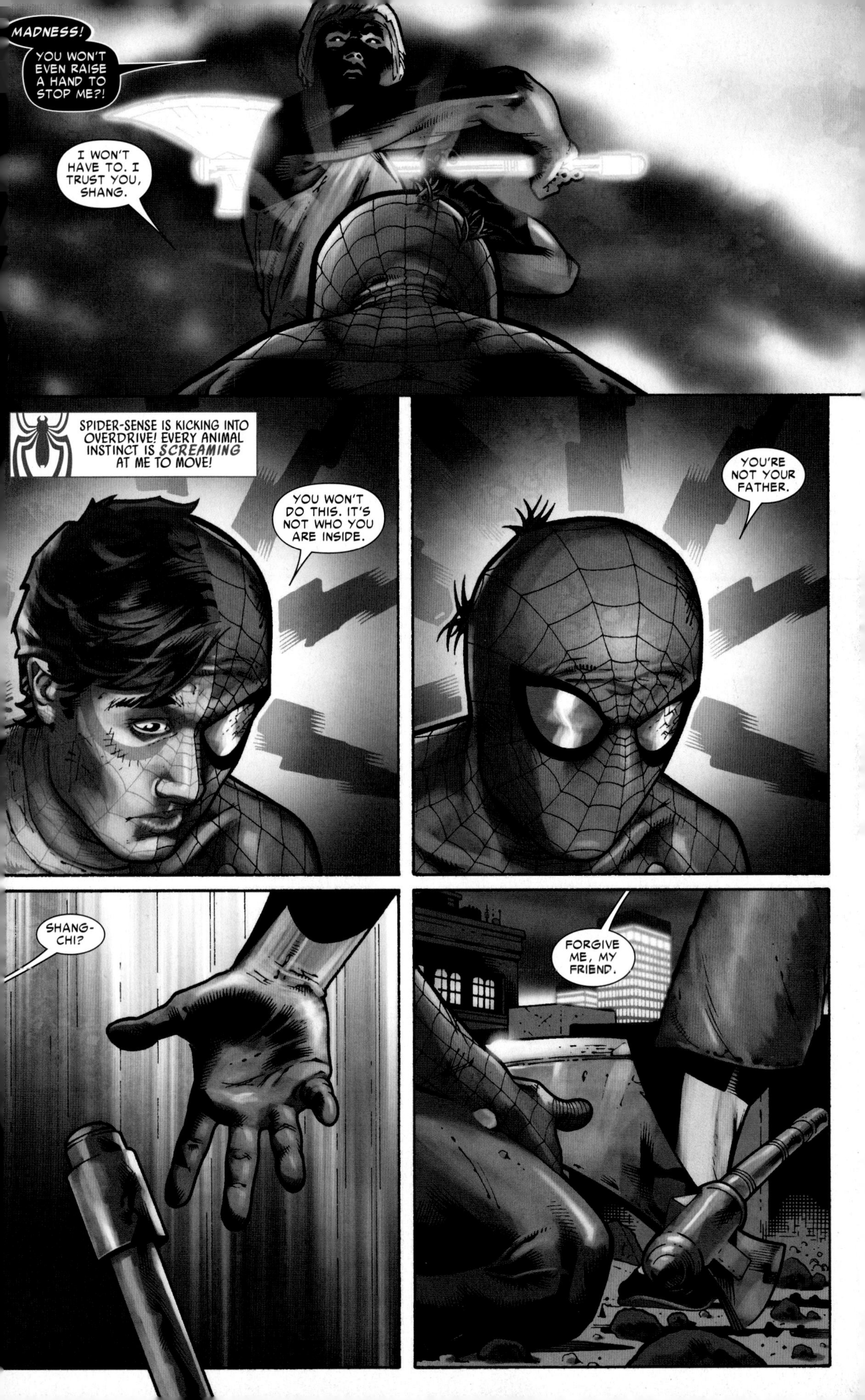
MADNESS!
YOU WON'T EVEN RAISE A HAND TO STOP ME?!
I WON'T HAVE TO. I TRUST YOU, SHANG.
SPIDER-SENSE IS KICKING INTO OVERDRIVE! EVERY ANIMAL INSTINCT IS SCREAMING AT ME TO MOVE!
YOU WON'T DO THIS. IT'S NOT WHO YOU ARE INSIDE.
YOU'RE NOT YOUR FATHER.
SHANG-CHI?
FORGIVE ME, MY FRIEND.

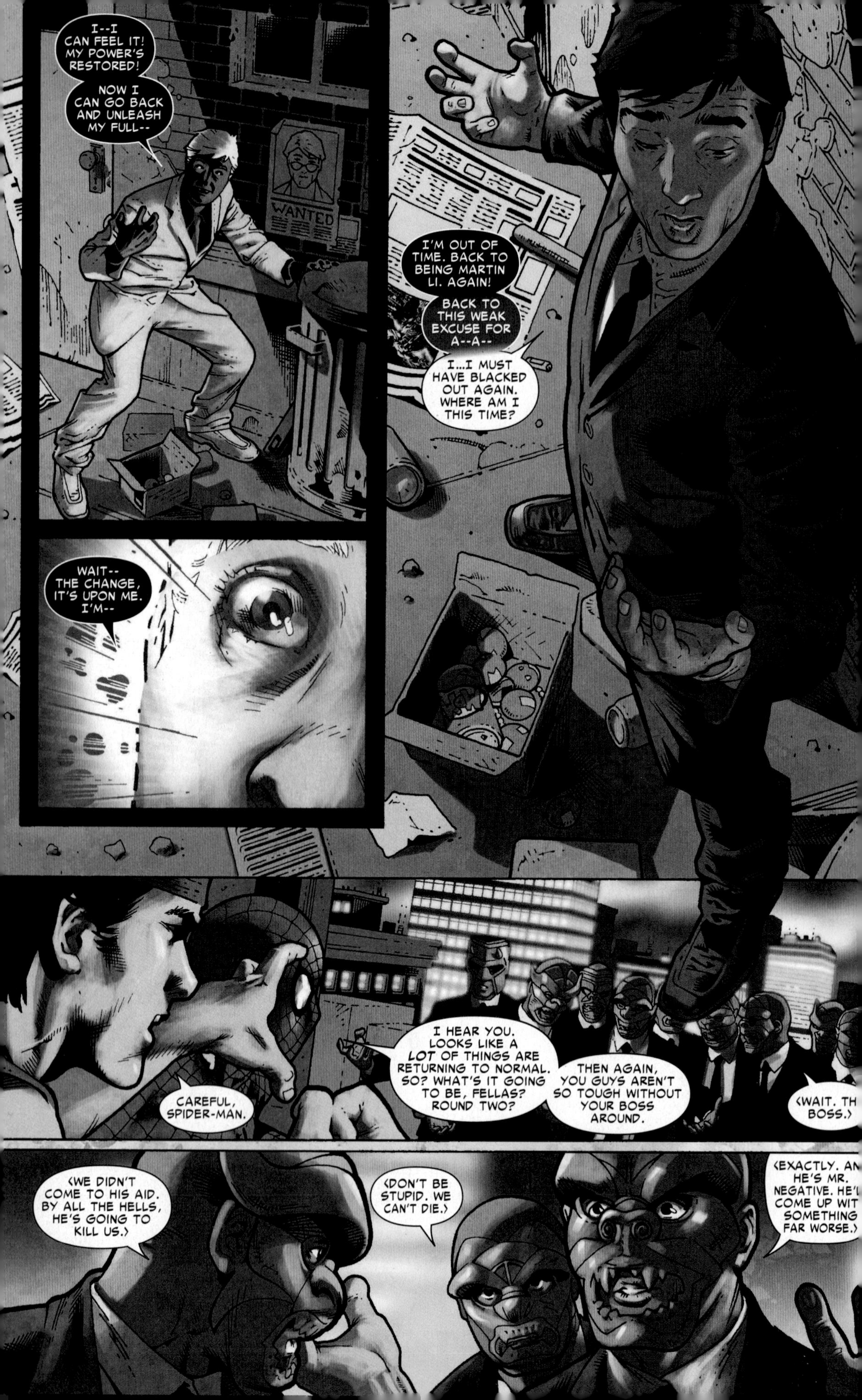
I--I CAN FEEL IT! MY POWER'S RESTORED!
NOW I CAN GO BACK AND UNLEASH MY FULL--
WANTED
WAIT-- THE CHANGE, IT'S UPON ME. I'M--
I'M OUT OF TIME. BACK TO BEING MARTIN LI. AGAIN!
BACK TO THIS WEAK EXCUSE FOR A--A--
I...I MUST HAVE BLACKED OUT AGAIN. WHERE AM I THIS TIME?
CAREFUL, SPIDER-MAN.
I HEAR YOU. LOOKS LIKE A LOT OF THINGS ARE RETURNING TO NORMAL. SO? WHAT'S IT GOING TO BE, FELLAS? ROUND TWO?
THEN AGAIN, YOU GUYS AREN'T SO TOUGH WITHOUT YOUR BOSS AROUND.
‹WAIT. TH BOSS.›
‹WE DIDN'T COME TO HIS AID. BY ALL THE HELLS, HE'S GOING TO KILL US.›
‹DON'T BE STUPID. WE CAN'T DIE.›
‹EXACTLY. AN HE'S MR. NEGATIVE. HE'L COME UP WIT SOMETHING FAR WORSE.›

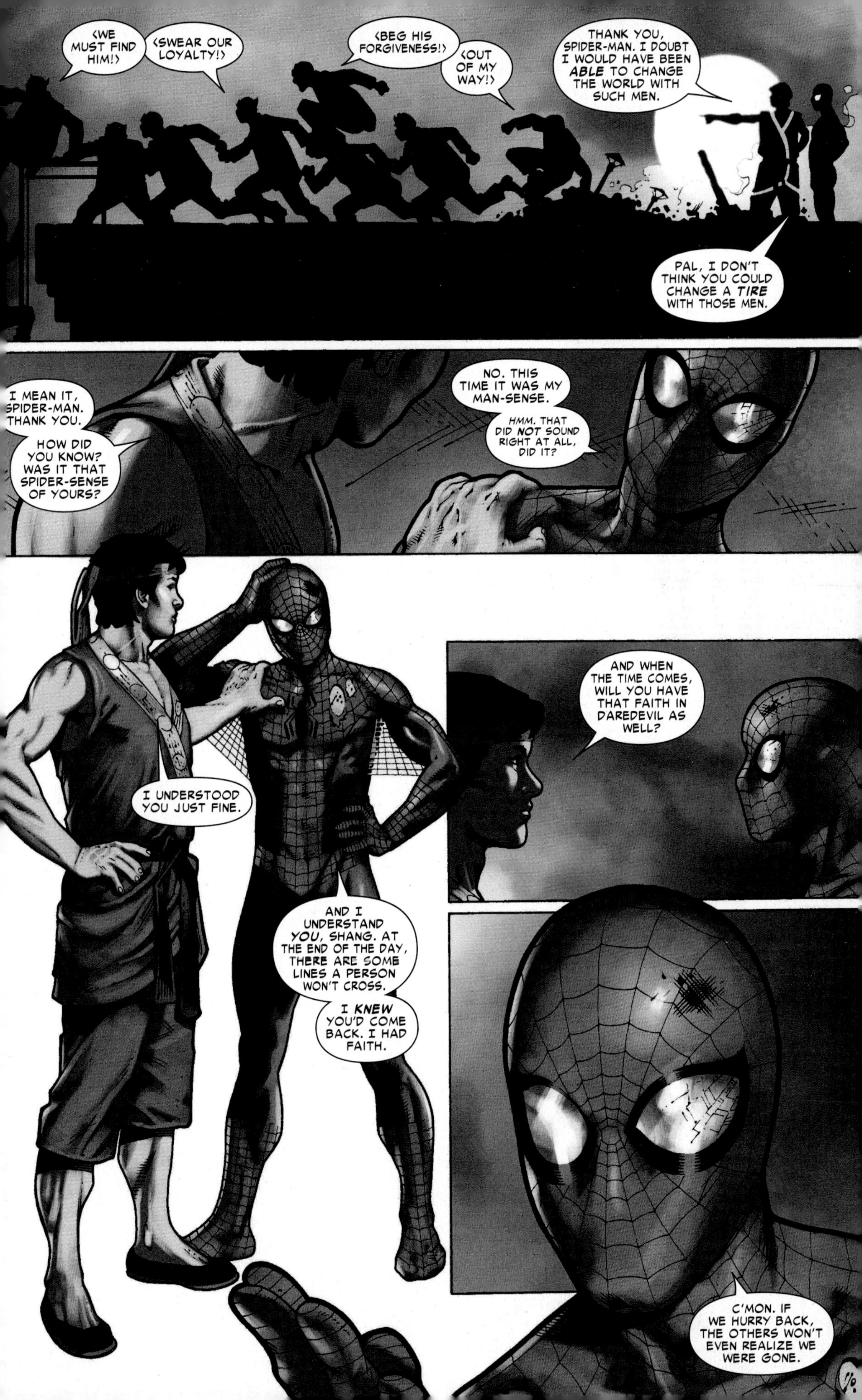

<WE MUST FIND HIM!>
<SWEAR OUR LOYALTY!>
<BEG HIS FORGIVENESS!>
<OUT OF MY WAY!>
THANK YOU, SPIDER-MAN. I DOUBT I WOULD HAVE BEEN ABLE TO CHANGE THE WORLD WITH SUCH MEN.
PAL, I DON'T THINK YOU COULD CHANGE A TIRE WITH THOSE MEN.
I MEAN IT, SPIDER-MAN. THANK YOU.
HOW DID YOU KNOW? WAS IT THAT SPIDER-SENSE OF YOURS?
NO. THIS TIME IT WAS MY MAN-SENSE.
HMM. THAT DID NOT SOUND RIGHT AT ALL, DID IT?
I UNDERSTOOD YOU JUST FINE.
AND I UNDERSTAND YOU, SHANG. AT THE END OF THE DAY, THERE ARE SOME LINES A PERSON WON'T CROSS.
I KNEW YOU'D COME BACK. I HAD FAITH.
AND WHEN THE TIME COMES, WILL YOU HAVE THAT FAITH IN DAREDEVIL AS WELL?
C'MON. IF WE HURRY BACK, THE OTHERS WON'T EVEN REALIZE WE WERE GONE.

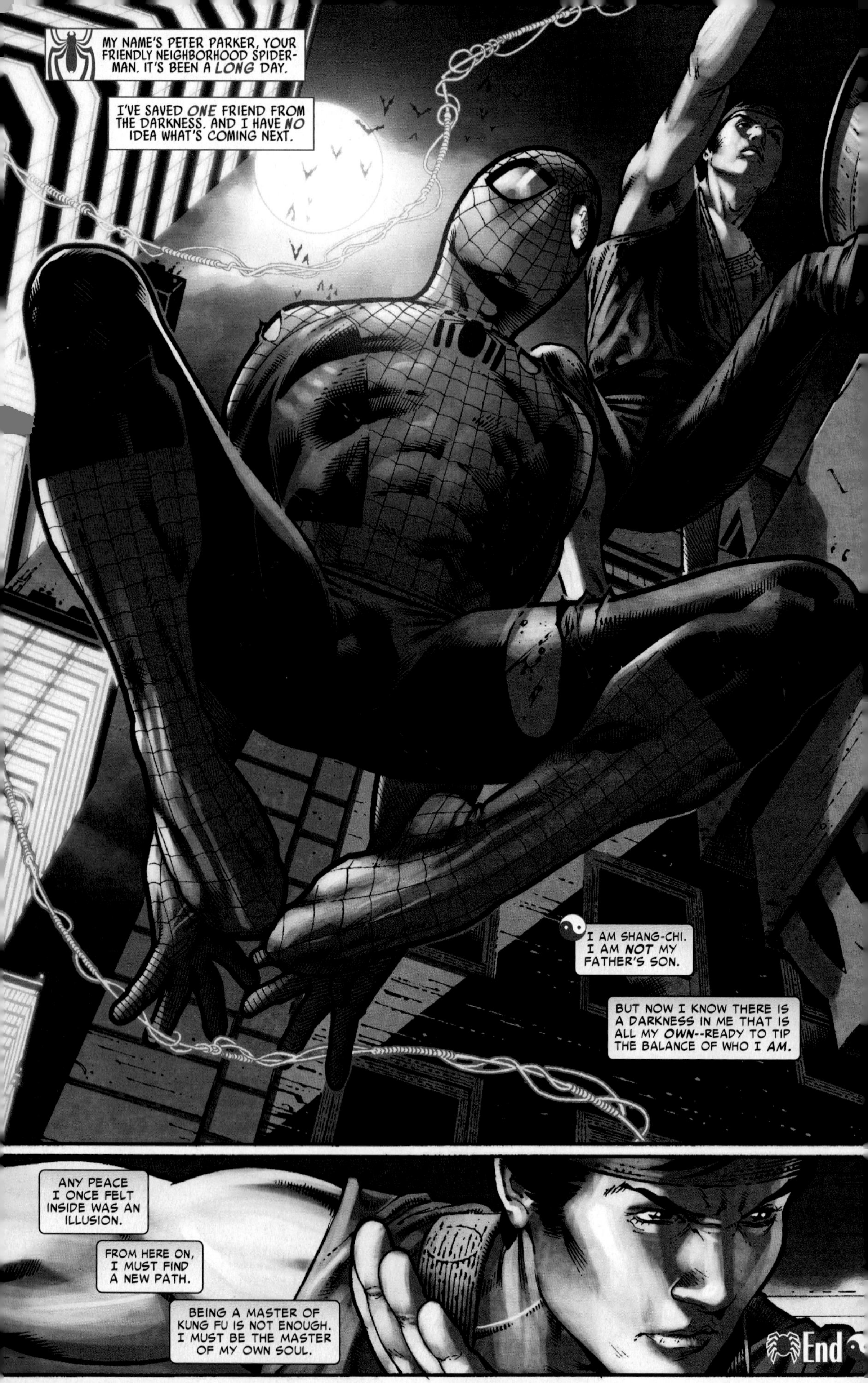
MY NAME'S PETER PARKER, YOUR FRIENDLY NEIGHBORHOOD SPIDER-MAN. IT'S BEEN A LONG DAY.
I'VE SAVED ONE FRIEND FROM THE DARKNESS. AND I HAVE NO IDEA WHAT'S COMING NEXT.
I AM SHANG-CHI. I AM NOT MY FATHER'S SON.
BUT NOW I KNOW THERE IS A DARKNESS IN ME THAT IS ALL MY OWN--READY TO TIP THE BALANCE OF WHO I AM.
ANY PEACE I ONCE FELT INSIDE WAS AN ILLUSION.
FROM HERE ON, I MUST FIND A NEW PATH.
BEING A MASTER OF KUNG FU IS NOT ENOUGH. I MUST BE THE MASTER OF MY OWN SOUL.
End

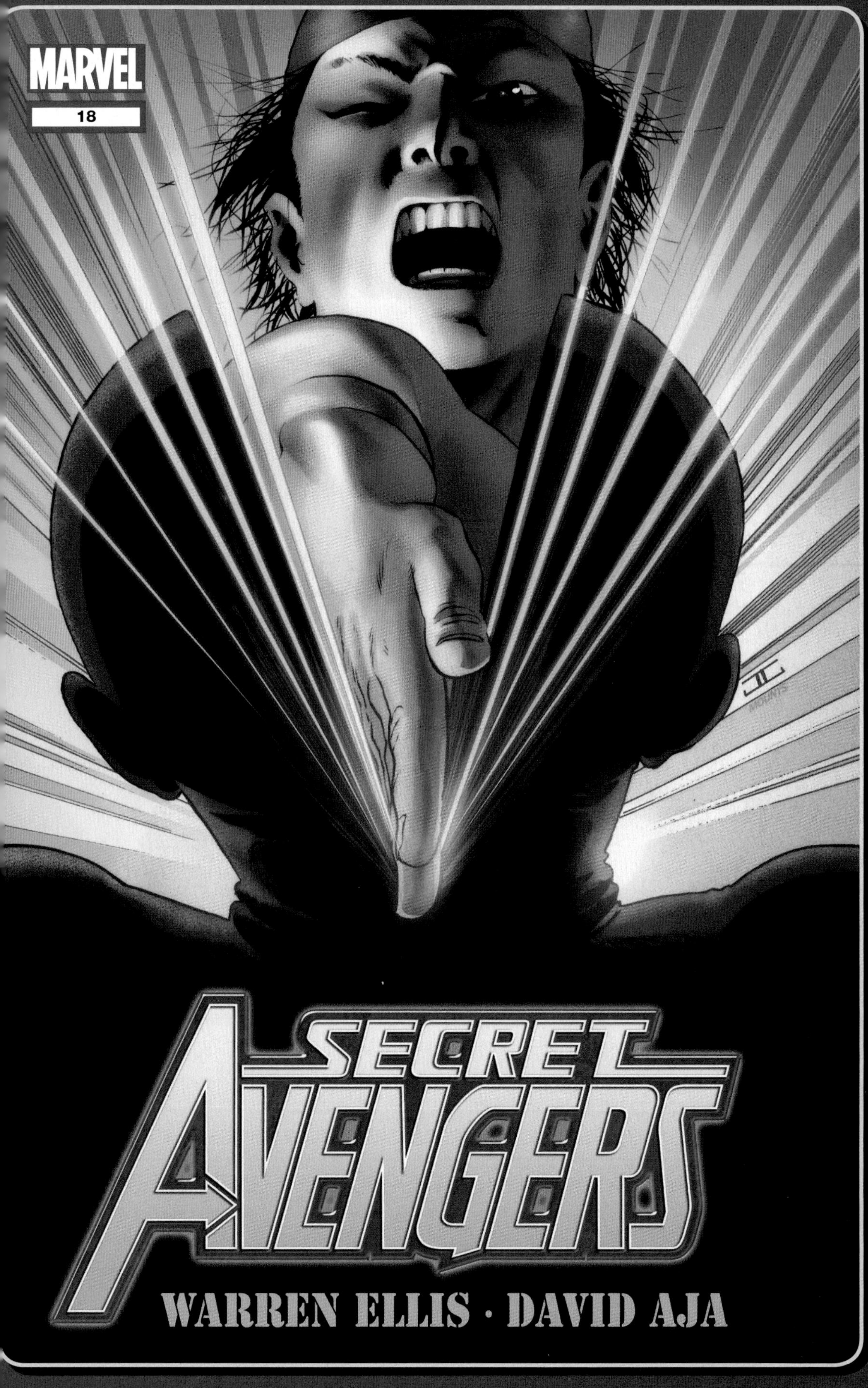
MARVEL
18
SECRET AVENGERS
WARREN ELLIS · DAVID AJA

THERE ARE HIDDEN PLACES WHERE THE END OF THE WORLD IS BEING BUILT.

THERE IS A SECRET TEAM DEDICATED TO BURYING DOOMSDAY THREATS BEFORE THEY HAPPEN.

THERE ARE MISSIONS NO ONE WILL EVER FIND OUT ABOUT. UNLESS THEY LOSE.

SECRET AVENGERS

"NO ZONE"

STEVE ROGERS
THE WORLD'S GREATEST
SOLDIER

SHARON CARTER
THE WORLD'S GREATEST
SECRET AGENT

SHANG-CHI
THE WORLD'S GREATEST
MARTIAL ARTIST

WARREN ELLIS
WRITER

DAVID AJA
WITH RAUL ALLEN
ARTISTS

DAVE LANPHEAR
LETTERER

JOHN CASSADAY
& PAUL MOUNTS
COVER ART

MAYELA GUTIERREZ
PRODUCTION

LAUREN SANKOVITCH
ASSOCIATE EDITOR

TOM BREVOORT
EDITOR

AXEL ALONSO
EDITOR IN CHIEF

JOE QUESADA
CHIEF CREATIVE OFFICER

DAN BUCKLEY
PUBLISHER

ALAN FINE
EXECUTIVE PRODUCER

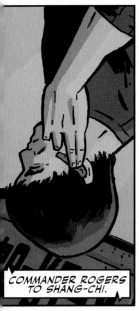

COMMANDER ROGERS TO SHANG-CHI.

SHIFT TO EXTREME COMBAT PROTOCOL WITH IMMEDIATE EFFECT.

INCAPACITATE ALL COMERS, PROCEED TO ZERO POINT.

"INCAPACITATE."

WE'RE IN A SEALED BOX, SHANG.

IF YOU JUST KNOCK THEM DOWN, THEY'LL GET UP AGAIN AND BACK US INTO A CORNER.

YES.

"YES"? WHAT DOES "YES" MEAN?

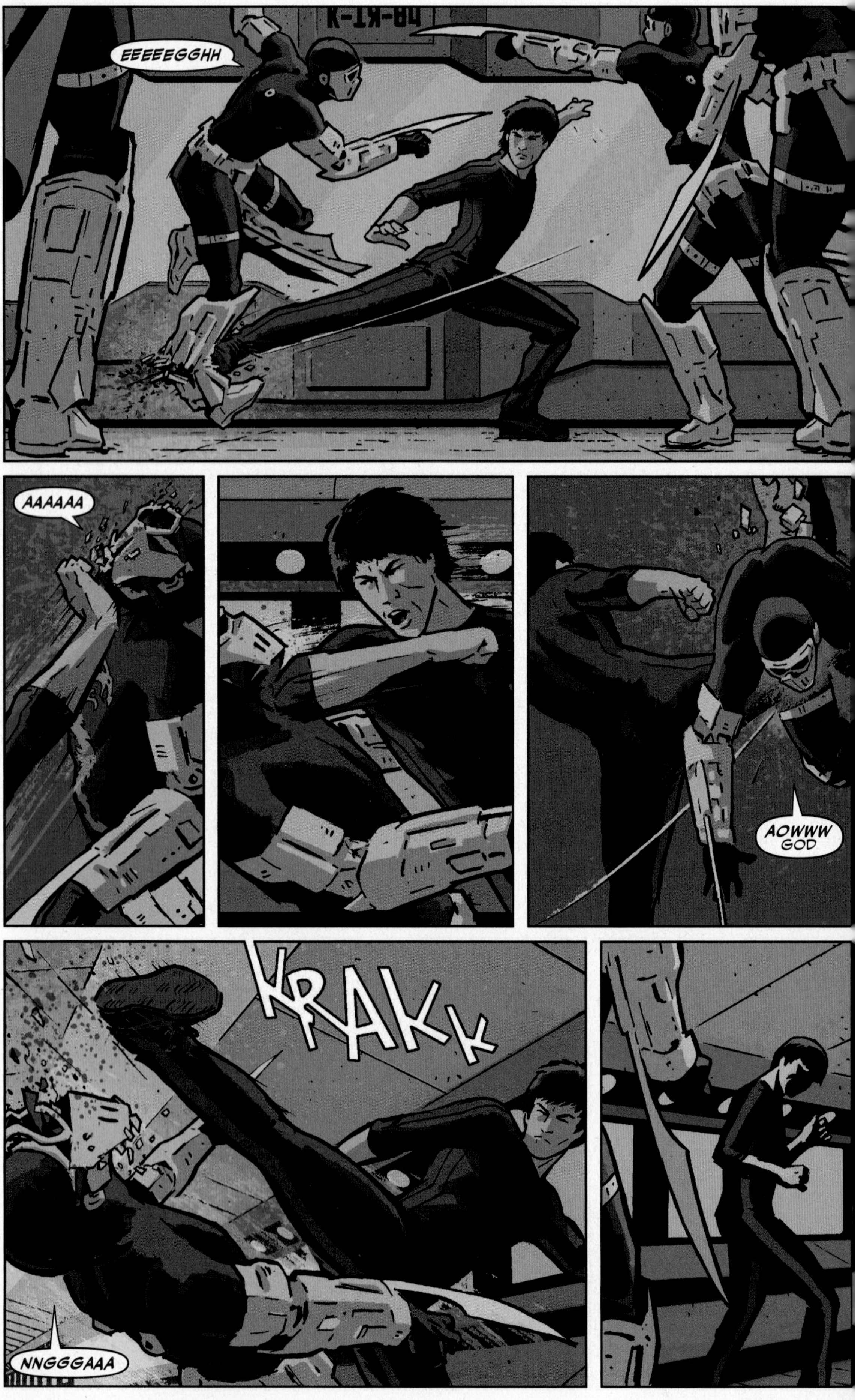
EEEEEGGHH
AAAAAA
AOWWW GOD
KRAKK
NNGGGAAA

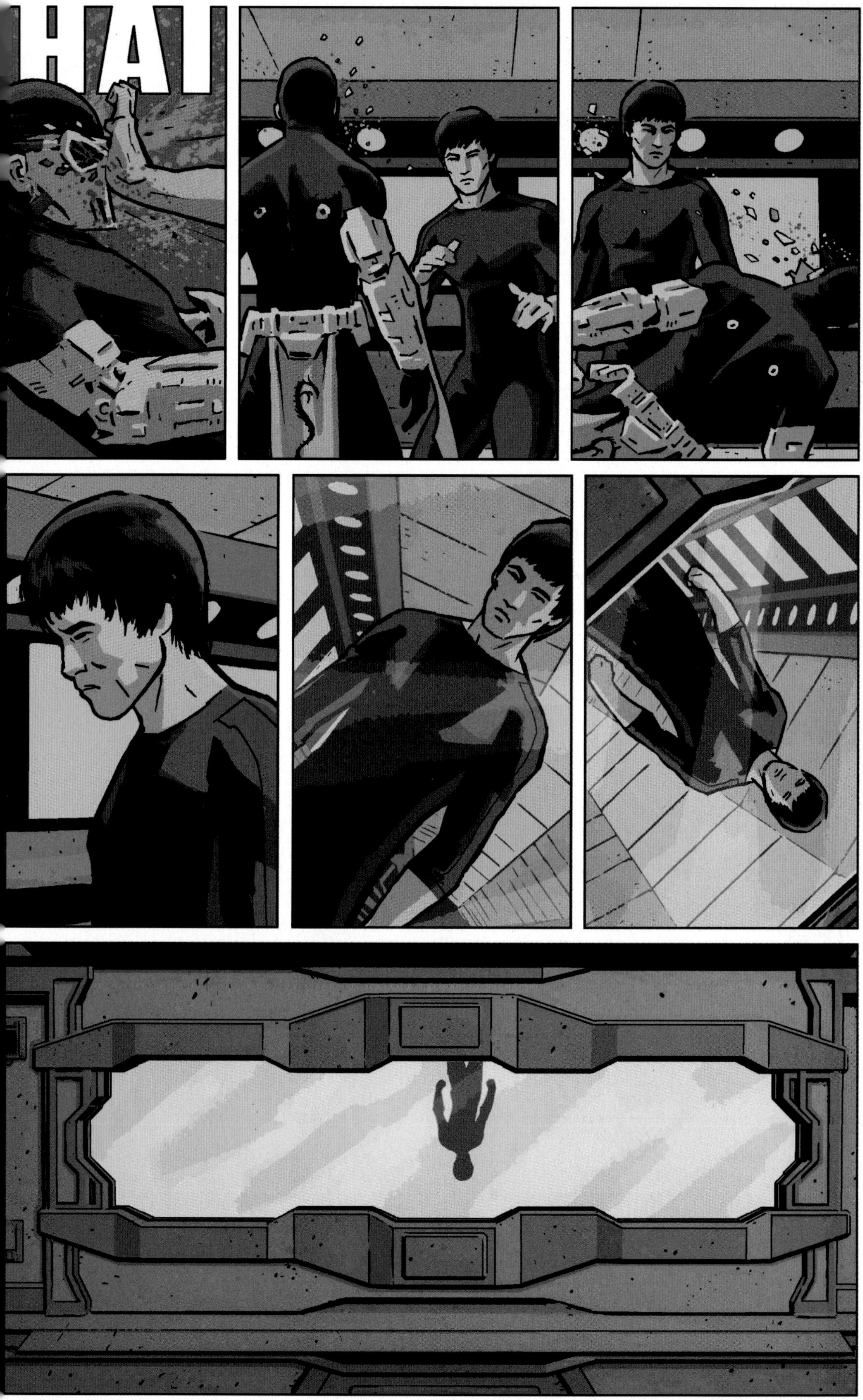
HAI

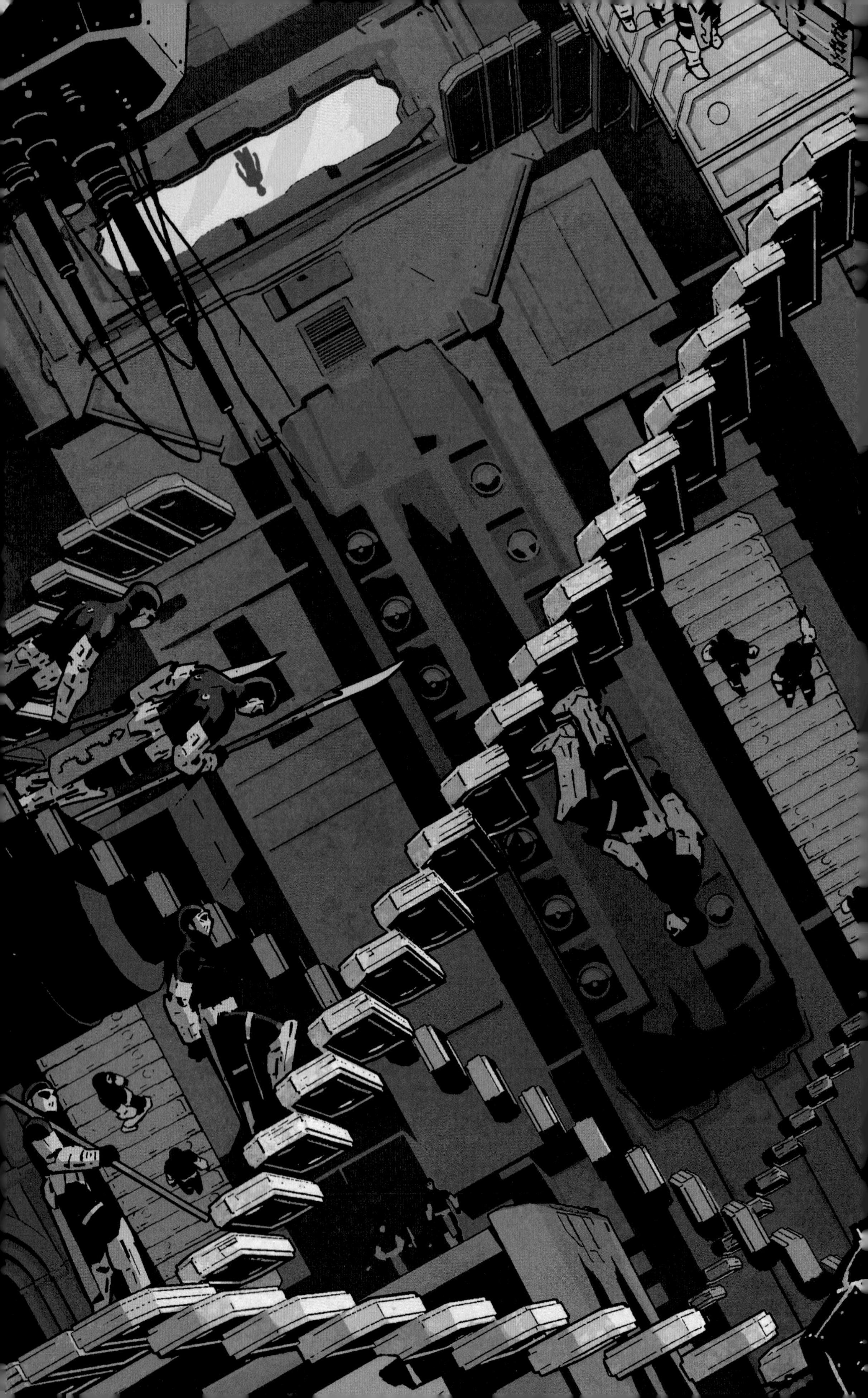

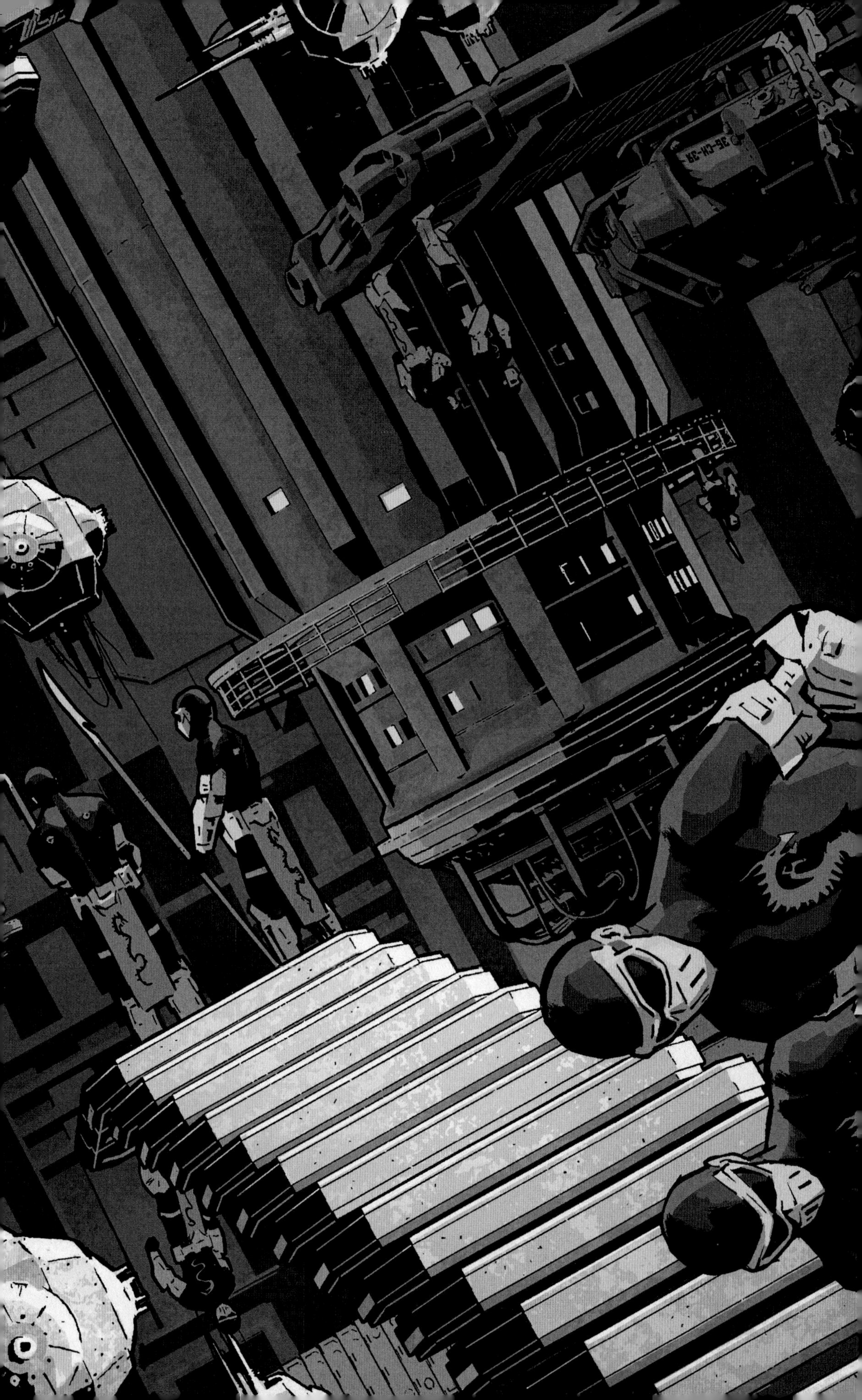

I'VE REVIEWED THE MATERIAL. I'M NOT AN EXPERT IN THIS FIELD, BUT I AM, SHALL WE SAY, SHALLOWLY VERSED IN IT.

THE MULTIVERSE IS A LIVING STRUCTURE. ENTIRE NEW UNIVERSES BUBBLE OFF OF IT EVERY DAY.

NOT ALL OF THEM HAVE A PERFECT BIG BANG. SOME EMERGE BROKEN OR MALFORMED. THESE ARE CALLED BAD CONTINUA.

THE NEGATIVE ZONE FAMOUSLY DISCOVERED BY REED RICHARDS, FOR EXAMPLE, IS A BAD CONTINUUM.

THE NEGATIVE ZONE IS VERY BIG. OTHER BAD CONTINUA CAN BE ONLY A COUPLE OF HUNDRED MILES ACROSS.

"YES"? WHAT DOES "YES" MEAN?

IT'S SHANG-CHI, STEVE. A MAN OF FEWER WORDS EVEN THAN YOU. WHAT CAN YOU HEAR?

BONES BREAKING. I GUESS WE'RE STILL GOOD.

GOD, I'VE NOT OFTEN WISHED MORE FOR A GUN...

THE STATION HULL IS TOO THIN, SHARON. EVEN THE FLECHETTE GUNS WOULD--

THE SHADOW COUNCIL ARE MINING TRANSMATTER IN A BAD CONTINUUM. THIS TRANS-MATTER, IT SEEMS, CAN BE ELECTROLYZED INTO NUCLEAR FUSION.

A TWO-GALLON CAN OF TRANS-MATTER, WHEN SUBJECTED TO A CHILD'S CHEMISTRY EXPERIMENT, COULD VERY EASILY STELLIFY EARTH.

STELLIFY?

TURN EARTH INTO A SUN.

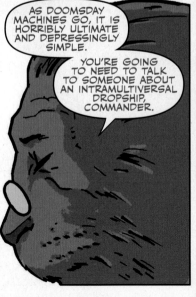

AS DOOMSDAY MACHINES GO, IT IS HORRIBLY ULTIMATE AND DEPRESSINGLY SIMPLE.

YOU'RE GOING TO NEED TO TALK TO SOMEONE ABOUT AN INTRAMULTIVERSAL DROPSHIP, COMMANDER.

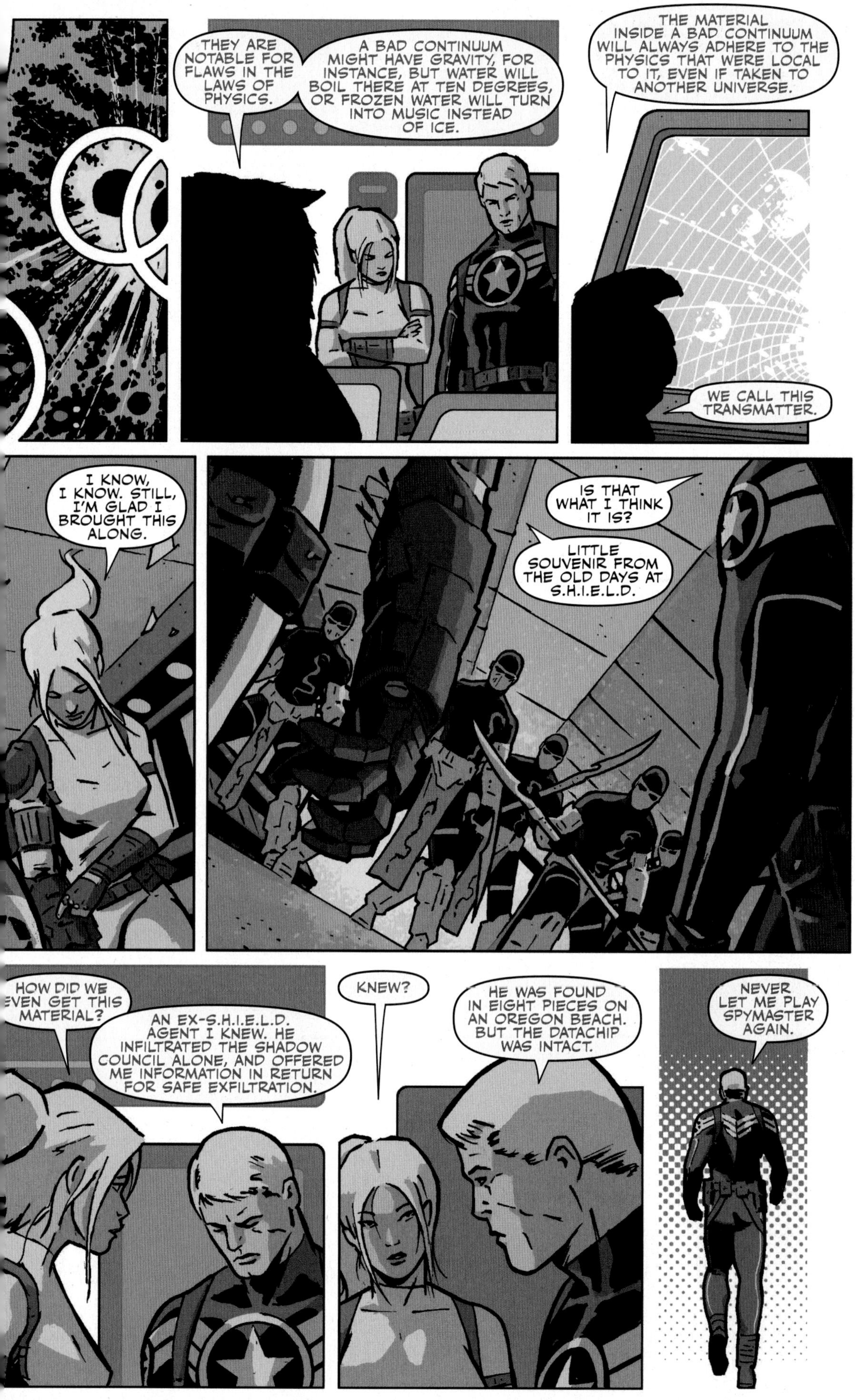
THEY ARE NOTABLE FOR FLAWS IN THE LAWS OF PHYSICS.
A BAD CONTINUUM MIGHT HAVE GRAVITY, FOR INSTANCE, BUT WATER WILL BOIL THERE AT TEN DEGREES, OR FROZEN WATER WILL TURN INTO MUSIC INSTEAD OF ICE.
THE MATERIAL INSIDE A BAD CONTINUUM WILL ALWAYS ADHERE TO THE PHYSICS THAT WERE LOCAL TO IT, EVEN IF TAKEN TO ANOTHER UNIVERSE.
WE CALL THIS TRANSMATTER.
I KNOW, I KNOW. STILL, I'M GLAD I BROUGHT THIS ALONG.
IS THAT WHAT I THINK IT IS?
LITTLE SOUVENIR FROM THE OLD DAYS AT S.H.I.E.L.D.
HOW DID WE EVEN GET THIS MATERIAL?
AN EX-S.H.I.E.L.D. AGENT I KNEW. HE INFILTRATED THE SHADOW COUNCIL ALONE, AND OFFERED ME INFORMATION IN RETURN FOR SAFE EXFILTRATION.
KNEW?
HE WAS FOUND IN EIGHT PIECES ON AN OREGON BEACH. BUT THE DATACHIP WAS INTACT.
NEVER LET ME PLAY SPYMASTER AGAIN.

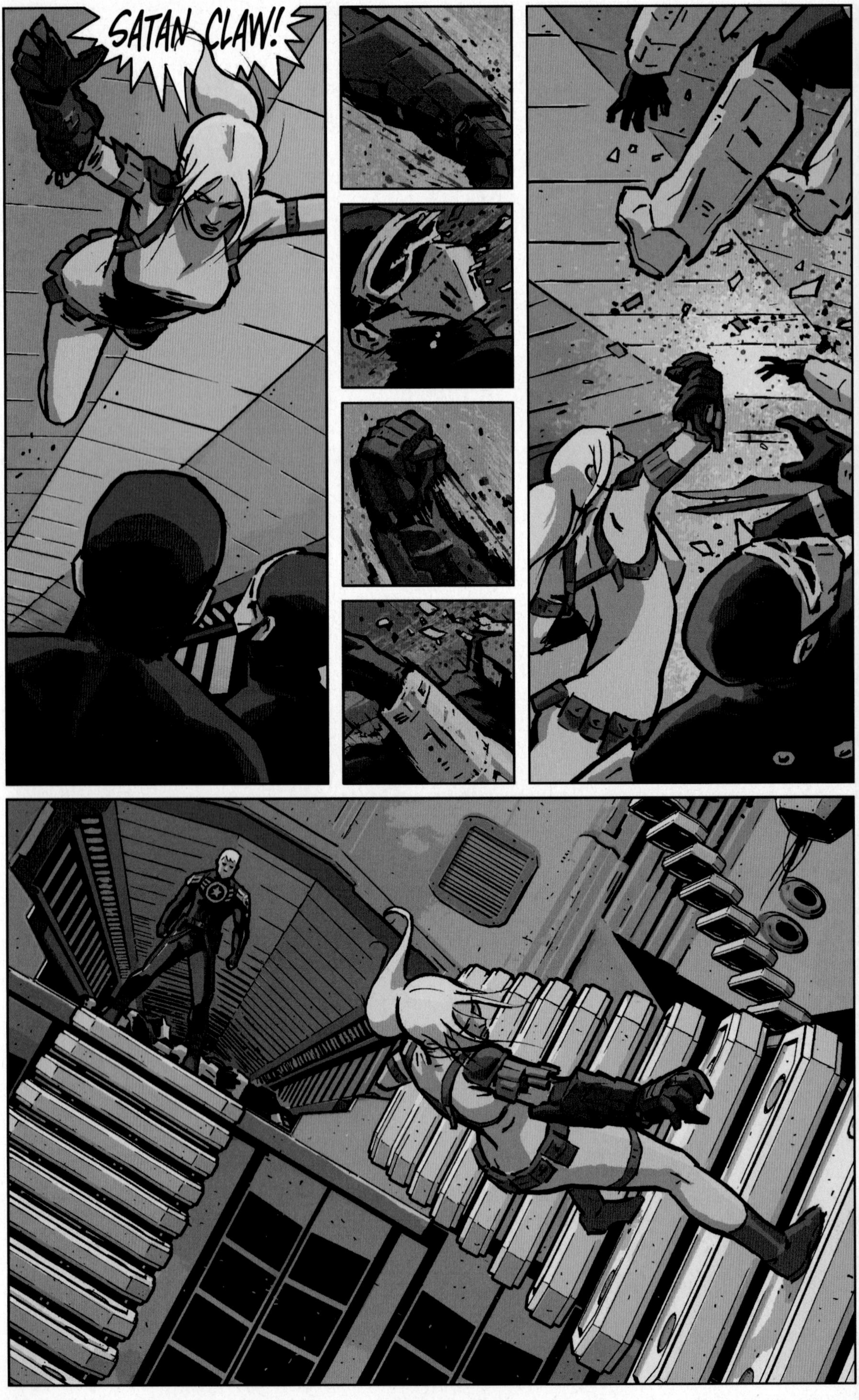
SATAN CLAW!

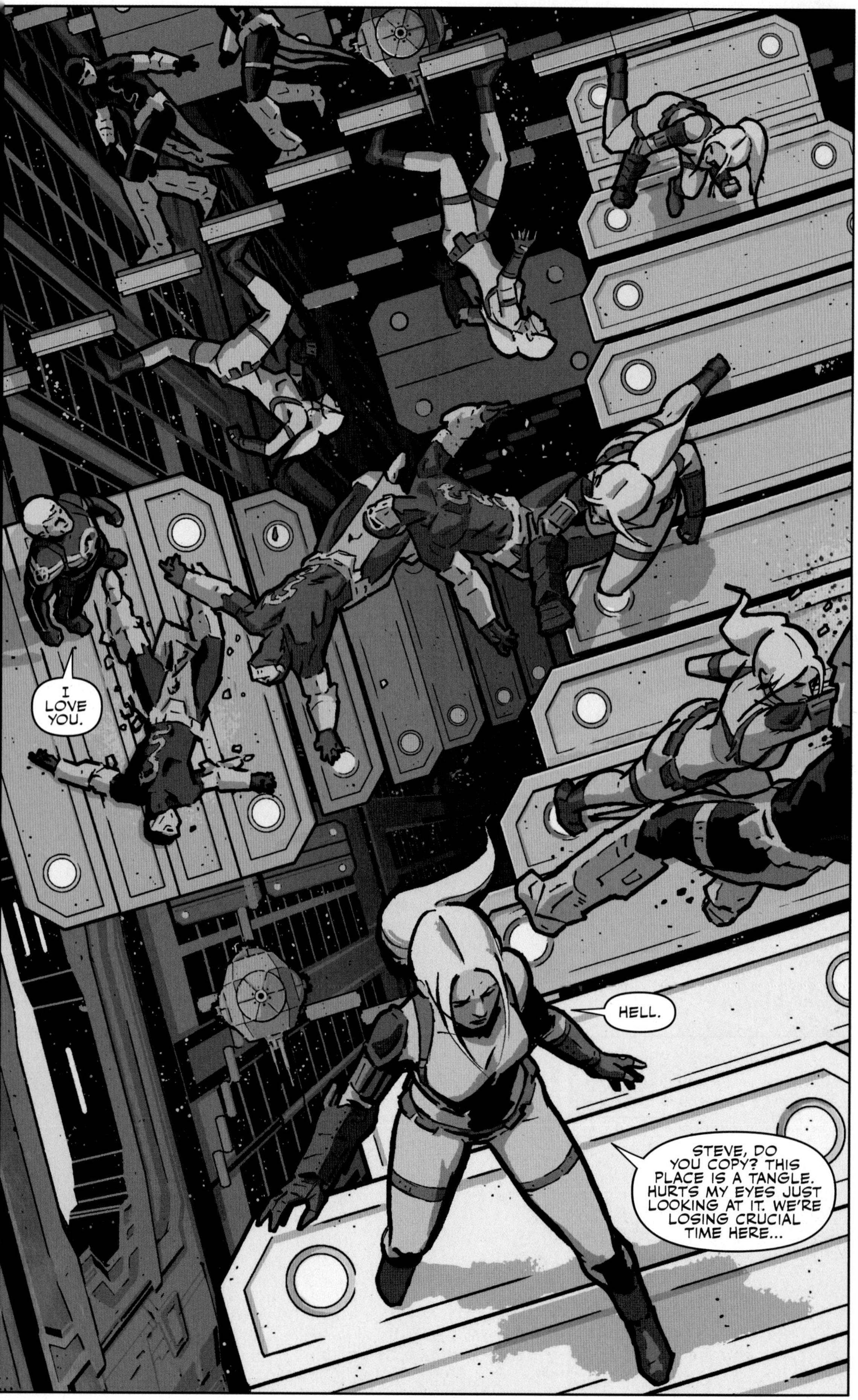
I LOVE YOU.
HELL.
STEVE, DO YOU COPY? THIS PLACE IS A TANGLE. HURTS MY EYES JUST LOOKING AT IT. WE'RE LOSING CRUCIAL TIME HERE...

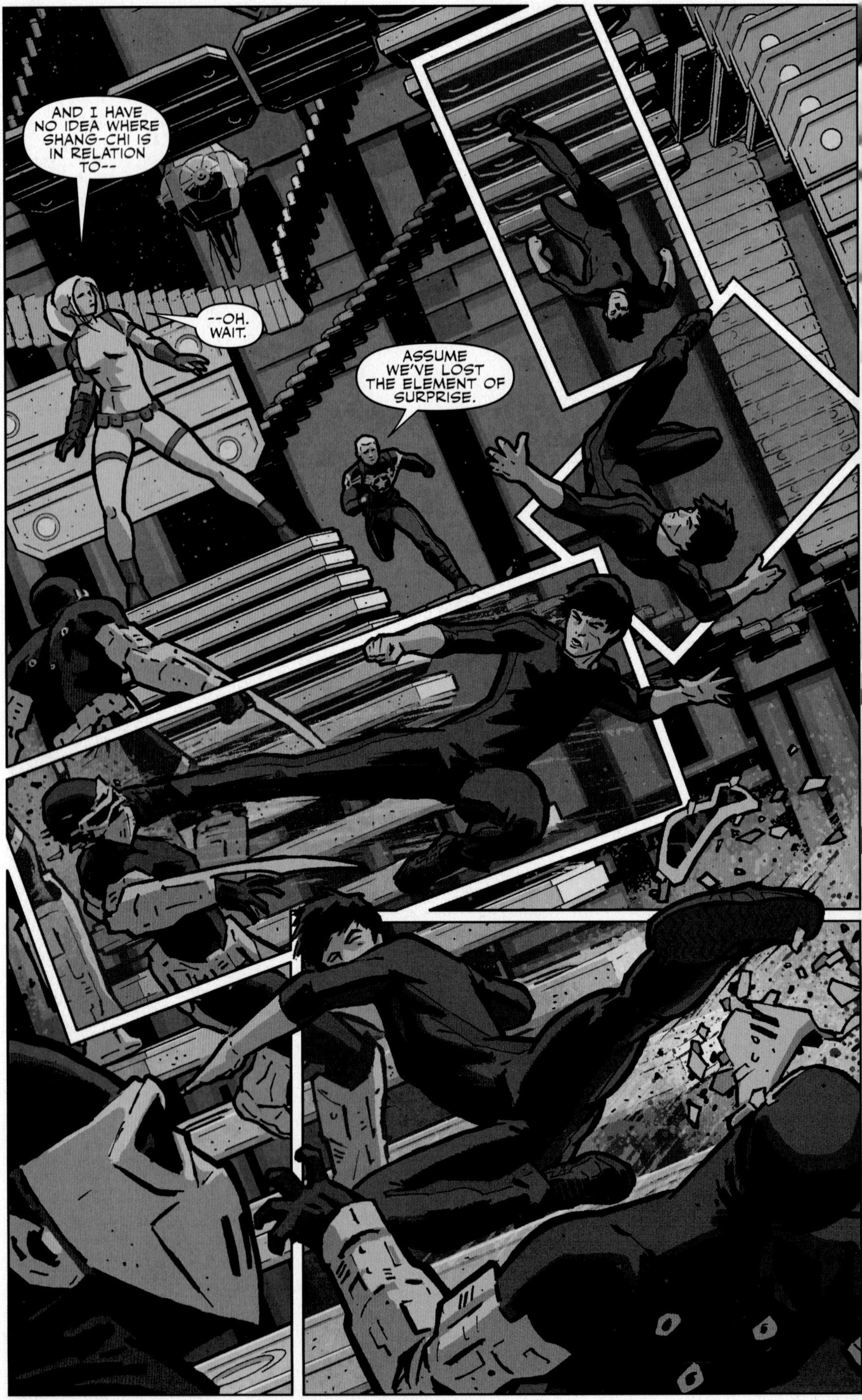
AND I HAVE NO IDEA WHERE SHANG-CHI IS IN RELATION TO--
--OH. WAIT.
ASSUME WE'VE LOST THE ELEMENT OF SURPRISE.

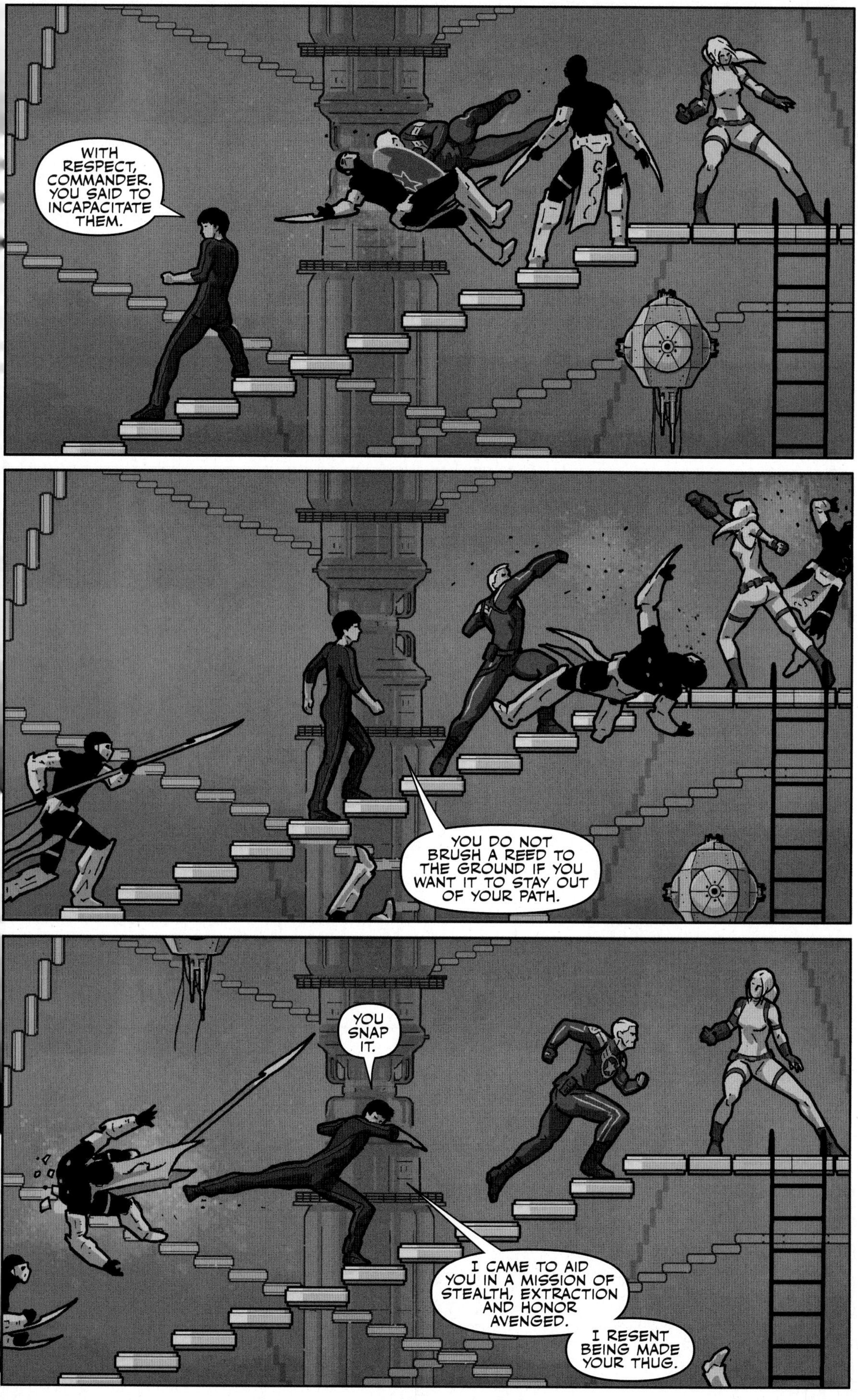
WITH RESPECT, COMMANDER. YOU SAID TO INCAPACITATE THEM.
YOU DO NOT BRUSH A REED TO THE GROUND IF YOU WANT IT TO STAY OUT OF YOUR PATH.
YOU SNAP IT.
I CAME TO AID YOU IN A MISSION OF STEALTH, EXTRACTION AND HONOR AVENGED.
I RESENT BEING MADE YOUR THUG.

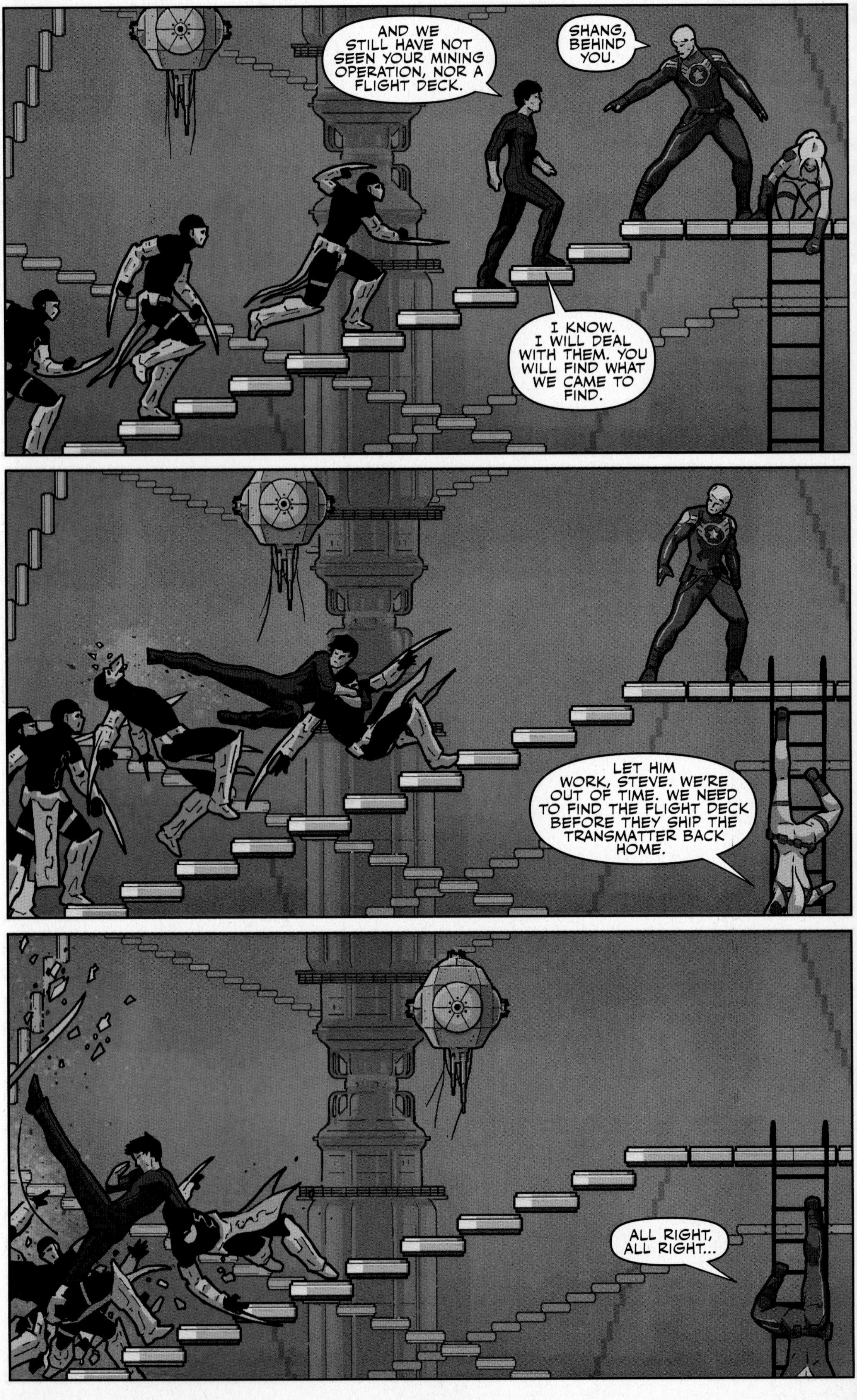
AND WE STILL HAVE NOT SEEN YOUR MINING OPERATION, NOR A FLIGHT DECK.
SHANG, BEHIND YOU.
I KNOW. I WILL DEAL WITH THEM. YOU WILL FIND WHAT WE CAME TO FIND.
LET HIM WORK, STEVE. WE'RE OUT OF TIME. WE NEED TO FIND THE FLIGHT DECK BEFORE THEY SHIP THE TRANSMATTER BACK HOME.
ALL RIGHT, ALL RIGHT...

GOD, WHATEVER HE'S DOING SOUNDS HORRIBLE...

YOU'RE THE ONE WHO SAID LET HIM WORK.

I COULD KICK MYSELF. AVENGERS SURVIVE THROUGH TEAMWORK, AND WE NEVER SEEM TO HAVE ANY.

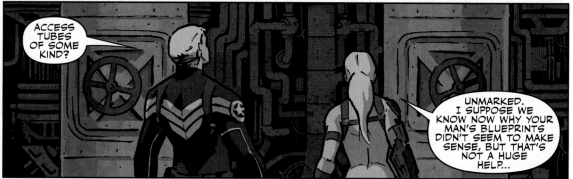

ACCESS TUBES OF SOME KIND?

UNMARKED. I SUPPOSE WE KNOW NOW WHY YOUR MAN'S BLUEPRINTS DIDN'T SEEM TO MAKE SENSE, BUT THAT'S NOT A HUGE HELP...

WAIT.

AAH! WHERE THE HELL DID YOU--

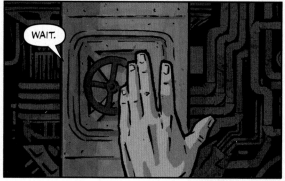

WAIT.

THIS ONE IS COLDER. IT CONNECTS TO A LARGE SPACE BELOW THIS CORRIDOR THAT IS OPEN TO OUTSIDE CONDITIONS.

FLIGHT DECK.

YOU SEE, SHANG? YOU'RE NOT HERE TO BE ANY KIND OF THUG.

YOU'RE HERE TO BE AN AVENGER.

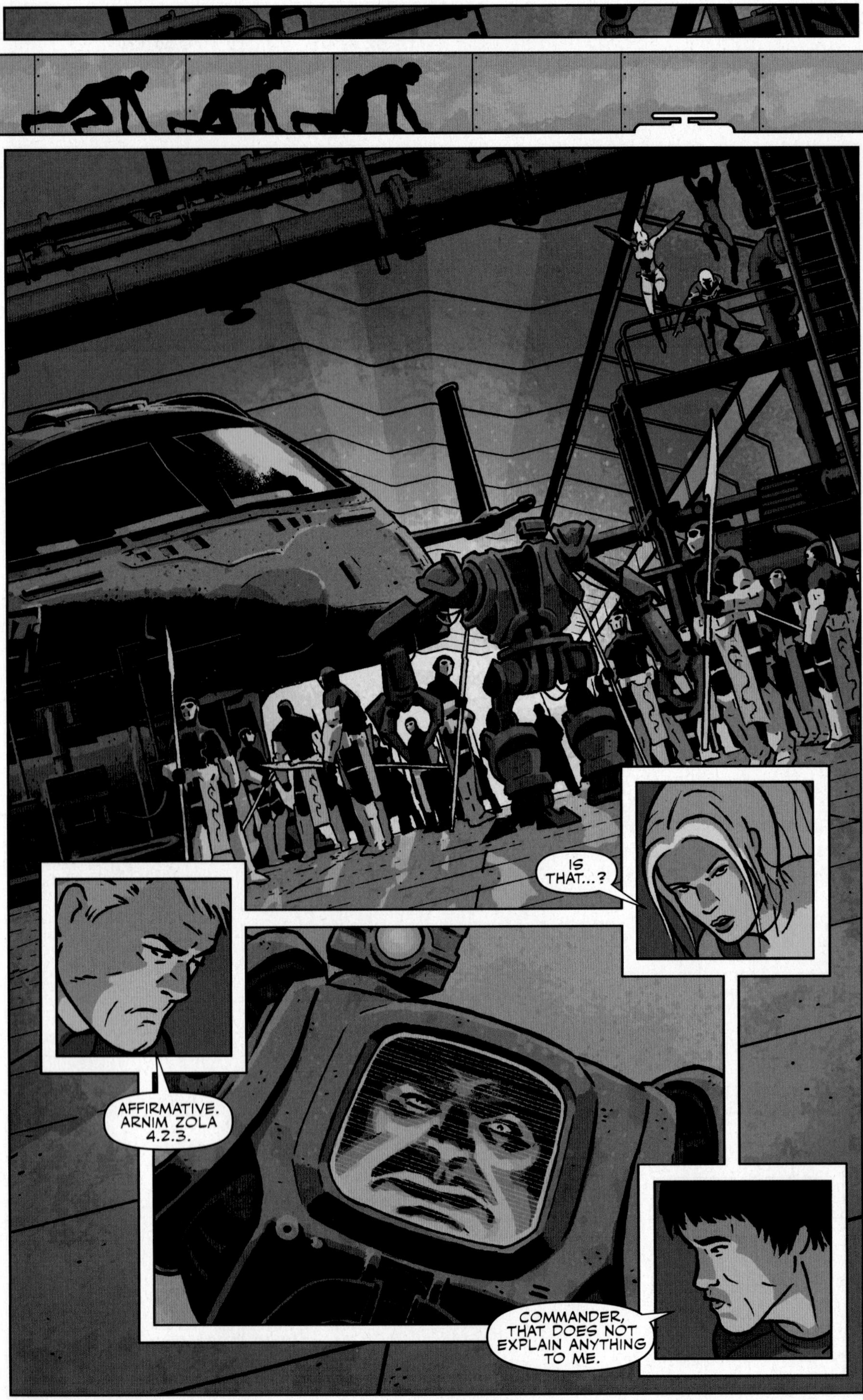
IS THAT...?
AFFIRMATIVE. ARNIM ZOLA 4.2.3.
COMMANDER, THAT DOES NOT EXPLAIN ANYTHING TO ME.

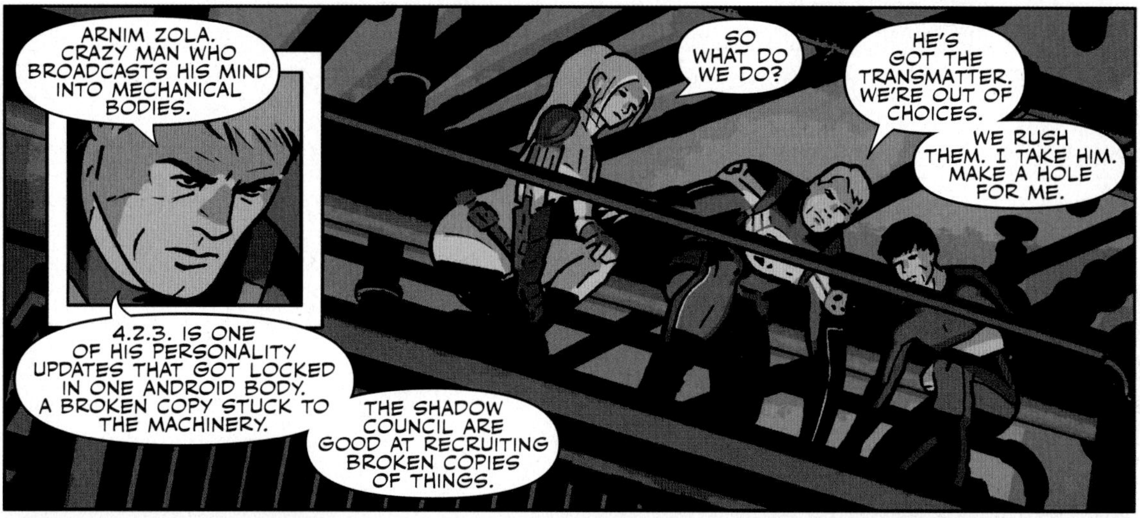
ARNIM ZOLA. CRAZY MAN WHO BROADCASTS HIS MIND INTO MECHANICAL BODIES.
4.2.3. IS ONE OF HIS PERSONALITY UPDATES THAT GOT LOCKED IN ONE ANDROID BODY. A BROKEN COPY STUCK TO THE MACHINERY.
THE SHADOW COUNCIL ARE GOOD AT RECRUITING BROKEN COPIES OF THINGS.
SO WHAT DO WE DO?
HE'S GOT THE TRANSMATTER. WE'RE OUT OF CHOICES.
WE RUSH THEM. I TAKE HIM. MAKE A HOLE FOR ME.

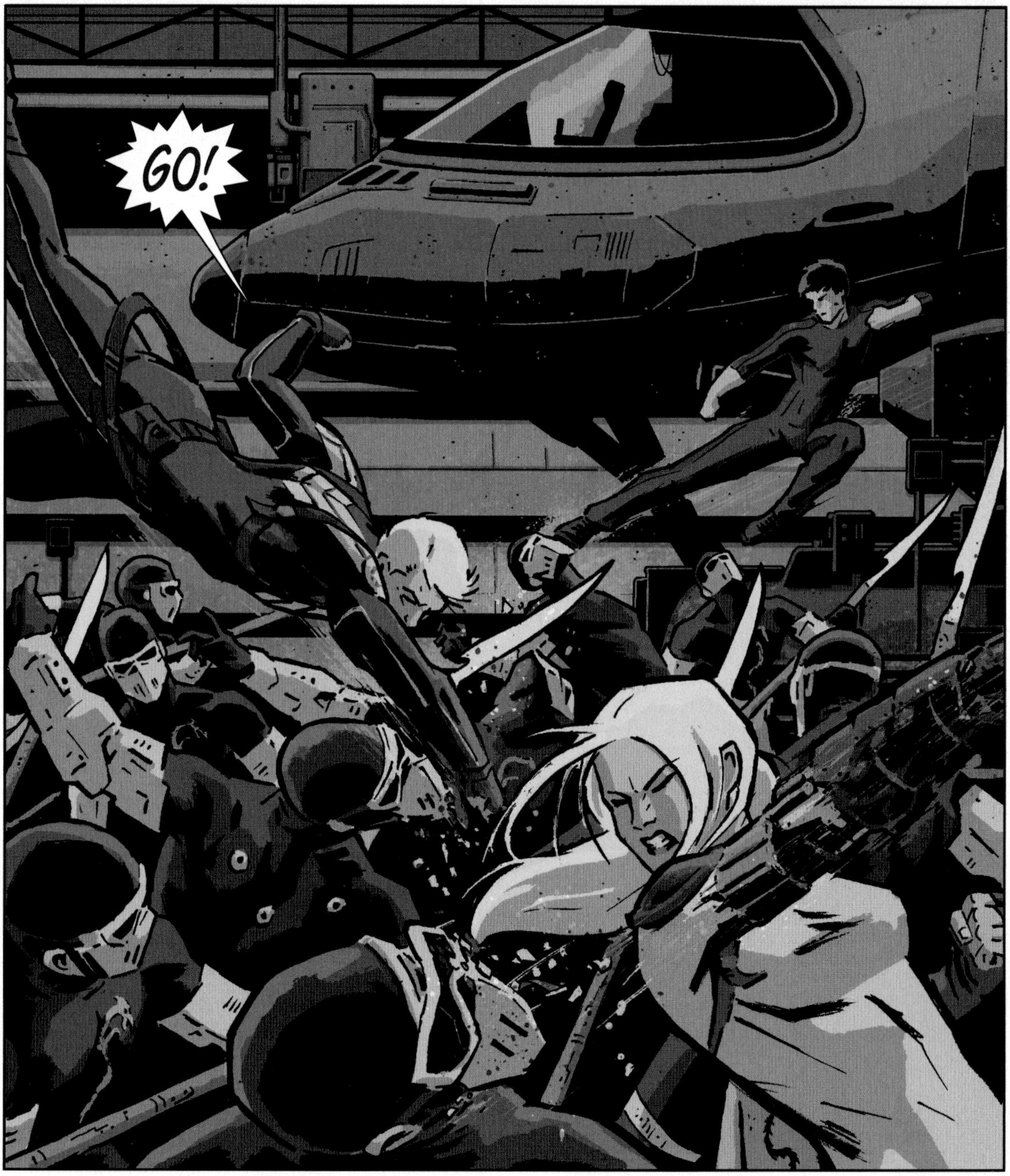
GO!

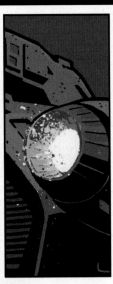

START THE
ENGINES!

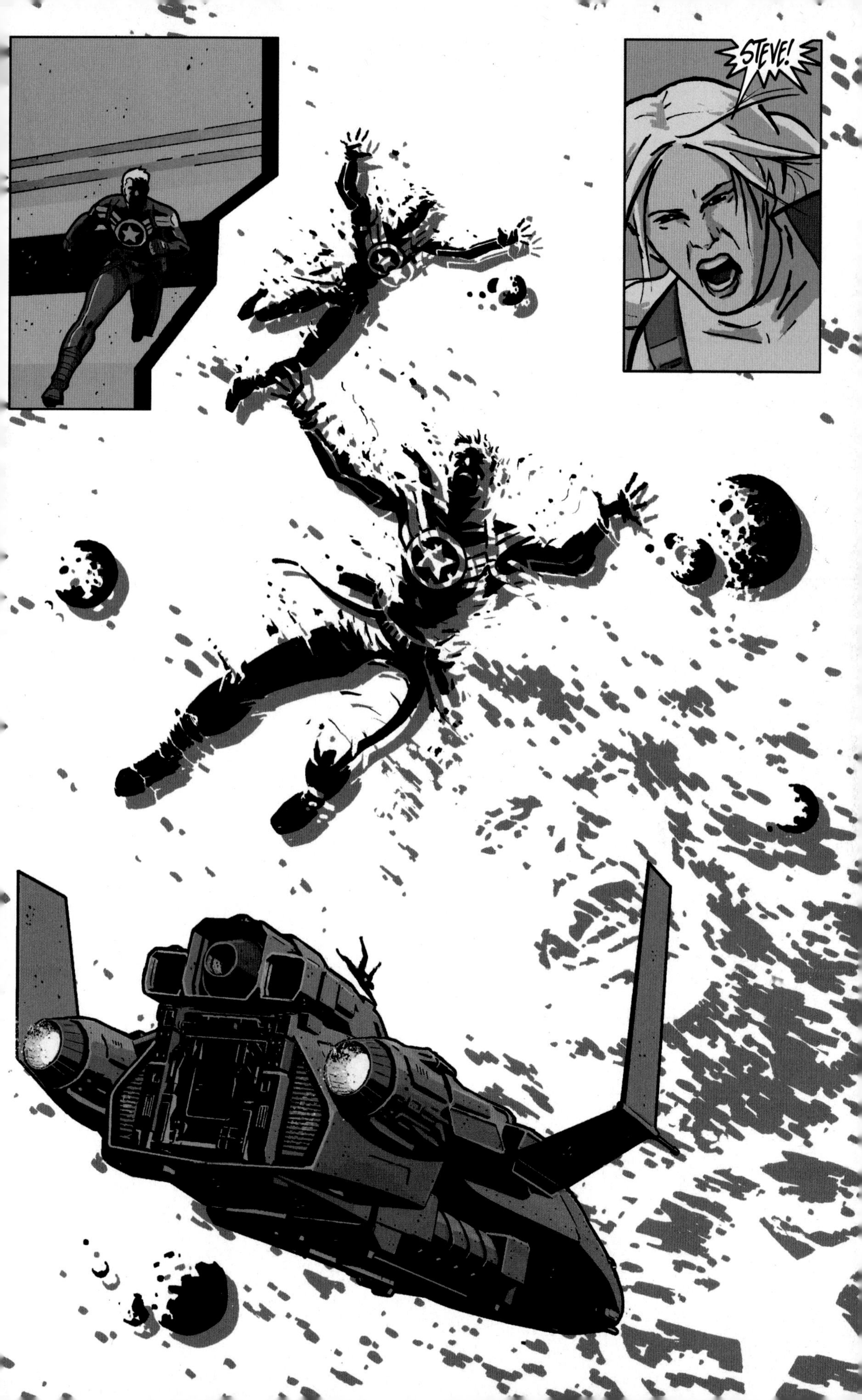
STEVE!

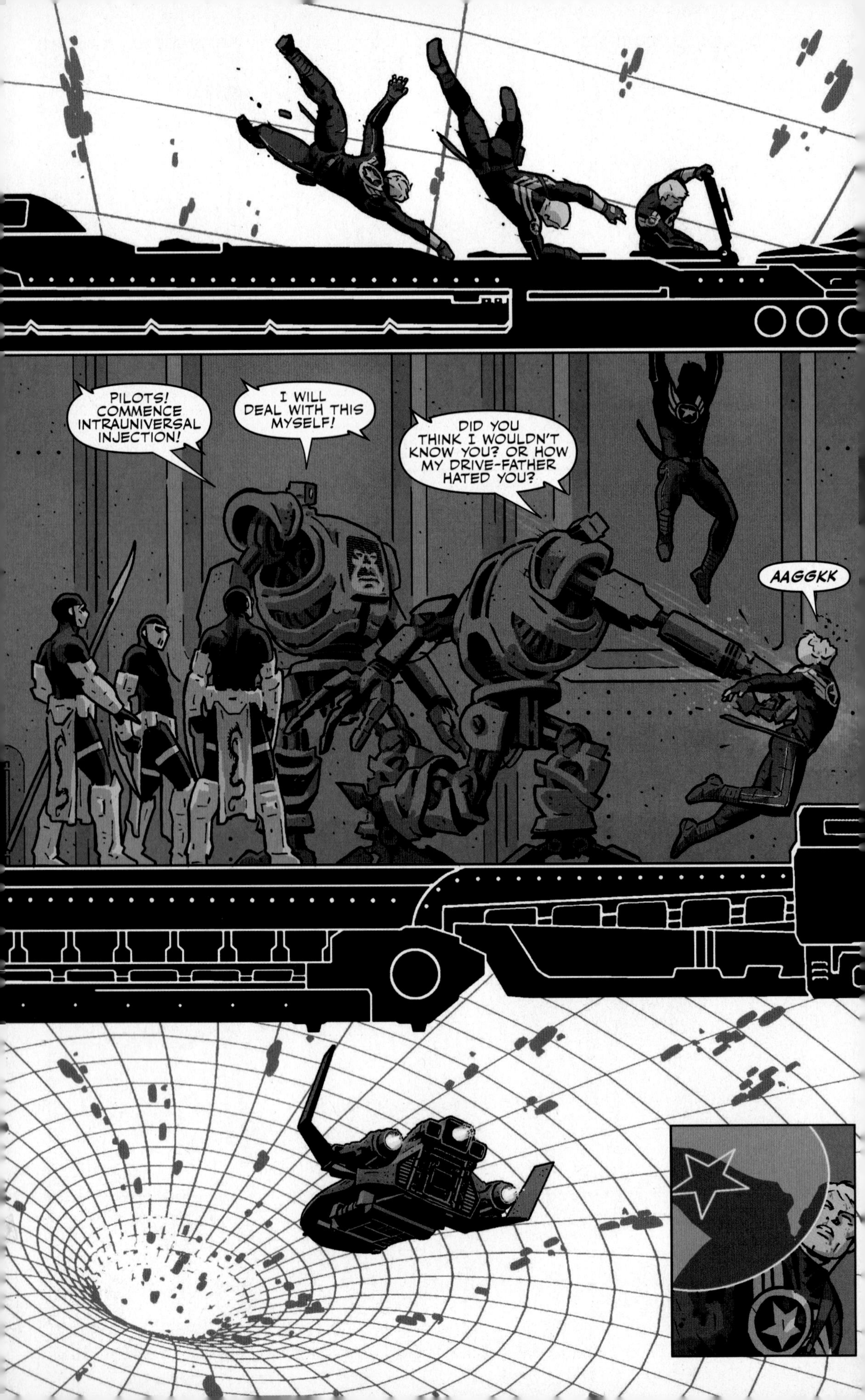
PILOTS! COMMENCE INTRAUNIVERSAL INJECTION!
I WILL DEAL WITH THIS MYSELF!
DID YOU THINK I WOULDN'T KNOW YOU? OR HOW MY DRIVE-FATHER HATED YOU?
AAGGKK

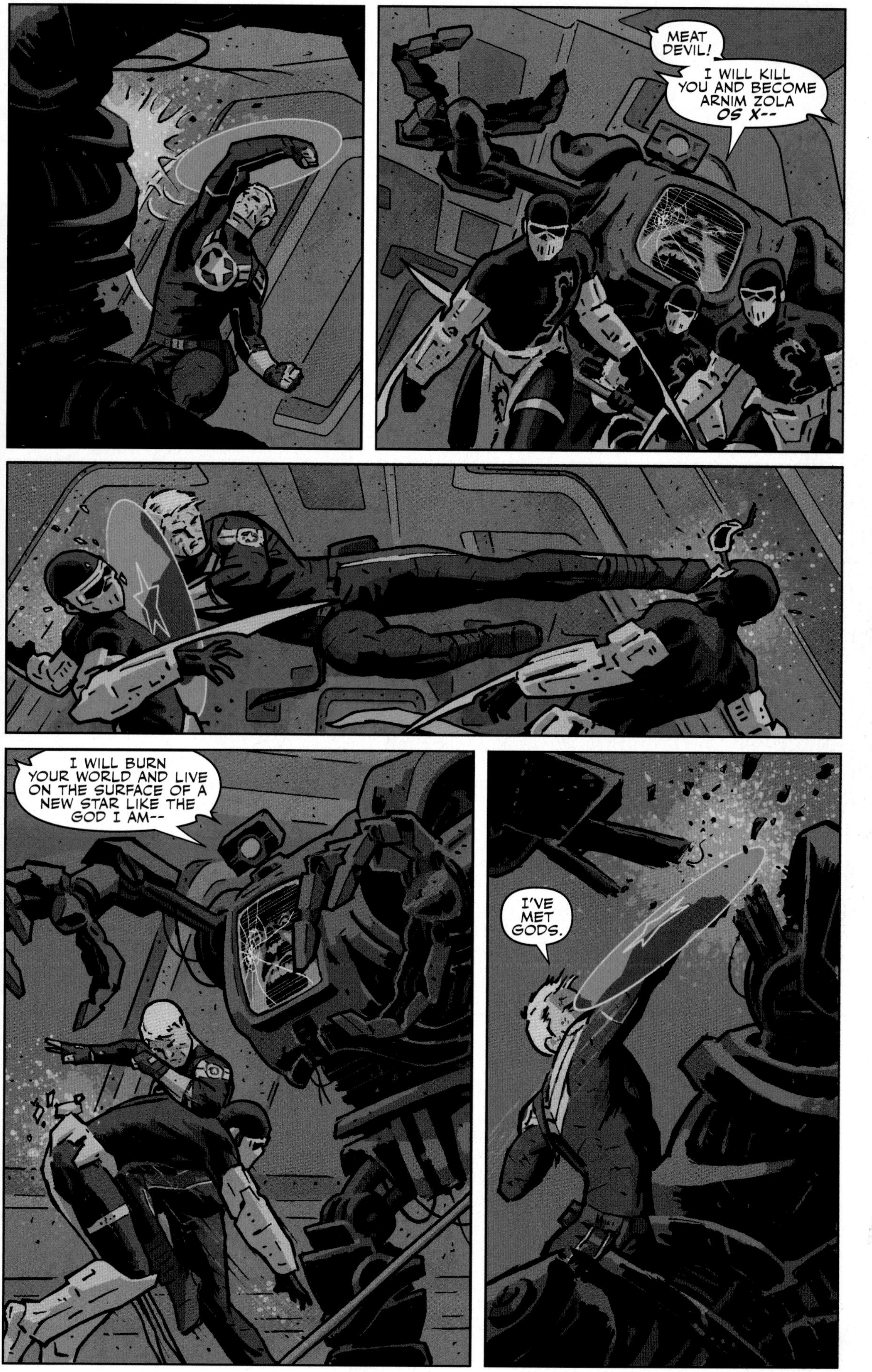
MEAT DEVIL!
I WILL KILL YOU AND BECOME ARNIM ZOLA OS X--
I WILL BURN YOUR WORLD AND LIVE ON THE SURFACE OF A NEW STAR LIKE THE GOD I AM--
I'VE MET GODS.

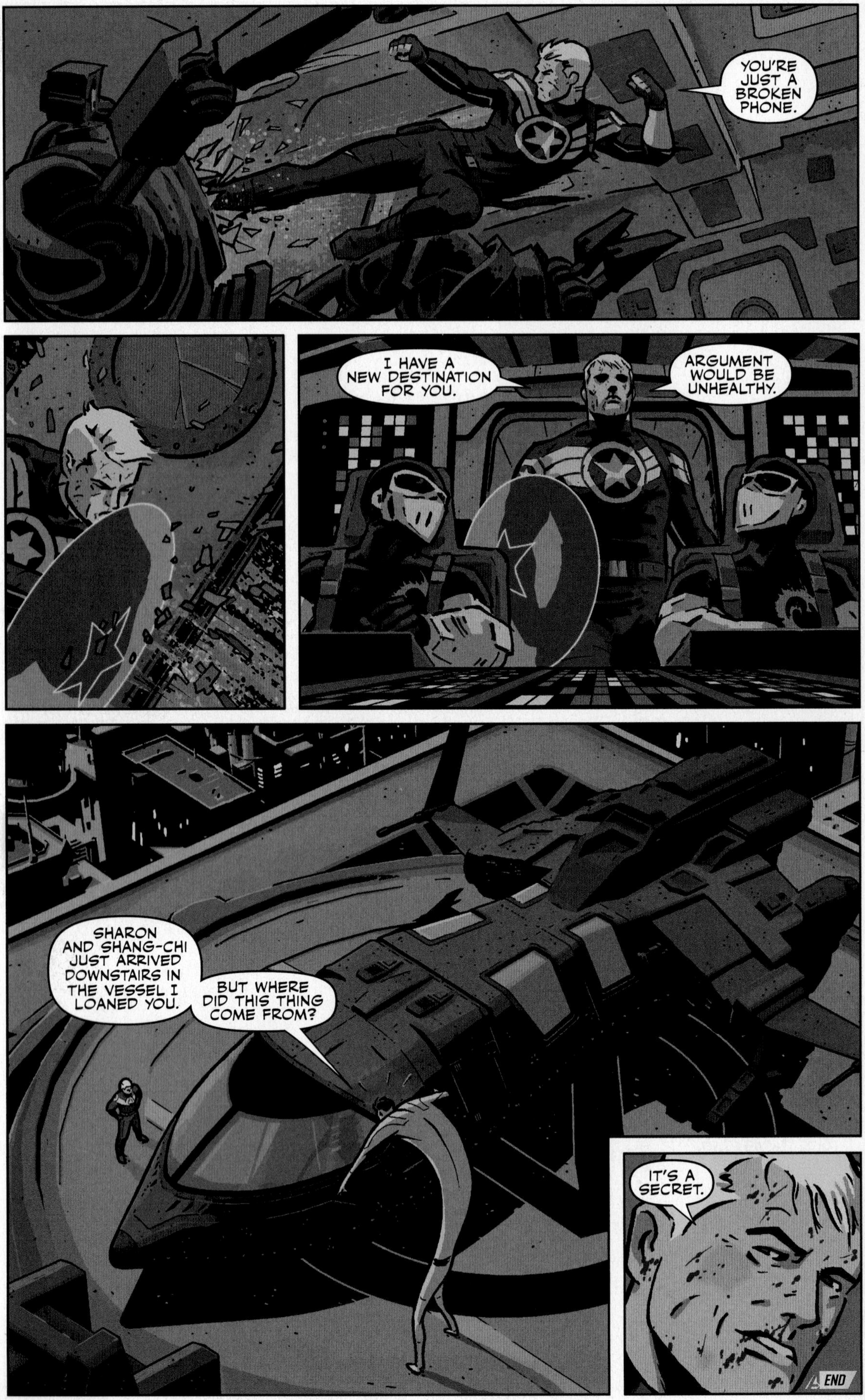
YOU'RE JUST A BROKEN PHONE.
I HAVE A NEW DESTINATION FOR YOU.
ARGUMENT WOULD BE UNHEALTHY.
SHARON AND SHANG-CHI JUST ARRIVED DOWNSTAIRS IN THE VESSEL I LOANED YOU.
BUT WHERE DID THIS THING COME FROM?
IT'S A SECRET.
END

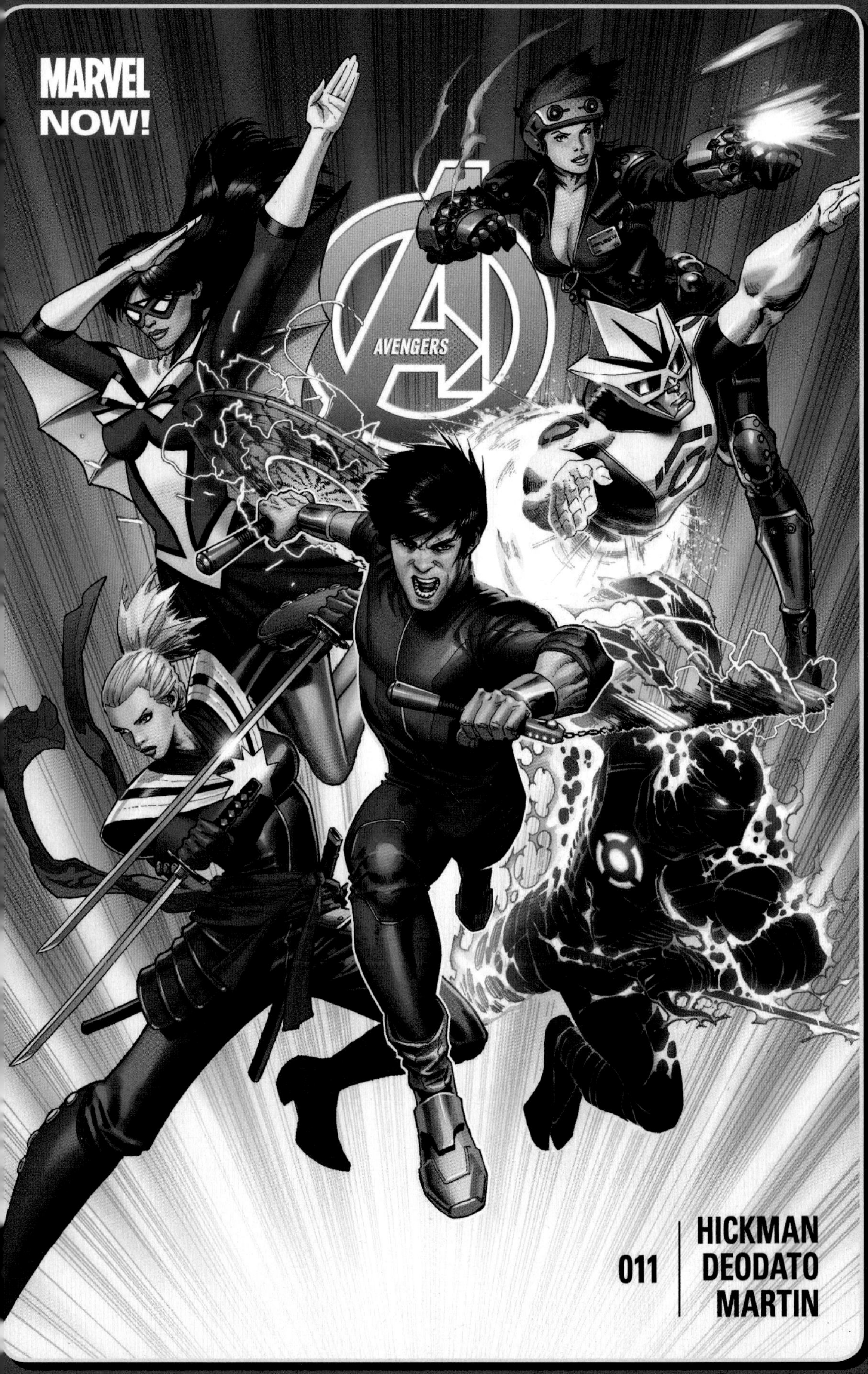
MARVEL
NOW!
AVENGERS
011
HICKMAN
DEODATO
MARTIN

PREVIOUSLY IN AVENGERS

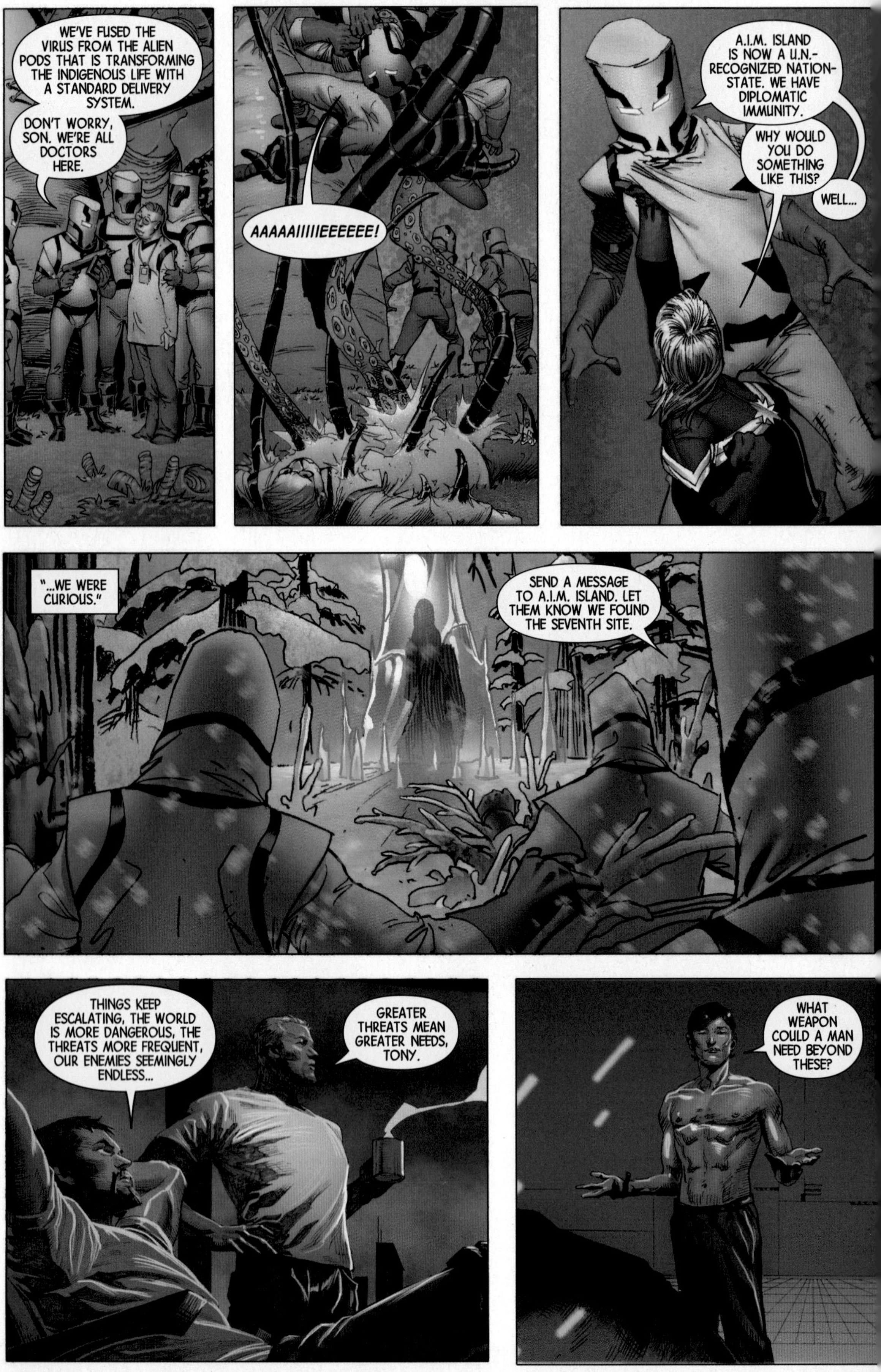
WE'VE FUSED THE VIRUS FROM THE ALIEN PODS THAT IS TRANSFORMING THE INDIGENOUS LIFE WITH A STANDARD DELIVERY SYSTEM.
DON'T WORRY, SON. WE'RE ALL DOCTORS HERE.
AAAAAIIIIIEEEEEE!
A.I.M. ISLAND IS NOW A U.N.-RECOGNIZED NATION-STATE. WE HAVE DIPLOMATIC IMMUNITY.
WHY WOULD YOU DO SOMETHING LIKE THIS?
WELL...
"...WE WERE CURIOUS."
SEND A MESSAGE TO A.I.M. ISLAND. LET THEM KNOW WE FOUND THE SEVENTH SITE.
THINGS KEEP ESCALATING, THE WORLD IS MORE DANGEROUS, THE THREATS MORE FREQUENT, OUR ENEMIES SEEMINGLY ENDLESS...
GREATER THREATS MEAN GREATER NEEDS, TONY.
WHAT WEAPON COULD A MAN NEED BEYOND THESE?

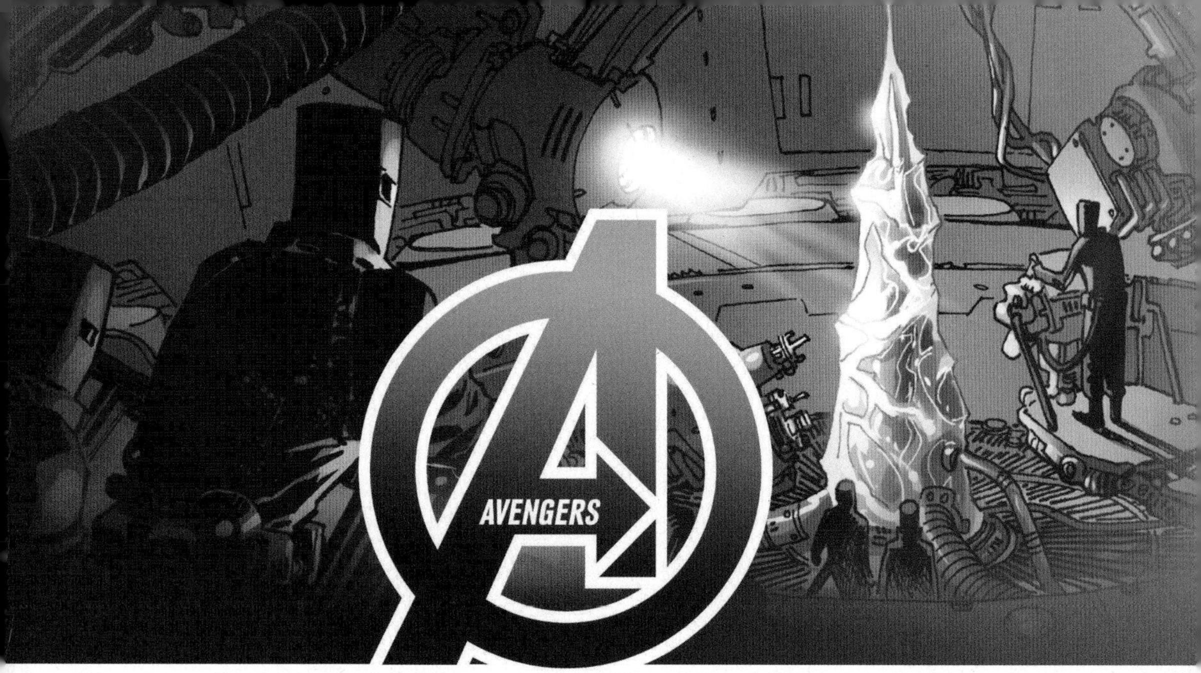
AVENGERS

"WAKE THE DRAGON"

WRITER: JONATHAN HICKMAN
ARTIST: MIKE DEODATO

COLOR ARTIST: FRANK MARTIN
LETTERER: VC's CORY PETIT
COVER ART: DUSTIN WEAVER and JUSTIN PONSOR
ASSISTANT EDITOR: JAKE THOMAS
EDITORS: TOM BREVOORT with LAUREN SANKOVITCH
EDITOR IN CHIEF: AXEL ALONSO
CHIEF CREATIVE OFFICER: JOE QUESADA
PUBLISHER: DAN BUCKLEY
EXECUTIVE PRODUCER: ALAN FINE

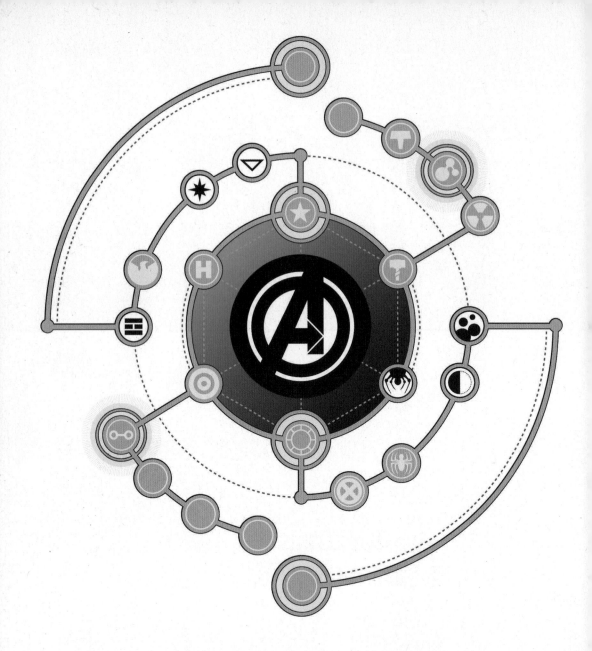

EARTH'S MIGHTIEST HEROES

CAPTAIN AMERICA · IRON MAN · THOR · HAWKEYE · BLACK WIDOW · HULK
WOLVERINE · SPIDER-MAN · CAPTAIN MARVEL · SPIDER-WOMAN
FALCON · SHANG-CHI · SUNSPOT · CANNONBALL · MANIFOLD
SMASHER · CAPTAIN UNIVERSE · HYPERION

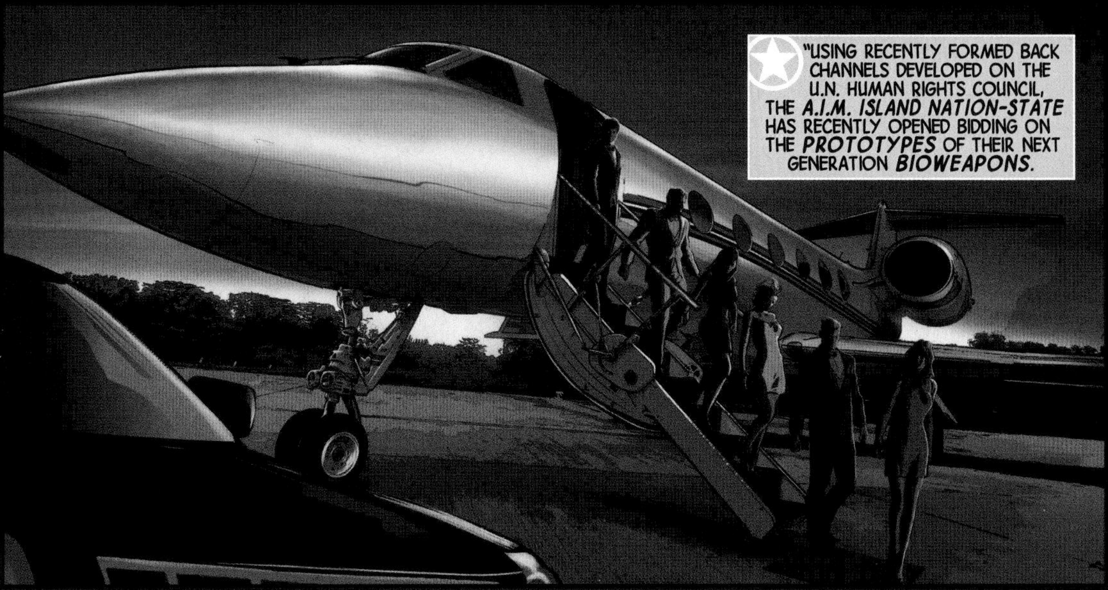
"USING RECENTLY FORMED BACK CHANNELS DEVELOPED ON THE U.N. HUMAN RIGHTS COUNCIL, THE A.I.M. ISLAND NATION-STATE HAS RECENTLY OPENED BIDDING ON THE PROTOTYPES OF THEIR NEXT GENERATION BIOWEAPONS.

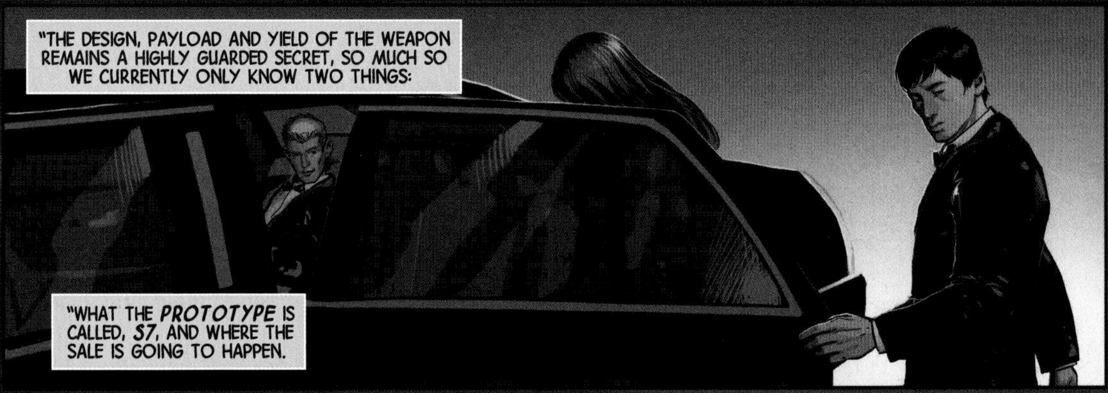
"THE DESIGN, PAYLOAD AND YIELD OF THE WEAPON REMAINS A HIGHLY GUARDED SECRET, SO MUCH SO WE CURRENTLY ONLY KNOW TWO THINGS:
"WHAT THE PROTOTYPE IS CALLED, S7, AND WHERE THE SALE IS GOING TO HAPPEN.

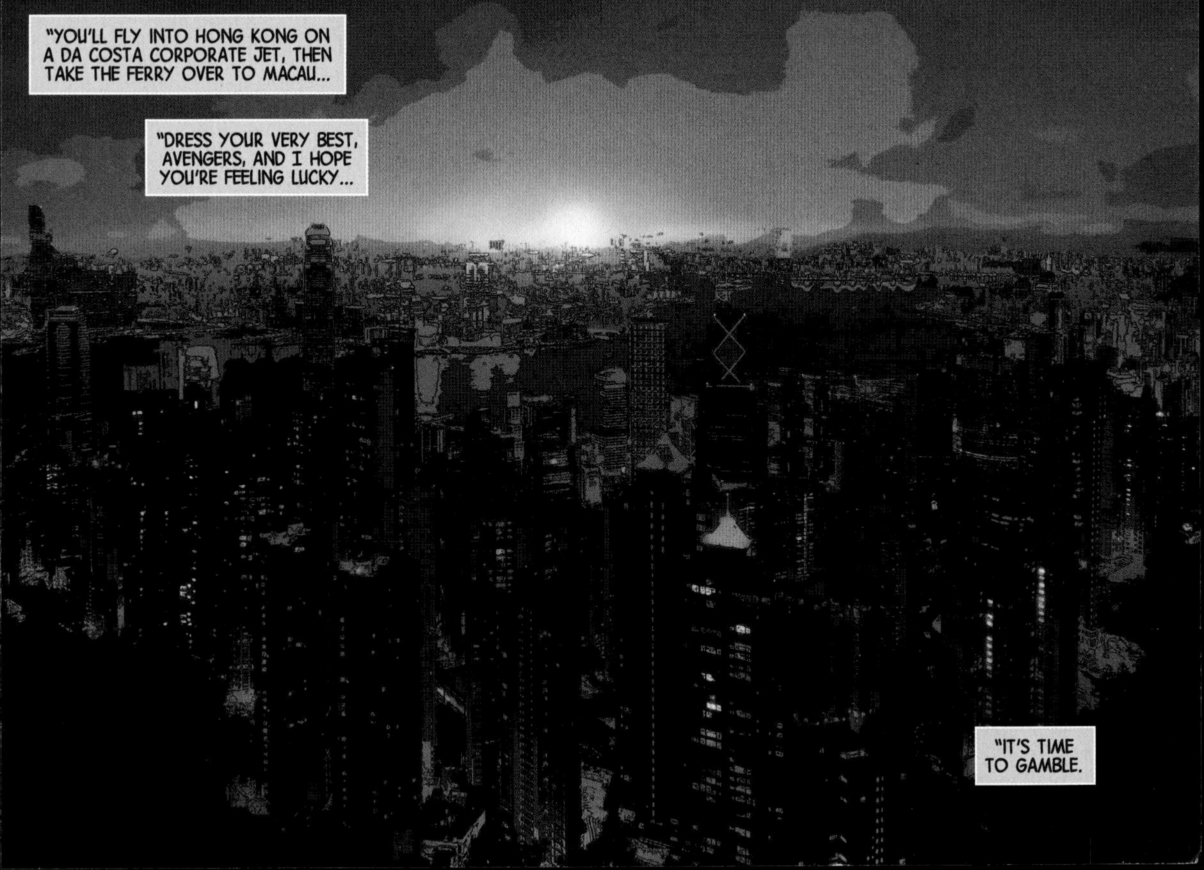
"YOU'LL FLY INTO HONG KONG ON A DA COSTA CORPORATE JET, THEN TAKE THE FERRY OVER TO MACAU...
"DRESS YOUR VERY BEST, AVENGERS, AND I HOPE YOU'RE FEELING LUCKY...
"IT'S TIME TO GAMBLE.

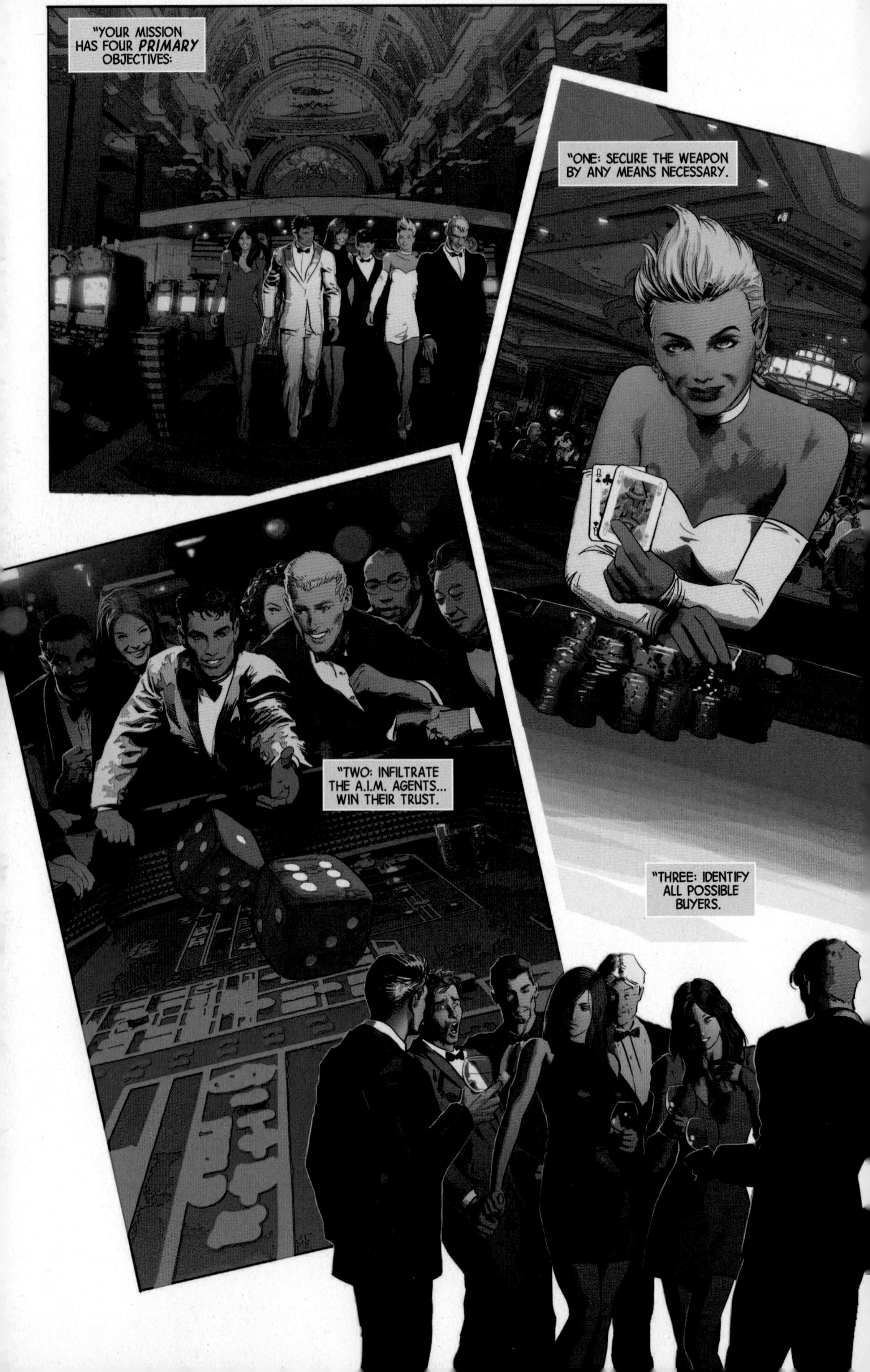
"YOUR MISSION HAS FOUR PRIMARY OBJECTIVES:
"ONE: SECURE THE WEAPON BY ANY MEANS NECESSARY.
"TWO: INFILTRATE THE A.I.M. AGENTS... WIN THEIR TRUST.
"THREE: IDENTIFY ALL POSSIBLE BUYERS.

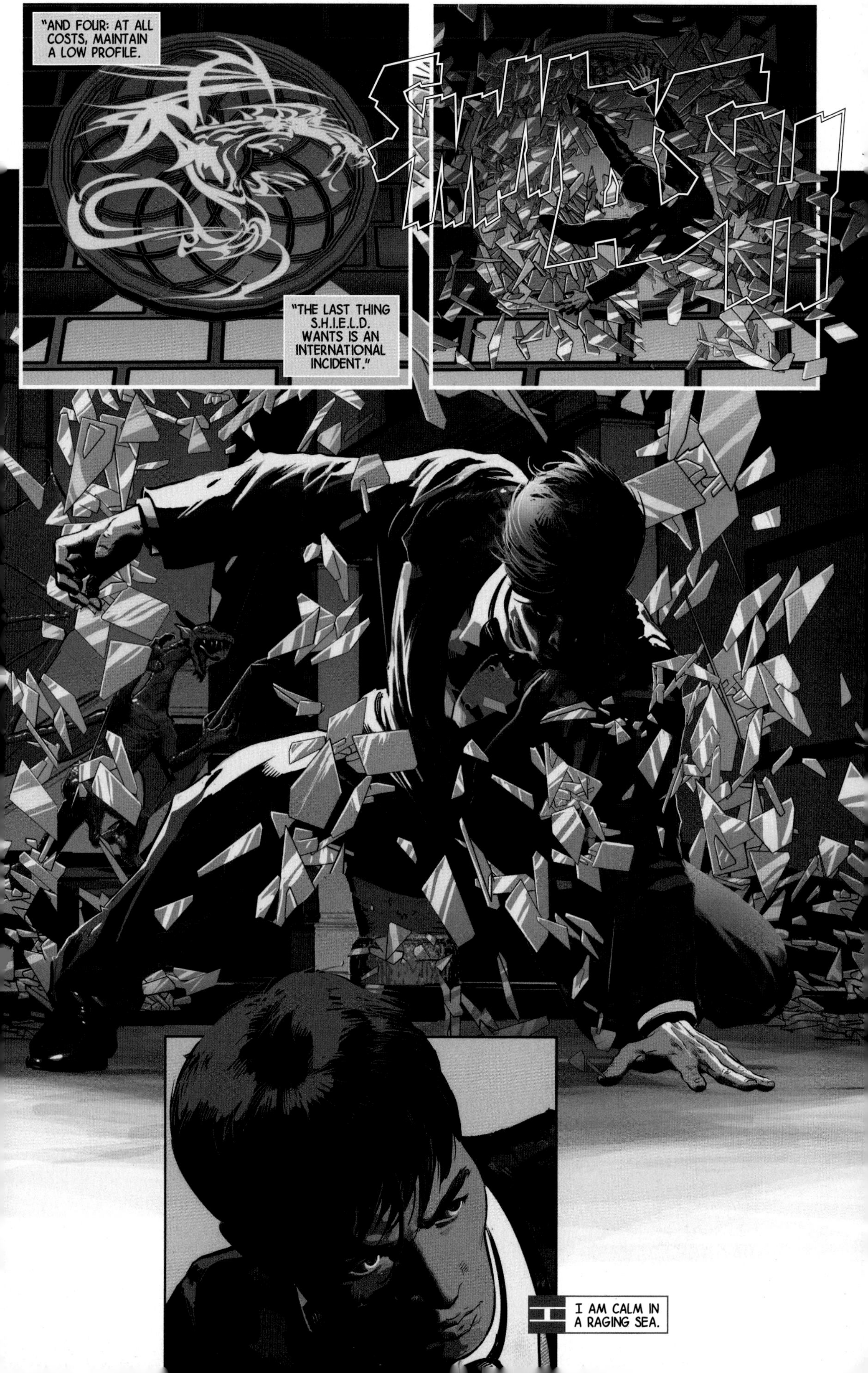
"AND FOUR: AT ALL COSTS, MAINTAIN A LOW PROFILE.
"THE LAST THING S.H.I.E.L.D. WANTS IS AN INTERNATIONAL INCIDENT."
I AM CALM IN A RAGING SEA.

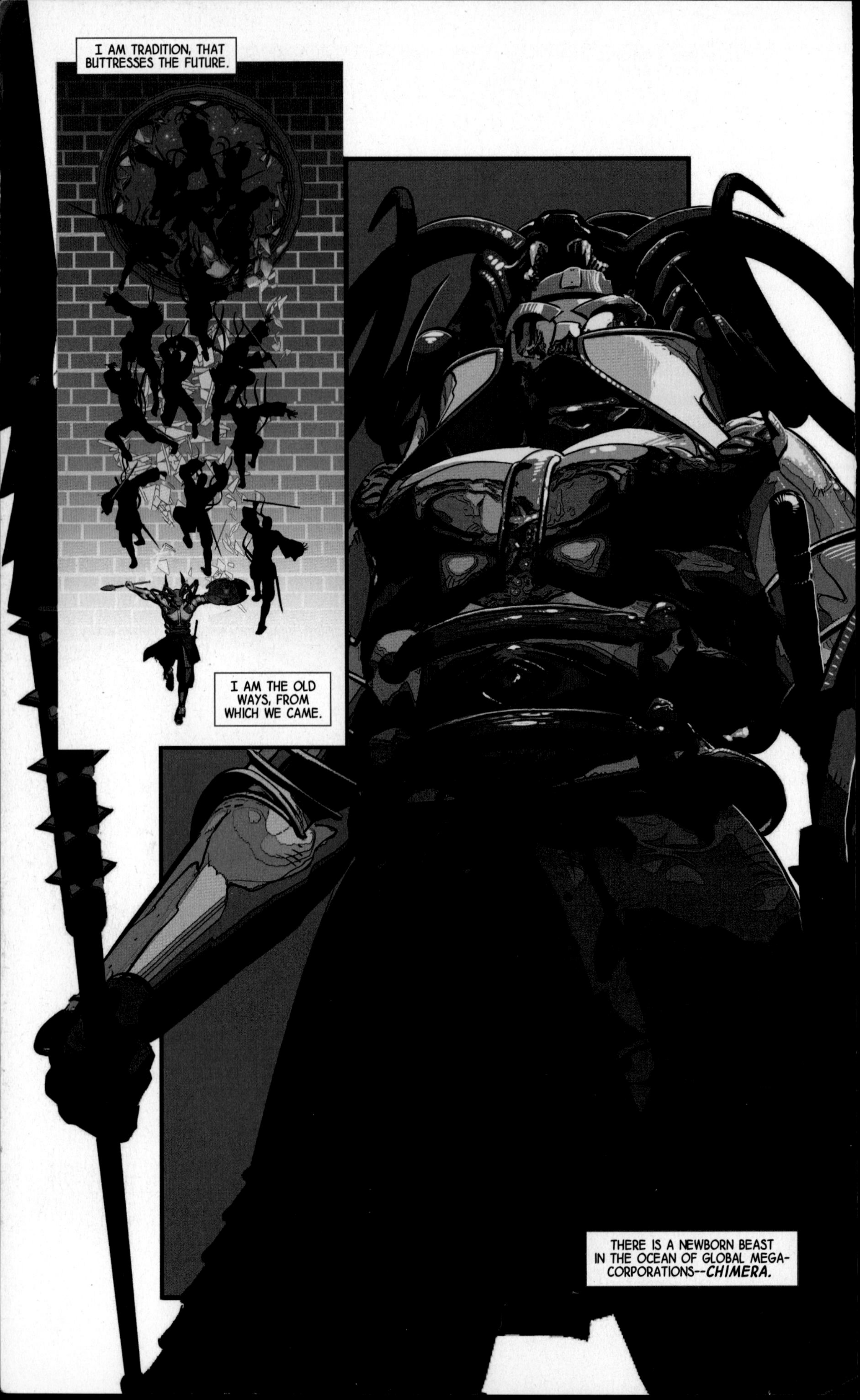
I AM TRADITION, THAT BUTTRESSES THE FUTURE.
I AM THE OLD WAYS, FROM WHICH WE CAME.
THERE IS A NEWBORN BEAST IN THE OCEAN OF GLOBAL MEGA-CORPORATIONS--*CHIMERA.*

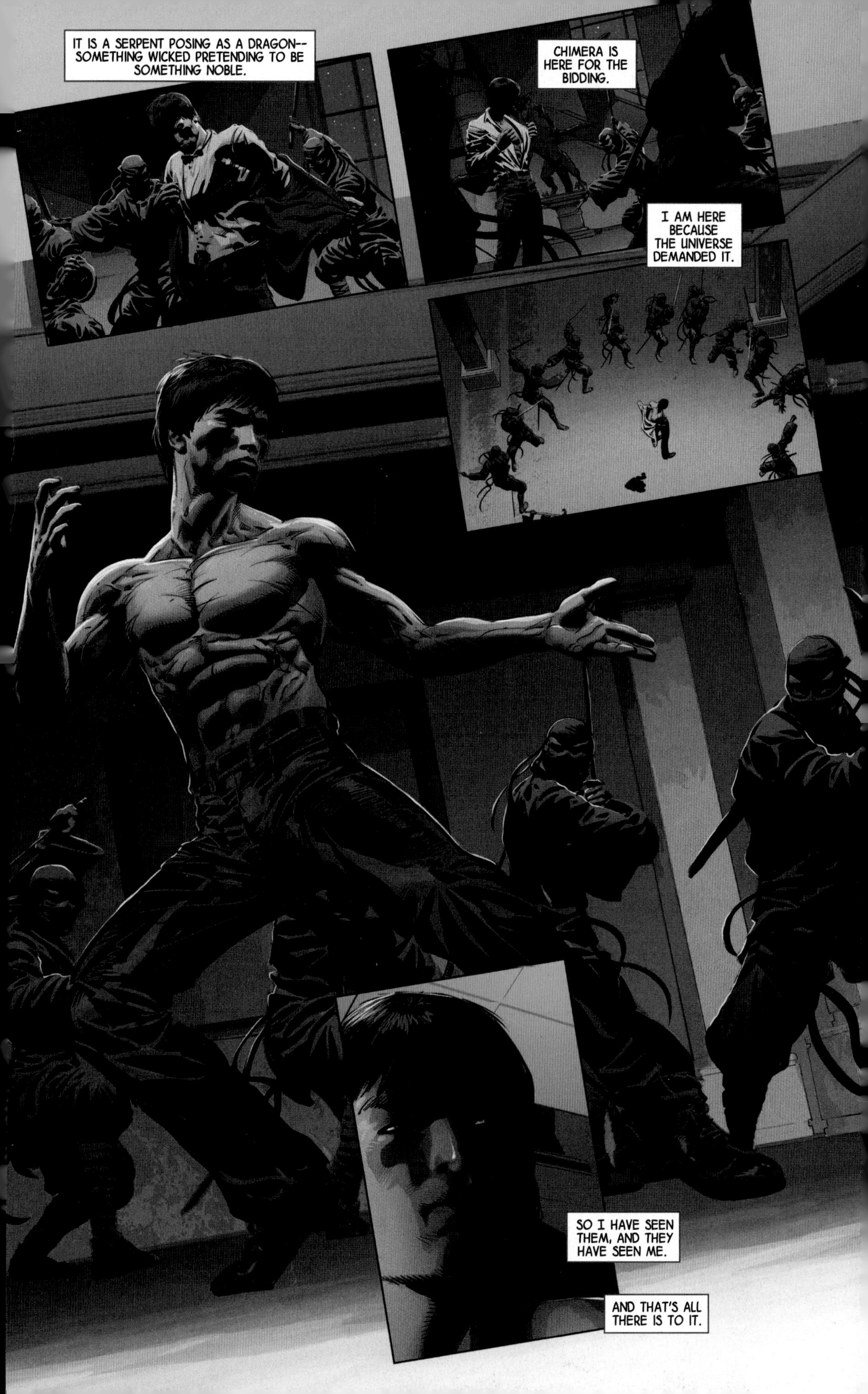
IT IS A SERPENT POSING AS A DRAGON-- SOMETHING WICKED PRETENDING TO BE SOMETHING NOBLE.
CHIMERA IS HERE FOR THE BIDDING.
I AM HERE BECAUSE THE UNIVERSE DEMANDED IT.
SO I HAVE SEEN THEM, AND THEY HAVE SEEN ME.
AND THAT'S ALL THERE IS TO IT.

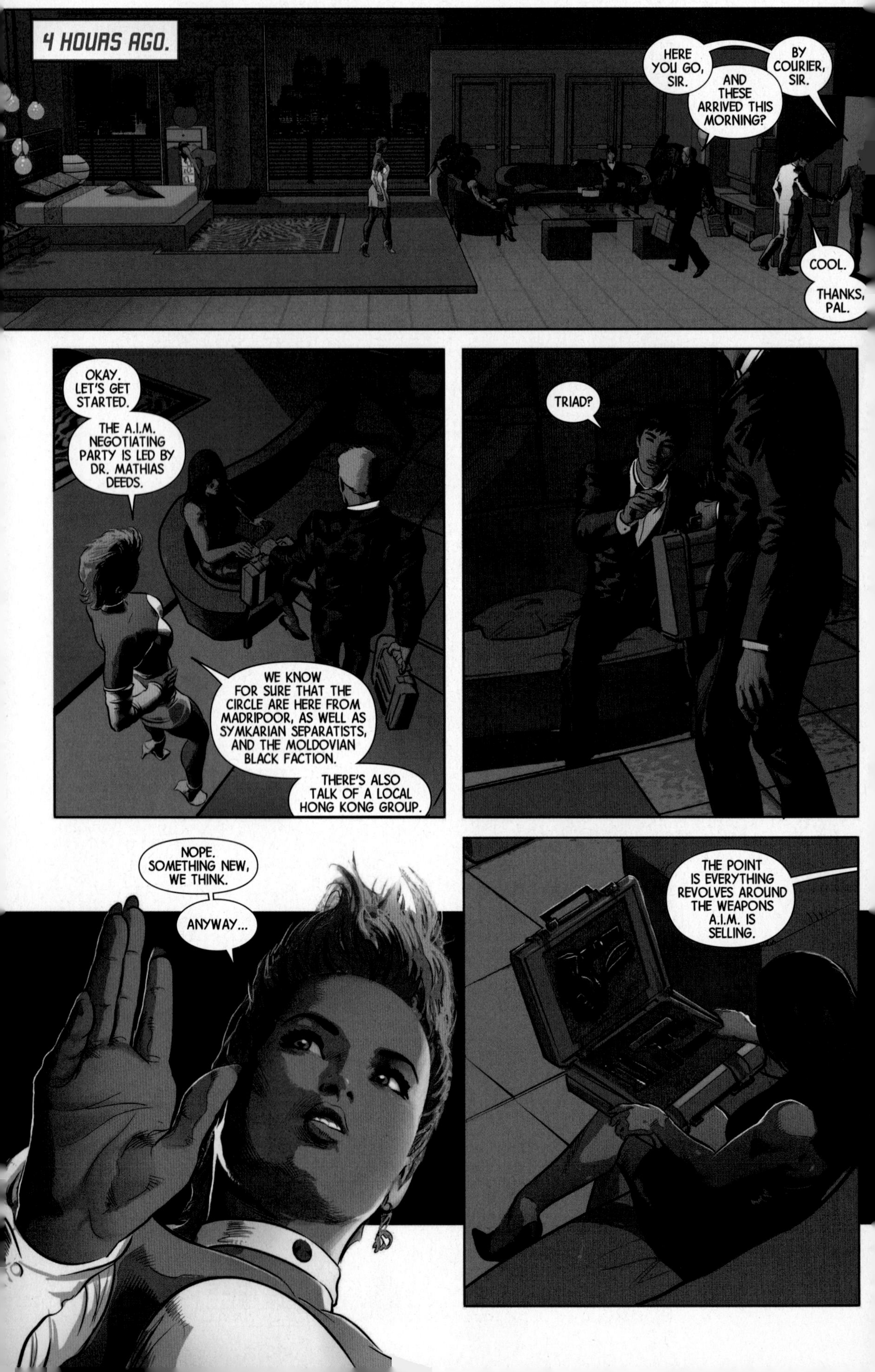
4 HOURS AGO.
HERE YOU GO, SIR.
BY COURIER, SIR.
AND THESE ARRIVED THIS MORNING?
COOL.
THANKS, PAL.
OKAY. LET'S GET STARTED.
THE A.I.M. NEGOTIATING PARTY IS LED BY DR. MATHIAS DEEDS.
WE KNOW FOR SURE THAT THE CIRCLE ARE HERE FROM MADRIPOOR, AS WELL AS SYMKARIAN SEPARATISTS, AND THE MOLDOVIAN BLACK FACTION.
THERE'S ALSO TALK OF A LOCAL HONG KONG GROUP.
TRIAD?
NOPE. SOMETHING NEW, WE THINK.
ANYWAY...
THE POINT IS EVERYTHING REVOLVES AROUND THE WEAPONS A.I.M. IS SELLING.

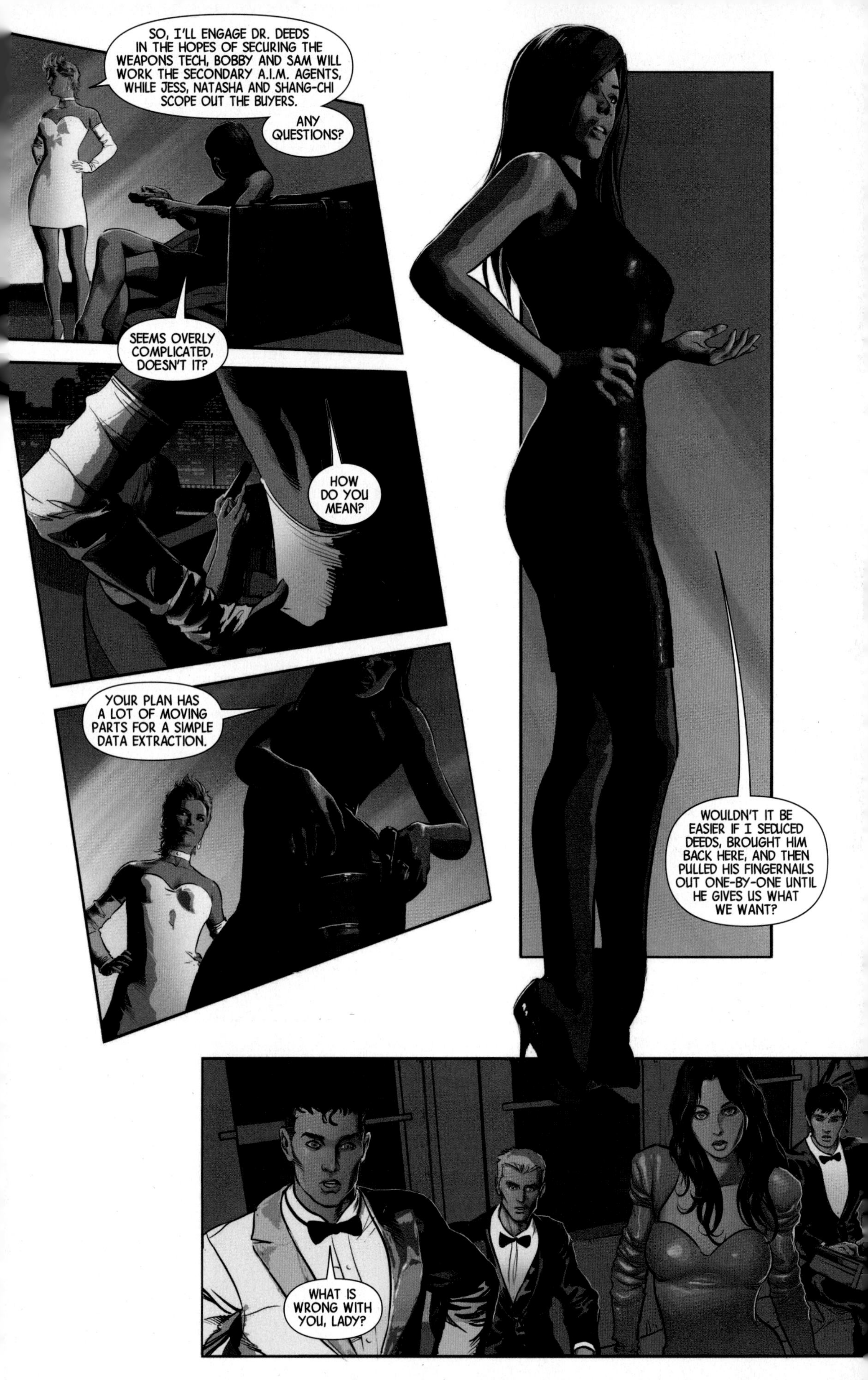
SO, I'LL ENGAGE DR. DEEDS IN THE HOPES OF SECURING THE WEAPONS TECH, BOBBY AND SAM WILL WORK THE SECONDARY A.I.M. AGENTS, WHILE JESS, NATASHA AND SHANG-CHI SCOPE OUT THE BUYERS.
ANY QUESTIONS?
SEEMS OVERLY COMPLICATED, DOESN'T IT?
HOW DO YOU MEAN?
YOUR PLAN HAS A LOT OF MOVING PARTS FOR A SIMPLE DATA EXTRACTION.
WOULDN'T IT BE EASIER IF I SEDUCED DEEDS, BROUGHT HIM BACK HERE, AND THEN PULLED HIS FINGERNAILS OUT ONE-BY-ONE UNTIL HE GIVES US WHAT WE WANT?
WHAT IS WRONG WITH YOU, LADY?

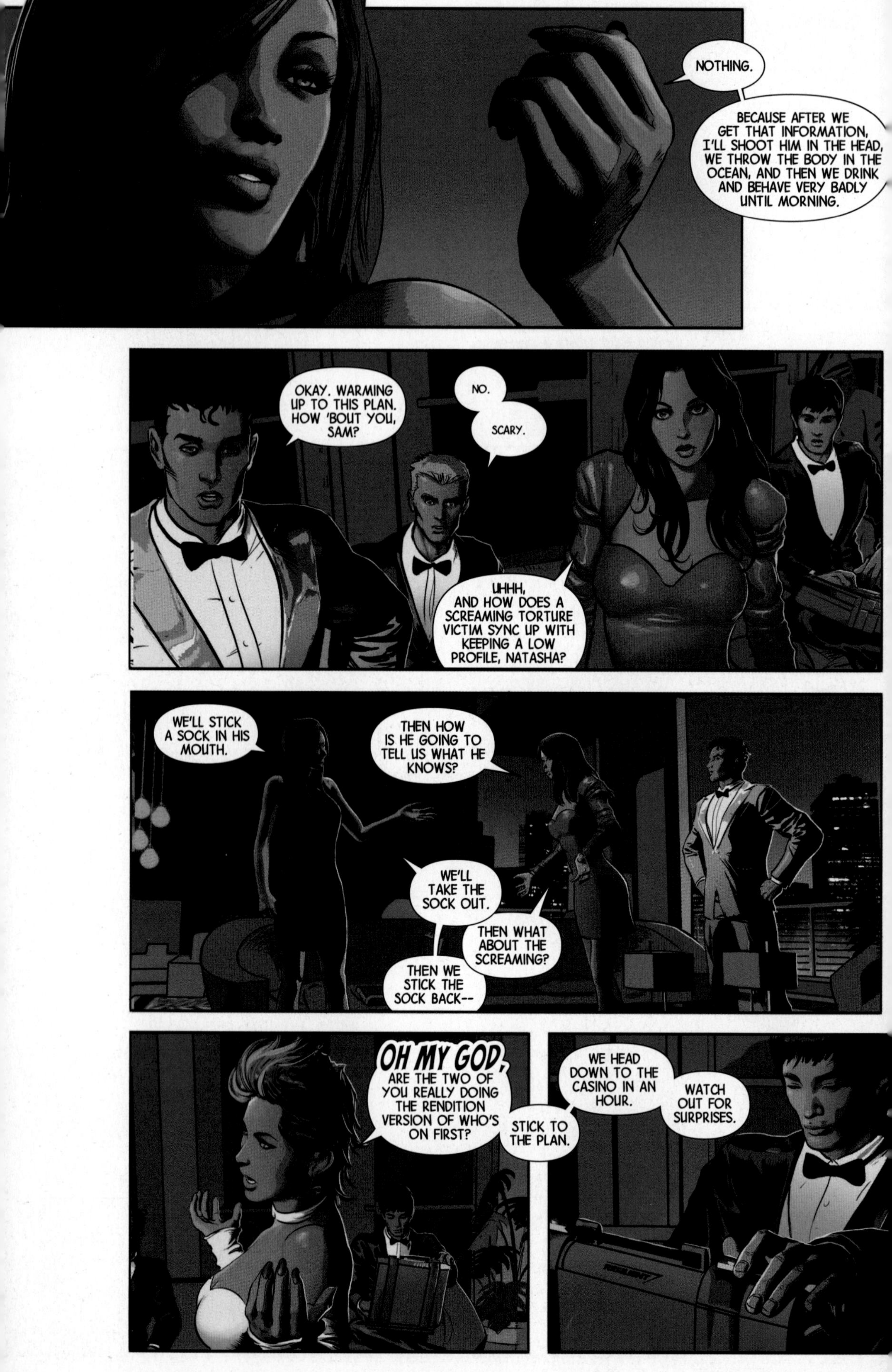
NOTHING.
BECAUSE AFTER WE GET THAT INFORMATION, I'LL SHOOT HIM IN THE HEAD, WE THROW THE BODY IN THE OCEAN, AND THEN WE DRINK AND BEHAVE VERY BADLY UNTIL MORNING.
OKAY. WARMING UP TO THIS PLAN. HOW 'BOUT YOU, SAM?
NO.
SCARY.
UHHH, AND HOW DOES A SCREAMING TORTURE VICTIM SYNC UP WITH KEEPING A LOW PROFILE, NATASHA?
WE'LL STICK A SOCK IN HIS MOUTH.
THEN HOW IS HE GOING TO TELL US WHAT HE KNOWS?
WE'LL TAKE THE SOCK OUT.
THEN WHAT ABOUT THE SCREAMING?
THEN WE STICK THE SOCK BACK--
OH MY GOD, ARE THE TWO OF YOU REALLY DOING THE RENDITION VERSION OF WHO'S ON FIRST?
WE HEAD DOWN TO THE CASINO IN AN HOUR.
STICK TO THE PLAN.
WATCH OUT FOR SURPRISES.

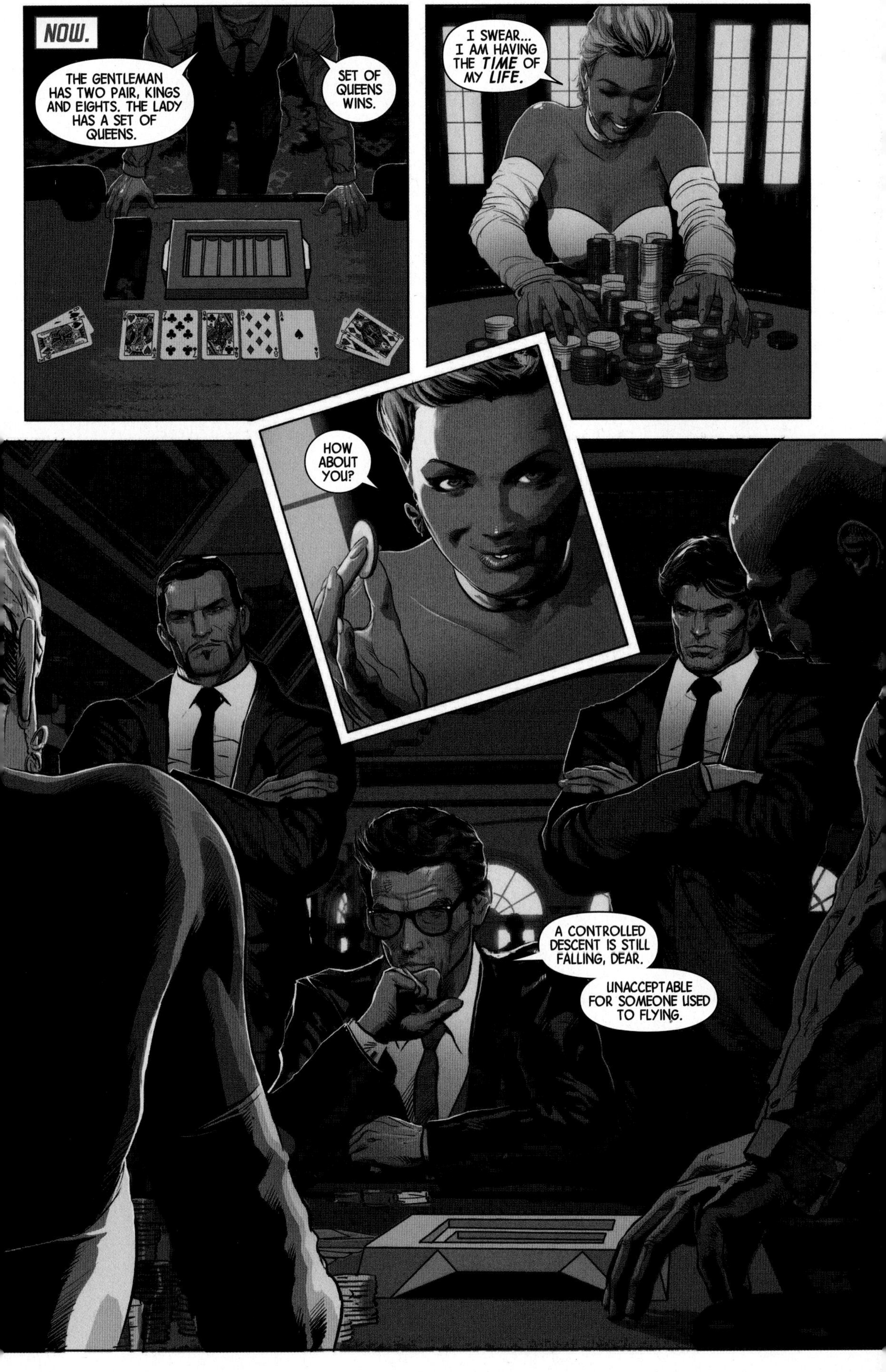
NOW.
THE GENTLEMAN HAS TWO PAIR, KINGS AND EIGHTS. THE LADY HAS A SET OF QUEENS.
SET OF QUEENS WINS.
I SWEAR... I AM HAVING THE TIME OF MY LIFE.
HOW ABOUT YOU?
A CONTROLLED DESCENT IS STILL FALLING, DEAR.
UNACCEPTABLE FOR SOMEONE USED TO FLYING.

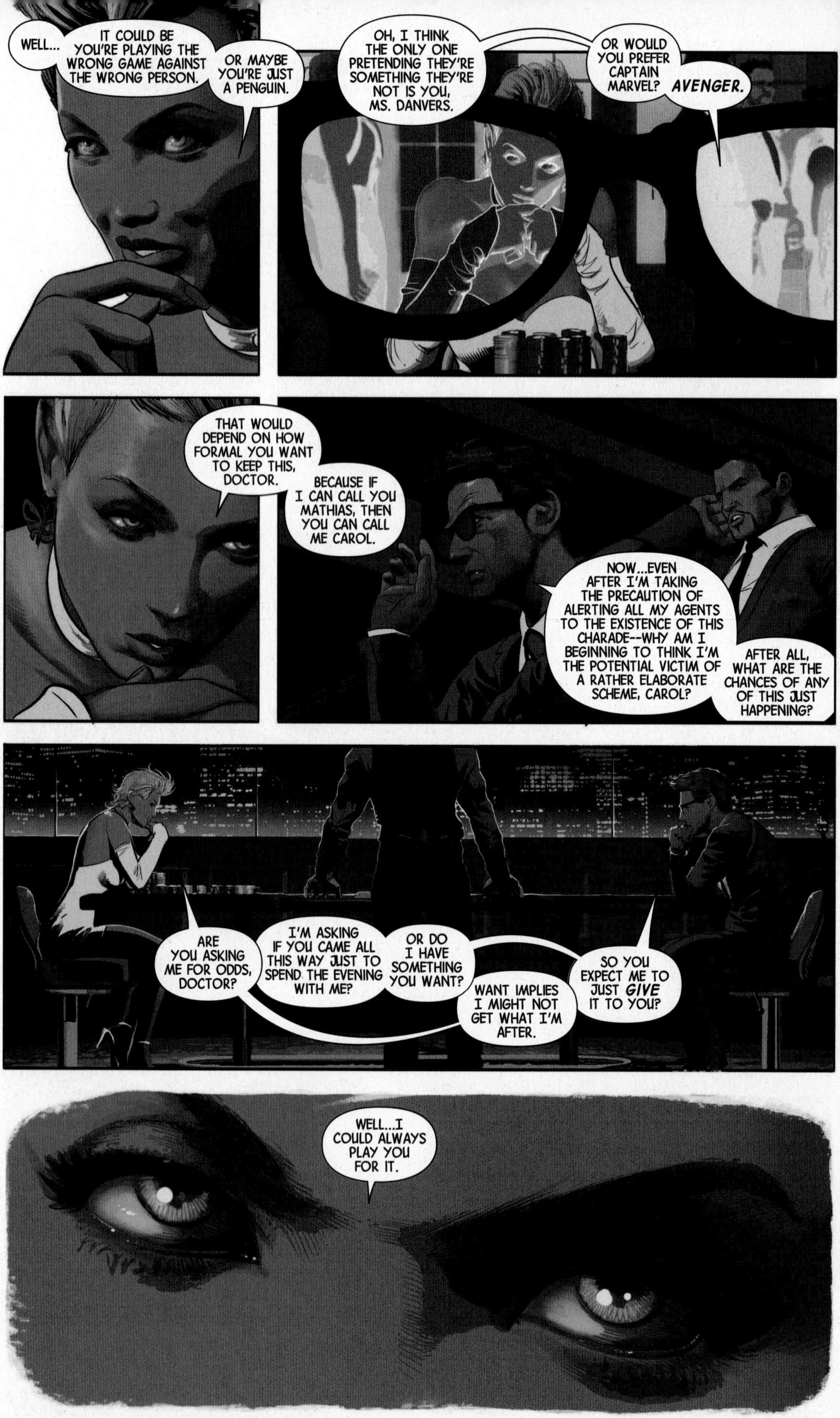
WELL...
IT COULD BE YOU'RE PLAYING THE WRONG GAME AGAINST THE WRONG PERSON.
OR MAYBE YOU'RE JUST A PENGUIN.
OH, I THINK THE ONLY ONE PRETENDING THEY'RE SOMETHING THEY'RE NOT IS YOU, MS. DANVERS.
OR WOULD YOU PREFER CAPTAIN MARVEL? AVENGER.
THAT WOULD DEPEND ON HOW FORMAL YOU WANT TO KEEP THIS, DOCTOR.
BECAUSE IF I CAN CALL YOU MATHIAS, THEN YOU CAN CALL ME CAROL.
NOW...EVEN AFTER I'M TAKING THE PRECAUTION OF ALERTING ALL MY AGENTS TO THE EXISTENCE OF THIS CHARADE--WHY AM I BEGINNING TO THINK I'M THE POTENTIAL VICTIM OF A RATHER ELABORATE SCHEME, CAROL?
AFTER ALL, WHAT ARE THE CHANCES OF ANY OF THIS JUST HAPPENING?
ARE YOU ASKING ME FOR ODDS, DOCTOR?
I'M ASKING IF YOU CAME ALL THIS WAY JUST TO SPEND THE EVENING WITH ME?
OR DO I HAVE SOMETHING YOU WANT?
SO YOU EXPECT ME TO JUST GIVE IT TO YOU?
WANT IMPLIES I MIGHT NOT GET WHAT I'M AFTER.
WELL...I COULD ALWAYS PLAY YOU FOR IT.

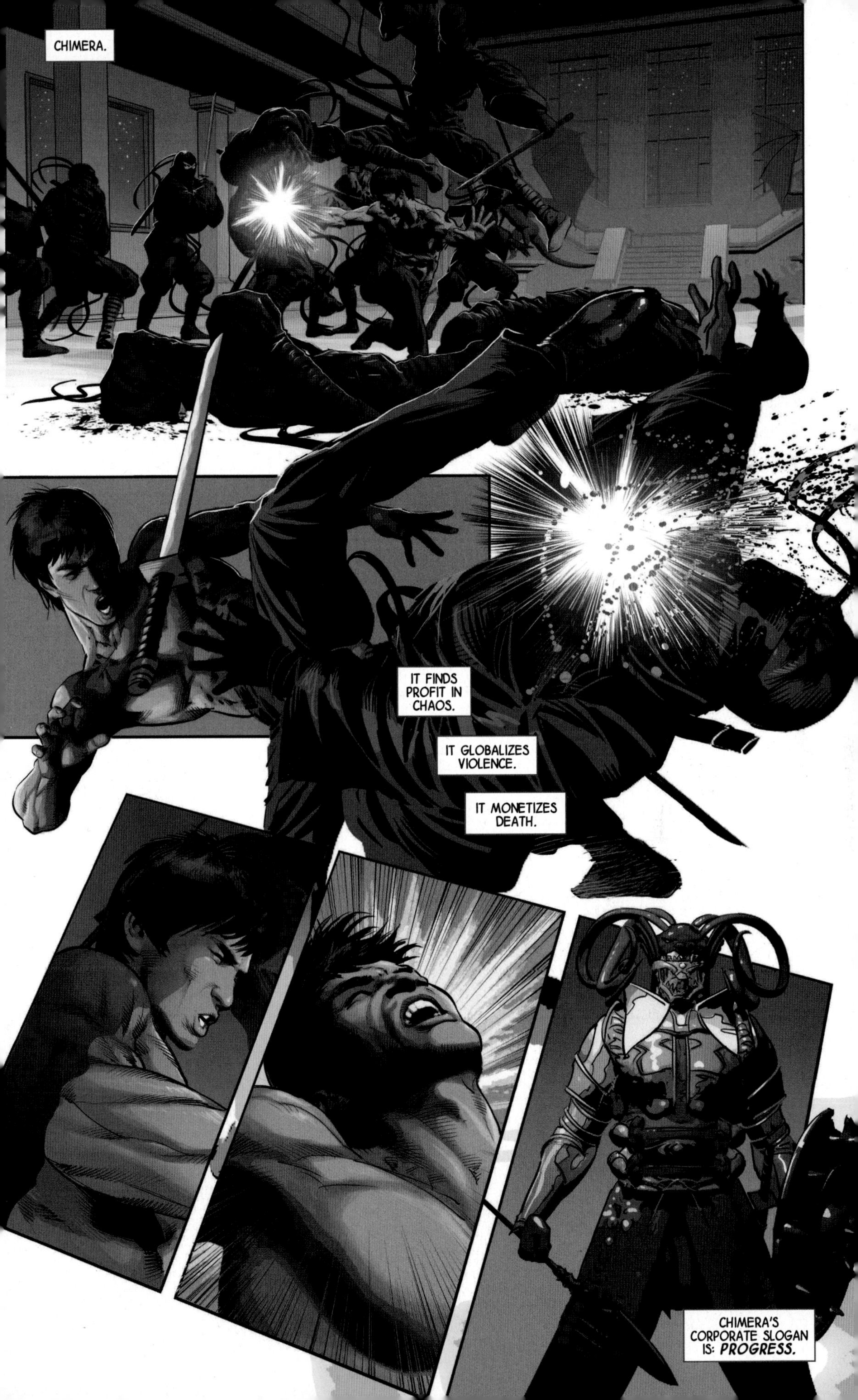
CHIMERA.
IT FINDS PROFIT IN CHAOS.
IT GLOBALIZES VIOLENCE.
IT MONETIZES DEATH.
CHIMERA'S CORPORATE SLOGAN IS: PROGRESS.

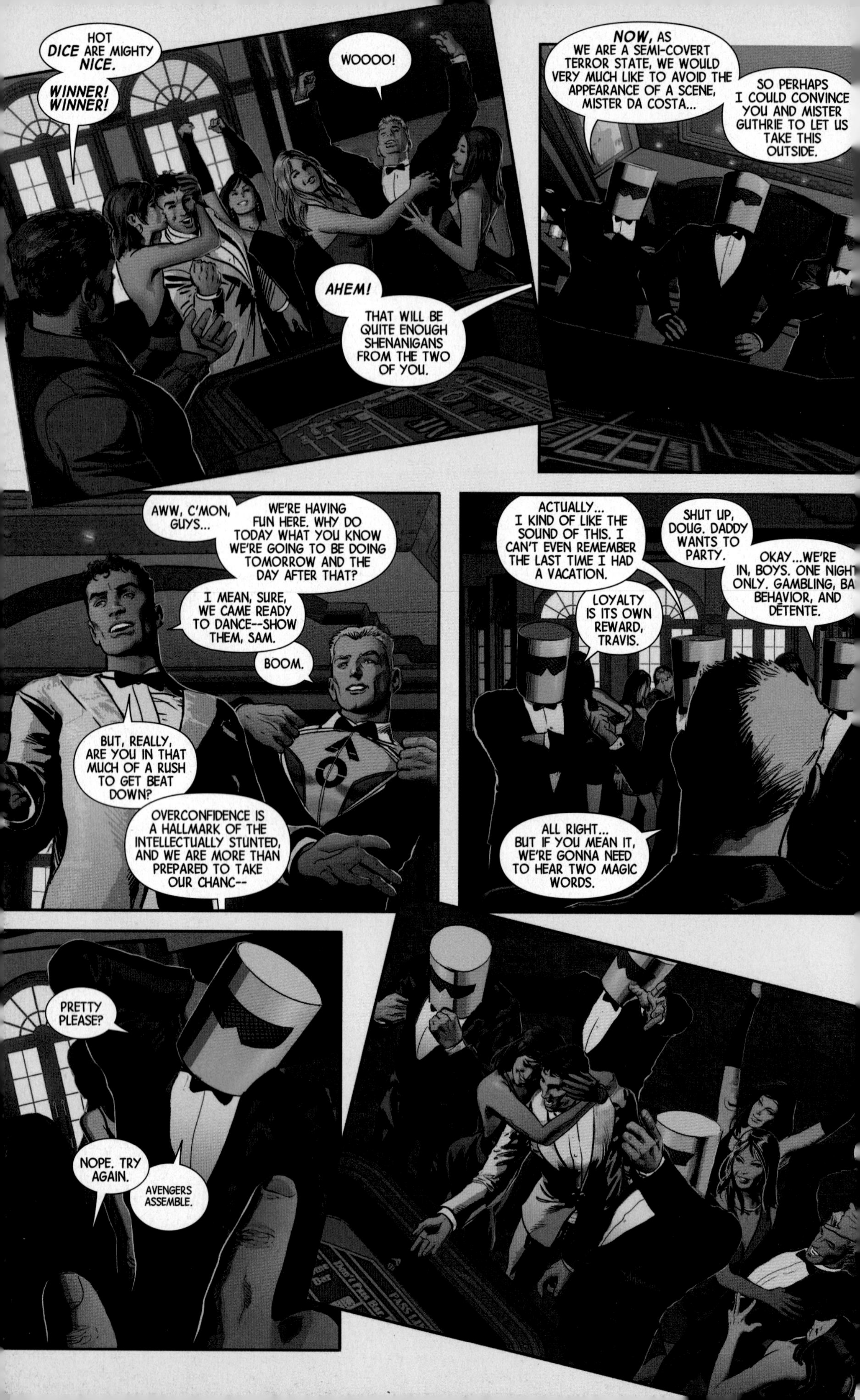

HOT DICE ARE MIGHTY NICE.
WINNER! WINNER!
WOOOO!
AHEM!
THAT WILL BE QUITE ENOUGH SHENANIGANS FROM THE TWO OF YOU.
NOW, AS WE ARE A SEMI-COVERT TERROR STATE, WE WOULD VERY MUCH LIKE TO AVOID THE APPEARANCE OF A SCENE, MISTER DA COSTA...
SO PERHAPS I COULD CONVINCE YOU AND MISTER GUTHRIE TO LET US TAKE THIS OUTSIDE.
AWW, C'MON, GUYS...
WE'RE HAVING FUN HERE. WHY DO TODAY WHAT YOU KNOW WE'RE GOING TO BE DOING TOMORROW AND THE DAY AFTER THAT?
I MEAN, SURE, WE CAME READY TO DANCE--SHOW THEM, SAM.
BOOM.
BUT, REALLY, ARE YOU IN THAT MUCH OF A RUSH TO GET BEAT DOWN?
OVERCONFIDENCE IS A HALLMARK OF THE INTELLECTUALLY STUNTED, AND WE ARE MORE THAN PREPARED TO TAKE OUR CHANC--
ACTUALLY... I KIND OF LIKE THE SOUND OF THIS. I CAN'T EVEN REMEMBER THE LAST TIME I HAD A VACATION.
LOYALTY IS ITS OWN REWARD, TRAVIS.
SHUT UP, DOUG. DADDY WANTS TO PARTY.
OKAY...WE'RE IN, BOYS. ONE NIGHT ONLY. GAMBLING, BA BEHAVIOR, AND DÉTENTE.
ALL RIGHT... BUT IF YOU MEAN IT, WE'RE GONNA NEED TO HEAR TWO MAGIC WORDS.
PRETTY PLEASE?
NOPE. TRY AGAIN.
AVENGERS ASSEMBLE.

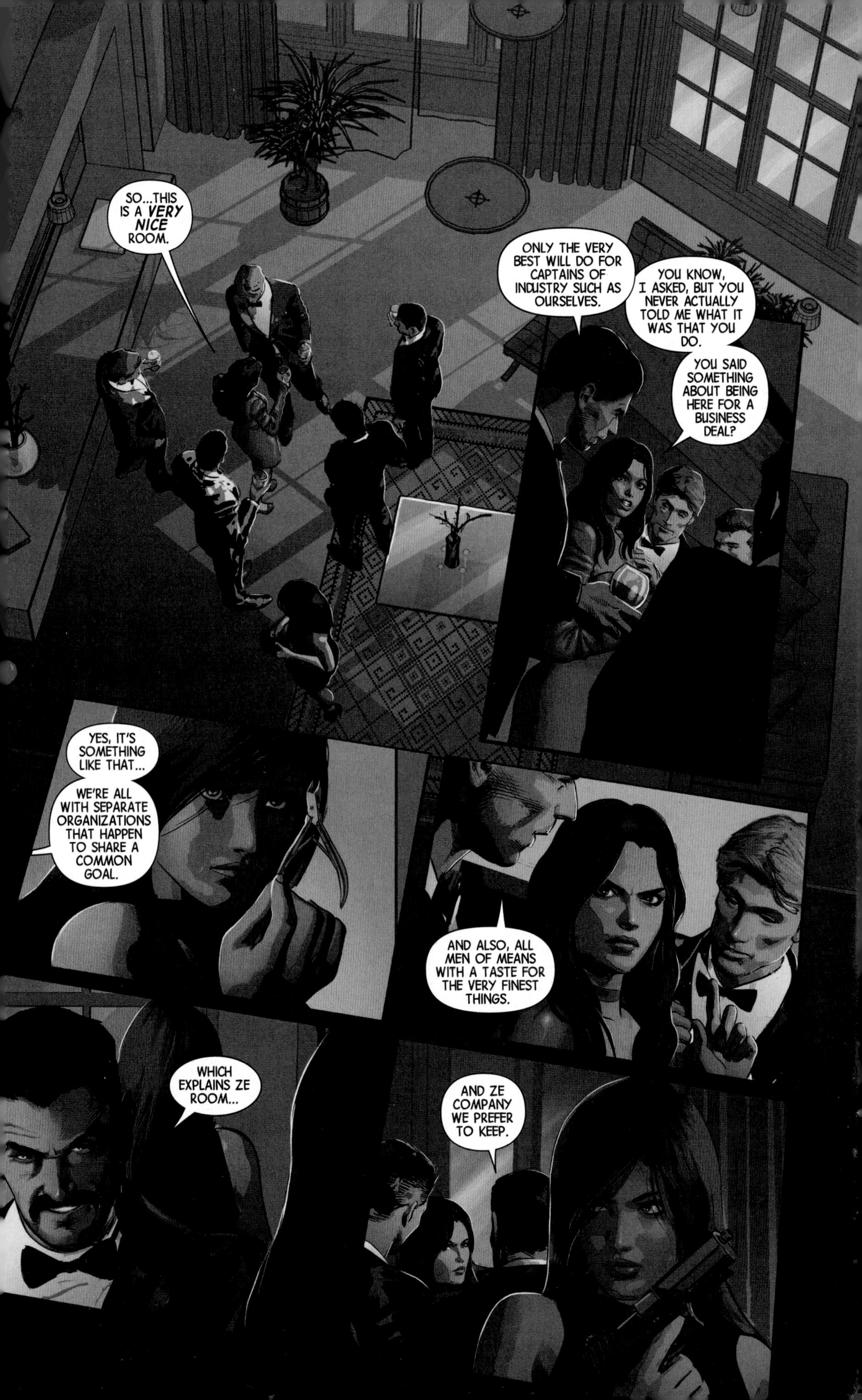
SO...THIS IS A VERY NICE ROOM.
ONLY THE VERY BEST WILL DO FOR CAPTAINS OF INDUSTRY SUCH AS OURSELVES.
YOU KNOW, I ASKED, BUT YOU NEVER ACTUALLY TOLD ME WHAT IT WAS THAT YOU DO.
YOU SAID SOMETHING ABOUT BEING HERE FOR A BUSINESS DEAL?
YES, IT'S SOMETHING LIKE THAT...
WE'RE ALL WITH SEPARATE ORGANIZATIONS THAT HAPPEN TO SHARE A COMMON GOAL.
AND ALSO, ALL MEN OF MEANS WITH A TASTE FOR THE VERY FINEST THINGS.
WHICH EXPLAINS ZE ROOM...
AND ZE COMPANY WE PREFER TO KEEP.

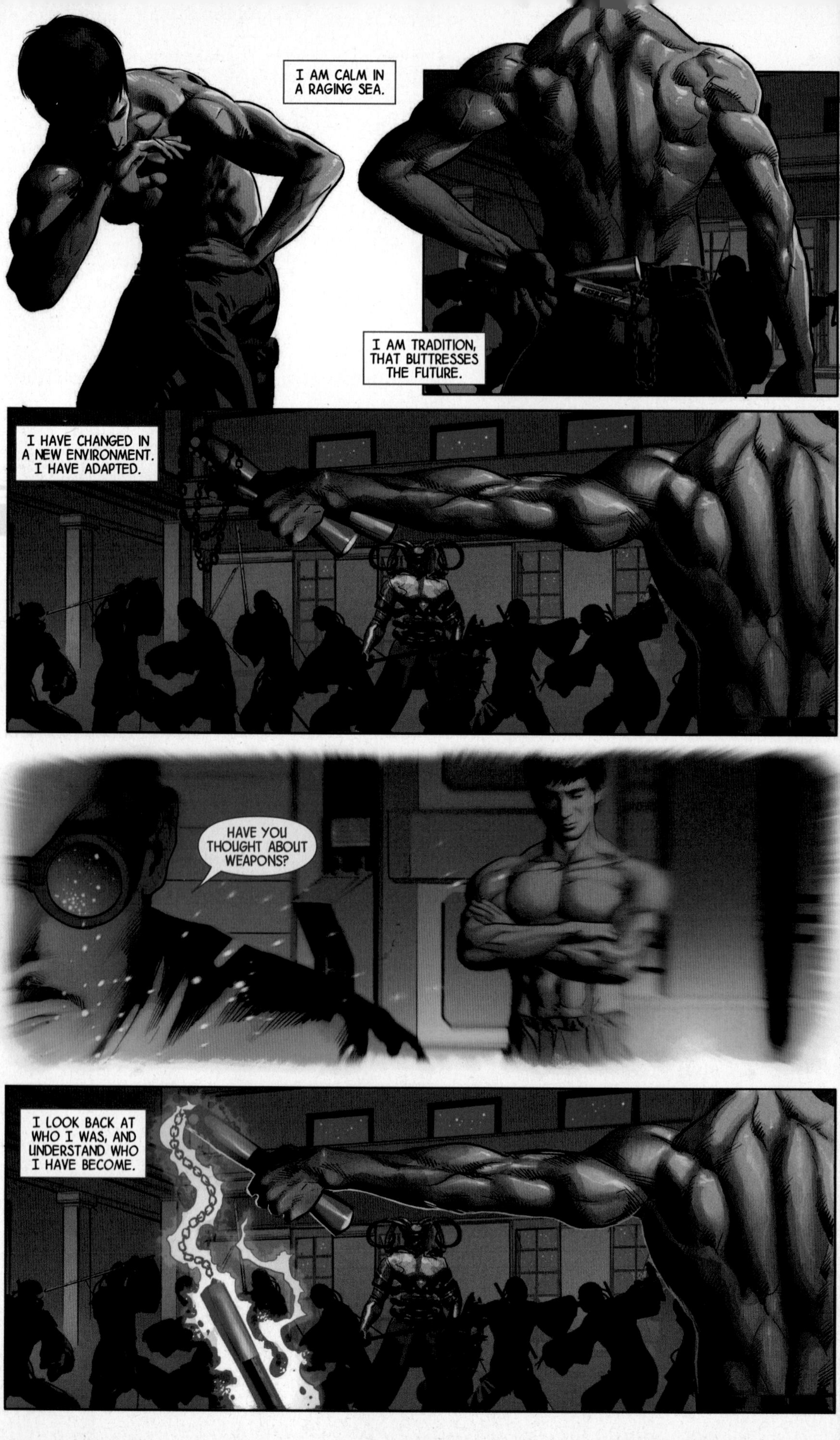
I AM CALM IN A RAGING SEA.
I AM TRADITION, THAT BUTTRESSES THE FUTURE.
I HAVE CHANGED IN A NEW ENVIRONMENT. I HAVE ADAPTED.
HAVE YOU THOUGHT ABOUT WEAPONS?
I LOOK BACK AT WHO I WAS, AND UNDERSTAND WHO I HAVE BECOME.

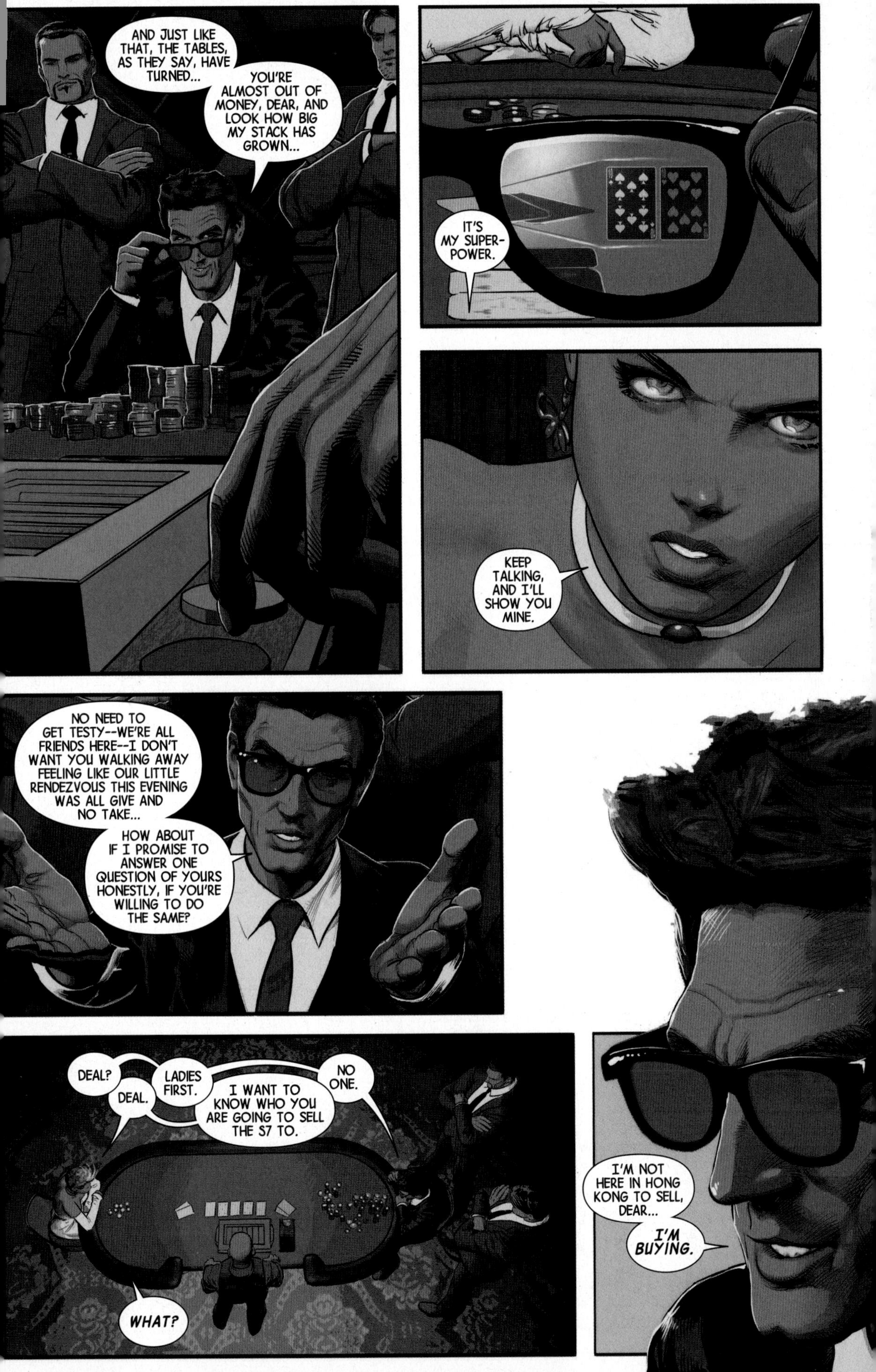
AND JUST LIKE THAT, THE TABLES, AS THEY SAY, HAVE TURNED...
YOU'RE ALMOST OUT OF MONEY, DEAR, AND LOOK HOW BIG MY STACK HAS GROWN...
IT'S MY SUPER-POWER.
KEEP TALKING, AND I'LL SHOW YOU MINE.
NO NEED TO GET TESTY--WE'RE ALL FRIENDS HERE--I DON'T WANT YOU WALKING AWAY FEELING LIKE OUR LITTLE RENDEZVOUS THIS EVENING WAS ALL GIVE AND NO TAKE...
HOW ABOUT IF I PROMISE TO ANSWER ONE QUESTION OF YOURS HONESTLY, IF YOU'RE WILLING TO DO THE SAME?
DEAL?
DEAL.
LADIES FIRST.
I WANT TO KNOW WHO YOU ARE GOING TO SELL THE S7 TO.
NO ONE.
WHAT?
I'M NOT HERE IN HONG KONG TO SELL, DEAR...
I'M BUYING.

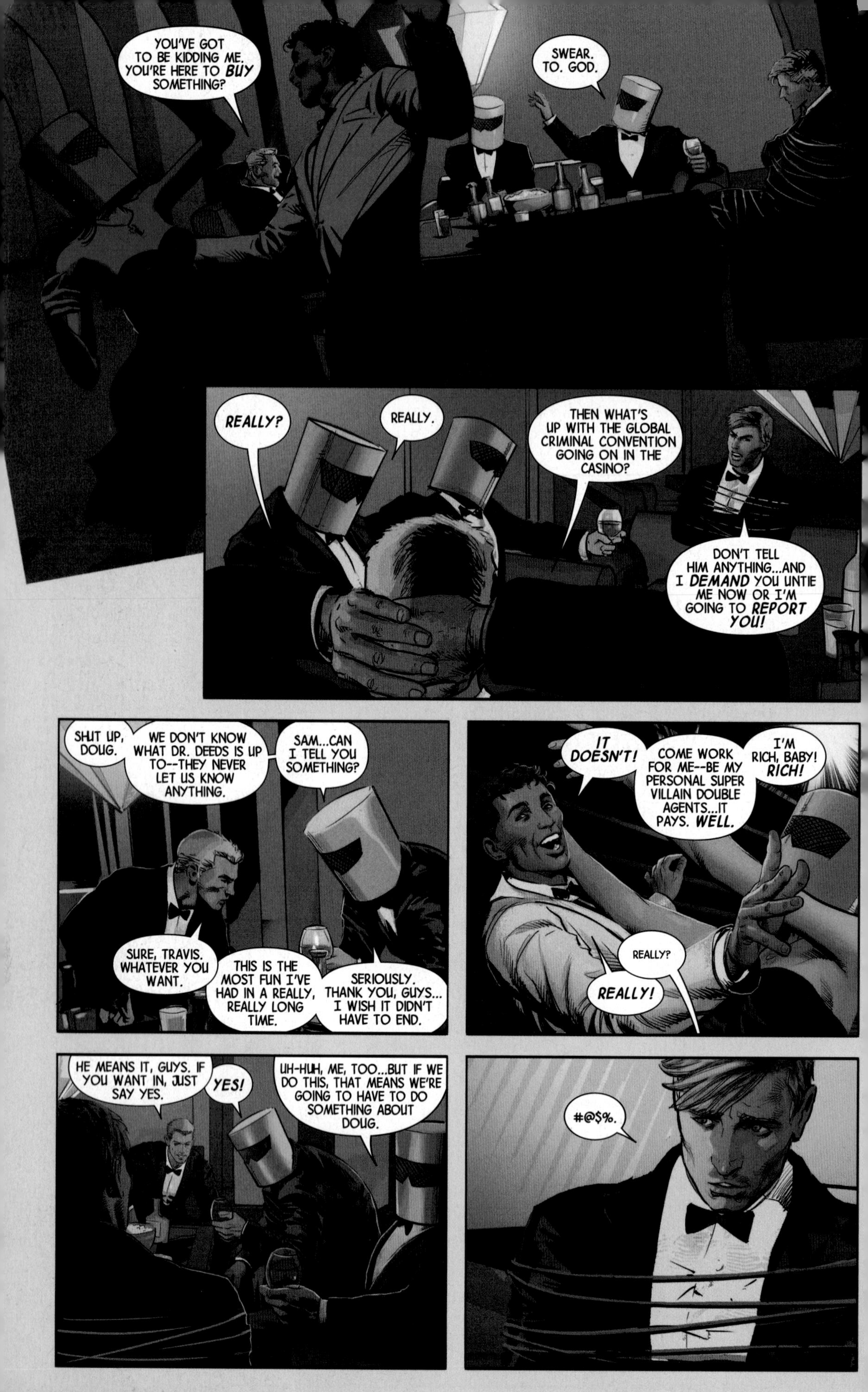
YOU'VE GOT TO BE KIDDING ME. YOU'RE HERE TO BUY SOMETHING?
SWEAR. TO. GOD.
REALLY?
REALLY.
THEN WHAT'S UP WITH THE GLOBAL CRIMINAL CONVENTION GOING ON IN THE CASINO?
DON'T TELL HIM ANYTHING...AND I DEMAND YOU UNTIE ME NOW OR I'M GOING TO REPORT YOU!
SHUT UP, DOUG.
WE DON'T KNOW WHAT DR. DEEDS IS UP TO--THEY NEVER LET US KNOW ANYTHING.
SAM...CAN I TELL YOU SOMETHING?
SURE, TRAVIS. WHATEVER YOU WANT.
THIS IS THE MOST FUN I'VE HAD IN A REALLY, REALLY LONG TIME.
SERIOUSLY. THANK YOU, GUYS... I WISH IT DIDN'T HAVE TO END.
IT DOESN'T!
COME WORK FOR ME--BE MY PERSONAL SUPER VILLAIN DOUBLE AGENTS...IT PAYS. WELL.
I'M RICH, BABY! RICH!
REALLY?
REALLY!
HE MEANS IT, GUYS. IF YOU WANT IN, JUST SAY YES.
YES!
UH-HUH, ME, TOO...BUT IF WE DO THIS, THAT MEANS WE'RE GOING TO HAVE TO DO SOMETHING ABOUT DOUG.
#@$%.

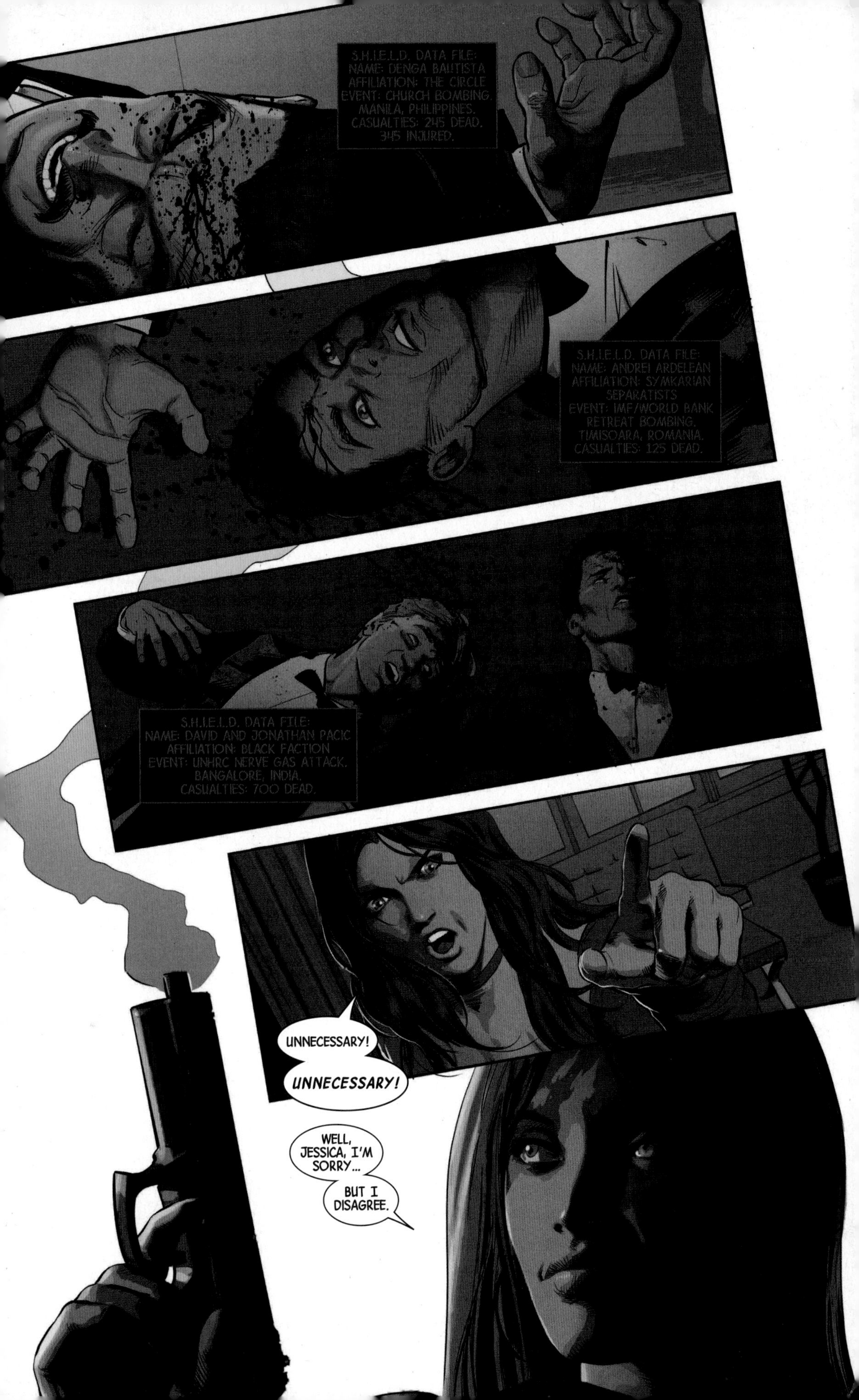
S.H.I.E.L.D. DATA FILE:
NAME: DENGA BAUTISTA
AFFILIATION: THE CIRCLE
EVENT: CHURCH BOMBING. MANILA, PHILIPPINES.
CASUALTIES: 245 DEAD. 345 INJURED.
S.H.I.E.L.D. DATA FILE:
NAME: ANDREI ARDELEAN
AFFILIATION: SYMKARIAN SEPARATISTS
EVENT: IMF/WORLD BANK RETREAT BOMBING. TIMISOARA, ROMANIA.
CASUALTIES: 125 DEAD.
S.H.I.E.L.D. DATA FILE:
NAME: DAVID AND JONATHAN PACIC
AFFILIATION: BLACK FACTION
EVENT: UNHRC NERVE GAS ATTACK. BANGALORE, INDIA.
CASUALTIES: 700 DEAD.
UNNECESSARY!
UNNECESSARY!
WELL, JESSICA, I'M SORRY...
BUT I DISAGREE.

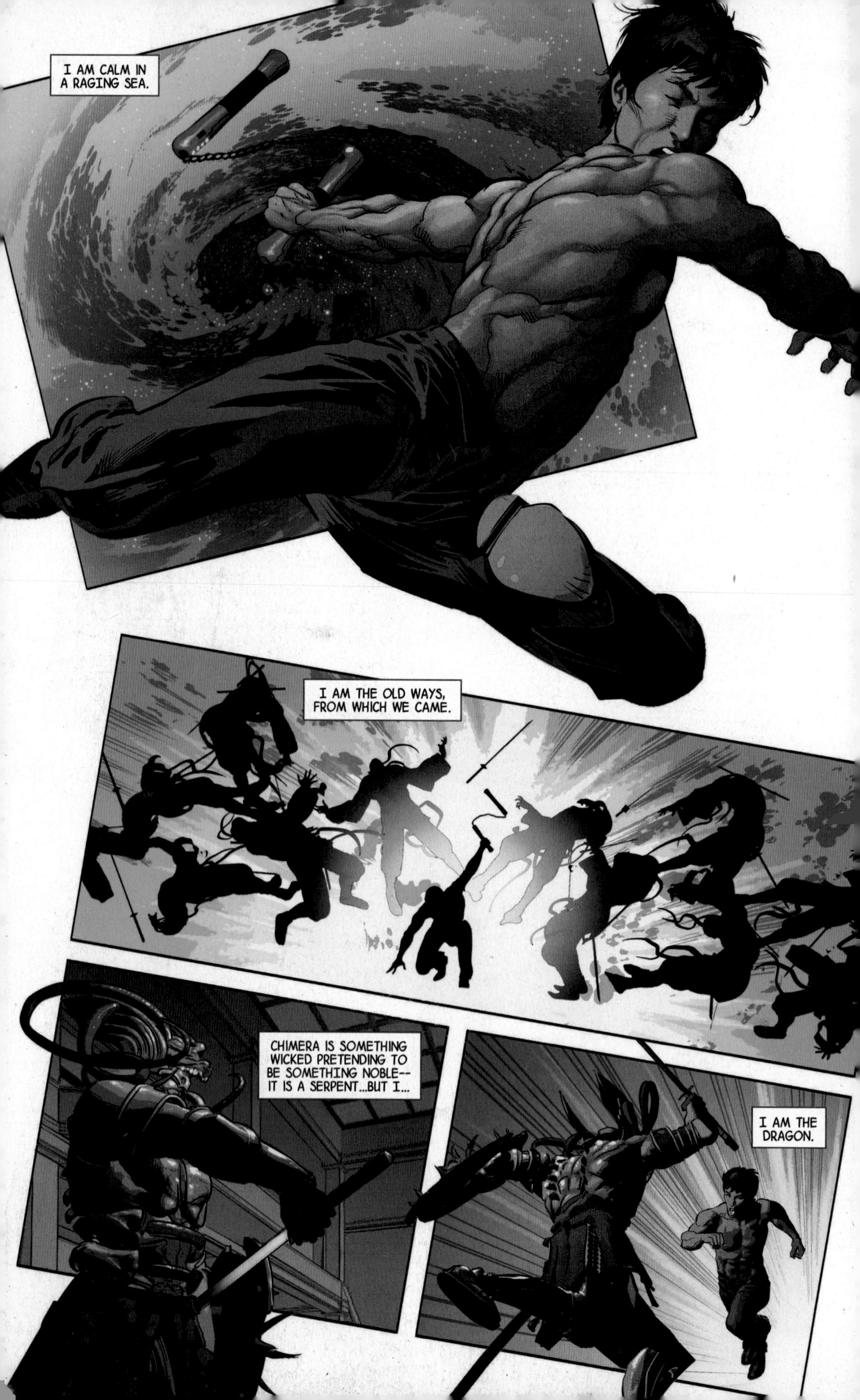
I AM CALM IN A RAGING SEA.
I AM THE OLD WAYS, FROM WHICH WE CAME.
CHIMERA IS SOMETHING WICKED PRETENDING TO BE SOMETHING NOBLE-- IT IS A SERPENT...BUT I...
I AM THE DRAGON.

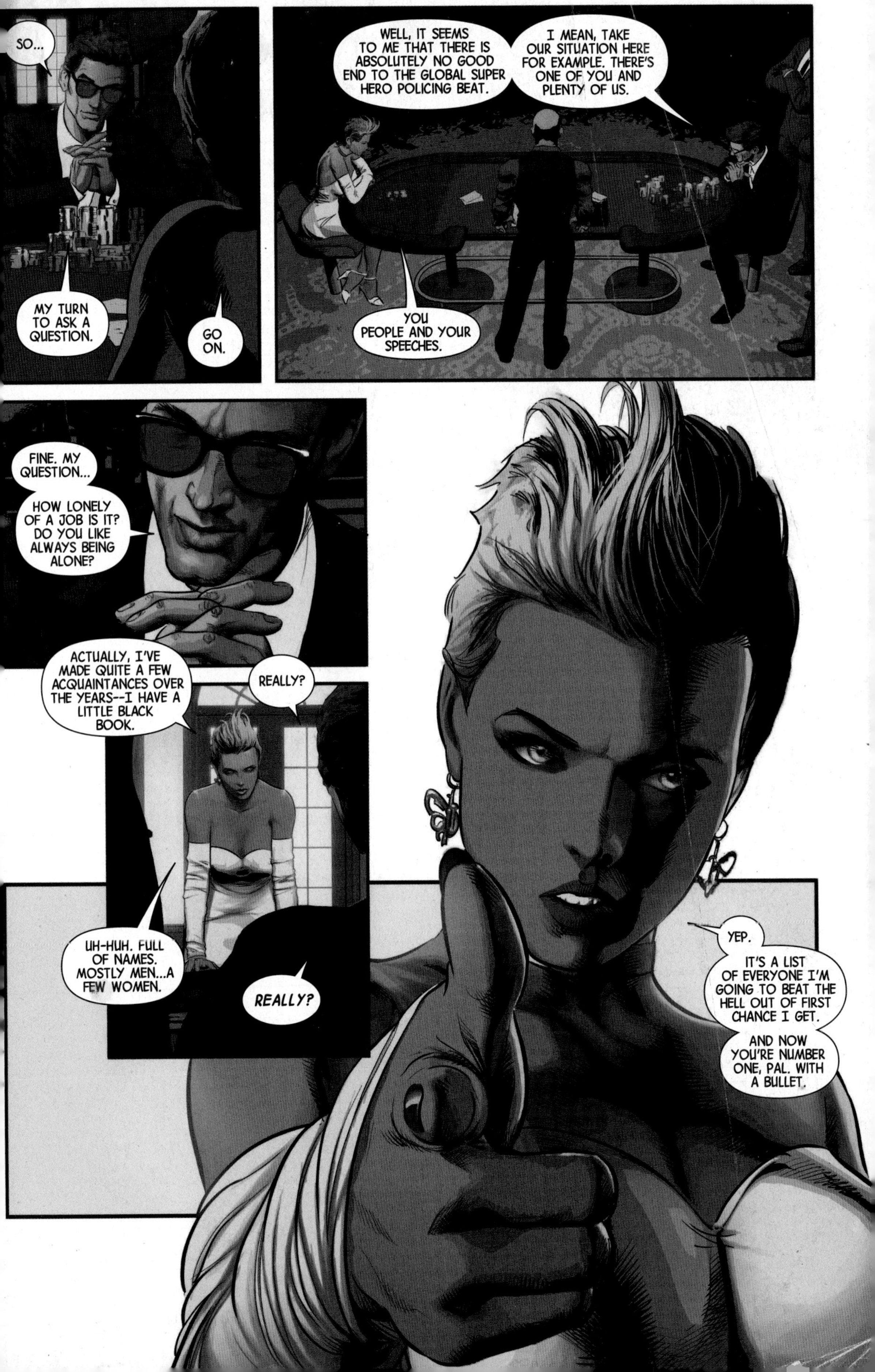
SO...
MY TURN TO ASK A QUESTION.
GO ON.
WELL, IT SEEMS TO ME THAT THERE IS ABSOLUTELY NO GOOD END TO THE GLOBAL SUPER HERO POLICING BEAT.
I MEAN, TAKE OUR SITUATION HERE FOR EXAMPLE. THERE'S ONE OF YOU AND PLENTY OF US.
YOU PEOPLE AND YOUR SPEECHES.
FINE. MY QUESTION...
HOW LONELY OF A JOB IS IT? DO YOU LIKE ALWAYS BEING ALONE?
ACTUALLY, I'VE MADE QUITE A FEW ACQUAINTANCES OVER THE YEARS--I HAVE A LITTLE BLACK BOOK.
REALLY?
UH-HUH. FULL OF NAMES. MOSTLY MEN...A FEW WOMEN.
REALLY?
YEP.
IT'S A LIST OF EVERYONE I'M GOING TO BEAT THE HELL OUT OF FIRST CHANCE I GET.
AND NOW YOU'RE NUMBER ONE, PAL. WITH A BULLET.

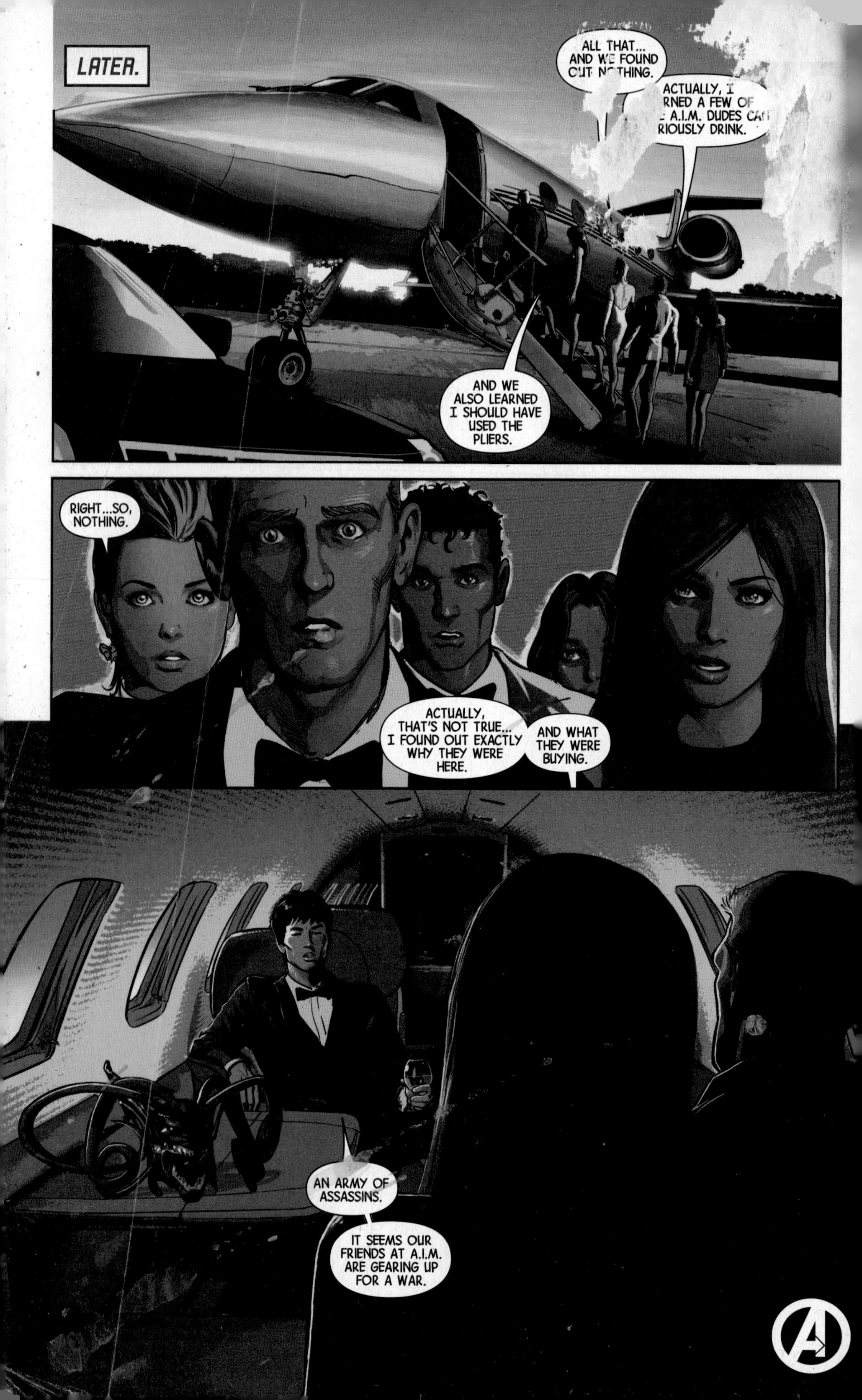

LATER.
ALL THAT... AND WE FOUND OUT NOTHING.
ACTUALLY, I
RNED A FEW OF
A.I.M. DUDES CA
RIOUSLY DRINK.
AND WE ALSO LEARNED I SHOULD HAVE USED THE PLIERS.
RIGHT...SO, NOTHING.
ACTUALLY, THAT'S NOT TRUE... I FOUND OUT EXACTLY WHY THEY WERE HERE.
AND WHAT THEY WERE BUYING.
AN ARMY OF ASSASSINS.
IT SEEMS OUR FRIENDS AT A.I.M. ARE GEARING UP FOR A WAR.